REMEMBERING BRADMAN

REMEMBERING BRADMAN

MARGARET GEDDES

VIKING
an imprint of
PENGUIN BOOKS

Viking

Published by the Penguin Group
Penguin Books Australia Ltd
250 Camberwell Road, Camberwell, Victoria 3124, Australia
Penguin Books Ltd
80 Strand, London WC2R 0RL, England
Penguin Putnam Inc.
375 Hudson Street, New York, New York 10014, USA
Penguin Books, a division of Pearson Canada
10 Alcorn Avenue, Toronto, Ontario, Canada M4V 3B2
Penguin Books (NZ) Ltd
Cnr Rosedale and Airborne Roads, Albany, Auckland, New Zealand
Penguin Books (South Africa) (Pty) Ltd
24 Sturdee Avenue, Rosebank, Johannesburg 2196, South Africa
Penguin Books India (P) Ltd
11, Community Centre, Panchsheel Park, New Delhi 110 017, India

First published by Penguin Books Australia Ltd 2002

1 3 5 7 9 10 8 6 4 2

Designed by David Altheim, Penguin Design Studio
Cover image by News Limited, reproduced by permission of the Bradman Museum
Typeset in 11.5/17 pt Jansen by Post Pre-press Group, Brisbane, Queensland
Printed and bound in Australia by McPherson's Printing Group, Maryborough, Victoria

National Library of Australia
Cataloguing-in-Publication data:

Geddes, Margaret, 1949– .
Remembering Bradman.

Includes index.
ISBN 0 670 91231 X.

1. Bradman, Donald, Sir, 1908–2001 – Anecdotes.
2. Cricket players – Australia – Interviews. I. Title.

796.3580994

www.penguin.com.au

Contents

Acknowledgements vii
Foreword by Mike Coward ix
Introduction xiii

1 **Hero of a Nation**
Bill and Barbara Brown 3   Keith Wotton 23
G. R. V. (Richard) Robins 26   Cecil Starr 45   Colin Brideson 49
John Wilkin 50   Sir Roden Cutler VC 51

2 **From the Shadow of War**
Percy Beames 55   Sir Alec and Eric Bedser 59   Bruce Bowley 71
Geff 'Nobby' Noblet 79   Neil Dansie 81   Neil Harvey 84
Sam Loxton 93   Arthur Morris 104   Doug Ring 115
Keith Sims 124

3 **Following the Game**
Alex Bannister 139   Dr Donald Beard 152
Ian and Ros Craig 160   Alan Davidson 170   John Statton 175
Dr John Lill 176   Rosie Lill 177   Len Maddocks 179
Colin McDonald 183   Jim Mellor 188   Nan and Rhyll Rivett 190
Bob Simpson 199   John Woodcock 205

4 **Senior Service**

Bill Scammell 215   *Doug Insole* 219   *Colin Egar* 234

Lou Rowan 248   *Ian Meckiff* 251   *Don Chipp* 259

Jim Tummel 264   *Bob Parish* 275   *Hedley Brideson* 279

Joan Ridings 284   *Mal MacPherson* 294   *Paul Sheahan* 301

Brian Cole 304   *Jill Gauvin* 306   *Bob Radford* 320

Graham Eccles 334   *Meredith Burgmann* 337   *Bill Jacobs* 341

5 **Out of the Limelight**

Greg Chappell 353   *Terry Jenner* 371   *David Frith* 378

Dr Ali Bacher 386   *Alison Steele* 387   *Graeme Pollock* 389

Rob Patterson 391   *Mike Coward* 397

6 **Towards a Century**

John Howard 403   *Lord Philip Moore* 408

David and Sam Parkinson 411   *Garry Barnsley* 416

Barry Richards 425   *Norman May* 429   *Jack Clarke* 433

Betty Joseph 438   *Richard Mulvaney* 441   *Charles Williams* 454

Alan Jones 461

Index 471

Acknowledgements

A project like this depends on the cooperation and goodwill of many people. I would like to thank everyone who gave their time and shared their memories.

Thank you to those I spoke to in Australia: Garry Barnsley, Percy Beames, Dr Don Beard, Bruce Bowley, Colin Brideson, Hedley Brideson, Barbara Brown, Bill Brown, Dr Meredith Burgmann, Greg Chappell, Don Chipp, Jack Clarke, Brian Cole, Mike Coward, Ian Craig, Ros Craig, Neil Dansie, Alan Davidson, Graham Eccles, Colin Egar, Jill Gauvin, Neil Harvey, Bill Jacobs, Terry Jenner, Alan Jones, Betty Joseph, Dr John Lill, Rosemary Lill, Sam Loxton, Colin McDonald, Malcolm MacPherson, Len Maddocks, Norman May, Ian Meckiff, Jim Mellor, Arthur Morris, Richard Mulvaney, Geff Noblet, Bob Parish, David Parkinson, Sam Parkinson, Rob Patterson, Graeme Pollock, Bob Radford, Barry Richards, Joan Ridings, Doug Ring, Nan Rivett, Rhyll Rivett, Lou Rowan, Paul Sheahan, Keith Sims, Bob Simpson, Cecil Starr, John Statton, Alison Steele, Jim Tummel, John Wilkin, Keith Wotton and to Dr Ali Bacher, who spoke to me by phone from his home in South Africa.

To the families of Bill Scammell and Sir Roden Cutler, thank you.

Thank you, too, to those who spoke with me in England: Alex Bannister, Sir Alec Bedser, Eric Bedser, David Frith, Doug Insole, Lord Moore, Richard Robins, Lord Williams and John Woodcock. I am particularly grateful to John Woodcock for trusting me with his treasured photographs.

Thank you to everyone who helped me in my research: to Colin Ingleby-MacKenzie, Michael Brock, Neil Maxwell, Malcolm Gray, David Richards, Lindsay Kline, Madeline Wiesner, Pat Statton; to Frank Prain in the *Age* library, the curator of the Lord's Museum, Stephen Green, and the curator of the Bradman Museum, Richard Mulvaney.

Thank you to Richard Donkin and Jim Robinson for access to their extensive cricket libraries. Throughout the project I have referred frequently to the following books: *200 Seasons of Australian Cricket* (Ironbark); *A–Z of Australian Cricketers* (Oxford); *Bradman*, Charles Williams (Abacus); *The Complete Illustrated History of Australian Cricket*, Jack Pollard (Viking); and *Barclay's World of Cricket* (Collins Willow).

Thank you to my friend Pauline Luke for her original suggestion, to my friend and neighbour Ron Steiner for his help and encouragement, to John Ross and Veronica Peek, to designer David Altheim and my editors, Peter Ascot and Nicola Young.

Finally, thanks to my husband, Dick Barnes, and my daughters, Lauren and Anna, for their loving support and tolerance.

Foreword

AT LAST, WORDS which give Sir Donald Bradman an identifiable humanity. It is ironic that in death Bradman has been given life by a diverse group of his friends and acquaintances who were prepared to share their special and often personal reminiscences of the greatest batsman. In the public arena, at least, Bradman's humanity generally was obscured by his awesome sense of infallibility and invulnerability and an obsessive pursuit of perfection.

And always it seemed he was primarily measured in cold, hard statistics – myriad variations on his career Test average of 99.94; Bradman the automaton. Invariably it was left to Jessie, his beloved wife of 65 years, to provide him with warmth and human manner.

By dint of her relaxed and respectful interviewing technique Margaret Geddes has elicited priceless material from scores of disparate folk who for one reason or another were associated with Sir Donald during his long and celebrated life.

And from it we can draw an unusually intimate and revealing portrait of Bradman the man.

For the first time we can reach some thoughtful and well-founded conclusions to why a man who spent the first 40 years of his life making certain of his immortality spent the rest of it trying to live with the uniqueness of his mortality.

This is not a hagiography and, with very few exceptions, the sycophants who made his life so challenging and his eventual reclusiveness a necessity are absent.

It has been said that we all have as many personalities as we have friends, and on the evidence before us this was true of Bradman. There may have been only one Bradman at the crease but on this reading there were often many more away from the middle. And the variations and contradictions on themes so thoughtfully pursued by Geddes are especially revealing and we see precious glimpses of Bradman as a husband, father, businessman as well as a batsman nonpareil. The thoughts of his godson, G. R. V. (Richard) Robins, alone make the reading worthwhile.

The son of perhaps Bradman's closest mate, the England all-rounder, captain and distinguished administrator R. W. V. (Walter) Robins, Richard speaks with affection and a frankness only permitted a member of an extended family.

As with so many of the interviewees, Robins relishes the opportunity to speak openly and expansively about Bradman. Of course, not one of them would have risked his displeasure by speaking in this manner when he was alive. There were, after all, certain protocols that had to be observed. Bradman was accustomed to everything being done on his terms and to having the last word.

It is stunning to read that Robins believes Bradman always considered cricket a means to an end and, while he liked to see himself as something of an English amateur, he detested the pomposity in the game. There is also splendid reading between the lines on everything from parenting to politics and, to this end, the interview with Meredith Burgmann, the president of the NSW Legislative Council who as a 20 year old was co-convenor of the Anti-Apartheid Movement in Sydney in 1971 is of particular interest and significance.

Given the intensity of Bradman's dislike for publicity and any intrusion into his private life it is instructive to learn of the extent of his relationships with leading figures in the media over many years and his affection for the provocative broadcaster Alan Jones. Inevitably, and quite properly, much is made of Bradman's imposing record as a letter-writer. Indeed, throughout the cricket community and far beyond there is an earnest hope that, in time, the family will give its imprimatur to the publication of volumes of Bradman letters. This would be a precious gift to future generations.

In the meantime, *Remembering Bradman* splendidly provides some of the insights into this remarkable Australian so many of us have long craved.

MIKE COWARD
SYDNEY

Introduction

Most of us know already that Sir Donald Bradman was a great cricketer. His batting history tells us that. Not only does he lead world
cricket's record books as a batsman, he leads by a large margin.

What will be new to many of us is that he was also an extraordinary man. A man of outstanding intelligence, he also had a
single-minded strength of will and a degree of determination that
dominated every aspect of his life. It made him a great cricket
administrator, a fine golfer, an accomplished pianist, a successful
businessman and a bridge player not to be trifled with. It did not
make him an easy man to befriend.

Sir Donald was a great man and we expect a lot of our great
men. But in fact they are human. They have their strengths and
their weaknesses, and though many of the controversies that
dogged his early career have faded with time, this was true of Sir
Donald as well.

Sir Donald's friends and colleagues have not lightly spoken of
him. He was a man who valued his privacy highly, and his friends
considered this when they shared their memories. Aspects of his
life that were previously little known – his philanthropy, for
instance – come to light. I appreciate the openness and generosity
of those who shared these insights.

Although blessed with extraordinary talent, Sir Donald did not
live a fairytale life. He lived with the personal tragedy of losing a
child shortly after birth and with the everyday difficulties faced by
his daughter Shirley, born with cerebral palsy. On top of that, his

fame, a consequence of his sporting success, brought with it for him a degree of aloneness. That he kept his feet so firmly on the ground is truly remarkable.

I set out to interview a broad cross section of people who knew Sir Donald in his cricketing, commercial and private life. The interviews begin with Bill Brown, who first met him in 1932 when the cricketing legend of Don Bradman had already been established. For some who spoke, it is a story they have told many times before. For others, it is an opportunity to share these memories for the first time.

Reflections on Sir Donald's many years as Australia's leading cricket administrator shed light on some of international cricket's gravest crises, including the throwing controversy, the cancellation of the 1971–72 South African tour of Australia and the emergence of World Series Cricket.

It would be impossible to write about Sir Donald Bradman without mentioning Lady Bradman, his partner in marriage for 65 years. All those who came within her orbit speak of this remarkable woman with affection and admiration. Clearly she too will always be remembered.

1

HERO OF A NATION

When batsman **Bill Brown** *played his first Test for Australia in 1934, 25-year-old Don Bradman was playing his 24th. Brown went on to play 22 Tests – 15 of them with Don Bradman – and he spoke to me the morning after a Melbourne Cricket Club lunch commemorating Sir Donald's birthday. He had recently celebrated his own 89th birthday and he laughed and made the stipulation before we began: 'Drinking – I'm not going to talk of it. Women – I'm not going to talk of it. I'll leave that to everyone else's imagination.' His wife **Barbara** joined us towards the end of the interview.*

I'D PLAYED AGAINST Don when I played for Marrickville against St George but the first time I actually met him was when we batted together on the Sydney Cricket Ground. They'd divided Sydney into four zones – north, south, east and west. I was in the same zone as The Don and I had talks with him out in the middle.

You went on to bat with Don Bradman many times during your career. What was he like to bat with?
He was excellent. You had to play second fiddle but that wasn't difficult, you couldn't keep up with him anyway so you became a very good running partner, as it were. Not that he wanted you to do that, but most people found him very hard to keep up with. He was so good and a very enterprising runner between the wickets and he could handle the bowling far better than you could, so you automatically slotted into the fact that you were there to run up and down for

him. But it was a wonderful spot to see how he played and how he handled the bowling, to watch from the other end, as it were. His footwork and his timing were always a revelation and an inspiration to you. He was so quick and he hit the ball so very hard and he refused to be subdued. He attacked the bowling, let's put it that way.

Tell me about the New South Wales team you joined in 1932.
There were some great players. There was Alan Kippax who was captain, Stan McCabe and of course Bill O'Reilly was in the side. Don Bradman. They'd be the main ones. Jack Fingleton. A chap named Wendell Bill would open with Jack Fingleton. It was not an easy side to get into. There were some very good club players around Sydney and if anyone faltered in the side, they stepped in very quickly. However, I finished up there.

I guess my main step on the ladder was playing for New South Wales against Jardine's MCC side at the Sydney Cricket Ground in 1932–33. Another young fellow from Cumberland and myself were the main run-getters in the first innings against Jardine's team, and that gave us a bit of recognition.

It was in the middle of depression years and at one stage our whole family was out of work and things were a bit grim. But we used to go down to the Town Hall once a week and get food coupons and things like that. And if I wanted to go to cricket matches, my uncles and aunts were very good, they would weigh in with sixpence or something if I needed it and you'd scale the trams. You got on the wrong side of the tram, you see, where the conductor couldn't see you. You hung out there and he was on the lookout too and he'd come out and he'd grab you and take you and sit you down inside and say that'll be threepence or whatever it was. So you'd give him your sixpence and he'd give you three back and then you'd get out at the cricket ground and you'd have to get another threepence to get in.

I remember going out when I was playing against Jardine's team. I had an old bag and a cricket bat and the conductor said, 'Where are you going son?' I said, 'I'm going out to Moore Park.' That's where the cricket ground was. He said, 'Oh you won't get a game of cricket there today son, there's a big match on and they'll all be there to see Jardine's team.' I didn't tell him I was playing against Jardine.

In those days you did all sorts of work to get a bob in. I used to put a sugar bag over my back and cycle round and pick up boots and shoes to be mended and I would get a percentage of the take. Then I'd deliver the shoes back again a couple of days afterwards. There was a big long hill at Stanmore Road in Sydney and I used to cycle up there and this dear lady would say, 'Oh you look so hot and tired, come on inside.' So she'd take me in and apart from giving me shoes to be resoled and reheeled, she'd give me an orange drink and say sit down for a minute.

The morning I was playing against Jardine's team I had to get up very early and mount my trusty cycle, put the sugar bag over my back and do my round before the game started. Anyway, a young chap named Ray Rowe from Cumberland and I were the only two that got any runs. Bradman got out, McCabe and Kippax, they all got out. Two of us got runs and we were sort of the flavour of the month, two young no-hopers.

As we were walking off the ground that night, unbeknown to this woman, my mother and father were in the stand sitting next to her, and she stood up and clapped and clapped and she said, 'That boy, that's my boot and shoe boy.' (laughs) There I was in front of about 40 000 people and all she could think of me was as the bloke on the bike with the sugar bag over his shoulder.

Who did you have to withstand that day?
Oh no, no, Larwood didn't play, Allen didn't play, Voce didn't play. I can remember in the dressing room, Allan Kippax said,

'I've won the toss, Bill, you and Jack' (that was Jack Fingleton) 'I want you to open.' 'Righto,' I said, 'Allan, ah, who's playing for Jardine's team?' 'Oh,' he said, 'it's not who's playing, it's who's not playing. Larwood's not playing, Voce is not playing, Allen's not playing.' Oh yeah, I thought, the grass looks greener, it's a lovely day, the sun's shining, I wouldn't be anywhere else in the world. Prior to that I'd been lying in bed at night worrying. I had a fairly heavy bat, you see, and I'd thought, God, I'll never get this up in time for Larwood, he'll hit me fair between the eyes and that'll be the end of me.

What would it have been like for Don Bradman when he first joined the New South Wales team?

I think to a certain extent it was a hard school. New South Wales had some pretty developed and experienced players and they accepted you but at the same time they watched you and said what's this bloke like? Worth a game or is he a flash in the pan? And Don without wanting to did so well that he threatened the hierarchy as it were, so they treated him a bit carefully. And then of course in 1930 he went overseas and set the cricket world on fire and came back right up there. So I guess a little bit of jealousy crept in, no matter how much they tried not to allow it to. You couldn't help to a certain extent other cricketers being envious of his tremendous success and popularity. He'd go to a town in England and there'd be a few thousand people there to welcome the team to the town and all you heard was: 'Is Bradman playing in this match? Oh, there he is there, there's Bradman.' In other words, 'Get out of the way,' (laughs) 'you're blocking the view.' Now that was not his fault and he didn't court it but he couldn't do anything about it, do you see?

In those days I would open the innings with Jack Fingleton and if we had a good day we batted to lunchtime, and after lunch we'd find the crowd had grown from say ten or fifteen thousand to thirty or even forty thousand, the reason being that the word had got round that Bradman'll be batting this afternoon at the Sydney Cricket Ground. They would give us half an hour after lunch and then they'd get restless because we were batting in Bradman's time, you see. And if you got hit on the pads, not only would the bowler and the fieldsmen appeal, but the whole thirty or forty thousand would appeal. Cries of 'Out! Out!' (laughs) But they wanted him in; they didn't want to watch us. And when you got out you got a most tremendous ovation, not because you played well but because you were getting out of the way. (laughs) There'd be a silence and then down the steps he'd come and out onto the field and there'd be an air of excitement. He very seldom let them down. He scored a century I think about every three innings.

Didn't you find that demoralising?
No, it didn't demoralise us, we got swept along with it, as it were. When you batted with him he sort of lifted your performance as well, even though you very much played second fiddle.

I read of the double century you made in the Sheffield Shield match against Victoria in 1934 when Bradman came in after Jack Fingleton was injured.
I think it was indicative of the man. He came straight up to me – I was about 70 – and said, 'Bill, we must get your hundred before the next new ball,' which came on at 200 runs, about another 40 or 50 runs away. And he just got a single here and a single there and allowed me to take over the scoring. He gave me all the strike. The result was I got my hundred and he was only about 10 or 15. Occasionally with the new ball you got an unplayable ball, so it was considered better if you could get your hundred before the second new ball. So he completely subjected himself to getting me to the

hundred and I remember I hit a four from a chap named Ernie Bromley who was a young Victorian player, and that made me 103. And Don was about 10 or 15 and when I was 128, I remember this vividly, he passed me and went on. (laughs) So in another 20-odd runs, he got about 90-odd.

But you went on to make 200.
Oh yeah, I wasn't batting badly, I was batting fairly well.

Was the Australian team as hard to make as the New South Wales team?
Oh yes, you had to do something special. I was very fortunate. I was probably the last player picked in 1934. Whether I took the place of Jack Fingleton, or whether they picked Ernie Bromley and then they couldn't fit Fingleton in – it's very hard to say. I think he felt that The Don may have voted for me instead of for him on the side. Not that Don was a selector, but at the same time he may have had a say in the selection of the side. Poor old Jack felt that as a latecomer, I hadn't been through the mill and didn't deserve a trip, and I must confess that to a certain extent I've got to agree, because he took quite a bashing in the Bodyline series of 1932 from Larwood and Voce and these fellows and stood up to it. I know he was very, very disappointed. Whether it meant putting me out or it would have meant putting that young Bromley from Victoria out, I'm blessed if I know. It wasn't my decision. But I did feel very sorry for him.

How old were you when you made that first tour of England in 1934?
I was 20 years of age and I was goggle-eyed at everything, coming from Marrickville, which was a working-class suburb in Sydney.

Was it during that series that Bradman became ill?

He became very ill. At one stage they thought he might die and they sent word to his wife, come quickly. Well she couldn't come quickly in those days, she could only get a ship. We knew he was very ill but there's nothing we could do. We had a program to fulfil. Stan McCabe had been appointed vice-captain and he stepped into the breach and we played under him. We liked Stan and respected him and he was a very good captain too.

Tell me about Stan McCabe's legendary 232 in the first Test in England in 1938.

Oh yes, he scored a double century at Nottingham. You can talk at length about that. One of the statistics was that he and the last-wicket man put on about 80 I think in 25 minutes or something, of which McCabe got all of the runs except about five or seven. And watching it, it was a really great innings. The strokes he played and the ease with which he played them, I'll never forget that. I think the boys were watching it on TV, they reckoned they got a better view because you got the close ups and that, and Don said, 'Oh come and have a look at this, you will never see anything better than this.'

Was that the same match in which you and Jack Fingleton were booed for stonewalling in the second innings?

It may be, there was one Test. I was accustomed to being booed of course, that didn't worry me. (laughs)

How do you get accustomed to being booed?

Oh well, you just shrug it off, it doesn't hurt me in any way. People say to me Bill what did you regard as your finest innings? And I say the day I set fire to the Sydney Cricket Ground. They think about that for a minute and they say what was that? We were playing

England in 1932 it was, and I was playing very slowly and it was a dull day, I'm not sure there wasn't a drizzle of rain. Anyway, the crowd on the hill piled the papers up in big mounds and set fire to them and they said, 'Can you see any better now Brownie?' And some of the papers blew onto the stand and set fire to the stand and they had to get the fire brigade out. So they were hosing the stands and the crowd on the hill were saying, 'Never mind the stands, turn it onto that so and so out in the middle.' (laughs) It was me you see.

You'd have been very young then.
I'd have been 19, 20 yeah. The New South Wales people watching cricket were very demanding. They had a very good insight into the game and they didn't suffer fools gladly and if you didn't have it, they told you very quickly what they thought of you. And if you weren't playing the way they thought you should, they'd tell you in no uncertain fashion. It was a very hard learning curve in a way but it toughens you up.

My reaction to English crowds – I remember missing a catch out at Lord's. I dropped this catch, it wasn't a hard one, Percy Chapman hit a very high one right to the outfield and I came in . . . (he puts his hands together) and phut! down it went. Oh, I waited for the burst of abuse I'd have got in Sydney. You know, 'What are you doing over here? Who put you in the side? Did you buy your way in?' And instead they said, 'Oh hard luck, young Brown.' I thought, God, I must have caught it. (laughs) They were so very nice about it. In Sydney they'd have really given me heaps.

Tell me about the match on the 1938 tour when England under their captain Hammond made the score of 903 against Australia.
That was at the fifth Test at the Oval. It was a good batting wicket and they had some very good players and we just couldn't get a breakthrough with our bowling. Of course, Len Hutton got 364

which was quite a contributing score. Hardstaff got a big score and they had a good side on the wicket on which it was extremely difficult to get people out. It was what you might call a very placid wicket; the ball didn't rise a great deal, it didn't spin a great deal and it was a matter of waiting almost for them to make a mistake rather than sort of knocking them over. And they just went on and on and on. Hutton batted for three days. They batted first and we had to bat twice after that.

You toured England with Australia in 1934, 1938 and 1948. Did Bradman mix socially with the team on the ship on the way to England?

Oh absolutely. He was after all a member of the side and it was everyone's duty, as it were. I don't think we were told that but it was everyone's duty to mix in well with the side and be one of the boys. Now he didn't head for the bar and put his foot up and have a few drinks. He very seldom drank. He may have had the odd glass of wine but I don't remember him indulging in any what you might call 'strenuous nights' with the gang.

They had two sections on the ship. The front section was where the ladies had afternoon tea and played bridge and Don was often seen up there playing bridge. He loved bridge. And down the other end was the smokers' lounge where all the riffraff was, singing away and drinking too I'm afraid. (laughs) He didn't spend much time down there. He didn't care for that sort of thing. He was a very intelligent man and he preferred something with a bit of meat to it, something he could analyse and think about, rather than some of the nonsensical things we used to get up to down there.

Were there others who kept apart like Don?

He didn't keep apart. He just didn't go with the riffraff down that end of the ship. As I say, he liked his bridge. Ben Barnett was a great bridge player; he was the second wicketkeeper on the ship, and there may have been others, I can't bring them to mind now. Don was a member of the side but there was no getting away from the fact that he was Don Bradman. He couldn't push that aside. That was it. He was Don Bradman and people looked at him differently to the way they would, say, look at me.

We used to play a match down in the south of England which was run by a gentleman by the name of Leveson Gower, pronounced Lewison Gore, and he was a bit of a big noter. Liked to be with the upper echelon and in 1934 we went to lunch on the first day when we were playing this match, and if you didn't know Bert Oldfield and Don Bradman well, you could mistake one for the other, because they both had reasonably sharp features, same build and everything. And he grabbed Bert Oldfield and he said, 'Come on, dear Don, you must come and dine with me.' And Bert Oldfield being the man he was winked at us and went off and sat down at the top table and this fellow was saying, 'Now Don . . .' not saying a word to anyone else but devoting his whole time to Don (as he thought he was), and Bert's looking down the table at us and winking. Anyway eventually this fellow was in the middle of a story to Bert and he sees Don sitting down the table with the rest of the team. He couldn't do anything, he had to go on with it. We're killing ourselves laughing. Don thought it was a great joke.

Then in 1938 (I think it was '38) Lindsay Hassett and I accepted an invitation to go to the Officers' Mess at Cairo with the upper echelon of the British Army. We went along and we had a very pleasant evening. It was not a backslapping drinko sort of evening, it was a rather quiet, very dignified and very nice, almost cultured, evening. The ladies were the wives of the colonels, lieutenant-colonels and many generals that were scattered around. They had a place in the hierarchy and you couldn't push them around. And they said they would love to see Don. We were very impressed with the ladies and the way they went about things, they were obviously well bred and knew their way around. They said if he would only come they would put on another evening. He'd been to these things before so he was reluctant but we said no, it's not like that, these people are very well behaved and you won't be under any stress or strain. So he went in and we followed him and in 10 seconds flat they had him pinned in a corner. They were all round him with autograph books and bits of paper and we had to go and rescue him. (laughs) He had 20 or 30 people around him. We were staggered because it was such a change of character for these extremely dignified people but that was the effect he had on people. Amazing really. It was accentuated as he went on. He could never disguise the fact he was Don Bradman. Everybody wanted to meet him and talk to him and get his autograph.

Do you think Don Bradman's personality was in any way shaped by his fame?
The fame came once he started to make big scores in cricket and he became 'Don Bradman'. I think the fact that he became so popular and that he had such a big following to a certain extent enhanced his exclusiveness and forced him into being a bit careful with his friendships and people. I don't think he was ever completely gregarious. You see, he didn't drink at all. I'm not saying that if you don't drink you're a no-hoper, but there's no doubt about it, it does help in men's circles in the making of friendships. You don't have to get blind drunk every night but a couple of drinks. Don could make friends without drinking, but the fact that he was Don Bradman, to a certain extent, put him in an awkward position with people. He had to be careful what he said. People listened to what he said and no doubt repeated it and wrote it down. So the leanings he had towards being one of the boys were probably short-circuited by the fact that he was Don Bradman.

How did you rate Bradman as a captain?

As a captain on the field, he was superb. He never missed a trick. He remembered things, he analysed the game, he always had his fast bowlers fresh and ready when they were called on a second time. He was a very, very astute captain on the field, there's no doubt about that.

Vic Richardson was probably the most natural leader of men that I played under. He was quite a character. A man's man and by sheer personality he kept everyone under his control and they all liked him very much. They liked Bradman too and they respected him, they respected Woodfull, but Vic was a sort of, how shall I say, he wasn't a bad boy, he just lived life to the full and sort of swept everyone along with him but he was still the captain and we all liked him tremendously. He led the team on and off the field, as it were. Bradman led the team on the field, and off the field at all official engagements of course. But he didn't interfere too much with the boys off the field, whereas old Vic, he'd be last out of the nightclubs, and (laughs) a lovely bloke.

Did you consider Bradman a friend or a team-mate?

Don and I were not team-mates in the sense that I would be with other members. Take Arthur Morris or someone, you'd say, 'G'day Arthur, how did you go last night? Have a big night?' 'Oh gees, I've still got a bit of a headache.' 'Oh yeah, you always were a bloody idiot.' You didn't talk to Don like that. But he was a very rewarding person to talk to. He had a very deep insight into the game, he thought about it, he respected it very much. He had a very, very keen intellect. He didn't suffer fools gladly but he wasn't the only one in that direction, there are lots of other people like that. There's no way in the world you couldn't talk to him. And he was the captain and he laid down the general principles for the tour, as it were, and we followed those. That's in the nature of being an Australian cricketer. You respect your captain and if he wants certain things done, you do them.

We didn't see an awful lot of Don off the field. His time was really taken up with official duties and everyone wanted him out to have dinner with them. He probably preferred to be with the team than anywhere else, but being Don Bradman he had a lot of commitments anyway without his captaincy commitments and he was very conscientious about answering letters and things like that. He worked long hours after midnight answering things that he felt should be answered. So that he was not a normal captain. Other captains sort of said Ah, to hell with that, you know, I'm going to go to the pictures tonight, they'll have to wait. He put his official things first.

Was it easier for you as someone younger than Bradman to accept his popularity than it would have been for the older players?
Probably, probably.

He seems to have found much more acceptance in the 1948 team.
Well, he was captain.

He was captain in 1938 too.
In 1938 he had a strong enclave of seasoned players – Hassett, O'Reilly, McCabe – they were the three what you might call 'strong men'. They were very aware of their job as players and what they owed to the captain. And they would always get behind him. There was O'Brien – he was another one. I don't know the real circumstances but the version that we understand is that, well, these fellows were to a certain extent – they weren't playboys, they didn't knock around with women and that, with all due respects to women, (laughs) but they did kick it around a bit in amongst themselves, you know, had a few drinks and then a few more drinks and

then a few more drinks. They regarded that as part of the deal. They worked like dogs on the field, they'd bowl as many overs as they were asked in the boiling sun, do whatever their captain wanted, but they reserved the right to have a few drinks when they felt like it. Somebody – I don't know who it was – got the idea going in the Board of Control that they were not pulling their weight, that they were not fit and all that sort of thing. So somebody in the Board of Control decided they would have a talk to the players. So they picked O'Brien, Fleetwood-Smith, O'Reilly and McCabe. All Catholics. I was just a young scrubber when I started and I didn't know who was Catholic and who wasn't. I didn't give a damn. But when you're captain like I was in New Zealand in 1946, you are a bit inclined to look a little more closely into that to see how you can make the best out of the team.

But these fellows were called up in front of the Board and sort of stood there like little schoolboys from what I can gather until Bill O'Reilly said, 'What the hell are we doing here? If you've got something to say to us, say it.' And that was Bill's idea of handling a conversation. (laughs) Anyway the thing sort of fizzled out but of course the newspapers got hold of it and it was blown out of proportion. Don said he knew nothing about it but the players felt he should have had more to do with it and said, 'All right, they're my team, my players, I want to know what's going on.' They said he didn't front up, he said he knew nothing about it, not until it was over. It's only come up again in later years. I knew nothing about it of course. I was a stupid young scrubber, all I knew was how many runs I made, whether I took any catches or not and the rest of the world went on around me.

Did you enjoy captaining Australia against New Zealand in 1946?
Yes, I did. It was most interesting. We had diverse personalities in the side. You don't manipulate them, you sort of try and assess

them and try and get the best out of them, let's put it that way, so from that point of view it's intensely interesting.

During the war, you spent some time in Adelaide, didn't you?
I joined the RAAF. I was a pilot, not a very good one but I got by without killing anybody else or myself and I was stationed at Parafield in South Australia for a couple of years at least. And Barbara (that's my wife) came over from Brisbane, because you never knew where you were going next or what was going to happen and she and Lady Bradman became great friends. One of the reasons was they both had boys about the same age, that was John and we had our son Geoffrey and the two boys knocked around together and got up to the usual things that boys about six or seven years of age get up to. Barbara and Jessie or Lady Bradman became very close friends as the mothers of children and she eventually became godmother to one of our children. We spent a bit of time out at the Bradmans' home. Eventually I was transferred up to Darwin, to fly something else up there, and Barbara went back to Brisbane.

I was posted to the transport squadron, which is the best thing that ever happened to me. I flew around looking down at the poor soldiers. You could go anywhere then and I spent a lot of time in New Guinea. I've got mates who got the DFC in England and all that sort of thing, but they had a different lifestyle to mine. I class mine as a gentleman's war. Never got dirty doing anything.

Did you feel you became closer to Don during that period in Adelaide?
I became much closer to him than I would have in the normal circumstances, but I don't think he regarded me as a bosom friend. I think he thought more or less, Old Will, you know, I'll catch up with him next time I see him. We spent a fair bit of time together by virtue of the fact that our wives were so friendly. Barbara went

back to Brisbane and I stayed on in Adelaide for a while and at one stage, I stayed out at his home for about a week in between flights. They were very good to me actually. Don was head of the Commonwealth Club, a group of businesspeople who worked for charities during the war and he got me to go to a couple of functions and we visited other cricketers like Tim Wall. He and Tim Wall were great friends.

Sir Donald said of his postwar cricket years: 'I was fired with a zeal that I had not previously experienced.'
I suppose anyone who lived through or was part of the war appreciated things far more after the war than they did before, things which they had more or less accepted as the norm. Then all of a sudden they found that it wasn't the norm, that you had to fight for things.

The 1948 tour of England must have been incredible. [Bill Brown missed the English series in 1946–47 due to injury.]
Yes, I think early on Don wanted to go through undefeated. I don't remember him actually laying down the law, but it became pretty obvious that he didn't want anyone to beat our side. That required two things. It required some good cricket on our part but also you didn't give them a bit of a sniff, you know, to see if they could win. If you were going to close the innings you'd close it in such a way that they'd have to do a tremendous thing to beat you. You can do that, you know, you can bat on and make the job almost impossible for them, although we didn't have to do too much of that because we had a very good bowling side and we seemed to win our matches fairly comfortably.

England still had rationing, but early on Don said we're not going to have any favouritism, we're going to eat the same as the English cricket team or the English people. The only time I remember deviating from that was when the chef at the hotel one morning said to us that a person who was a great follower of Australian cricket had acquired, bought or had imported 16 or 17 steaks and he wanted us to have them at dinner that night. Attendance at dinner is not compulsory, if you've got something better on, well, you go, but I well remember this night they were all there, bright and early.

I remember another occasion at a golf club. We played this game with the members, all very pleasant, and went and had a few drinks and there was quite a lot of talking amongst the members. We said, 'What's going on? What's happening?' They said, 'Haven't you heard? There's ham tonight. Ham!' They were all excited. So we didn't live on the fat of the land, but it was all right. We got a bit of an idea of what the English people went through and we were just lost in admiration for them. They didn't say much but if they got an idea in their minds that they weren't going to leave London, you could bomb, you could do what you like, and they wouldn't leave. Blow people up and everything. Oh gee, they were tough. We got some idea of why they were too much for Hitler and his gang.

Did you ever play golf with Sir Donald?

I'll never forget one occasion Don and I played R. W. V. Robins and another fellow. R. W. V. Robins was chairman of selectors of English cricket at one stage and a very strong force in English cricket. He was the captain of Middlesex in England, and came out to Australia in 1936–37. He was a very good slow bowler and an aggressive batsman, not a maker of big scores, but a dangerous player and he and Don had this thing going, they played squash against one another, and they got stuck into it, and they played billiards against one another. A lot of fun but a great rivalry.

On this occasion, Don had put me up about 10 yards from the

green and Robins' bloke had put him over in the trees somewhere and he said, 'We've got them Bill, it won't get on the green from there.' He said, 'Just put it up on the green as near the pin as you can and we'll do them.' So I duly played a seven iron or something, but I lifted my head, you see, and hit the ground behind the ball and sent it about 18 inches. Whether by accident or design, I was out of the next Test. (laughs) I don't know whether it was the golf or not. He didn't play with me many times after that, I think he regarded me as a bit of a loser. I couldn't help it, I just lifted my head. He was not amused.

Did he have a similar relationship with the English cricket administrator Gubby Allen?
G. O. Allen, yes. They were both men who regarded cricket in a very high vein, they didn't just play it. They regarded it as a country's honour at stake and all that sort of thing, whereas some of us probably thought it was a good day out to make you thirsty. (laughs) They had much higher ideals about it; they kept the game on a very high plane. Didn't leave it to the hoi polloi to drag it down.

I remember dear old Arthur Mailey once walking in, we were all sitting in the lounge. Arthur Mailey was a spin bowler like Grimmett only he was a bit before Grimmett's time, but we all knew him and he was a pressman and he was very much liked by the team. He walked into the lounge this night and he said, 'I've got some free tickets here for the concert at the Albert Hall, anyone like to come?' And we said, 'Oh, what's on Arthur?' He said, 'Well it's Beniamino Gigli, the Italian tenor.' Now he was the world's greatest tenor of his time, and we said, 'Who?' He said, 'Beniamino Gigli.' 'Oh, thanks Arthur,' we said, 'but we're going down to the Roxy cinema, Bing Crosby's on down there.' I thought I saw a pained look come over his face as if to say,

God, who am I associating with here? Here's Beniamino Gigli, the world's greatest opera singer and I'm giving them free tickets to go to the Albert Hall and they're going down to hear Bing Crosby. (laughs) I don't think Don was there. This was after dinner and we were kicking it around in the lounge. I think Don had slightly more intellectual things than a Bing Crosby picture down at the Roxy. No, this was the riffraff that were left. He got the wrong group. (laughs) Don played the piano and he played it very nicely. I think he knew his music very well. I've no doubt he'd most likely have wanted to go.

Barbara Brown had rejoined us by this stage, having returned from a shopping excursion with a brand new hat to add to her already splendid collection.

BARBARA BROWN: Have you heard the story that Don tells on one of those tapes [recordings of after-dinner speeches] about the little boy who had to write an essay on a great musician? I think it was Bach. He wrote: He was a very great man and he led a very busy life and he had eight children. He used to practise on an old spinster in the attic. That's the funniest story I ever heard Don tell. He wasn't really a funny fellow, he had a droll sense of humour.

BILL BROWN: Oh he was all right, yeah, he was all right. It was just that he was forced into being Don, Sir Donald, probably something he didn't entirely want.

BARBARA BROWN: When he was knighted, the conservative Adelaide people were not awfully happy. In those days they all wrote in to the papers and said that had he been Colonel or had he been Commodore that would be acceptable, but there had never been a sportsman in Australia knighted before Don and it must have been very difficult for him to get this kind of criticism when he'd been given this big accolade. When they knighted Lester Piggott, everything was all right, you had two sportsmen. But they haven't knighted many sportsmen in Australia, have they?

Did you play bridge with the Bradmans?
BARBARA BROWN: No, I wouldn't have dared. With anything he took up, he really did it well, didn't he Bill? He played wonderful billiards, he played wonderful golf. That was Don.

BILL BROWN: He naturally applied himself to anything, very much so. He was the first one to envisage scores of over a hundred, although Ponsford did to a certain extent too, but Don made it his lifestyle. If we got a hundred, we thought how damned lucky we were to get a hundred and we got a rush of blood to the head and got out, but he went on and on and on and played better and better and better until he got 300 and up to 400.

BARBARA BROWN: A couple of years ago when they had the Invincibles reunion in Brisbane, we were all taken out to the races the next day. We had lunch in the dining room and then we were taken to the secretary's office to meet somebody and we didn't see a horse or a race or anything, so we were coming home at about 4 o'clock and this fellow came up to Bill and said, 'Aren't you Bill Brown?' Bill said, 'Yes.' He said, 'Well I've been wanting to see you for years, you're the reason I never saw Bradman bat. I came down from Cunnamulla on the train all night and I went out to the cricket in the morning and,' he said, 'you were batting. You batted the whole afternoon and Bradman didn't come in.' He said, 'I had to catch the train back to Cunnamulla that night so I never ever saw Bradman bat.' Bill thought he was going to say I used to see you play . . .

BILL BROWN: No, he told the truth, he got stuck into me.

BARBARA BROWN: Up there, in Brisbane, if openers didn't get out and let Don come in on a Saturday afternoon, they'd be furious. And if you got there and saw everybody coming away, you'd know Bradman was out.

Didn't that make Bradman unpopular within the cricket fraternity?
BILL BROWN: He was just a very great player, it was just who he was and there was nothing he could do about it.
BARBARA BROWN: When I first met Bill, I knew about Don Bradman but I didn't know about Bill Brown or Fleetwood-Smith or any of those people. The whole world knew about Don Bradman.

The young Don Bradman found a mentor in his father's employer Alf Stephens, president of the Bowral Town Cricket Club, a mayor of Bowral and owner of a backyard pitch on which young Don used to practise. Alf Stephens' son-in-law **Keith Wotton** *spoke to me in Bowral where he has lived for the last 67 years.*

MY WIFE PEGGY was Alf Stephens' daughter. He was Don Bradman's first cricket captain and he helped him get accommodation in Sydney and so on. Peg's dad had about eight trips to England – every time the Australian team went over, he went over. And the family went over in 1934, I think. At any rate, the girls were at a private school, a ladies school in Granthem in Lincolnshire, and Peggy didn't like it. Neither did her sister Joan. They thought Mum and Dad are tripping around, why can't we be with them? One day Peggy was sent for by the headmistress. She told me she was in fear and trembling, she didn't know what she'd done wrong. The headmistress said, 'Sit down, Peggy, now would you like a cup of tea?' Peggy didn't know what was going on so she said, 'What have I done wrong?' She said, 'Nothing, but is it true Don Bradman is coming to visit your aunt this weekend?' (Peg's mum and dad were staying with Peg's mother's sister). She said 'Yes.' And the headmistress said, 'Well would you do something for me? Would you get his autograph?'

Peg's dad helped him a lot so when they were going to name the Bradman Stand in Sydney, we were members of the cricket ground and Peggy said she'd like to go down for Dad's sake. We were down at lunchtime. He was very busy and he couldn't say very much. He said, 'You've got to excuse me.' They had an idea I played with him but I never did. See, he was eight years older than I am and by the time I got to Bowral in 1935, he'd gone to Sydney.

I remember though when I was about 12, Mother had been out to visit one of her friends with whom she used to play croquet and at teatime she said, 'Oh, there was a nice young man turned up today at Mrs Sherry's.' 'Oh yes,' I said, 'What's his name?' She said, 'His name was Don Bradman.' 'Don Bradman!' She said, 'Yes, he played the piano for us and he played beautifully. I said to him, "Mr Bradman I'd rather hear you play the piano than watch you play cricket."' 'Oh gee Mum,' I said, 'you didn't, did you?'

One thing Don Bradman and I had in common, we were both in St Jude's Choir at one stage. Don was a boy soprano, I think he used to get sixpence a service. I was strictly amateur. I understand they tried to find a reason not to pay the boys for misbehaviour and so on, so they were docked sixpence. I don't know how true that is.

I saw him play I'd say a dozen times and I'll tell you one thing about Don Bradman, how many people have mentioned his fielding? He was a brilliant fieldsman. I never ever saw him miss a ball or drop a catch and I don't know why he had that wonderful ability, he was moving into position before the ball was played. I reckon he was one of the most brilliant fieldsmen I ever saw and fielding is an integral part of cricket.

Don had an uncle, George Whatman, and the old-timers always maintained he was a better cricketer than Don. But in those days there was no money in cricket and he was an expert horticulturalist. He opened the batting for Bowral, he kept wickets for Bowral and when they couldn't get a chap out he'd take the gloves off and bowl slowies. I never saw him play but I had a bit to do with him. A very gentle person. Don's father worked for Peg's dad and he did all the fencing for him.

How did you feel about the Bradman Museum when it was first proposed?

I fought against it. We went to court about it and it cost us a lot of money. I didn't want it for various reasons I feel strongly about. They make too much of a fetish about Don Bradman. I wrote one letter to the local paper. I said, 'There's a Bradman Museum in Cootamundra, there's Bradman Place and so on here.' I said I thought it was overdone. At any rate, they got it. But I do think it is extremely well done. So we've mellowed a little bit and a few pieces we had that were Peg's dad's, we gave to the museum.

Did you meet Sir Donald when he came down to open it?

As a matter of fact, I was an official guest at the dinner they had on the Saturday night. I was sitting at a table with Bill O'Reilly and I found Bill O'Reilly a delight. A typical Irishman. He kept referring to the Little Bloke. I said, 'Who are you talking about?' He said, 'The Little Bloke.' Well, Bill gave the most wonderful after-dinner talk, he never referred to Don directly, it was always the Little Bloke. To open the pavilion, the revamp of the Bradman Oval, Don was to shape up and Bill was to bowl him one ball. A joker said to him, 'Bill, now what are you going to do if he hits you for four?' He said, 'He won't reach it.' And he was that far outside the leg stump. They weren't very good friends, Bill O'Reilly and Don Bradman. Bill O'Reilly came from this area, from Winslow. That's just the other side of Moss Vale. I never played cricket with him either. (laughs) But I was the president of the local association and captain of the district cricket team. I made a lot of friends playing cricket. We had good times together.

I was in the Bank of New South Wales and when we were stationed with the bank in Campbelltown, we knew Don's sister, Mrs Sproule, who made that famous statement: 'I don't know what all the fuss is about, he only plays cricket.'

Pity Peggy's not still here, she could tell you a lot about him.

England Test all-rounder R. W. V. (Walter) Robins and Sir Donald Bradman became close friends in the 1930s and their friendship developed over the years as both became engrossed in the administration of cricket. Robins served as an England selector and MCC team manager, as well as representing Australia on the Imperial (later the International) Cricket Council in England and organising the itineraries for Australia's English tours between 1948 and 1964. His son **G. R. V. (Richard) Robins***, Sir Donald Bradman's godson, spent two and a half years in Australia in the 1960s training as a journalist with the ABC. We spoke over a cup of tea off Sloane Square, London.*

I THINK FATHER and Don were very great friends for a variety of reasons. Largely because they both came from the sticks, became internationally famous at exactly the same time, were roughly the same age, had a clear view of the pomposity which existed in the game among the people who ran it in those days, and a healthy disregard for that. And they just hit it off.

And I think Don loved the fact there was somebody there who would take the mickey out of him. If anybody else ever tried, he wouldn't take it. He'd snap and shout pretty quickly but he'd allow my father to take outrageous risks with him and say some of the most outrageous things and get him to do things which he would never do, never have done, with anybody else. And when Don was in this country Father would take him to a nightclub and make him drink more than he was meant to do and get up to all sorts of high jinks and Don would always say that he behaved properly and my father didn't.

The Australian team used to stay at the Waldorf in the Strand and Don would have a palatial apartment there. In one case they came back very late one night and they were going up in the lift at about 2 o'clock in the morning and Don in that high-pitched voice of his said, 'Oh it was a great night. We shouldn't be drinking all that stuff so late at night, Robbie, I'm not used to it.' And there was another chap in the lift. My father thought it was an ideal opportunity to have a bit of a go at him so when the chap got out on the second floor and the lift door shut, Father said, 'Don, boy, don't you know? Going over the top a bit there, you know, we're still in rationing in this country. Not allowed to do that sort of thing. And do you know who that chap was? He's the Deputy Head of New Scotland Yard.' And Don's face fell by a mile. (laughs)

And they would swap autographs, because they looked fairly similar and people didn't know the difference between the two of them. Don would sign 'R. W. V. Robins' and my father would sign 'Don Bradman'. And they had some pretty exciting times when Don would put my father up in Australia, and they'd have some pretty lively dinner parties. All sorts of activities used to go on late at night and they were riotous good friends.

Of course my mother was very fond of Don and my father was very fond of Jessie, and they both got married in the early 30s, roughly at the same time. And the story is always told that Don, my mother and father went out to dinner in 1930 before they were married, very young people, 23, 24 I should think. What happened was that Don had been introduced to this attractive girl that my father proposed to marry and he apparently said to my father, 'Oh you'll never marry her, she won't have you, Robbie.' And he said: 'Well, she's told me that if I get you out in the Test match, she's going to marry me.' And of course Don says that the reason he got out in the second innings of the second Test against my father in 1930 was so my mother and father could get married. And he always used to tell that story and he always said, 'Oh, you know, my bat got caught up with my pads and I couldn't quite get it out in time,' and 'Nothing to do with the ball. I could have played it any . . .' And of course the next Test match, at Lord's, when he got 254 and played his flawless innings, my father, fielding at cover, went up to the captain Percy Chapman when Don came in to bat and he said, 'Give me the ball. I know how to get this chap out,' and bowled a leg-breaker with the first ball and Don hit it straight back at him and it went straight back and hit the picket fence in front of the pavilion like a rocket. And he was there to show that he was not going to make that mistake again. Absolutely. He hit my father all over the ground and played that wonderful innings. But it didn't alter the fact that off the field the friendship grew.

Father didn't go on the Bodyline series tour, because he'd just got married and my mother was pregnant with Penny, my elder sister. Which is a great pity because I think Father's sense of humour and sense of good fun off the field would have been a very good thing to have out there. When the pressure was beginning to rise he could have perhaps stopped it and let off a bit of steam with some humour. But there was no humour with Jardine around because he was a very tough man.

Father did go back to Australia in '36–37 as vice-captain under Gubby Allen and that was a very happy series. Although something happened. Don was extremely beastly to Gubby at the end of the series and did something or said something, which Gubby never forgot and Don always felt very guilty that he'd done it. I don't remember what it was but something happened between the two of them at that stage, but then they had to patch that up because for the next 20 years they were in charge of the game together.

And they did patch it up?

Yes they did, but again there wasn't the friendship, anywhere near the friendship. I read some of the letters from Gubby to my father when he went to Australia: 'I've tried to find the great man and he just doesn't seem to be available whenever I try to contact him.' And that could never have happened with Father.

Somebody has described your father as being almost all the things that Sir Donald wasn't, that it was a very complementary relationship, that he was spontaneous and funny whereas Sir Donald was more serious and always planned ahead.

There's a lot in that and I think that they both saw the advantage to each other in pursuing the friendship. Father was able to prick the pomposity and get behind the wall, more than anybody. John [Bradman] has often said that my father was perhaps the most . . . not irreligious but he was prepared to do anything, have a crack at anything. And that would really make Don sit up and listen because he was so used to having things structured and organised and set out in a proper fashion. Father would come in and say, 'You can't do that, Don. I mean that's absolutely ridiculous.'

Father was very clever and I think Don also appreciated that Father was an extremely able man and was prepared to see things from both sides of the coin. Whereas perhaps Gubby Allen, from his background, represented more of the old style patrician method of controlling cricket which Father and Don had no respect for and had contempt for. And the pricking of the pomposity was something that Don could really appreciate because that was 'Yah!' you know? And he'd quite often say, Robbie, I wish I'd said that. I'd have loved to have done that. I'd love to have been there when you did it.

Was the Don Bradman you met postwar the same man your father knew in this pre-war period?

No, I think it's important to remember that like a lot of people whose lives straddled the war, the Don Bradman before the war and the Don Bradman after the war were two very different people. The pre-war man was a very different character to the person that I got to know and to become very fond of.

How would you describe that difference?

Always with me he was cheerful and light-hearted and good fun. I think that he'd learnt to make a distinction between what he was going to be privately and what he was going to be publicly, whereas perhaps before the war he hadn't quite drawn the line and he was trying to be tough right the way through, with everything. After the war he developed more of a balance in his life. Sport wasn't the overpowering and important thing that perhaps it was when he felt that he had such a responsibility to Australia in the pre-war period. And he was taking over more on the administration side, where you have to have a broader view.

Many of the 1948 Australian players I've spoken to mentioned your father, saying: 'Oh we'd go off and do something or other and Don would go off with Robbie Robins.'

I have, I suppose, 60 to 70 letters written by Don to my family. There's a letter from 1948, when he finally agreed that he would come on the '48 tour and he wrote to my father and he said, 'Dear Goldie,' (in their letters to each other they called each other 'Goldie' and 'Snow') 'For the first time in your life you've been proved to be right. There is sentiment in cricket and it is only sentiment that is taking me to England for this tour and your letter was the defining influence in this.'

My father had said: 'This country needs to be cheered up, to be brought out of its sort of depression that it has been through during the war and your appearance and the appearance of your great team will do a great deal to affect the nation's feelings at the moment. It will bring them out of themselves.'

Don had said, 'I'm not coming. I'm not playing cricket any more. I might play some cricket in Australia but I'm not going abroad again, ever.' And so Father finally persuaded him and then he said, 'Oh, I'm only going to come if you're there all the time to look after me and help me through, because it's going to be absolutely terrible. I've got to have you there.' And so Father and Don used to creep off to hotels and strange places and talk about how the next stage of the cricket was going to go. Don did very much rely on Father who was on the selection committee, and captain of Middlesex.

Everybody thought that Father should captain the English team that year because he knew Bradman's psyche better than most people. But Father didn't think he was a good enough player, so he excluded himself from the selection process even though he was selected, and then said, 'No, I won't play. Norman Yardley should captain the side.' And Father stayed in the background. But as my father used to say, he was a stunning schoolboy cricketer, a brilliant club cricketer, an average county cricketer and a rotten Test cricketer.

That's harsh!
Well he was very harsh on himself, Father, very harsh on himself. But that was the right thing to do. He stood aside.

He must have been really important to Don at that time.
Well, he was. Don was always ill, always ill and it was ridiculous. Later he would always write to me and the first thing he would say was, 'Oh we've got bad news in Australia here. My legs are playing up', or 'I'm not well' and this sort of thing. And yet right up until

the last time in 1999 when he was just a very tired, little old man, I used to see him and there they were. Like the previous time, in 1995, he was there in his shorts and his long socks and Jessie was there and the house was full of flowers and it was absolutely wonderful. He was on the top of his game and he was as spritely as ever, and yet he had been writing to me for 30 years, always starting it off saying, 'Oh, I've got bad news from Australia. I'm not too well.'

And he'd been ill for the longest period of all time, because he was a hypochondriac. That time he had his appendicitis or whatever in 1934, he'd got something into his mind that he was always ill. Like a lot of great sportsman there was always a nagging problem. He felt when he came back into the game after the war that he wasn't going to be able to play anywhere near as well as he played before and he was worried about that. He was also worried that he wasn't a fit man and the fact that he hadn't been able to play sport prior to the war. And the fact that there were lots of people talking behind their hands saying, 'Oh bloody old Don, all he did was turn up at the recruitment place and sign a few memos going around and really didn't do anything in the war', I think that upset him.

So he needed his old carousing pal, because he didn't really have too many of those, to guide him through. He wanted to make all the speeches, he made 54 speeches. And Father would go round and make sure that everything was okay and that Don was under control and he'd come to stay with us quite a lot at Berkeley House, which is our house near Burnham Beeches Golf Club, near Slough basically, not too far from the centre of London. He really did rely on Father.

When he came over to this country in 1948, Don arrived at our home and he's brought all these packing cases with him. And he's sitting there and my mother's opening them and another ham comes out (laughs) and another ham comes out. He brought a whole stack of food from Australia because the Australians felt the

English were suffering so badly. During the Second World War my father sent my sister to Australia where she was put up by the Bradmans, and she would be telling Don and Jessie how desperate things were in England. They were so generous. They felt that we had to be looked after.

I notice that when he broke his ankle while on tour in '38 he went and stayed with your parents.

That's before my time obviously but yes, he did, and he'd always rag my father and mother about the quality of the lifestyle that they had. But remember, what Don was looking for was very much the same sort of quality of life that Gubby and my father had established. He saw cricket as a means to an end, and that he wanted to be a stockbroker, and he wanted to sort of be like Robbie. And he buys this plot of land and he builds one of the only two-storeyed houses in Adelaide. Everybody else has got bungalow-style houses and he's 'Oh Robbie and Gubby have got those houses, you know, I want two floors'. And yes, he saw cricket as a way of establishing himself, creating a home for himself in Adelaide, a family life, all that was exactly what he wanted. And then he wanted to be the businessman and if he was able to use the connections that he'd made during the cricket career, like Robbie and Gubby had done, well all to the good. Like Peter May who went into insurance broking, and Colin (Cowdrey) who went into the banking world, it didn't do any harm for their business, the fact that they were who they were. So Don saw himself as that sort of English amateur.

What was your father's profession?

He was an insurance broker and Father was chairman of our family business, which is a Lloyd's broker. Don was always fascinated to know how the Lloyd's brokerage business was going. And they did a certain amount of swapping. Father would get close to a chap in

England who would have a business in Australia and he'd write to Don and say, 'Get in touch with such-and-such because he's got a big business out there and he's going to need a stockbroker. You might get some business.' So through yet another channel their friendship was useful. They did quite a lot of trading off each other.

And it was a sort of David and Jonathon friendship. Both complemented each other, both had talents which the other could use and Father would use Don, quite obviously, when he wanted to put a point across to the MCC committee. My father represented Australia for 20 years on the International Cricket Council in this country and Don would say, 'This is what we want done' and Father would put the point to the ICC committee. Also Father, between 1948 and 1964, organised all the itineraries of the Australian cricket teams to this country, so that he would arrange the tour programs and Don would say, 'No, we're not doing that, and we're not doing that.' And so the two of them had all sorts of reasons, apart from pure friendship, to be regularly in touch.

What are your earliest memories of Sir Donald?
He came to us in 1953 when we were still living in Burnham and he was just this giant. Tiny man but a giant presence for a very small boy. But the first time I really remember him was three years later when he came back and stayed with us when we'd bought this big house in Hampshire. It was during the Olympic Games, which were in Australia but we watched them on the television with Don. Father would go and play golf and he would take Don to watch the local cricket team play. And what I did, which he wrote about in his book *The Art of Cricket*, I was a mad keen Australian cricket supporter, mad keen, and I didn't have an Australian cap. All I had was a green cap that my father had swapped with a South African player when they played South Africa in the thirties and I cut the

Australian badge out of the tour itinerary booklet and I stuck the badge on the front of the cap. Don saw this and he said, 'Why are you supporting Australia?' I said, 'I've always supported Australia, Uncle Don.'

At that time England was playing Australia at Manchester. It was that famous Test match where Jim Laker got 19 wickets, and I couldn't stand the fact that Australia was being beaten so badly. So I went into the garden where I'd rigged up my own pitch with a net behind it and did my own bowling with my own commentary. Did my own match. And after the game, when the Englishmen were coming off congratulating themselves on beating Australia so easily, apparently I walked into the drawing room where Don and my father were sitting and I said, 'Don't worry about the match that's on the television because Australia's just won in the garden with no trouble at all, and I got all 10 wickets.'

He thought that was the funniest thing and because I came in with this cap on, he said, 'Hey you can't have that. You've got to have a proper Australian cap,' and so for my 10th birthday the following year he sent me his 1948 touring cap. I loaned it to the Bradman Museum at Bowral and it's now sitting there, a very valuable piece of Australian cricket memorabilia.

So we sort of hit it off then and I perhaps saw him only a couple of times between then and 1965 when I went to Australia to live. I was fortunate to come into his life in the mid-60s when my father's life was ending, because he died very young [in 1968].

What were you doing in Australia?
For two and a half years, I worked for the Australian Broadcasting Corporation, training as a journalist. And when I got to Adelaide, Don put me up. Basically Don and Jessie let me have the run of the house. They were my 'mother and father'. I took all my pals around and he was absolutely wonderful. He played the piano and we played

snooker and I'd tick him off about how some of the Australians used to bat and he'd say, 'Ah they don't bat like that. I'll show you how they bat,' and Sam Loxton would come to supper or Richie would come to supper. Looking back now, there's me, as a 19 year old, sitting at the same dinner table as Richie Benaud and Don, talking about the subtleties of the game. And Jessie was wonderful and of course John was around a lot in those days and he and I played for Kensington Park in the grade side there, and in one match I outscored Bradman because John got nought and I got four. So I've always thought that was a tremendous success. But he was extremely good fun and the swimming pool at the back was always available.

My sister flew out for the last Test match in 1966 and Don put us all up in Adelaide and then I didn't see him again in Australia until about 10 years later. But we wrote a lot, and he came to England, I think in 1970. I took the cricket team to Australia in 1975 with my wife and again he put us up and that was wonderful stuff.

The man that I knew was a very much different person to the person that was on parade. He was just very funny. Very funny. And he'd tell us all these stories about what he got up to. He had a very broad range of interests and he often enjoyed his wine. But there was a very distinct difference between the man when he was on court and he was being serious and even playing games. He was very serious about playing his games. Very serious on the golf course.

And did you play golf with him?

Yes, and he played golf with my nephew William and they were level with two to play. He knows his course like the back of his hand of course in Adelaide, and Winkie (William) is a very good golfer as well. And they'd come to the seventeenth and Wink says, 'What should I use here Don?' and Don says, 'Oh I should think it's a two or a three from here you know. Got to give it a whack.' And of course Wink gets it out, gives it a whack and hits it miles over the creek and Don won the hole. Yes. Won the round. And Wink was absolutely furious. Stormed off the ground and I got a note from Don later saying: 'We've just had young William to stay. Not only did he drink all the vodka but his manners on the course could be improved by some distance.' (laughs) He was absolutely competitive, absolutely competitive.

It's been said that he would get a bee in his bonnet about certain issues like the front-foot rule.

Yes he would, he would worry a point to death if he thought that he had it right and the person on the other side of the argument was wrong. Absolutely. But it's fun that Father, and I to a certain extent, could say, 'No Don, you're absolutely wrong about that' and he would take it, but if somebody else tried that they wouldn't half get a flea in their ear.

Was that because he was used to being agreed with?

I think he was always agreed with and even in my company he would always correct Jessie. There was a classic in 1995 when we were having supper together and it was amazingly hot in Adelaide and Jessie says, 'Yes, you're quite right, it's been extremely hot. I think this is the hottest I've ever known since we've been here,' and Don's at the other end of the table. 'No,' he says, 'we had three days like this in 1934.' And he's serious. He's serious. And even to the end. We had dinner in Adelaide in 1999 and John is sitting on one side of him and I'm sitting on the other and I said, 'Now come on, Don. I don't want to hear about all those runs again and boring old stories, I want to hear about those two wickets you got. Now remind me what they were.' 'Oh,' he said, 'I got Wally Hammond out once, you know. He just under clubs it to mid-on and I got the wicket.' And John then butts in and says, 'Wasn't he standing at extra cover?' and Don turns around and says, 'No, shut up John, this is serious.'

It sounds like your father was one of the few people that didn't agree with him all the time.

Father was not a great politician, because he would say what he thought, but you see Don and he, by the time they were both dealing with the administration of the game in the fifties, they'd already been friends for 25 years, and so they'd grown into an agreement phase. They would basically think pretty much along the same lines. They both wanted one thing only out of cricket – that it should be an attractive and exciting game. It wasn't there to win at all costs, although when you were on the field there was nobody tougher than Don, and Len Hutton once told me that you could stick pins in Bradman and he wouldn't bleed. He was absolutely ruthless. But they both played the game in exactly the same way, which was entertain the public, give them what they want, that it was a positive game and not a defensive game. And they were both very scared that the growth of professionalism in the game would close it down and make it more of a defensive game, because you didn't have that breath of fresh air which was provided by the amateur approach.

But largely they came at life from the same perspectives. For cricket they had the same perspective, married young wives at roughly the same time, they both had two children before the war, they both saw cricket as a means to an end, as opposed to just being a game. They saw to it that their lives would develop in stockbroking or insurance thanks to the springboard that cricket had provided. And they both wanted desperately to give something back to the game which had given so much to them.

Gubby, the other great friend, was an astonishingly rich man. Very narrow-minded, bachelor all his life, with the old patrician view of how the game was played. He believed that. And a lot of the views that they had were absolutely fine, absolutely right, but there was always a sort of feeling in the back of Don's mind, 'Oh well, they're rather looking down on us. I'm not having that. Not being pushed around by those blighters.' So as I said that view on pomposity, which Father and Don agreed with so much, helped. So from a whole range of perspectives, they hit it off.

Don's relationship with Gubby has been described as essential for Australian and English cricket because Don represented Australian cricket and Gubby represented English cricket and between them they used to work out everything together. Where did your father come in that?

Usually as trying to keep them apart. (laughs) And I have no doubt that Don would use Father when he would write and say, 'I've had a letter from Gubby which says XYZ. Surely he can't really mean this and surely there's a way we can work round this.' And then Father would think it through and Gubby and my father would have rows about the management of the game, famous rows, ongoing, ruthless rows and yet underneath they were good pals because they respected each other and they were both great all-round games players. And so Gubby would listen to my father's views when he was trying to create a sort of meeting place between the two. I mean there were things like the dragging controversy and the lbw law and all sorts of things that Don was absolutely vicious about. And the throwing controversy was nipped in the bud in 1960 because Don said, 'We've all got to agree to this. If there are any throwers out there they are watched by the umpires before the Test match has started, and if there is any suggestion of it, they're out.' They controlled it, and they were probably lucky that they didn't have the intrusive press that you have these days.

It was just changing in the sixties, and of course then my father died. How he would have coped with the 'Stop the South African tour' and the Packer business I don't know.

*Do you think that perhaps Sir Donald liked to have a friend in
England as opposed to one next door?*

It may well be true to say he had more friends abroad than he had
in his own country. But I think that in any life it is very difficult to
have more than three or four very close friends. The rest of them
are acquaintances. It is not as though he stayed in an ivory tower
and didn't move out. I went to a Rotary Club meeting with him in
1975 and there were hundreds of people there, and he was just one
of them. I sat next to him and they all said: 'G'day Don, how are
you?' and that sort of thing. No real celebrity status.

But he did keep himself very, very much to himself, even when
he came to stay with my mother when he flew back for the last
time to this country. The Lord's Taverners invited him back on
their 50th birthday and he was surrounded by the Huttons and the
Comptons at this big dinner, and when he came down to the Isle of
Wight to stay with my mother he wore his coat collar turned up
and his hat pulled down when he was walking along the beach
because he didn't want anybody to recognise him. That was one
side of him. And yet there's this lovely photograph we have of Don
drinking a glass of wine at the dinner table at dinner that night,
from the wrong side of the glass, to see if he could do it. So there
you go. A lovely balance of how he would be. When he was private
among great friends he was one sort of person but if he just
stepped a toe outside the door he was different.

*He seems to have been almost afraid in the last years of the
demands of the press and the demands of people in general.*

In 1995 he was fine because Jessie was still alive and he was still
bouncing around but when I saw him in '99 he was saying: 'Oh,
I'm very lonely' and the trouble was that he had to keep the door
closed because he'd built up in his mind this awful problem that if
he did open the door just a fraction the world would pour in.

A lot of what Bradman was about can be traced back to where he came from. The family came from Suffolk very close to where I live, and they were a classic close-knit East Anglia family, used to getting on with their own thing, keeping quiet, not allowing too many in. It is classic of all the farming community up in East Anglia, you'll find groups of families who haven't changed in decades, generations. The same names would come up in the villages, because they're such a close-knit, almost inbred community. Very suspicious of anybody who comes in from the outside. Very religious, very suspicious, very inward-looking people. And now East Anglia has had a bit of air breathed into it by motorways and things like that coming into it. But Don Bradman reflects very much the Bradnam [sic] family which he came from, from Withersfield in Suffolk. And it needed somebody who was a meteoric character to draw him out of himself. You know, 'Come on Don, you can't do that. You can't sit inside when it's a wonderful morning. Come on, let's go and do this.' And that's really how the friendship was, Father lit the fuse so that Don would actually get out and have a bit of fun. And Jessie would say, 'Go on, yes, why don't you go out with Walter?' Father would say, 'Come on Don. Come and play some croquet' or 'Come and watch the cricket' or 'Come and see my son playing'. Anything like that. Or, 'Why don't we go out tonight and have a few drinks?'

Was Sir Donald someone who always had to be busy?
Yes always, always. Always had to do things. Even when we were staying there after breakfast he'd do three or four hours with his correspondence, then we'd have a break and go out for lunch and then he'd take us to somewhere and show us around and then he'd come back about 5 o'clock, he'd go and have a bath, have a drink before supper and quite early to bed. That would be the way he would run his life.

How did your father and Sir Donald treat their children?

I had the good fortune to deal with my father after the Second World War, when effectively he had become a much more mellowed character. But in that tough way that both Robins and Bradman approached dealing with their children, my father gave my elder brother a terrible time as a young man, a really terrible time, very much in the same way as Don treated John. I'll give you two examples. My brother wanted to marry a girl at the age of 22 and my father said, 'You're not doing it' and he refused to give his support. And secondly when my brother was elected captain of Middlesex for the 1960 season, my father stood up at the committee meeting and said no, I'm not going to vote for him. And so my brother didn't get the job. And he said it would upset his mother, because 'If he gets a run of bad scores and things go wrong and the papers get on to it it's going to be very upsetting for her'. Basically what he said was he's not a good enough player, and that's it. And so they selected somebody else.

That sounds very harsh.

It is very harsh, but that's the way that Don and my father both treated their children. They were very hard on them. They believed that was the right way to bring them up. It may not have been particularly nice but it was the right thing to do.

And you could argue that my brother wasn't up to it and (it's the old Australian theme) you've got to be able to earn your place before you're considered for the captaincy. And Father agreed with that just as much as Don did.

Don was the toughest man that you could possibly imagine. He was ruthless with his children, he was ruthless about the way that he ran his life. It was run to clockwork and it was run to an organised timetable. But during and immediately after the war, things *were* very hard and their approach only reflected what was happening in the world at that time.

Everything changed in the mid-60s when the world changed and instead of looking on your parents with reverence, you looked on your parents with something near disdain. Since then, families who use that old truculent approach have been laughed at by their children.

Both your father and Sir Donald were cricket selectors, a very demanding role which must have taken them away from the family.
Don always found time. Always found time. My father loved his business. He adored being in the office and nothing would drag him away from the city. He would make room for cricket in the evenings or at other times but those big sporting characters had to sacrifice a lot and put the responsibility on their wives to look after the family. And after all, that's what men did in those days. That is the way middle-class families ran their lives and the wives had to accept the fact that not only did these characters go to work during the day, they went to committee meetings in the evening, and they'd play golf (or squash, until they got too old) with their pals at the weekend.

Your father and Don both played squash, didn't they?
Yes, and Don was a very fine squash player. My father was a good squash player but I remember my father telling this story about Don and Gubby coming back from playing squash and I think Gubby had won because Gubby was one of the great players. And Don said, 'I played squash with Robbie the other day. Pretty good player, you know.' And Gubby was driving his Bentley and said, 'Merely a retriever old boy.' (laughs) I'm afraid Father was really like that. He was very, very fit and very low centre of gravity, and ran like a hare, but he was basically a retriever and he wasn't a thinker about the game.

But they played a lot of squash together and golf, but particularly golf. When the Test team had arrived from Australia, Father would always entertain them all for a weekend at the home in Berkeley House and there'd be a golf day and the team would play golf at Burnham Beeches and they'd be paired off with various other people.

How do you rate Sir Donald as a cricket administrator?
It's a fascinating era in cricket, between 1930 and 1970, before the game changed entirely and professionalism became the norm. It was a wonderful period. I think that you could have found that cricket could have run into an awful lot of problems between '45 and '65 if Bradman hadn't had the helm. Lots of things could have gone wrong.

Basically the main change was from being an amateur game with a few professionals into being a professional game. But he always took great credit for everything. He was never wrong. He would always say, 'No, you're wrong about that. No, it wasn't like that at all,' and he was never wrong about anything. It was a huge joke and we just laughed but people actually took it very seriously, because Don was serious about it. He could be very, very pedantic, very boring about going on about his own subject, so that it really did need somebody to breathe a bit of fresh air in there, or else he would have, he could have been, an extremely, unattractively dull and bitter man.

But Father was able to get at him and I think one of the great sadnesses is that the two of them weren't able to grow old together because very, very few crept into the inner circle. But he always had Jessie.

And I'd have thought Jessie could prick the bubble a bit.
Yes she always said, 'Oh Don, don't be so stupid' and 'Don't be so stuffy, Don' and that sort of thing and he would actually take that on board. He would listen. But it is that boundary between his personal life and his professional life which is the key to it because once he crossed that line he was an entirely different person.

And the trouble is that too many people who he knew on his professional side were journalists or went into the journalistic world and gave the world an impression of Don which was, to my mind, inaccurate. He was almost a closed book before the war except to my father. It was only after the war that he began slowly to open out a bit, thanks largely to Jessie. Slightly to Father but largely to Jessie. Jessie made him come out.

Because you do know, he's a little, ordinary man when you cut him off from that public figure, he's a little, ordinary man who delighted in conversation and friendship and meeting old friends. He loved his golf, loved his snooker, loved his wines, loved having pals and friends over for supper and that sort of thing. And he loved his music – Don would always play a bit after supper – and his cricket, but it's like turning a light off, the moment that he was on court it was an entirely different approach. And so few people were given the opportunity to see the private side of him because of the absolutely cast-iron wall that came down between himself and the outside.

Interestingly, the competition between my father and Don, they played six times together at Test level and it was three-all. And Father was once asked why Bradman was such a great man and he said he was great for three reasons: as a cricketer, as an administrator and as a man. And that's a very nice epitaph to have.

Cecil Starr was the one to bring up his age when I interviewed him at his home in Adelaide. 'At 94,' he said, 'I think I am the oldest living member of the South Australian Cricket Association.' He played for South Australia and served on the South Australian Cricket Association with Sir Donald as well as acting with him as state selector.

SIR DONALD WAS picked in the New South Wales side in 1927 and I was picked in the South Australian side. New South Wales had sent their team first of all up north and then they sent them across by train and the reason they did that was because they'd stop and play a game at Broken Hill. And from there on they came down to Adelaide and played South Australia.

Was it your first year with South Australia?
Yes. I finished up as 12th man, so I didn't play. He made 114 or 118 in his match.

Did you play against him again in Sheffield Shield before he came to South Australia?
No, I don't think I did. I played against Bill O'Reilly – does that name ring a bell? – at his first game at the Adelaide Oval and his last game on the Sydney Cricket Ground.

Did it cause a great buzz in Adelaide when Bradman came to play for South Australia?
Oh yes, I think it did really. I had a fair bit to do with him because I was one year older than him and when he got married, he had a son [in 1939] and both his son and mine (I've got a daughter and a son) went to the same boys' college, St Peter's College, and were in the same class.

What was he like to play against in club cricket?
Very nice. Really good. A really top competitor, really excellent. Yes, no complaints.

Were you batting at number three for South Australia when he joined the team?
Yes, I opened up for a while and I batted down the list a bit. I used to have a lot of trouble with my right eye, I used to get a recurring ulcer on the pupil and that kept me out of a lot of cricket. I didn't

bat with Sir Donald. He definitely changed the South Australian side by coming, for sure. They built into a very good side and they won the Sheffield Shield for at least three or four years. I played after the war. I played one set of tours. We did Victoria, Sydney and Brisbane, all in the one stint, straight after the war, in 1946.

Were you on the state selection committee with Bradman?
I had two stints as a state selector, seven years pre-war and eight years after the war. Phil Ridings, Bradman and myself sat on the South Australian selection committee for eight to ten years each. We'd have variations of opinion, we wouldn't agree on selections, and some things, but I can't say that in all my contact with him I ever saw him get angry.

How would you describe the role of selector?
It's different to anything else on a cricket committee really because you are dealing with individuals personally all the time. I was on it when I was playing a bit but if you weren't a player you had to be prepared to go and see a match every Saturday, so it was quite demanding in that area.

You were both involved in the South Australian Cricket Association for a number of years. What was Sir Donald like to sit on a committee with?
Excellent. Very helpful, very knowledgeable. Probably he would be the best all-round committeeman that I've ever sat with on any committee. He was very meticulous and on any subject that he wasn't clear on, he would make sure he found out a bit more about it before he got too involved. He was so capable overall and he had a very strong financial brain. He wasn't dominating.

If he had anything to say and what he had to say wasn't confidential, he would say it, and it was always pretty sound. You could either take it or leave it, no harm done. I think he would have been an outstanding committeeman in any sphere and I know a lot of organisations and sporting committees would have liked him on their board for sure.

Was he demanding of others?
Not so demanding but if they didn't contribute as committeemen, he wouldn't go out of his way to help them at all.

Did he delegate?
Oh yes, he wasn't one of the fellows who wanted to be number one all the time.

Was he interested in cricket across the board?
Oh yes, although there wasn't much he could do across the board once you got past state cricket. He couldn't do much for country cricket unless he got on the committee and he didn't want to do that, he was too involved with Test cricket, state cricket and even club cricket. Country cricket is a separate issue down below that.

You both must have had a lifetime of cricket committee meetings.
(laughs) Yes, that's true. It wasn't unusual to be tied up three or four nights a week sometimes in the cricket season. It didn't happen that often, but it did happen because there were so many subcommittees in the cricket association because they had to hand it down to the running of district cricket, 'A' grade teams, country teams – that all emanated from the cricket association itself. It's not quite so demanding these days, because they've got computers and machines that have taken a lot of the work.

Did you enjoy cricket committees?
I did, I liked it.

Over the years, did you feel close to Sir Donald?

We would go to cricket functions but we weren't socially very close. He was quite a retiring person really in that respect because he had such a lot of demands on his time. I don't think he looked for a wide circle of friends.

Do you feel Sir Donald's fame influenced his personality?

Well, first of all he was an outstanding cricketer all his life – schoolboy, state, country – outstanding. And I think that all just dovetailed in and followed on one from the other. I can't see anything that could take away from that.

How do you rate Sir Donald's overall contribution to South Australian cricket?

Well, it would be impossible to measure, it was so great. And to me, it's quite noticeable now where South Australia are not as prominent in the cricket world in general as they were when Bradman was there.

*Retired headmaster **Colin Brideson** was a schoolboy in pre-war country South Australia when he first saw Don Bradman in action.*

I REMEMBER THE first time I saw Bradman bat was when the South Australian team went to Strathalbyn. That was where I was born. I would have been in primary school and we had a holiday from school and a new turf pitch had been put down and all the town gathered around. Bradman was there with the team. I'll never forget it because Vic Richardson was on the microphone and in real country style you had the motor cars around the oval and Bradman made his hundred. (laughs) He belted the ball everywhere. I remember Vic Richardson telling the people to move their cars back so that they wouldn't get a ball through the windscreen. Then Bradman told the local captain, because it was a local team they were playing, 'Put a man out there.' He was a hundred and something and he belted the ball and it would have gone for a six but the guy was just where Bradman had told the captain to put him. That was in about 1938.

John Wilkin *represented South Australia in cricket and golf and recalled seeing Don Bradman play for the district club Kensington before the war.*

THE GREATEST INNINGS I've ever seen Bradman play, I was only 14 or 15 at the time, I think it was 1938. It was a district cricket match. He was playing for Kensington and they were playing at the Kensington Cricket Ground which was a very big ground – I think it's either wider or longer than the Adelaide Oval – and he used to live right next door to it. In those days they used to start at 1 o'clock and if you didn't score 400 in a day, you'd think you'd get beaten on the first innings. He went in first wicket down at quarter past one and he got out at five to six, he was caught on the sightboard, 301. On his own. Three hundred and one. We've heard all his wonderful scores, but this day he'd hit the ball no higher than this roof for a six. They weren't these dolly sixes. And he broke the pickets with his fours, he had about 20 fours and 20 sixes. It was just a magnificent innings. He wasn't a big man, he wasn't that strong. He just had magnificent timing and he used to have that extra second – he'd get into position where he could place the ball between the fieldsmen. When I played golf with him, I said to him of all the innings I've seen you play, I've never forgotten that innings. I suppose it stamped itself on me because I was young, but I said, 'Do you remember it?' And he said, 'Yes, I do as a matter of fact, because it was the first time they'd asked me to use a steel-shafted bat.

I must say they did bang off it that day.' Oh, it was just a magnificent innings.

*Decorated war hero and governor of New South Wales from 1966 to 1981, **Sir Roden Cutler VC**, spoke to me only weeks before he died in February 2002. He struggled to recall a relationship which had grown over more than 50 years into a mutual deep respect.*

I SUPPOSE THE first time I met him to talk to would have been before the Second World War.

What did you like most about Sir Donald?
I liked his frankness. It's hard to say. He was to me a hero always. And I suppose still a hero, even though he's dead. I sought his company every cricket match and then it came later that he sought mine at every match.

So you became friends?
Oh deep friends. He used to drop me a note or ring me or write to me with his views on this, that and the other. We became very close.

What was he like to watch cricket with?
You kept out of his hair, you didn't tell him that was wrong and that was right. He'd say 'Rubbish. He did the right thing. He's decided to bowl inswingers,' and things like that.

Did you agree with his views on cricket?
Oh, he knew best. I didn't argue with him. He would say, 'He started at the third ball that had been bowled in the fourth Test,' or something. He knew about every ball bowled in his lifetime.

Did he have views on most subjects?

Oh, I suppose he did. Very definite views on most things and that was that. He was very much up to date with world affairs and what was happening or what he thought should happen or would happen. I'd say, 'Don, they said this in the *Herald*.' He'd say, 'Yes, I know. They were wrong, weren't they?' And bang, that was the end of that. Yes, he was very much a man of the world.

Did you know Lady Bradman?

I knew her very well. She and my wife were friends. She was a wonderful woman and my wife was very fond of her. She was often our main contact.

Did you often visit them in Adelaide?

Many a time. Although strangely enough I never met him at his home. I was pretty busy.

In that case you had a lot in common with Sir Donald. He must have related to the demands made on you.

I think so, yes. I know I'm a perfectionist, to the point of being a nuisance, and Don Bradman, I think, was the same. You did a thing properly and went over and over it, time and time again until you could do it exactly, properly.

What attitudes to cricket did you share?

The decency of it. Anyone who didn't play the game according to the game was not wanted.

2

FROM THE SHADOW OF WAR

*Don Bradman encountered sporting journalist **Percy Beames** in his guise as both journalist and the captain of the Victorian cricket team in 1946. Percy Beames covered cricket for the* Age *until he retired in 1976. He was approaching his 90th birthday when we spoke at his home in Glen Waverley.*

I WENT TO the *Age* newspaper in 1946 and I was captain of the Victorian cricket team that year. Naturally we went round Australia with the teams when the English Test team toured under Walter Hammond in 1946–47. We flew over and picked them up in Adelaide. Even when he was captain of Australia Bradman stood back, he wasn't one of the captains that really mixed with the press. He didn't ignore them or anything like that, but he stayed in what you might call his position. He did the things that had to be done, perhaps he might help announce the Test team or things like that. Hammond was captain of England and obviously from the start of the tour there was a lot of dislike between the two men, Hammond and Bradman. They had respect for each other in their playing ability but there was a lot of difference in the way they treated the players and the way they treated each other.

Hammond was employed by a big car manufacturing firm in England, Packard or something like that, and from the start he picked up a car in Adelaide and he and the manager of the team travelled together with the property steward. They left the control of the team from that point on to the baggage man, to travel with the team on the trains. Bradman didn't appreciate that for a start. The other thing that he disliked was the fact that whenever there was a match coming up, a Test match particularly, and they'd go out to toss, Hammond always wore a brown felt hat with his white clothes. That infuriated Bradman, but he covered it up very properly. So there was this dislike between Bradman and Hammond. As quality players, there was a certain amount of competition between the two as to who was the better player. Of course Bradman's figures proved that, but Hammond was a very good player too.

So the feeling started straight away. And then of course in the first Test Australia and England played at Brisbane, Bradman went on and made that big score and there was a grave doubt about his dismissal or should-have-been dismissal at 28. I think he might have been out too, but he was justified in holding his ground until given out because there was a certain amount of doubt. And of course when that happened they all appealed and went up there and the effect of it was Hammond was accusing Bradman of being a cheat. So that worsened the feeling that already existed, so from that point on they were never going to get together again, not as cricketers, you would imagine, would. He wasn't forgiven.

Did you have the chance to get to know Bradman as a cricketer?

I became the captain and a selector of the Victorian team in 1946, and that was the year Bradman became manager of the South Australian Sheffield Shield team. It was the usual thing for the captain of the visiting team to sit with the manager of the home team when the two teams had a lunch together on the day of the match so I sat next to Bradman whenever we played South Australia. I got to know him better still because Jack Ryder was manager of the Victorian team at that stage and he and Bradman were Australian selectors for the Test team. Ryder used to convey one or two thoughts back about discussing the team with Bradman.

It was Bradman, Ryder and [Chappie] Dwyer from New South Wales. For instance, at that particular time we had a fellow, Bill Johnston. There was a great controversy when in 1946 we picked Bill Johnston from Richmond to play for Victoria. The Richmond Club were so incensed about the move that they were going to report us, the selectors, to the Victorian Cricket Association, because they considered we were going to ruin his progress by changing him from a fast-medium left-hand bowler to a quick. The same thing happened in Sydney, we had to use Johnston as a fast bowler and he did very well. New South Wales had Morris, Lindwall, Toshack, Lush, almost the cream of the big side, and we played a draw with them. Prime Minister Menzies was there. He was so impressed by the way the young fellows had performed that he decided to give us all a dinner in Melbourne at the old Hotel Australia. There were 13 players as well as Bob Menzies and his brother Fred.

When Bradman saw Victoria play against South Australia down at St Kilda, Bill Johnston came on later in the day after our alleged fast bowlers had bowled the quicker stuff, Johnston came on and he bowled slow and then he bowled quick on this particular occasion. Bradman said, 'Tell Johnston to forget about his slow bowling, he's a fast bowler.' And Bill Johnston turned round from that point in his career, changed over to quick bowling, and then he bowled for Australia so it was Bradman who influenced him in that case.

I got to know Bradman a little bit better when Victoria played South Australia on the Melbourne Cricket Ground and Bradman had come back again to lead the South Australian team. There was Bradman, there was Grimmett, there was Ward. They had a very strong side. I think Grigg was captain of our side, Lindsay Hassett was in the side, Keith Miller and a few others and we batted first, and we were in a bit of trouble. The early batsman failed and then

Keith Miller and myself came in. At that stage we'd have been five or six down. We went on, that first day and Miller I think was 90 not out and I think I was something up that way. The next day we came out and we continued on and both of us went on and made our hundreds and then got out and we'd amassed a reasonably good score by that time. You know, 480 or something like that, we thought we had a good chance. Bradman and Babcock went in and they practically wiped the whole score off before we got them out.

Did you cross paths with Sir Donald when he was a journalist?
I saw him later in England when Australia toured there. You might recall he went over to do the *Daily Mail*. We didn't see anything of him before the Test match but he would arrive just before the game started, he would sit right up at the back there, not try and get down the front. He had one of the chaps from the paper with him, and at 4 o'clock, obviously when the edition time was due to come out, no good him staying any longer, he would just quietly get up and go and you wouldn't see him there until the next morning. He never mixed with the rest of the press. I didn't see him at any stage in a conference or sitting around with the others.

You probably know too that there was a feeling among a certain section of the players. I knew Jack Fingleton very well, I did his copy for him in South Africa the first time I went there in 1949–50. He didn't want to go because South Africa was still minor in the Test field so he said would I do it for him and I said yes. I got to know him, and many a time there would be reference made to Bradman. O'Reilly, Fingleton, Chuck Fleetwood-Smith. I think the thing that got in their gullet was the fact that when he received the £1000 on the 1930 tour, he never bought a drink for the players. I think that was the key that set them back absolutely. But I could not name one person to you that would have a genuine bitch that would stand up to justification to Bradman. It was really remarkable that all the young kids in that 1948 side spoke so highly of him.

It might have been the fact too that Bradman had always had that country person's reluctance to come out and big time. It's not so much now, because we've got TV and so on, but in those days the country person, you always waited to be asked or advised or something like that, whereas others like O'Reilly and Fingleton, McCabe, they wouldn't hesitate about walking in on someone or taking a liberty or expressing their views or any of those things. I don't think he ever lost that reluctance.

Among Sir Donald's closest cricketing friends were the English Test bowler, selector and team manager **Sir Alec Bedser** *and his twin brother* **Eric**. *Over the years, the brothers have visited Australia 28 times. We spoke in the house in Woking that they helped their bricklayer father build in 1953–54, only half-a-mile across Horsell Common from the cottage in which they grew up.*

When Alec and Eric Bedser turned 80 in 1998, Sir Donald contributed the following to the publication that celebrated the occasion:

I FIRST MET these remarkable brothers in 1946 when Alec toured Australia with the 1946–47 English touring side. In a January Test in Adelaide, in a temperature of around 105°F, Alec bowled me for a duck with the best ball I faced in my whole career. It swung in, pitched to right leg stump and took the off bail. It was only one of many such balls he bowled during his long and illustrious career. Since that now-famous occasion our friendship has remained staunch and true and during the passage of the years we have remained closely in touch by phone and mail, augmented by the annual visits Alec and Eric have made to Australia. My wife and I looked forward to those occasions. Sadly she was recently called to a higher service but I know she would have loved to have joined me in sending this brief tribute to these remarkable brothers as they reach their 80th milestone.

Both men have given a lifetime of service to cricket for which our great game should be grateful. Cricket has a wonderful habit of creating lifelong friendships. In the case of the Bedser brothers I think their outstanding contribution to cricket and to life in general has been their transparent honesty and sincerity. They exude an integrity which is the hallmark of great citizens and they are outstanding examples for young players of all ages to follow. I am delighted to join with their many friends in sending congratulations and paying a tribute to this remarkable couple.

SIR ALEC BEDSER: I first met him in Adelaide in '46 when we played against South Australia at the Adelaide Cricket Ground. I didn't actually play in that game and that's when I first saw Don and young John, he was six then, and Jessie, you see, so I've known them since then. I was quite friendly with young John even then. I have a picture somewhere of him sitting on my knee watching the cricket. Then of course we played against each other in '46 and '48 and we weren't so close then.

What was he like to play against?
SIR ALEC BEDSER: He was just a damn good player.
ERIC BEDSER: Difficult, I suppose one would put it. (laughs)
SIR ALEC BEDSER: Yes, of course he wasn't too well in '46, he'd been ill and I think it was a bit touch-and-go whether he was going to play, but he got 100 at Brisbane. So I think that decided him that he would carry on. If he'd have got out cheap at Brisbane I think he might have packed it in. And then his health got better and he played then and improved, and of course he came to England in '48, which

was the best thing that happened. Best thing for cricket that he came to captain the side. It made the tour, because he was held in the highest esteem here and you can imagine, just after the war and everything, the first big tour of England. In England, Australia was *the* Test series and the Australians were the great attraction. And no one had seen anything of course for five or six years and the crowds were enormous. We were still on rationing and all that sort of thing.

What was it like to bowl to Don Bradman?

SIR ALEC BEDSER: Well you had to bowl pretty well really. Any ball that was loose or anything he scored from it, so it made you bowl properly, that's what he did. It was a good education really, when you were beginning and you realised what you had to do to be a decent bowler, and that's what it amounted to.

I got him out a few times. I mean I'm not a theorist or anything like that. I rate cricket as a simple game and all you can do in bowling is if you bowl and control length and direction and if the ball does something, well it's a lucky day, you get someone out. But the point is you've got to be consistent and for the largest percentage you've got to be damned near a bat. With Don, I got him out with being persistent, I suppose.

He spoke very highly of you.

SIR ALEC BEDSER: Yes he did, yes, he was very kind. See, I bowled him out in Adelaide in '47 when the ball swung and pitched back and he went back and he missed by about that much. And of course I nearly did it again in the second innings when he came in. Nearly for a pair, you see, but it just missed the second time. But from then on he realised I could do it, so I think that affected the way he played as far as I was concerned. And then we got him caught out on the leg side but people said it was a trap – well it wasn't really. When he first came in to bat he always wanted to push the ball for a single on the off side so we thought well, if we can try to stop him doing that, and in the process we put two or three fielders there. As it happened the ball moved, and if the ball moves there isn't anyone really can control where it's going, not even he, if it moves late. And that's what happened. It moved late. Simple. Three in the same place. Three running. So everybody said, 'You had a trap'. Well, hit the ball at the pitch right and it swung and he played the stroke and it happened to go straight to the fielder there. It could have gone wider, but it didn't. But it happened three times running which was great. In point of fact I got him out six times running.

So he had reason to fear you . . .
Yes. He had the last innings in Sydney in '47, then he came over here and he played against Surrey, and I got him out. He got 100 then. That was twice. Then I got him four times in succession in the first two Test matches so we met six times in succession. He got 200 in the process. He got 100 against Surrey and he got 100 at Nottingham.

      Then in 1953 he came over here to work on the *Daily Mail* with Alex Bannister, and then after that when I'd finished playing, when I became chairman of selectors here and managed three sides to Australia, then I got to know him. I really got to know him from about '56. I got closer to him when I became a selector because . . .
ERIC BEDSER: . . . he was a selector at the same time you see, for Australia.
SIR ALEC BEDSER: Yes, he was selector in Australia and he was chairman of the Board and he was in an official capacity and I was then, you see.

The role of selector seems to be bit of a thankless task.
SIR ALEC BEDSER: Yes it is, but I enjoyed it. You can only do as well as you can. I mean, there's a lot of rot talked about it, you know, if

you haven't got the players well you can't be any good. I mean you can't make . . .

ERIC BEDSER: We say to people: selectors don't make cricketers. We can only select what you've got there. That's what it amounts to.

SIR ALEC BEDSER: But he was very friendly with both of us. He's been here. He came here with . . .

ERIC BEDSER: Yes, with John and Jessie.

How did the friendship develop?

SIR ALEC BEDSER: I think it was just the passage of time and the fact that you were doing side-by-side jobs really. I mean he didn't make friends easily, Don, and he obviously must have taken to us and respected us.

ERIC BEDSER: But it took a while. The thing sort of gradually built up. We didn't push ourselves and he didn't but it just came gradually. It just developed.

SIR ALEC BEDSER: We corresponded regularly and of course the more we went to Australia the more we saw of him and so it developed that way. And we were very friendly with Jessie. Jessie was a lovely person. I should imagine Jessie had a lot to do with Don's success.

ERIC BEDSER: I think that it's fair to say that Jessie helped to knock the rough edges off of Don in the early stages, but he learnt very quickly.

SIR ALEC BEDSER: A lot of things were said about him. Obviously he had a pretty hard start in the bush and he had to look after himself and everything else and he didn't drink when he was playing, he didn't smoke and he didn't like going to pubs or anything like that, so I mean he was often accused of living a life on his own. Well in point of fact he did – he didn't go out and mix with the Fingletons and the O'Reillys who were in his team and used to go and have a drink in the pubs. He didn't do that you see, but that was his life.

He wasn't a bloke's bloke, was he?
THE BEDSERS: No, not at all. No, he wasn't.

Was drinking with the boys as important in English teams as it appears to have been in Australian teams?
SIR ALEC BEDSER: Well, we don't . . .
ERIC BEDSER: If someone doesn't want to we never bother.
SIR ALEC BEDSER: But of course the social life in England was different before. I mean, our pubs before the war were totally different to what Australian pubs were. The pubs here were more-or-less clubs, particularly then, but in Australia if a chap went to the pub before the war and just after the war, they were just drinking places and The Don obviously didn't want to do that. So I think the social side of it was a bit different. Just after the war the typical English pub was a sort of little social club. People from the various villages, they'd all go down to one of the pubs in the evening for a couple of pints of beer and just socialise and it was just a means of people meeting up. In Australia they used to close at 6, you see.
ERIC BEDSER: Whereas here they were open to 10, half past ten.
SIR ALEC BEDSER: So there wasn't the rush to gobble down as many pints as you can, the 6 o'clock swill. Here most fellows who played cricket, they'd always come and have a drink. Some of them might even have a soft drink, but basically they'd have something. An enormous number of people would just meet at the pub. Whereas in Australia, the only way for men and women to basically get together, they had to go to someone's house. That's what life was like.

Did you manage the team to Australia in 1962–63?
SIR ALEC BEDSER: When the old Duke of Norfolk came, yes. Basically the Duke was put in as the manager and I was supposed to be the assistant. Well he didn't know anything about it. He's a wonderful bloke, I mean he's a magnificent chap but I had to do all the

work. Because he was the Duke of Norfolk, he went down well with everyone, and the great thing about it was he owns a lot of race horses and he was boss at Royal Ascot and everything else, so he went down well even from the racing point of view, which was all right for me. He used to take me and the red carpet would be out for him to go to Flemington and all these places. So it was a good tour. They were all good tours as far as I was concerned.

Was Don Bradman's relationship with Gubby Allen important to English cricket?

SIR ALEC BEDSER: Yes I think it was, yes, because they were both much on a level seniority-wise in the two boards, although Gubby Allen was MCC, which is a private club, whereas the Australian cricket was a board, in those days. But they were pretty close. And he was close to R. W. V. Robins, who was the godfather of Shirley, I think, and he used to stay with Robins.

ERIC BEDSER: Robins played for England as well.

SIR ALEC BEDSER: And he was a chairman of selectors and he was on a lot of MCC committees and that sort of thing.

ERIC BEDSER: Of course in those days MCC ran English cricket, not the board of control as it is now. Whereas Australia has always had a board of control.

Sir Donald was involved in various controversies in international cricket: the throwing controversy, the cancellation of the South African tour and World Series cricket.

SIR ALEC BEDSER: Yes, he didn't have much to do with Packer. He kept away from that.

There is some resentment that he didn't speak out about that.

SIR ALEC BEDSER: Well, I never asked him about it, but I've somehow got it in the back of my mind that he didn't want to get too involved because if he got involved in that he could have put himself in a hell of a position. He was a director on the Board, wasn't he, and Packer was a big, influential man, I mean where would it all lead to really? I suspect that's what he thought. He probably thought he'd better keep out of it, but I never asked him so I don't really know.

ERIC BEDSER: I think at that time Don had started to free himself of the positions in the Australian cricket side, the administration and everything, he was easing out at that time.

SIR ALEC BEDSER: And I often wonder if perhaps he didn't want his family to get involved, perhaps he didn't want Jessie to get involved. I think it's probably just a decision he made.

Coming back to that first tour of Australia in 1946–47, was there hostility between Hammond and Bradman?

SIR ALEC BEDSER: They didn't like one another, no. But I never . . .

ERIC BEDSER: It wasn't apparent.

SIR ALEC BEDSER: Wally Hammond never said much anyhow. I mean he never confided with any one, Wally didn't, I mean he was a very unusual sort of chap. He very much stuck to himself a lot, Wally. Never said much.

ERIC BEDSER: Of course it may have come about before the war, I think, probably things happened then actually, I don't know what. After the war it was a sort of a hangover I think because then Wally was 40 so he wouldn't have worried too much I don't think.

SIR ALEC BEDSER: Oh, he was 41 when he came out.

ERIC BEDSER: And Don was 38. I think it must have been some quite deep-founded thing, I don't know what it was.

SIR ALEC BEDSER: They weren't friends, put it that way. But all the time I was with him in '46 there was nothing apparent that Wally Hammond had anything against Don, he just didn't talk to him. Never discussed it.

A journalist who covered the series suggested it was because Hammond wore a brown hat out to the toss.

ERIC BEDSER: Yes, that was unusual.

SIR ALEC BEDSER: Yes, that would have upset the Australians as a whole because certainly in those days they were very . . .

ERIC BEDSER: . . . sticklers for always wearing the Australian cap.

SIR ALEC BEDSER: Which I reckon is right, you see. And that's one of the things I've got against everything today. Everything revolves around money. I mean, our captain of England now, Vodaphone is sponsoring the English side and all you see everyone wearing is Vodaphone caps and the captain of England gets on television, he hasn't got England's cap on, he's got the Vodaphone cap on.

ERIC BEDSER: They go and toss up and they've got a Vodaphone cap on. I think that's all wrong.

Do you think the game loses something?

THE BEDSERS: Oh, absolutely.

ERIC BEDSER: The honour of the whole thing and the privilege of wearing it.

SIR ALEC BEDSER: You see, all we saw when we were kids was this English blazer and England thing.

ERIC BEDSER: And that's what you wanted.

Was Sir Donald as you saw him a man who bore a grudge?

SIR ALEC BEDSER: I don't know about that. I think he was the sort of chap who was very straight himself so I think if he was let down, well, that was the end of it, as far as he was concerned.

ERIC BEDSER: You wouldn't call it a grudge but I'm sure, as my brother said, if you really let him down badly he would just finish with you.

And was he demanding as a friend?

SIR ALEC BEDSER: No, not with us. Never asked anything. But he'd do anything for anyone else. I mean the things he did, sign things for people, spent hours and hours.

He did sign a lot, didn't he?

SIR ALEC BEDSER: Oh yes, I mean he would do anything if anyone wrote and asked him. Of course, they all took advantage of him. Everyone does now. Now they sell his blinking things.

Did that surprise you then, how much he was prepared to reply to demands for his signature?

SIR ALEC BEDSER: Well it did me yes, I mean I used to say to him many times, 'Crikey you overdo it.' You know I mean every Tom, Dick and Harry. Once you start one, you see, they tell all their mates and they all write, you know. Oh yes, you write to Don and he'll write back, and he spent hours doing it.

ERIC BEDSER: He used to say, three or four hours a day he used to spend writing.

SIR ALEC BEDSER: He was telling us one day, wasn't he, that he went three times a day to the post office. You're talking of 300 or 400 letters a day you know, coming in at certain periods.

ERIC BEDSER: And on the '48 tour here, they say he used to get 600 letters a week, 600 or 700 a week.

So there's no unwritten law that every cricketer must reply to everything?

SIR ALEC BEDSER: Oh no, if you're a decent fellow you do the best you can but some of them just chuck them away and don't bother. I mean Denis Compton never answered a letter. A lot of them just won't bother. And they want payment for everything now. They won't sign any autographs now without signing rights.

ERIC BEDSER: Don was a meticulous chap, he was.

SIR ALEC BEDSER: And he was very kind to us. When we went in 1950–51 I got the flu in Perth and it must have been in the newspapers that I'd had the flu with a temperature and I wanted to go on to Adelaide and be there with the team. It must have been in the paper because when we landed early at Adelaide airport Don was there to meet us and he said, 'The hotel rooms won't be ready until 12. You'd better come home and go to bed in my house.' This was 7 o'clock in the morning. I mean, he was very thoughtful. A lot of people don't know that side of him. That's one of the things which I think hasn't been shown enough because he wouldn't tell anyone of course. He'd do these things.

ERIC BEDSER: And he was very careful with whom he did it because he didn't make friends easily.

SIR ALEC BEDSER: And I think he would have hated it if anyone took advantage of him.

He must have been in an awkward position. I mean there's only one Don Bradman.

SIR ALEC BEDSER: Of course the difference is, you see, that never happens here. Because London's a bigger place and there isn't that same adulation of sportspeople. There wasn't when we played. I mean, you played cricket and if you were amongst cricketers they'd sort of know you, but the general public wouldn't know you probably from Adam if you played for England, whereas in Australia with Don, everyone knew him.

Cricket is much more widely played . . .

SIR ALEC BEDSER: Yes and the population is smaller. I mean take where he lived in Adelaide, I mean everyone knew where Don Bradman lived in Adelaide and everything else, whereas if you live in London they don't care less where you are.

ERIC BEDSER: You know with all due respect to the Australians, in London Don Bradman would be one of many so-called celebrities. You've got the top of the acting profession and the top of the law and everything here.

SIR ALEC BEDSER: You've got big American so-called stars coming here and everything else, something happening all the time.

He chose to live in Adelaide . . .

SIR ALEC BEDSER: Well basically to get a job because he didn't want to play cricket for a living. He had a chance to be a pro, Lancashire League, but he always said he never wanted to play cricket for a living so he wanted to get some sort of solid thing, a business. In those days of course there wasn't the money. I mean, cricket in Australia was performed by chaps who played who had another job and by the time they got to about 28 they had to pack up cricket to get their livelihood.

ERIC BEDSER: But now there's a professional set-up, you know.

SIR ALEC BEDSER: But now they're staying on you see, like the Waughs, they're 40 nearly, 38–39. Don stayed on longer than any one of his predecessors because they all had to go and get a job. That was one of the reasons why people say, 'Oh Australia always gives youth a chance'. What it was, it was economic necessity. I mean someone who is good, he had to get a job. If he left it too long it would be too late to get a job anywhere. Phil Ridings for instance. He was chairman, general manager of his company. All of them, even if they had to go and start a sports business, like Bill Brown, it meant they couldn't run away to play cricket when they were trying to run a store.

So explain the difference in England. How many would play as professionals?

SIR ALEC BEDSER: We always had a professional set-up here, each county, since about 1900, 1890. At Surrey we had about 22 on the staff, professionals.

ERIC BEDSER: Yes, of varying degrees. Youngsters coming up and the actual county first-class side.

SIR ALEC BEDSER: Similar to a state side.

How long could you survive in cricket?

SIR ALEC BEDSER: As long as you were good enough. But when you got to the late thirties obviously you began to wane – your form – but seeing that was your living, a lot of blokes were left high and dry. They played on until they were 40 then they were too late so all they could do after that was either be umpires or coaches or something like that.

ERIC BEDSER: They used to go to public schools coaching. What we call public schools, you call private schools.

SIR ALEC BEDSER: But then that's changed now because there's so much money in it. And of course in our day there was no such thing as media, and no such thing as television. Nowadays it's just another world.

*South Australian batsman **Bruce Bowley** was 13 years old when his father woke him one morning saying, 'Come on son, out of bed. Don Bradman's coming to play for Kensington.' 'Dad,' he said, 'you've made a lot of statements in your time to try and get me out of bed, but that's the biggest joke of all time.' We spoke at his home in Adelaide.*

MY DAD PLAYED with Don in that first game. He played cricket for South Australia and at this stage of his career he was practice captain for Kensington and I used to go along and keep time for him. (You might have 30 fellows out there batting and they all have say ten minutes, then you call them in, you call them out.) The first night Don came out I worried my dad, 'Dad, introduce me to Don Bradman', because earlier he'd taken me down to the Adelaide

Railway Station one day just to see him at close range getting off the train.

The first time I played against him was at Kensington. In those days pre-war they used to have a state Colts team. They were promising lads from all districts and I was the only one from Kensington. We played against Kensington and they beat us outright. They had 40 runs to get in about 15 minutes. Bradman and another state player Ross Moore (he was killed during the war) came in to bat and they got the runs. And in getting the runs Bradman cover drove one past me like a rocket. Went to the fence and the coach called out, 'Why don't you get behind the ball, boy?'

As time went on, I used to go and watch him. I watched him make over 300 one afternoon. And it was his son John's first birthday.

Did you have any contact outside cricket?

My dad was a house painter and decorator and when I first left school I went to work for him. In 1939 we were painting the Bradman house in Holden Street Kensington, inside and out. It's a two-storey house and I can still remember trying to get to a window or something near the front room to paint every morning because Don used to sit down and play the piano. He was a beautiful pianist. He'd be waiting to be picked up by Harry Hodgetts, H. W. Hodgetts, a sharebroker who he came here to work for. Then Harry or his sons beeped the car and he'd stop and away they'd go.

Did he know you were listening?

Yes, he did. But the maid of the place was an attractive young lass and he reckoned I was there trying to get her eye, (laughs) so he was wrong, I wasn't. I was 18 on the first of January 1940 and we were painting his house when I went in to join the air force in early February.

Did you return to cricket after the war?

I spent five and a half years in the air force and came back from the war in early October 1945. It was at the beginning of the cricket season so I went in to see the secretary of the South Australian Cricket Association, Mr Bill Jeans, and said, 'Here I am, Mr Jeans, who do I play for?' 'Oh,' he said, 'you were a Kensington bloke.' I said, 'Well I never played "A" grade for Kensington before the war, I played "B" grade.' I said, 'I was in the Colts to play "A" grade.' 'Oh,' he said, 'you'd better play for Kensington.' If you lived in the district you had to play there in those days, you had no option. He said, 'Go around and see Don Bradman round in Grenfell Street.' It was Don Bradman & Co., sharebrokers, at that time. Poor old Harry had got into a bit of financial trouble. (We painted his house too before the war. He had a two-storey house up on Park Road Kensington.) So I went around to see Don and he said, 'I'll need you to play on Saturday.' Now this was a Tuesday. I'd only been home two or three days. I said, 'Oh, I haven't got any gear or anything, Don.' He said, 'Well get some. Go and see Cecil Starr in at Myers and you buy your cricket gear.' He said, 'I'll ring the secretary of the cricket club, Clem Harris.' Anyway, to cut that story short, we played East Torrens and I made a hundred. And I couldn't walk for about three days. I hadn't had a bat in my hand for three years.

Don was quite ill for a while with fibrositis and he had a break from cricket. When he came back we were playing Glenelg at the Glenelg Oval. I remember in the Friday night's paper, a media fellow from here had written an article making statements that five of us members of the cricket club – he named us – had made a statement about Bradman's future. We'd never even spoken to the fellow. When we got to the oval on the Saturday, we were most embarrassed, we would have crawled in the locker and locked it, you know? He sensed this and before we went out onto the field, he called us together and said, 'Now look, boys, I just want you to know I realise what was written in last night's paper was definitely not true. I just want to clear your minds of that before we go out on the field.' We felt a lot better.

We got Glenelg out at about 5 o'clock. Back in the dressing room he said to our fellow who was captain when he wasn't there, he said, 'Well Garth,' (Garth Burten who was also a first-class cricketer for South Australia) 'who's your opening batsmen?' Garth said, 'Martin Chappell,' (that's the father of these three boys) 'and Bill Bird.' He said, 'Righto Martin and Bill, put the pads on and in you go. Now who's your number three?' 'Ooh,' he said, 'Bruce is number three.' 'Righto Bruce, put the pads on.' I thought gee whizz, number three, that's his position, not mine. But I can remember on the Thursday night before this match we went out to give him a hit in the nets at Kensington and it was wet. He said, 'Well, even though it's wet and the wicket's not going to be too good I just want to have a look at the ball, that's all.' And it was just a terrible practice for him.

So out the opening batsmen went, Martin and Bill, and it wasn't long before Bill Bird got out. Now there were 5000 people at that ground for a district cricket match. We were lucky if we used to get ten people. Five thousand people were there just to see Don Bradman and of course they all stayed because we got Glenelg out. And as I went to walk out on the field, as I got to the gate and I walked through – I'll never forget it – they yelled out, 'Get off the ground, ya mug, we didn't come here to see you.' (laughs) So I quickened my step up a bit to get out there.

Not long after that Martin got out and they were happy. In the master came. And he had to take strike to a very fiery fast bowler. And I was at the other end and he bowled this first ball and it was going for his off stump and he was outside of his off stump, which is not the right thing to do. Pretty easy to get in behind it, you see, not even this side. I thought oh, here we go, first ball. He turned it round to leg and we got two. Next week he got a hundred and oh, I finished up with 60 or 70 I think. That was the first time I played with him.

After that I used to make a lot of runs with him. A lot of batsmen, if he was at the other end and they came in they used to freeze purely because he was there watching. For some reason it didn't ever bother me and so it was a valuable experience to bat with him.

He had a theory. You went in and you wouldn't get a strike for two or three overs. He would take all the strike. He'd work it singles and whatever at the end of the over and let you get used to the atmosphere. Then as the day wore on, suddenly he'd have a period where he wouldn't have the strike. You'd have all the strike because he would have a rest and that I believe is one of the sound reasons why he used to make these big scores. Because there wasn't much of him, he was a smallish man and he wasn't a robust fellow.

I remember one day up at Kensington we were playing against Prospect on a very bad pitch and Charlie Puckett who had been a Test cricketer played for Prospect. We had been having trouble. When I went in I started hitting the ball up in the air and all over the place. Got away with it. Don wasn't very happy about this situation because the wicket was a bit bad. It didn't seem to bother me. (laughs) Anyway he called me up in the middle of the pitch and he said, 'Bruce, have you ever stopped to realise that there's only one more recognised batsman to come? Now you go back and hit the ball along the ground.' Those were his exact words. And I went back and I hit the ball along the ground. I think I got 80-odd that day. But batting with him was an education. He was so easy to run with. His calling was precise. I nearly ran him out that particular day. I hit the ball to mid-off and said yes and he just got in.

It's a pretty crude word to use I suppose, but I always believed the man was a freak. He used to see that ball. He didn't put the ball where the field was set, he always hit it where the field wasn't. He had that photographic mind. He knew where they were. I always thought that he used to see that ball that split second earlier than the normal man.

How did Kensington perform in the postwar period?

We won the premiership the first year after the war but he wasn't playing that year. He played in a final match at the Adelaide Oval, a semi-final we played against West Torrens who had a pretty strong side. Phil Ridings was the captain. He was my state captain and I had a lot of time for him too. I know when I went in Bradman came out, which he wouldn't normally do, and he said, 'Have you played Norm King before, Bruce?' This is a leg-spinner. I said, 'Yeah, plenty of times,' and I think it was the third ball I went down the pitch (laughs) and I missed and that was the end of that. West Torrens made 325 I think it was, I know we fielded on to the Tuesday night from half past four until 6 – until your innings was finished, that was the rule in those days. I had quinsy and I suffered, I went out on the field on the Tuesday night, and felt like I wanted to die.

When we were batting, we were nine-for, I think, and we must have been about 150 short of the West Torrens total. This lad went in to bat, he was a great mate of mine, and he didn't like the fast bowlers, he was a bit scared. He used to back off a bit, you see. And Bradman was batting with him and while Peter made 9, Bradman made the rest. And we beat them. The greatest innings I've ever seen, it was. And the first ball after we passed their score, West Torrens threw overthrows and Peter doubled his score and Bradman made 212. And when they came off, we were all 'Well done Don', and this reporter that I mentioned earlier who had made statements about us when Don came back to play his first match happened to walk in the room. Don was hot and sweaty, sitting down, and he looked and saw him and he said, 'Clem,' (that's Clem Harris, our secretary) 'remove that man from the room,' and then Clem had to go up and escort him out.

The press used to tell lies like that. My old dad was a simple-minded chap who I worshipped and being a state cricketer himself, and a country boy, he said, 'Son, always beware of the press. They'll make you, then overnight they'll break you.' Those were his exact words. Young John Bradman became a bit of a cricketer when he went to St Peter's College and at that stage I was the coach up there. Every January they used to run a competition from all the districts of these under 17 schoolboys. I remember the first game we played was down at the Albert Oval against Port Adelaide. Young John was in our team and the scribes were there, worrying hell out of him. I said, 'Look, why don't you leave the lad alone?' But because he was Don Bradman's son . . . I can quite understand why the lad changed his name. Eventually he just didn't play cricket. The lads in our team didn't worry but all the papers in the world were there to talk to Don Bradman.

Kensington used to go to the eastern states and play in Melbourne over the New Year. And in 1949 he was knighted. It came out in the New Year's honours. And that was my birthday, the first of January. He was over there to attend an Australian Cricket Board meeting. He was staying in a different hotel to us of course and we all got up in the morning and walked over to his hotel up to his room, that's the manager and all the players to congratulate him. In his pyjamas, he was. We were probably the first to physically congratulate him on his knighthood. Up to that stage I used to call him Don but after that I called him Sir Donald, always.

I played in Bradman's last first-class game [the Arthur Richardson Testimonial] and I was batting with him when he got out. Arthur Richardson, the Test cricketer, was my uncle. I didn't know much about Harry Hodgetts' troubles but I know my uncle lost his life savings. I couldn't see where Bradman would have had anything to do with it. Arthur at this stage, he coached and he played Lancashire League cricket in England, he coached in New Zealand, he coached in the West Indies, he coached in Western Australia, and South Africa. In those days he became a fairly wealthy fellow. What he used to do is send his money back to Harry Hodgetts to invest for him and Harry went up and so did Uncle Arthur Richardson's money. He didn't die a pauper but from a fairly wealthy bloke he finished up with nothing really. Kensington gave him a testimonial and the SACA gave him one too and I played in that game against Victoria. Dear old Arthur was there.

Did you have any contact with Sir Donald after you finished playing cricket?

Eventually I went to work at Rigby where I stayed for 37 years. And Bradman presented me with my 25-year watch. He was then chairman of directors of our company. I used to attend the board meetings to take the minutes. I could tell you a lot of stories (laughs) about Sir Don and members of the board. He was a yard ahead of them all the time. He was a very smart and studious man. He used to do his homework. Early on the old managing director used to pull the wool down over the eyes of the directors. My face must have gone red a few times, I'll tell you. And then Bradman got on the board and he used to say 'Yes, but what about this?' The old chap used to sit there and suck his pipe and he stopped doing it after that because Bradman had done his homework. It was a very interesting situation.

I used to see Bradman about once a year in later years and we'd sit down and have a bit of a chat. Lady Jessie was a graceful lady. A beautiful lady she really was. I went there to get things signed too. All my books are signed by him. I think it's *The Bradman Albums* where he wrote 'To my friend Bruce with best wishes, Don Bradman'. I treasure all those. We published a couple of books at Rigby about him. In fact I edited one about his 1930 tour of England, before the Bodyline series. The last time I went to see him we sat in his sitting room, I saw the grand piano over in the corner, and not thinking I said, 'Oh do you still play the piano, Sir Donald?' 'No, Bruce,' he said, 'the old arthritis has got to my fingers,' but he still had a piano there.

*The lanky Australian bowler, South Australian coach and administrator **Geff 'Nobby' Noblet** played under Don Bradman and went on to serve with him on the South Australian Cricket Association. His wife Betty, who sat with Lady Bradman and Joan Ridings at the Adelaide Oval, was with us when we spoke at his home in Adelaide. 'Not bad for 84, am I?' he said, as he waved me goodbye.*

BRADDLES WAS MY first captain when I played for South Australia. We played against Lindsay Hassett's Services team in 1945. He was an excellent captain. He told me where to place the ball. He said that what I was doing was all right for the district but for these fellows I needed to do something more and five or six balls later I got a wicket.

What was the advice he gave you?
He told me that I was bowling at the stumps and the batsman did not have to move. He said I could make him move across by bowling on a line a quarter of an inch outside the off stump. I bowled there from then on.

Did you play against him?
I only bowled to him three times and he made a hundred each time.

What was Sir Donald like to serve with on the SACA?

When I first went on the committee in 1959 or 1960, Braddles was a vice-chairman and he became chairman while I was still a junior member of the committee. He was a remarkable man. He knew everything and wasn't frightened to put in any effort to find out what was going on. And he never promoted that he was an Australian Cricket Board member. It was part of his duties and he accepted it. At our meetings he might say, 'Now the Board wants this,' but it would be the Board, not Don.

He liked good discussion. He used to say, 'Whoever's got something to say, please say it because that's the only way we'll get on.' He was a bit like his batting; he wanted to make sure things were moving in the right direction all the time. There was no sitting back and saying everything's okay, he wanted to progress. And he knew how to dot his i's and cross his t's all right because that's why he became so good in business life. He was that way inclined all the time.

I think the point with his batting was that he was such a quick thinker and that's everything in sport. Your brain directs and he had such a great brain and was so quick with it and he developed it all when he was young. So it follows on. He knew what was going on all the time.

Tell me about the last time you saw Sir Donald . . .

While I was on tour with Australia in South Africa in 1949–50, I was working for a bank and in those days you had to verify signatures. I'd learnt to do this for four or five years and of course you got to know writing. Going over on the ship we had to sign about 500 sheets of autographs and I used to get a piece of paper and I could do everybody's autograph except Hassett's. His letters were very interwoven, it was the only one I couldn't do.

When Don was still signing those odd days down at the

SACA office, one of my relations through Betty's family wanted a bat autographed by Bradman so I rang up the office and I said, 'When's Don coming in?' I went in that day and Don's in there with a girl who's sorting things out and as I walked in we shook hands and he said, 'Just the man I want to see.' I said, 'Why's that, Don?' He said, 'You can help me out, because you could sign my autograph when you were young, couldn't you? You've done it a few times.' And I held up my hand and said, 'Not now, Don. See that?' (He holds up his shaking hand.) Of course he wouldn't have allowed me to do it. But that time we stayed and had a good chat with him.

Former South Australian batsman, administrator and selector **Neil Dansie** *had flown back to Adelaide from Europe only a few hours earlier when he turned his mind to his memories of Sir Donald. He had first played for the Kensington Cricket Club in 1942 when he was 15.*

I PLAYED THE last game Sir Donald played in district cricket with him. Because of his commitments to South Australia and Test cricket, he didn't play a lot of district games and I'd have played two or three games with him at the most. The last was in January 1949 and Kensington were playing Port Adelaide at Port Adelaide. I was batting down the other end when he got out. I remember it as plain as today. It was the first ball after drinks. He got caught behind and the crowd booed the umpire and they all went home. Whenever he played, people would ring up to see if Kensington were batting or not and if they were, they'd all come and watch. It was nothing to have three or four thousand people at a game. And then when he got out they'd all go home and only a few handfuls would ever stay.

What was it like batting with him?

It was an education. I can remember when I came in, his exact words were, 'Sonny,' (he called me Sonny) 'I'll let you have a look for a little while,' and for the first four overs, I never faced a ball. Like he'd just keep the strike and take the single off the last ball so I could look at what was going on. Then after a while he said, 'All right, you can have a look now,' and he let me have perhaps one or two balls towards the end of the over. He was just so good he could do these sorts of things. He was very strong physically and mentally, I think he was extraordinary. But I saw the key to it was that he could see the ball quicker than anyone else. One of the English bowlers told me he'd never move the field when he was bowling to him, because he said if you moved the field he'd hit the ball where you moved the field from, and make you look silly.

If something went against him on the field, he'd never show it. If he received a bad decision, he'd just smile. He said, 'You never show your feelings on the field. Perhaps you may say something or do something in the dressing room, but in front of the public you must always show respect to the umpires.' He was very firm on that. He never sledged, never criticised, never. On the field, he just acted the complete gentlemen as he was. You see him doing these things and you say to yourself you've got to be the same.

Did he offer batting advice?

He just loved talking about cricket and if you wanted to know something he'd talk to you for hours, about administration, about cricket. He would never try and change you but if you were doing something wrong, things that might improve you, he'd tell you. But he wouldn't go up to you and say listen, you should be doing this and this and this.

I can remember when I was first chosen in the interstate side, he rang me up and he said to me, 'Neil, you hook and cut a lot, and no doubt you'll get out many times playing that shot, but whatever you do, don't give it up, because you'll score hundreds of runs.'

And when I became a selector for South Australia in 1976, he rang me up and he gave me some advice. 'Now Neil,' he said, 'selection is a very enjoyable job, you get a lot of pleasure out of it, but never make comments to the press about players that you're going to choose or who might be chosen or who are near to being chosen because circumstances can change so quickly. Somebody could get sick, somebody could get injured, somebody could lose a bit of form, and everything you've said goes out the window. So never make a lot of comments to the press on selections because you get egg on your face.'

Did he ever coach?
Yes, he coached the state team for one year. I can remember the headlines now in the paper. I'd come back from England in 1956 after two years in the Lancashire League and the papers said South Australia hope to improve, they'll have the 3 Ds – The Don, Dooland and Dansie. I've got the cutting at home. That season, if he said, 'Be in the foyer at 9.30', everyone would be there at 25 past nine. That's the way he was looked upon. And after practice, he used to have a hit and everybody would try and bowl him out. We couldn't, but if we got one ball past him we'd think that was exciting. He was manager of my team once too. It was in Perth round about 1957.

So did you win?
(laughs) I don't think so. We didn't win too often, I can tell you that.

Did Sir Donald's son John play for Kensington when you did?
I was captain when John played cricket at Kensington. He had a lot of potential but he gave it up. He was hounded by the press. Sir

Donald kept right out of the way but there was so much pressure on him he didn't have a chance. Earlier I remember wheeling John around the Kensington Oval when he had polio when he was about 12. He was in this big frame, encased in plaster from head to foot and he just lay flat all the time. Sir Donald would wheel him from home to the cricket at Kensington Oval because it was just round the corner and I'd take him for a walk, just to break the day for him.

*Nineteen-year-old batsman **Neil Harvey** was the baby of the 1948 Australian team that toured England under Don Bradman. He went on to become a selector of the Australian team from 1967 to 1979, serving on the panel with Sir Donald for four years. We spoke at his home in Sydney.*

MY FIRST GAME with Bradman was in 1947 when an Australia XI team played India on the Sydney Cricket Ground, and that's the game when he made his 100th century. It was my first game for an Australian XI, so it was quite an honour for me to play in that particular match.

Was it daunting?
Yes, it was actually. I was very privileged. I was the first young bloke to get a go after the war. They don't pick guys my age any more, mainly because I guess there's so much money in the game and players are playing longer, but in those days we all played for the same amount, which was nothing, and to be the first young guy selected after the war was a great privilege.

In that series I was selected to play in the second Test match in Sydney here, I was 12th man, I was 12th man again in Melbourne. I played my first Test match in Adelaide as a 19 year old against

India in January '48 and I played the last match in the series in Melbourne and they were both played with Bradman.

In 1948 you were selected for the tour of England.

Yes. In those days they picked 17 players and we had a manager and a baggage man/scorer, old Bill Ferguson who had been doing it since 1930, I think, lovely bloke. That was our lot. We didn't have any physios, or psychos, or coaches or any of that stuff they cart around these days. The team assembled in Melbourne and hopped on an old DC3 and flew over to Tasmania and that was the start of the tour. We played two matches against Tasmania, one in Hobart and one in Launceston. They were nowhere near getting invited into the Sheffield Shield competition then so these two games helped to promote the game.

Then we came back to Melbourne and we flew over to Perth in a DC4, the old propellers going round and round. In those days it used to take about 14 hours to get from Melbourne to Perth where we'd play this four-day match against Western Australia. After that match the *Strathaird* was waiting for us down at Fremantle and we went off on the 28-day voyage to London. The Cricket Board in their wisdom used to send us first class, which makes a hell of a difference, I can assure you. I did four trips to England and fortunately for me, they were all by ship. The one under Bradman, the one under Lindsay Hassett in '53, Ian Johnson in '56 and Richie Benaud in '61. And from then on it was air travel. I loved going by ship. It gives you time to get to know your fellow players on the way over and by the time you get to the other end, you're all pretty good mates and you're ready to get off and play some pretty good cricket.

On the way over Bradman didn't appear on deck once before lunch and since he's never been a real good sailor we thought he must have been seasick. But come lunchtime he'd have lunch with the fellows and he might come out and have his game of deck quoits and he might have a practice in the nets with us with the rope ball and whatever the crew used to make for us.

When we got to England we found we had 12 days from when we landed until we played our first match and there was a luncheon or a dinner organised, black ties, for every one of those days. Sometimes a luncheon *and* a dinner, and here's us trying to get some practice in. Bradman had been to England three times before, and he knew what to expect and the reason he didn't appear on deck during those mornings was the fact that he was preparing his reply speeches to all these welcoming speeches that he was going to receive on behalf of the English public. In my mind not only was he the world's greatest ever cricketer but he's also got to go down as one of the best after-dinner speakers. Because some of those functions we went to, the Poms could turn on some first class after-dinner speakers and you've got to be good to be able to reply to them.

We had this great amount of mail waiting for us in London. Being the first Australian team after the war, everybody wanted autographs and things and half of it was probably directed at the team, the other half personally at Bradman and he's never been one to knock back answering his own mail until almost the day he died. So he's trying to get his practice in, he's trying to do all these reply speeches and he's also got this problem answering his own mail. Do you know he was up until one and 2 o'clock in the morning doing them? He got them all out of the way. He was a freak that fellow, an absolute freak.

How did you rate him as a captain?

He had a great team to captain, you know. It's been judged the best sporting team of the century so I suppose that made his job a bit easier. I only played four Test matches on the field with him. Two against India and the fourth and fifth Test matches against England in 1948. I couldn't see myself ever breaking into this team on the tour of '48 but you never know what's going to happen – Sid Barnes got this ball smacked into his kidneys at the third Test match so he couldn't play at Headingley. That's the only reason I got a game.

In those days there weren't team meetings. The first of the team meetings started under Richie Benaud when we had dinner the night before with the boys and we'd discuss the opposition and how to bowl to them. But in Bradman's time, he had to do it all on his own. Maybe Lindsay Hassett was consulted, being vice-captain. But he could work out players' weaknesses and he didn't have to look at them all that long to work out what they were. This is why he became such a great selector as well. He obviously knew the weaknesses and strengths of the opposition that we were going to play against. All these things are taken into account and that's one of the things I learned when I was a selector with him.

Looking ahead, you made 100 runs in 106 minutes against South Africa in Adelaide in 1953, which was very much in Sir Donald's style. Did he comment on that?
He was funny in that regard. When he picked the side and you were in the best team for the country, then he expected you to do a job and you never got too many personal accolades if you did it probably nearly as good as he could, you know? He sort of expected you to do it, how you did it was entirely up to you. He'd never been one to tell you personally. Even when I got my first century at the age of 19 at Leeds, he didn't say all that much. He just said, 'Well played,' and shook my hand and that was it.

And he's never told me anything in his life, strangely enough, about how to improve my game. During my initial first couple of matches in England in '48 I was having a little bit of strife because I wasn't used to English conditions, and I think I was averaging 7 after about three games. I didn't know what to do. I wasn't game to go to Bradman, he was twice my age, and I was a bit scared to ask him. I was rooming with Sammy Loxton and he was a good mate of Don's, so I said to Sammy, 'Look, I'm not making too many runs at the moment, can you do me a favour? Will you go and ask the boss what I'm doing wrong?' So Sam went to Bradman and said, 'Hey George (he always called him George), my little mate's got a problem. He's not making any runs, can you tell him what he's doing wrong?' And he didn't tell me anything. He said to Sam, 'You go back and tell your little mate, the only thing I can tell him, if he keeps the ball on the ground, he can't get out.' And that's the only thing he ever told me about batting in my life. I suppose on reflection, it's not bad advice really.

And you didn't need any more?
Later on I didn't no, but at the time I felt I needed something because these different conditions were upsetting me a bit and I wasn't coping all that brilliantly.

Is it a captain's role to look after the younger members of the team?
I think in those days it probably was, even though he probably didn't like to do it. It should have been his duty if he found some-one was struggling to offer a little bit of advice, but he was always reluctant to do it. He was like that. He never offered anybody any advice unless they asked for it. Because if he saw a bloke was doing something wrong and he said, 'I think you've got to change some-thing,' then if the bloke continued to fail he felt he was going to be to blame because he couldn't improve him. Nowadays they've got coaches to fix these little problems with the batting techniques, or bowling techniques or fielding techniques.

Did he mix with the team on the tour in 1948?

On tour you'd probably call him not a boy's man. He had all these English friends. Say we'd be playing a match at Lord's, well Don would be first showered and dressed and he'd be off to Gubby Allen's place or Walter Robins' place, whereas the boys would be sitting around having a crate of beer between themselves. I've never seen Don have a beer. Not one. I've seen him have sherries and I've seen him have wines but I've never seen him have a beer, he just didn't like it. And of course nobody's ever seen him in a public bar. You can imagine going into a public bar and somebody recognises him and all of a sudden there's about 20 blokes around him, slapping him on the back, so he just didn't do it. So on tour on the field he was a team man, very much so, but off the field he didn't mingle with the boys like the other fellows did.

Gubby Allen used to live alongside Lord's and Don used to go to his house for dinner. If we were in London, every Sunday he and Gubby would play golf. They were very good mates. Gubby became very influential in the Marylebone Cricket Club and that suited Don as well. In those days they didn't have the International Cricket Conference; it was just up to the countries involved to work things out and being good friends they could sort of work things out between them. And they were both hell of a good cricketers. Walter Robins was another one, played for Middlesex and England, a leg spin bowler, he was a very good friend of Don's too. I think between the three of them they worked out quite a lot of things that kept England–Australia relations on a pretty good footing.

And you went on to serve as a selector with Sir Donald . . .

I got to know Don Bradman much better as a selector than I did as a player, and I've never struck a more knowledgeable bloke about the game of cricket. He was a great administrator. He was on the cricket board for years and years, he was an Australian selector for years. He put a hell of a lot back into cricket that a lot of people don't bother to do.

I'd called quits playing at 34 and a couple of years after that they asked me to be a New South Wales state selector. And after I'd been on a couple of years at state level, they decided to give me a go on the Australian panel and they dropped Dudley Seddon off. So I became a selector with Bradman and Ryder. I was only about 38 and to get on the panel with these two guys . . . We had a marvellous few years together picking sides.

That must have been quite an experience, because Jack Ryder was a legend too, wasn't he?
Absolutely. It was just one of the highlights of my life because if you can't sit down with these two guys and talk about cricket and learn something, there's something wrong with you. They can teach you so much about, not only selecting sides, but how to rate players and all that sort of thing.

What was it that you learnt from Bradman as a selector?
Well. I suppose it's the make-up of a cricket team for a start. You've got to get a balanced cricket team. The way they work out how players are better suited against the coming opposition, that you probably wouldn't even think about until you talked to these two guys. So it was the make-up of the side and how to judge a cricketer's ability. I think most of us, if you know anything about the game, have probably got that little bit of inbuilt ability to judge a cricketer anyway. But these guys had so much experience doing this job – pre-war the pair of them were doing it together – and you could sit around the table and you could learn a lot. You weren't left out in the cold. They asked you an opinion, you gave an opinion and sometimes you won, sometimes you lost, it was as simple as that. But they were a couple of beaut blokes to work with.

We were all delegated to watch matches around the country and you got a point of view over. If Don agreed, fine, if he didn't agree, well there'd be a little argument then it was up to the third bloke to give the casting vote. (laughs)

You and Sam Loxton were on the panel with Sir Donald in 1970–71 when you replaced the Australian captain Bill Lawry with Ian Chappell. Was Sir Donald a good man to make a hard decision with?

These things are discussed, probably during the course of a Test match that the three of us are watching together; they're not just made up on the spur of the moment. And this thing was in the wings for quite a little time actually. Because at that time the game needed a bit of a pep-up. We imagined that Bill Lawry was a bit on the negative side and although he did a fine job of opening the batting for Australia, Australian cricket in those days was in the doldrums a bit. It needed a bit of spark to get it underway again and we felt that Bill Lawry wasn't the right bloke to do the job. Of course it didn't help his cause that he ended up making a pair in the Test match after we discussed this, so that sort of sealed his fate more or less. That was when Ian Chappell was brought into the captaincy and as we all know Chappell sort of turned the game around a bit and the players played for him. So that's basically how things worked in the case of Bill Lawry.

Was that a particularly difficult decision?

It was. You sort of sit there and say we're going to get a hell of a lot of criticism for dropping the captain because it has never been done before. Bill Lawry took it quite hard for a period of time but it's all forgotten now. Bill and I are good mates again. We didn't have a lot of harsh decisions to make during my period with Bradman and Jack Ryder. It was good.

It must be very hard being a selector, is it? You seem to cop it from all quarters.

You do. You get letters in the mail from people and they abuse you and they don't even bother to put their name and address on it. Usually you pick these things up, read the first line and then throw it in the garbage.

Do the press tend to blame selectors?

Yes they do. As soon as the team loses, it's not the team's fault it's the selectors' fault. They're the blokes that bear the brunt of all the abuse and I suppose you've got to be fairly broad-shouldered to weather the storm.

When was the last time you saw Sir Donald?

It was at a '48 reunion arranged by Terry Jenner in Adelaide and Don didn't come to the dinner because at that stage he wasn't feeling all that brilliant for public appearances. And the Governor put on this morning tea party at Government House and he came along. He drove his little Holden Astra himself. We were all delighted that he found his way clear to come. We had a ball. He talked to two blokes at a time. Not everybody converged, and he stayed a hell of a lot longer than we thought he would. He was still there at the finish with the rest of us. And when we got outside he said to me, 'Gees, I can't find my keys.' His car keys. He'd gone through his pockets and he couldn't find them. I said, 'Maybe you left them in the car, Don.' Of course the car was parked inside the grounds, so it was perfectly safe. So I walked over to the car with him, opened the door, and there they were in the ignition. That was three years ago.

Sam Loxton played 12 Tests from 1947 to 1951 and went on to be a
Victorian and Australian selector and a Victorian Liberal Member of
Parliament for 24 years. He is a storyteller by nature and there are few
stories he likes telling more than his first encounter with Don Bradman.
His first cheeky comment led to a friendship which lasted a lifetime.
As he says, 'I think I made him laugh occasionally.' He was in
Melbourne for speaking engagements when we spoke.

I HAD ESTABLISHED MYSELF in the Victorian side by 1947–48, and
we went to Adelaide to play South Australia. Lindsay Hassett was
our captain of course, and we'd made a mess of it on Friday, we'd
batted, and we were all out very early on the Saturday morning.
South Australia commenced their first innings. They lost a wicket
and in he came and of course he was going through his normal
procedure, scoring runs and so forth. We went to lunch and he'd
felt, I suppose, that he was handling things pretty well.

After lunch Bill Johnston was bowling from the river end and a
fellow named Fred Freer, who is not with us any more, he was
bowling from the cathedral end. And we weren't making any
impression. Then Lindsay Hassett beckoned me. I was fielding in
the covers alongside Neil Harvey who'd broken into the side well
and truly by this stage. Obviously, being beckoned by Lindsay
Hassett towards the bowling crease, I knew what that meant.
I looked up at the batting end and there was my hero. As I left, Neil
Harvey said, 'Bad luck.'

I got over to Lindsay Hassett and as I approached him – normally bowlers do these kind of things – I said, 'I'll have two slips.'
'Just a moment, I'm the captain of this side,' Hassett said. 'I should
place the field. As a matter of fact, I'm not too certain it's going to
make much difference where they field.' Well, of course, I teetered
back on the heels a tad with that one. Then he said, 'You'd be better served marking out your run.' I was about to do that when he

stopped me, and said, 'Oh, and by the way, you're going to need this,' and he handed me the ball. (laughs) As he did that he said, 'We will do our very best to get it back to you as quickly as we can.'

By this stage, I was overcome by the obvious confidence that my captain had in me. I marked out my run and I turned and I hurled myself at the bowling crease. (They used to have one in those days.) I have vivid recollections of this particular delivery. As it left my hand and was disappearing up the pitch, I saw that the seam was upright, where it should be, I knew that the ball had great pace and that the direction was perfection, you see, and I had a vision. I had a vision of this ball passing through what is termed, in cricket parlance, the 'bowler's gateway to heaven' – between bat and pad – when something got in the road. It was only four and a quarter inches wide and it only weighed two pounds two ounces – that's very important, a very light bat, not like they use today. And the ball sped at the speed of light behind square leg, to the fence and bounced back a tad or two. (laughs)

Of course I'm standing off the pitch, well away. You don't stand in the batsman's way having delivered the ball, you either get behind the stumps to effect a runout or you move out of the way to let the batsman have right of way, different to what happens today. And of course Bradman was under tremendous pressure, the tension must have been enormous, and to ease the tension after seeing the ball disappearing towards the fence he came trotting down the onside of the pitch with a smile on his face. None of my team-mates heard this conversation, but I thought it was about time I introduced myself to my hero, so I said these famous words, 'Turn it up, that was a pretty good nut.' To which he replied, still with a smile on his face, 'But a better shot, Sammy.' The fact that he even knew my Christian name when we hadn't been introduced surprised me. I think from that moment on, we struck a chord. I can't be certain if it was the smile on his face, or that he'd hit me for four that had caused me to introduce myself. But I'm jolly pleased I did because he certainly didn't hold it against me.

But next week, it was one of those amazing things, Neil Harvey and myself were both selected in an Australian XI game at the Sydney Cricket Ground to play against India. It was the match in which Bradman scored his 100th first-class 100. And that in itself was a wonderful thing. All of a sudden within a couple of weeks I'm playing against him, bowling my first ball to him and then being captained by him the following week.

Bradman was the skipper when we went to England in 1948. (This 'Invincibles' tag, we'd love to know who coined it, but we haven't got the faintest idea how it started.) It was a magnificent side, not only the ability of the players, but the fact that with the exception of Neil Harvey, who was only a baby, the rest of the fellows in one way or another had served in the war. Some in actual theatres, like Miller in the air force and Lindsay [Hassett] in the desert, and so forth. There was a tremendous bond and there was a tremendous desire to play the game. It was breaking new ground. When we finally got on the ship, I think we had the one and only team meeting of the tour. They have a team meeting every time they take a wicket today. (laughs) He gathered us all together and put on a little tea and nuts and a few drinks and so forth and just spelled it out. I mean, he never mentioned the opposition. Nor really did he mention the task ahead, he just said that he hoped that we would all enjoy the tour and that success would come from within. There would be outside influences of course, the press and so forth, but that if we all played as a united team then success was sure to come. And it did, it did. There was the odd little occasion when we ran across a wicket that was not all that flash. Wickets, I want to tell you, were vastly different to today. We had some trouble finding the pitches we had to play on and they were all uncovered.

In 1948, we finished up bringing back a record amount. Our manager Keith Johnson came back with £64 664 – well, you could have bought Victoria for that in 1948. We had record gates at county games, they were packed, records at Test matches. Being away for eight months, we were paid £600, but quite frankly the tour was such a joy that I think if they'd have paid the rent at home and given us a few bob for a few drinks we would have gone over there for nothing.

Did you have much contact with Sir Donald during that tour?
The majority of my sporting life I've been an asker. I've been prepared to say is there a better way I can go about this? Now I did that in England. I enquired about back-foot play and so forth. I'd watched these fellows and they seemed to be doing it a little differently to what I was, and I asked him a question. I said, 'How do I go about this?' And he said to me, 'Sammy, how many runs have you made?' and I was able to tell him, and he said, 'And what's your average?' Oh, I said it was 50 and he said, 'I think we'll continue to play your way.' I've never forgotten that. That's how he was.

The Test match at Leeds in 1948 was the greatest Test match that I can remember. We were in a reasonable amount of trouble because we had to make 404 in 345 minutes on the last day of an uncovered pitch. And Arthur Morris got 182 and Braddles 173 not out. It's not a bad effort for a man in his 40th year. Of course the bowlers weren't bad either. People like Bedser and Laker and so forth. Wonderful, wonderful bowlers in England. Bedser was a wonderful bowler anywhere but Laker was a far better bowler in England than he was anywhere else.

I'll never forget the ovation when Bradman went out to bat. In fact I think the English people were more fascinated than we were. They just couldn't believe there could be anybody like this. Because in 1930 he'd made 334 in a day at Leeds against Larwood,

Tate and Geary – there's three reasonable trundlers – and in 1934 he'd made 304. They absolutely loved this man.

In the first innings in 1948 he received the greatest ovation I've ever heard. They thought this is the last time we'll see him. But rain had affected the pitch overnight and he got out for 30 odd. That was the start of my little mate Neil Harvey's great career. I was up the other end. We were room-mates and the fact that he got his 112 in his first Test match against the English was the highlight of my tour. But then Braddles went out in the second innings and got 172 not out, so you can never tell in this game of cricket. But I was privileged to have been there and to have heard that reception.

There is one statistic about Bradman that is not generally known. He went to England four times from 1930 to 1948. That's 18 years. Now in itself, that's a remarkable feat. But he went to England and in those 18 years he played in 89 first-class games, including all Test matches, all on uncovered pitches. He batted 120 times, so in other words there were 31 occasions where he had to bat a second time. (laughs) Only 31 because he made so many runs in the first innings. But he had 18 not outs. And if my memory serves me correctly in those 89 matches, he scored 9837 runs at an average of 110.5 runs per match. Now they talk about the 99.94. Of course that's never going to happen again, but when I repeat those figures to people, their mouths fly open. One hundred and ten and a half a match! Of course when you divide four tours into 89 you come up with about 22 matches. Well, our tour of England was 34 first-class matches. He's got to have a spell sometimes.

One of the remarkable things about it was I don't think he'd have gone to England in 1948 if it hadn't been for the war. Yet he went in 1948 in the interests of the game of cricket. He loved England, he loved the people (although when he was batting you wouldn't have thought he did but he did) and he felt that it was his duty to resume cricket here after the war when he was far from well.

Did he offer advice to young batsmen?

He recognised ability and he never proffered technique. As a youngster he was self-taught as far as cricket was concerned and he learned, I'm quite certain about this, by watching what the other great players of his youth did. He worked it out himself. And that's been one of the things that a lot of people have felt Bradman could have done. They believed he could have helped a lot of other people. Now there are problems associated with that and I'll do my best to explain them. Firstly, if you felt you had a problem, you only had to ask him and he would proffer his help. However, he wouldn't see a fault and suggest to a player. Even at my old age now, I'm vastly different because I've been involved in helping kids at a very, very low level. But he had a problem and the problem was this. Imagine being told by Bradman that it would be advisable to do ABC and you do your very best to do this and go out and get three very low scores. The opportunity is there for a player to say, 'I was only doing what Bradman told me to do.' So I think this is why he was always reluctant to proffer advice. He was pretty canny, and knew there was a possibility that something like this could happen.

I can remember one player who was going through a period when he wasn't going too well. I said to this player, 'Look, I want you to do something.' He said, 'What's that?' I said 'I want you to ask me if I would be good enough to ask Sir Donald to have a word with you.' He said, 'Would you do that?' and I said 'Yes, I would.' So he said, 'Good, well I'd like you to arrange that.' So when the great man arrived from Adelaide, I knew that the player was going to be 12th man for this Test match, and fortunately our boys had won the toss and were in the field. So the 12th man was left in the dressing room on his own on the first day and I said to the great man when he arrived that he would like to have a bit of a word with him. The first thing he said to me was 'Are you sure that he has asked me to have a word with him?' I said 'Yes.' (laughs) So he said, 'Fine.'

Consequently I wasn't involved in the conversation. I went away to watch the game and they probably watched the game through the glass and later the great man joined me. I said 'How did you go?' And he said 'Fine, we had a good chat.' I said 'What did you tell him?' I was anxious to hear. 'Well,' he said, 'firstly I told him that when he entered the game I admired the way he hit the half volley through the off side and back over the bowler's head for four and so forth.' And he said, 'I also told him that he reminded me of Walter Hammond on the off side and whilst he wasn't strong on the on side, he was adequate and this could be improved with experience.'

I could imagine where this player's chest was when he said he reminded him somewhat of Walter Hammond who was a magnificent player. Not in 1946 when he came out here, he was far beyond it then, but he had been a magnificent player. In fact, I think that Bradman scored 37 double centuries in his career, and Hammond scored 36. Of course, that included a lifetime in county cricket, but it was still a magnificent performance. So that was just one little episode where I was able to get a player to seek the great man out – in a devious way.

I'm the only player alive who played in Bradman's last six first-class games. You had to be Victorian to do that because the last one, the Arthur Richardson Testimonial in Adelaide, was the South Australia versus Victoria Sheffield Shield game. Arthur Richardson was a former coach of South Australia and this was the testimonial and the great man decided, yes, well he'd make it his last. He'd played in his own testimonial down here at the Melbourne ground. He'd played the Kippax/Oldfield Testimonial in Sydney – they were both pals of earlier days when he was playing with New South Wales and Australia. He'd had no practice or anything like that for the last game but he played and they had forty-odd thousand people there on the Saturday to see him bat, which was a magnificent tribute. By strange coincidence I'd played

South of England, I'd played against the Gentlemen's XI and I'd played the last first-class match in England, Leveson Gower's XI at Scarborough. And then I played the three testimonials.

After 1949, I was captain of Victoria and I continued to see a lot of him because he was a selector and he attended matches. He'd come into the dressing room and we'd have a natter and so forth. He was interested in the boys and he liked to be introduced to them and so there were more or less no boundaries, it was cricket.

Then later on, towards the end of my career in 1956–57, I became a VCA selector. I was terribly fortunate that my mentors, as far as selection was concerned, were the great man and before the great man Jack Ryder. I played district cricket as a kid when Jack Ryder was the captain of the VCA Colts – we were a district side in those days. (The war turned that over and the VCA Colts never reassembled after the war.) My youth as a budding cricketer was improved immensely by the fact I had a fellow like Jack Ryder who was in fact Bradman's first captain when he played for Australia. There was a tremendous amount of admiration between those two.

I would be a manager of various teams when we went to Adelaide or wherever we happened to be and he might be there as a selector, so once again we had plenty of time to chat about all sorts of things. By the time it got around to 1970 dear old Jack Ryder retired as an Australian selector and I got the job.

So we've gone from an upstart, to being captained by him, and then the tour of England, and more or less a friend during the period leading up to that time I was appointed a selector and of course it gathered momentum then. All these opportunities came along for a genuine closeness. When I was drawn for a game in South Australia he would meet me at the train in Adelaide, he'd drive me home for a cup of tea then we'd go down to the ground. I didn't have hotel accommodation, I stayed with him and Lady Jessie. And it was marvellous. We played golf, of course. In those days there was no play on Sundays so we'd have a game of golf. Then there were Test matches where there were rest days and when there was a game in Adelaide we'd all go up to Yalumba.

We never argued. (laughs) There was never an argument at a selection committee meeting. There was discussion about various things. He'd say something and I'd say, 'Well I don't know whether I completely agree with that.' I said it on purpose because he was inclined to make a comment and I wanted to know more, and he'd then give me chapter and verse. I don't know if he ever twigged to this but half an hour later, I understood the problem fully.

What he gave up in the interests of the game of cricket and the country are unbelievable. He worked it out and I've got no reason to doubt him when he said that cricket cost him seven years in total away from home. Unbelievable. That's when you take in the tours. And let's face it, he toured England four times but he never toured anywhere else. You take into consideration duties to the South Australian Cricket Association, duties to the Board and so forth. Seven years, it's a tremendous amount of time, and especially when he is trying to run a business. I mean, can you imagine a leading stockbroker in Melbourne today being able to devote that amount of time away from the office in the interests of Australian cricket?

John Arlott must have been the most perceptive bloke. I think he summed this bloke up as I don't think anyone's ever done before. One of his comments was: 'When any word a man might say may be the subject of publication and misinterpretation, conversation becomes an art indeed but it ceases to be a pleasure.' Now that almost sums this man up to a tee.

I'm not going to say for one moment that he didn't suffer fools, that is well and truly overdone. But he chose his friends. He'd been through a period in his cricket life where he couldn't sit down in the dining room and have his soup without somebody coming up with an autograph book at dinner and he just signed the book. (laughs) He mightn't have said it's a pleasure, but he'd sign the book and he'd go on.

He was a director of many companies, especially in Adelaide. He was what I would term a working director. I think he used to count the petty cash. He knew what was going on in any endeavour that he took on. Of course he was sought after because they knew his worth, his skill, his stockbroking experience.

What was he like to play golf with?
(laughs) Oh, my word. It was good to be on his side because he was as competitive on the golf course as on the field. I never saw him playing golf with Gubby Allen, but they used to play a lot (laughs) and the competition was fierce, I know it was. They were great pals but when they got on the golf course . . . I don't think they played for anything, I don't think they even played for a ball, but they both played to win and that was how he was. He played to win. There's no other way to play as long as you play according to the spirit of the game. One side's trying and the other's not, there's no enjoyment. He was a tennis player, a squash player – even playing billiards, there was no quarter given. No, it was marvellous and you wouldn't want it any other way.

How would you describe his sense of humour?
I'll let you judge for yourself. (laughs) I've got a letter at home. He said: 'Just a little trivia to hand with the passing of Lindsay [Hassett]. You have now become the 16th eldest Australian Test player alive.' And he went on to say I'm the oldest, Leo O'Brien, Billy Brown and so forth – etcetera, etcetera. I read this and I thought I wonder if I fit into the 16th category so I got Wisden down, and I did. Anyway years later – of course we'd lost Leo O'Brien, Freddy Freer, we'd lost Len Darling, we'd lost Mervyn Harvey, and so forth, and with all these fellows gone, I thought, hello, my word, I'd better drop the

old bugger a line. So I said, 'I got a letter from you a long time ago, I think it was round about '93,' I said, 'Just a little trivia to hand tells me that with the passing of so and so and so and so, my ranking has improved remarkably and I'm now the 10th eldest.' (laughs)

He was full of humour. There was one night I invited him and Tim Caldwell for dinner. I think Tim was chairman of the Board then. He was from New South Wales and we always used to laugh because we were both ES&A bank employees, though he was a little bit better that me, (laughs) he became manager of New South Wales. My wife cooked a curry. One of his favourite wines was Yalumba because he was a pal of Wyndy Hill Smith's who was Yalumba in those days. He always loved a Yalumba red whether it was straight claret or a cabernet sauvignon, it didn't matter. Anyway, we were enjoying ourselves at dinner and he decided that stumps should be drawn. I had to drive him back to the Windsor. And there was a candle on the table. The wax had melted but the candle was still burning, so in other words, play was still under way, you see. (laughs) So just by way of drawing stumps, he picked the candle up and . . . (he blows) What happened was, he brought the candle close to him and he's got his blinkers on, you see, and when he blew it the wax went round and it completely covered his glasses. (laughs) His first words were 'I'm blind' and we said, 'We know,' and then we realised how blind he was. He couldn't see through his glasses. We never let him forget that. That was one occasion when stumps were drawn in a most peculiar way. He was great fun but you had to know him. I was just blessed. It's the old, old story, isn't it? Being in the right place at the right time. We had so much fun.

I've got a letter at home where he was pretty disenchanted in one particular tour with the behaviour of certain players. But I suppose we were a different ilk. I mean to say, no player today plays more fiercely than Lindwall and Miller, and these fellows. But it was the spirit in which the game was played that was so terribly important and people had such respect for people like the great man, and Hassett. Lindsay was a character off the field, but my word, on the field, dear oh dear oh dear, if anything he was a tougher captain than Braddles. You just had so much respect for these kind of people that there was nothing you were going to do on the field that was going to bring discredit upon them. Because the captain is responsible for his players and their behaviour. And that's the one big thing that's forgotten in this game today.

But it was the privilege of my sporting career to be associated with him. He was a great bloke and of course the love of his life, she was something else too. She was a magnificent person. I used to give him a bell once every three or four weeks, just to see how he was. This had been going on for a long time. The last conversation I had with him, we [Neil Harvey and Loxton] did a show at Cootamundra. And it was decided that we should go down to the house where he was born. This is now a museum in Cootamundra – the room and everything where he was born and they've got some lovely memorabilia there too. Anyway, I had a mobile phone and I got up to the gate and I said I've got to ring him.

And I rang him and of all things, he was ill. But he answered the phone. He had an attack of food poisoning. We were only moments on the phone. And that was the last time that I actually spoke to him. He said, 'Sammy, son, I'm violently ill,' and I said, 'All right mate, okay, but I just wanted you to know that I'm standing outside where it all started at Cootamundra.'

*Left-handed opening batsman **Arthur Morris** played 46 Tests for Australia, 14 of them with Don Bradman from 1946 to 1948. When I rang to arrange an interview, he said, 'It's a bit like the Easter Bunny really. I'm beginning to think I imagined it all.' We spoke at his home in Cessnock on the eve of his 80th birthday.*

I met Don Bradman probably much earlier than anybody else in Australia. I would have been eight or nine and he was travelling for Mick Simmonds [sports store]. He was in Dungog where my father was a schoolteacher and the local stationer had a little afternoon tea party for him. And of course my father went along and tagged me along too. I would have been barefooted, and as 'Giddy' Lough said, 'You were a little snotty-nosed schoolboy in those days' so I probably said, 'Hello Mr Bradman.' So I can claim to having met him – what, more than 70 years ago.

And The Don remembered it well of course.
(laughs) He remembered it very well, yes. But I never even mentioned it to him. He at that time had come back from England in 1930 where he'd broken all these records and he was the hero of every young boy so it was a marvellous dream for me to meet him. That I would ever be in the same team and playing for Australia with him, that would be the most astonishing daydream any child ever had!

You were only 18 when you played your first game for New South Wales in 1940. Would you describe Stan McCabe and Bill O'Reilly as your mentors?
Oh yes, they were very good to me, particularly Bill O'Reilly because I was playing in St George, his side. Stan McCabe was my first state captain. Bill O'Reilly I think was vice-captain, but you know, they were both very good to me and I admired them very much. They were great cricketers and great personalities.

Did you encounter Don Bradman in any of those early state games?
No I didn't. I think probably the next time I would have met him was as a selector when I came back from New Guinea at the end of the war, but only to say, 'Hello Mr Bradman'. But he captained us – I'm

sure he captained us – in an Australian XI match that we played in Melbourne before the Test match series started in 1946–47 and I got 100 in that game. I got a century against the Englishmen in '46 so there was a chance of me getting picked for Australia I would have thought, but there were three selectors: 'Chappie' Dwyer from New South Wales, Jack Ryder from Victoria and Don Bradman.

Of course you were selected and in the first couple of Tests in 1946 you . . .
. . . failed miserably.

I was going to say 'had difficulties'.
(laughs) Yes, failed miserably. Things didn't go too well.

Did Bradman offer you advice?
No, not at all, no. He just let it be, and you don't really feel very good about it. I mean the first Test when Sid Barnes and I opened, we roomed together up in Brisbane. We both didn't get any runs really, he got 20 or 30 or something, but he could see that I was upset about it and he said, 'What we'll do, we'll go back to our room, and we'll lock the doors, bolt the windows, take the phone off the hook and we'll sulk.' Which made me laugh straight away so I felt better about it from then on. So you just take them as they come. I had scored a couple of hundreds as the war started, for New South Wales v Queensland, but Bradman wasn't playing at that particular time.

You shared the crease with Bradman more than any other batsman. What was he like to bat with?
Very good, yes, and we both obviously ran well together because neither of us ever got run out in our partnerships, so that proves something I think. I was considered generally as a good runner between wickets. I had plenty of experience in grade cricket but

O'Reilly would have picked me up quick early enough if I'd been running people out.

It must have been amazing to be in England in '48.
Oh it was, yes it was. They were thirsty for sport and everything. We had big crowds wherever we went, mainly because of Bradman I think, but even if Bradman hadn't been there I think we'd have got good crowds because they wanted to see Test cricket again, after the terrible pounding they got during the war. There was a lot of damage there of course, still obvious in '48.

In the fourth Test at Headingly in Leeds in 1948, you made 182 in a second-wicket partnership of 303 with Bradman which lasted four hours, and you are credited with having seen Denis Compton off.
Bradman was picking it wrong. He got dropped once and nearly got caught again in slips. So what I wanted to do after lunch was to get after Denis Compton and get him off, because though he wasn't a regular bowler he was their best bowler on this wicket. It was turning a lot on that particular day and, knowing that he was not a regular bowler, you can take risks and get after them because when you get on top of them they don't quite know where to bowl the next ball. And I got after him after lunch and got rid of him, took 30 or something off a couple of overs. Anyway, Yardley the captain took him off and he didn't come back on again. I know E. W. Swanton said he should have been kept on and he could have won the game for them, yet I'm sorry he wasn't kept on because we would have won the game earlier.

Had you played him in the previous Tests in Australia? Is that why you handled him so well?
No, I think I was a good player of spin. In fact it has been written by people that I put him out of the game in England for two years.

So I gave him a bit of a touch-up and he was their main spinner, but I like batting against spinners so, you know, I was up the wicket. I could play backwards and forwards at them and was always playing shots at them, in other words I wasn't anchored on the front foot, but I chased them. I was after them. In fact I was always pleased when the other bowlers went off and the spinner came on, because I tried always to not allow them to bowl a length and to make them have to change their length all the time, which meant you get up, right up, or you get right back.

One of the things said about Bradman is that he hogged the bowling.

Well he never did with me, I always got my fair share. Sid Barnes had that reputation too, but neither of them in any time in my batting with them ever did that. That particular day when they put Len Hutton on he grabbed him. I couldn't get up the other end to have a go at Len Hutton because he was hitting him for fours, but that's how it goes.

You hit 20 fours in that innings.

Yardley was going for a win and he had the field in so it meant once you passed the infieldsmen, there was no one out there. So that all helped that to happen to a great degree. It was a bad wicket, a last-day wicket and it spun a lot but fortunately it spun slowly. I think it was the one game we could have lost in 1948, in all sincerity about it. All the press, the local press said: 'At last England is going to win a Test match'. That's the way the press was writing, and that gave us great satisfaction to prove them wrong of course. But it just went along. In the morning our batting was to save the game then after lunch to get on top of it and then after tea we could see that it wasn't going to be a loss, it wasn't going to be a draw, that we had a chance of winning it, a good chance of winning it and that's how it unfolded. I mean we didn't go out there sort of saying we're going to do this and we're going to do that. You can't do that. So it unfolded as something you couldn't script. I'm sorry I didn't last to the end but Neil Harvey hit the winning run and he got a great 100 in the first innings, so altogether it was a great Test for Australia.

The most-quoted piece of advice that I hear of Bradman's is that if you hit the ball along the ground you won't get caught. You tended to lift the ball, didn't you?

I think he was quite happy with seeing that I was able to lift the ball very safely.

In the fifth Test in England in 1948, Bradman made a move in the field which resulted in Denis Compton being caught out. Would you tell me about that?

Well, I was just fine of the square leg umpire. Compton was coming out to bat and Ray Lindwall was bowling. He moved me about three metres finer and Ray bowled him a bouncer which he hooked straight at me, which I caught thank God, otherwise it would have gone through me. And nobody took any notice of us in those days, you know, nobody came up and hugged me and patted me or anything. Lindwall was talking to Miller and I said to Don, 'Why did you move me?' 'Oh,' he said, 'I remember back in 1938, Compton hooked down that line against Ernie McCormick' (he was the fast bowler in 1938). I said, 'Jeez, you've got a memory like a bloody elephant!' Extraordinary.

We were having a meal together years later and I said, 'Remember when you moved me and I caught that catch off Lindwall and caught Compton?' He said, 'Oh God yes, I remember it well.' He said, 'It was at Lord's.' And I said, 'No, it was at the Oval because you could see the gasometer in the background. I can still remember it.' 'I'll bet you £100,' he said, 'it happened at Lord's.' This was back in the pound days and he's not a betting man. And

£100 to me was a lot more than it was to Don so we got it down to 50, 20 and then £10 and I thought, I'll take it. And in my mind if somebody refutes him they're gone, you know, because I know how good his memory is. Anyway, next week a cheque for £10 came in the mail. He was wrong. But he didn't retract it.

I showed the cheque to Bill O'Reilly and he said, 'You should frame it' and I didn't know quite what he meant by that. (laughs) So even Don's memory could go. It was an interesting thing with him too. He was jealous of his memory, and as he got older, if the recollections of somebody didn't coincide with his, he was very caustic about it. He'd feel as if somebody was having a go at him. Understandably, because he believed firmly in his own memory, but he could have been wrong. But he wouldn't admit it at all.

You played under Bradman and then Hassett.
I was vice-captain with Hassett for his career.

How did you rate Bradman as a captain?
Like every other good captain. Australia has always had good captains and there should be half a dozen fellows on the field with the experience to captain the side on the field. It's very important off the field and I think that's where the captain, a real top captain, is. But most of them . . . I've never struck a bad captain yet in first-class cricket. Bradman was pretty conservative but then he'd come through some pre-war matches when England got 900 or something. I think it was always in the back of his mind what Mr Barnum said years ago, 'Don't give a sucker an even break'.

Had England's captain Hammond burnt something into him with that score of 903 in the final Test in 1938?
I think there was a certain amount of rivalry between them that came from the 30s, you know, because they both played against

each other so often and Hammond was a great player. I don't think he ever forgave Bradman for bowling him out on a full toss one day. Hammond was determined he was going to hit it not only over the pickets but out of the ground – and missed it. One of those terrible things that can happen.

Was Sir Donald supportive enough of the young players when he was captain?

He was very supportive, yes, and you could go to him any time and talk to him and you could depend on him if it were personal and private, you know. There'd be no words, you could trust him. He was a bit different from other captains. He probably didn't mix very much. Lindsay Hassett did it and more so, but for most of us Bradman was our hero in the 30s so it was different. He was a private person and besides that he had an enormous amount of mail to answer. Bradman wasn't a bloke to go down to the pub. I mean if we'd go down to the pub he'd probably be up there answering letters and signing autographs, you know, that sort of thing. But he was very easygoing with you at breakfast, lunch, dinner, and a wine at night and good value, good fellowship.

People talk about him not mixing much. He couldn't. He had thousands and thousands of letters to write. Incredible. And if he was going to do something, he was going to do it properly, and when he made a speech he really worked hard at it. He'd probably have about 50 drafts I should imagine until he got exactly what he wanted to do. And he was called on all the time to make speeches. There were no managers to make speeches with Donald Bradman in the team because nobody would put up with it; it would be Don Bradman who would have to do it, naturally.

They do it very well over in England because you've got top speakers like Mr Justice Birkett, he was in the Nuremberg Trial, brilliant man, delightful man, and you've got Lord Brabazon.

They have a leading speech maker and that's it. Poor devils come out here and we give them the works. They go up the country and the secretary does his and then the president gets up and then the captain of the side gets up and then the vice-captain, and they all say the same thing: 'And we're very happy to see you and we're really looking forward to the game tomorrow.' That's the Australian way. Everybody can't wait to get up and speak. So Don would have to be producing a top-line speech, every time.

Was religion still an issue with the Australian team when you started to play?
No, we had I think four Roman Catholics in our side and nobody ever worried about it. The only thing, Ernie Toshack used to come down early on Friday mornings and get stuck into the sausages. That's the only time he ever came down early. And the other Roman Catholic boys would say: 'But it's Friday!' 'Oh golly, is it?' Because they only had fish on Friday. (laughs)

But I think in the administration it was still living on in some of these representatives of outer districts up into the fifties.

You went on to be vice-president of the New South Wales Cricket Association and deputy chairman of the Sydney Cricket Ground Trust. Did you have contact with Sir Donald in those capacities?
Oh yes, yes. If he ever came across we'd have him to lunch or he'd have a day with us at the Sydney Cricket Ground Trust. He'd have spent the rest of the time with the cricket association. But he'd come over and as we would in those days, we'd invite people, you know, leading cricket authorities, cricket players, even cricket writers! (laughs) to partake of the luncheon with us. I resigned from the association when the Packer thing started, because I had a conflict of interest and I had to get off one. I got off the association because what I was doing at the Cricket

Ground was very important, we were building the ground and I was well and truly involved.

How did you rate Sir Donald as a cricket administrator?
Oh first class. Tremendously knowledgeable about cricket and a great studier of the game. He really did go into things and very thoroughly, and everybody went to him for advice, I think. He was a first-class member of the Board of Control and first-class chairman, first-class selector and he did a tremendous lot for the game. He was always thinking of something that would improve the game and improve the game as a spectacle. In fact, it would be good if every game could have a Bradman who had been such a great performer on the field to be such a great administrator off it. Not many people do that, spend their life really, devoted to the game.

Many feel that they've done enough.
Yes. 'I've had it. Let somebody else have a go.' So yes, he was an outstanding administrator.

Did your relationship with Sir Donald develop into a friendship?
Yes, and the friendship continued because we continued to meet through my involvement with the Trust and going to the various venues like Melbourne or Adelaide from time to time. I was always delighted to see him. If I'd go to Adelaide he was always charming and I'd have dinner with them. I don't think we would have discussed cricket very much when we'd have dinner. I suppose we had interests in politics, and we'd discuss all sorts of things. If you went to his place there was always a couple of very good bottles of red or something. He knew his wines. That was another thing he was very interested in. See he didn't drink until after the war but all he drank then was the grape. He went deeply into it. There were no

half issues with him. As I said earlier, whatever he went into he went into very thoroughly.

During the Test in Adelaide, we used to take the rest day out at Yalumba. I remember one day we were running a little late, and Don and Jessie Bradman were taking Judith and myself out by car and on the road we were accosted by a hit-and-run goat. It flew across our windscreen, across the bonnet, hit a car that was travelling along the same way inside us, in the inside lane. And of course when we arrived there everybody had a few drinks under their belts and to be told by us that we were just hit by a hit-and-run goat, I think they thought we'd had a few before we got there.

Do you think Sir Donald was inhibited by his fame?
I think he was aware of fame and he handled it very well, but it made him very private, because it got to the stage where it didn't matter where he would go, he'd get trampled into the ground. We stopped off in India on the way over on the ship and there were 10 000 everywhere on the wharf as the ship came in. He couldn't get off the ship; they would have swamped him. And as always we enjoy fame but I think it overcame him really. He was a private person and it made it very tough for him. Of course, he had the most wonderful wife and I think that was a tremendous help to him.

Did you find that the Bradman 'mania', for want of a better word, increased as time went on?
Oh I think it's always been there but probably everything has increased with colour television and sponsorships, advertising. Everything in the whole game and in nearly all sports has. Certainly in regard to people like myself it has, in regard to 'the Invincibles'. Up until a few years ago, I used to be Arthur who? but now I'm Arthur Morris. There's a difference, you know.

Spin bowler and all-rounder **Doug Ring** *played in 13 Tests, and was a member of the 1948 Australian team that toured England unbeaten. At his home in Melbourne, he showed me a pile of letters he was posting which had come for his autograph. 'It's getting more and more,' he said, amused. He summed up Sir Donald Bradman in one word: 'elusive'.*

I WAS SITTING in a deckchair on the *Orantes* on the way home from England after the 1948 series in England and Bradman came along. I was on my own reading a paper or a book or something or other and he said to me, 'Do you mind if I sit down and talk to you?' And I said, 'No, by all means,' and I got his life's history from him. He went through from the time he started in 1926 when he came down from Bowral. When he went to Sydney he found it very difficult as a country boy going into the city on his own. He was obviously, even then, showing the signs of greatness and in the New South Wales team there were about six players in the Test team and they all treated him very guardedly – they were very suspicious of him. He didn't dislike them but they didn't embrace him either and he found that very hard. I think it coloured his approach to people. He became very guarded. And despite being uncomfortable, he started to dominate the play. That was obvious after the 1928–29 series, when he started with an 18 I think and got a 79 and a 112. (laughs) Half a dozen of that team were dropped out of the team that went to England in 1930, and he was phenomenally successful, extraordinarily, but he was a country lad and he was suspicious of just everybody.

But he relaxed a little in our tour in 1948. And this was the substance of what he spoke to me about on the *Orantes*. He said that this was the happiest tour he'd ever been on (this was the fourth tour), that most of the chaps had accepted him for what he was. He was a genius as a player. He was so far better than any of us, and there were some great players, but he said he was accepted.

And he *was* accepted. In England we were playing in Sheffield in Yorkshire, and we stayed about 15 miles out of Sheffield at a place called Grindelford which was the most beautiful spot in England. It was just the pub and a couple of farmhouses dotted around the place and we had a great night there. Bradman played the piano for us all and we sang songs. He really relaxed, and I think he found it very difficult to relax. There were many times when he played the piano to us. He played it pretty successfully, modern stuff and some of the classics. He had the music in front of him and he played by it. I don't say he was an expert. My stepfather was a musician and he played the piano a lot better than Bradman, but he was pretty good.

He also discussed the selection of teams. He'd been a selector in 1945, 1946, 1946–47, 1948. He said that the team selections in those years were most interesting. [Jack] Ryder and ['Chappie'] Dwyer were his two confreres. He said, 'I usually found opposition to my selections. I invariably thought that the other two combined against me.' I thought that was an extraordinary thing to say to me, that there was generally opposition to his views from the two older men. He said that may have been because they were brought up in a different era and had a different philosophy and he said, 'I found that they invariably got their way.' I thought it was a most interesting, illuminating thing to tell me, that he didn't get the team he wanted, although he was captain. Having heard that, I mused to myself that he might have not had his way when I was selected. (laughs) Really. I thought that when he was talking. I thought I wonder what you thought, whether I should go or not, because there were others.

You didn't ask him?
I didn't ask him. He talked to me for an hour. But that was really the only time he spoke to me one to one, man to man. I was a good

listener. I thought he was most interesting. But I don't know why he picked on me to expand on his views. I think he liked me, yeah. I'm easy to talk to.

I think his upbringing affected him. His family were church people, they were country people, very solid people. I think his whole personality was such that his family meant everything to him. But his livelihood was geared to cricket and he played methodically. His methods were different from any of ours. His grip was different as a batsman. He could concentrate to the exclusion of everything else. He shut everything else out, totally. And his technique was extraordinary. He lectured to us early on in the tour and said, 'You know you fellas are out caught a lot. It's the wrong thing to do. Six out of ten batsmen get out caught.' He said if you hit the ball into the pitch, into the ground immediately, you eliminate six of the ten ways of getting out. He said if you don't run yourself out and your defence to the ball bowled at the stumps is perfect, you eliminate practically all ways of getting out. Now I'd never heard that expressed before. Six out of ten. (laughs) And that's the way he batted. His grip was such that his hand was turned over on his top hand further than any of our batsmen so that any time he hit the ball, he hit it into the ground. And that's the way he approached it. He was deliberate, methodical with just one approach to the game. He impressed us with that. 'If you don't hit the ball in the air,' he said, 'you won't get caught.'

Did you change the way you batted?
I did. I applied that principle. He taught me quite a bit.

Did it change the way your team-mates batted?
I don't know. It's hard to get into the minds of people but it probably had some influence. He was critical. I know a couple of times

on the tour he reproved batsmen. He'd talk to them in the dressing room because they'd got out caught. He said don't hit the ball in the air, keep it on the ground, they can't catch you. That's the way he approached it.

Did you have much contact with him during the 1948 series?

In a game he might talk to us, give us an idea of what he fancied, but that's the only contact we ever had with him. We attended a number of functions in England. Bill Johnston and I talked to Douglas Jardine at a function. We had a chat for quite some time and we thought he was a pretty decent sort of fellow, pretty affable and he invited us out to dinner. We had a team rule. To accept any invitation to a function from anybody outside the team, we had to get Bradman's approval. It wasn't schoolmasterish, or anything like that, but we had to get his approval. So after we said to Jardine that it would be okay with us, we'd have dinner with him, we said but we've got to get the approval of Bradman so excuse us. We wandered over to Bradman at this function and we said Douglas Jardine wants us to come and have dinner with him. And he looked at us and he said, 'You like him?' 'Oh yes,' we said, 'he seems a pleasant sort of a guy.' He said, 'Well you can't go.' He said, 'Make your own excuses, but you're not going.' So that was that. There was obviously a deep-seated enmity arising from the Bodyline series.

He never ever forgot a darned thing. Really. There were people he didn't like. It was obvious in that conversation on the *Orantes* that there were people he didn't like, he said so. I'm sure he never forgot a person or any of their attributes, or whether they'd offended him. He never ever forgot and he wouldn't forgive at all. He was a strange man. He was elusive, you couldn't pin him down. I don't think we ever really understood him. He concentrated on the game. Everything was planned.

I played only in the fifth Test in that series. We came out of the Piccadilly where we were staying and he came over to me, and they hadn't announced the team and he said, 'You're in the team. Come with me in the cab and we'll have a chat.' And he outlined to me his plan to attack the Englishmen. He said, 'I've got three pacemen in the side, Lindwall, Miller and Johnston, and you're the fourth.' He said, 'I want to bowl you from one end exclusively, the three pacemen will bowl in short bursts from the pavilion end and that's the way we'll approach the game.' He thought that under English conditions that was the way to go and it's the perfect way to go. And going down to the Oval, he outlined this theme of his. The English batsmen would get no peace, the three pacemen would attack them. And I said, 'All right, I'll do that.' But the interesting thing was that at the start of that game there was a little bit of moisture in the pitch and he wasn't absolutely sure if he won the toss what he'd do. He said, 'I have never won the toss and not batted first,' but he wasn't sure. And we had a chat in the dressing room, we exchanged views, and we thought it would be a good idea, that we could bat on it. But they won the toss and batted and in the first innings they made 52. Lindwall was a beautiful bowler, he took six wickets. The game evolved and in the second innings the wicket flattened out, it was only slightly moist. And England batted a second time. I bowled for four hours from one end and I was just told to flatten out and keep them quiet and he bowled the three paceman down from the pavilion end. In short bursts. Furiously. Really giving them everything. They made 188. Nine wickets fell to the pacemen and I took one. But I bowled 28 overs for 44, which is reasonably economic, and I bowled 13 maidens. He subsequently wrote an article in an English newspaper in which he outlined his idea of a perfect Test team. There were six batsmen, a wicket keeper and four bowlers – only. He said you don't need any more than four bowlers. Three pacemen and one spinner and you bowled that way. He proved his point.

Did you resent not playing in the earlier Tests?

I think I was pretty happy just to be there. I don't think anybody felt that way. It was a pretty happy team, it was a pretty good team, we were pretty hard to beat. To be on the fringe of that Test team was something and then to finally make it in the fifth Test. I was to play in the first Test, I think I'd taken more wickets than anybody on the tour at that stage, and it rained. I was in the team and I was excluded and my room-mate Bill Johnston was picked and he bowled so well, he took five or six wickets on this slightly moist pitch.

How would you compare Hassett to Bradman as captains?

Well, Hassett was a happy sort of a fellow, never imposed his will on anybody, never instructed anybody. He was more relaxed about the game and we lost only one game on the whole series in 1950–51. If we hadn't lost that we'd have matched the '48 tour. But I don't think he ever used me very well. (laughs) And I don't think he was a very good captain, not like Bradman was.

Bradman was a great admirer of Billy Woodfull who captained him in 1930 on the tour of England. And Billy Woodfull taught me at Melbourne High, and tried to teach me maths. Oh, what a tyrant he must have been. He was the toughest teacher I ever experienced. As a master he was frightening. Silence in the grade. Utterly.

Did you share any interests outside cricket with Don Bradman?

I played golf with him once with Ray Lindwall and Ian Johnson in a four ball. I think it was in Slough in '48 on the tour. We had a game off and we muscled up a foursome. He probably thought that I'd hit the ball fairly well, and I did, but I hit it inaccurately. I hit the ball a long way, always, but not too straight and Bradman had to recover my bad shots, exclusively, and he didn't enjoy it at all. But he did it magnificently. He was a pretty good golfer, he played off about three. But I wasn't. (laughs) But we beat them. For a small wager. He didn't enjoy it, he took it very seriously. The three of us enjoyed it tremendously but not Bradman.

We played golf up in Scotland and he played it exactly the same way. I don't think you can enjoy golf. Bradman certainly didn't, but he played with us on a number of occasions.

Then in 1950 we were in Brisbane playing against England in the first Test and I took a couple of tickets that were on offer to the team to see Handel's *Messiah* at the Town Hall. I was the only one who took them, I canvassed the whole team and not one of them wanted to go. Not that they were averse to me, they just didn't want to go. Bradman was a selector in 1950–51 and he was in there and he said, 'I believe you've got a ticket spare for Handel's *Messiah*.' And he and I went to see the performance. And oh dear, I was most amused at the attention we got. If Ring the cricketer here were just given a ticket, nobody would take any notice of it but I was with Bradman and we were ushered to our seats down at the front. At the interval the manager came down to see Bradman and said, 'Would you like to come backstage? Eugene Goossens would like to talk to you.' The conductor. We went backstage and talked to Goossens who surprised us with his knowledge of the game. He was an enthusiast. Most unusual for a man of his background. We had quite a chat, mostly Goossens with Bradman. He got a lot of attention he didn't want.

I don't think he gave an interview on the whole tour in 1948 with a newspaper or a journalist. He was very happy to talk at conferences and functions and he spoke eloquently, very freely, but he never gave an interview. Not one. Which was frustrating for the Englishmen but he wouldn't do it. He just didn't trust them. He said he'd be misquoted. In 1947 he spoke at a conference, and he wrote to me actually by way of explanation and pointed out that they'd misquoted what he said. He said that Ring could be regarded as too old to tour England. 'Could be regarded'. And he elaborated on that. And they just quoted 'Ring too old to tour England'. And shortly after that I was picked.

I interviewed him after he'd retired for *World of Sport*. And I know that Ron Casey sold it to England and round Australia so it was a bit of a scoop. It was interesting. The interview was done at the Parliament House. Sam Loxton who was a member of our team organised it. I interviewed Bradman for about 20 minutes and I played the whole thing on the *World of Sport*. I can't recall exactly what he said but I know he ranged over a number of topics, quite freely, and I don't know why he consented for me to do it but he did.

He was not a selector in 1953 when we went to England again. He wrote for an English newspaper and they syndicated it of course, they made a fortune out of him. He mixed very freely with us, no trouble. I think the nucleus of the 1948 team were in the '53 team. Oh yeah. He was pretty friendly, but by golly, I don't think anybody knew him.

Elusive. He was a very quiet man, very shy. He spoke eloquently in an Australian accent, but I rate him as one of the shyest men I've ever met. If he was invited to a function in 1948, he'd take two or three of us with him. They only wanted to talk to Bradman but he took some support. He was devoted to his family, and he kept to himself. He mixed with us in the dressing room then when the game finished at the end of the day, we wouldn't see him. But he kept in contact with us. He was almost reclusive and he was scared. He used to go out through the back of the Piccadilly Hotel, through the kitchen into Oxford Street. I don't know what started him but he was very frightened of the press. He wouldn't get in the cabs with us. He didn't want to be interviewed, and that was his method.

It sounds like a tough existence.

Well, it was tough. For instance, we enjoyed ourselves on the tour. We went out, we weren't excluded from doing what we were used to. But he didn't. He just concentrated on the game.

Was it a team of hard-drinking men?

We enjoyed ourselves. (laughs) It was not long after the war and 15 of the 17 had been in the forces. It was a younger team. But there were no curfews, no rules laid down by Bradman, we were left to our own devices. We didn't abuse the freedom we had. If we were to play in a Test match, the game before, from that time onwards, no drinking. We respected Bradman and his views, and we reacted accordingly. Neil Harvey was a lot younger than most of us. He was 19. He disapproved of some of our antics in '48. He didn't quite understand them. He bellowed. (laughs) He disapproved of our drinking.

The team was unbeaten on the tour.

Halfway through the tour Bradman said to us, 'I think we could go on this tour unbeaten,' and from then on playing against the strong counties, he picked the Test team, so he wouldn't be beaten. We were nearly beaten in Yorkshire when he wasn't playing and he sent Hassett a telegram. (laughs) 'What's going on?' He did, he sent us a telegram because he thought we were probably playing up. Well, we weren't actually, we were trapped on a bad wicket, and we got home. We got the points as it happened. But from that game against Yorkshire, he picked the Test team against the powerful counties. And he always picked the Test team in the match before the Test. Always.

The English didn't like it. But he was human. He was responsive to the pleas of the county secretaries, of the poorer ones and the not so good, that he would bolster the gate if he played. And he played where he could. He played more matches than perhaps he should have and I don't know whether the tosses were organised in those games, but he always batted on the holiday, on the Saturday or the Sunday. I think the toss was purely perfunctory to ensure a good gate. And he always played in the game before the Test match, to tune the side up.

The side was too strong for the English county teams even though we had the same food, which was pretty meagre. We handed in our ration tickets to the pubs we were stopping at. We had exactly the same menu. We'd go in the dressing room after having had a slice of toast and a mushroom on toast, that was breakfast.

It must have been extraordinary in England at that time after the war.
It was more extraordinary in 1953. We watched the Coronation from Shaftsbury Avenue, 50 metres down from Piccadilly in a bombed-out building that was still not rebuilt; they had canvas along the walls. London was still razed to the ground in '53. Some of the other cities were just as devastated. We played in Bristol and several miles of the city were just devastated in '53. That was eight years after the war and they still hadn't rebuilt it. In Coventry in 1948 we saw people living in tents.

Did you ever play against Bradman in the Sheffield Shield series?
I'm nearly 83. I played before the war. I started in 1938. Many of the players had played the Bodyline series. I was just a boy. I got Bradman out in Adelaide when I was 20. He was on 64. I remember it. It's seared into my soul. Bradman bowled Ring, 64. (laughs)

*When **Keith Sims** returned to the civilian world in 1946 he found that Hodgetts & Co., the stockbroking firm he had worked with, had been declared bankrupt and in its place was Don Bradman & Co. We spoke at his home in Adelaide.*

UNDER THE GOVERNMENT ruling with returned servicemen, if you were employed by somebody when you enlisted, and that firm was still going, they had to re-employ you. But I was employed by H. W. Hodgetts when I enlisted and of course when I came back . . . Then I went and saw Bradman and he said yes, he'd be quite happy. Len Bullock and a chap who did a lot of the operating were the only two on the staff that had any connection with H. W. Hodgetts, where Bradman was previously employed.

Of course when Hodgetts went broke in '45, I don't know the full circumstances but I know for sure that the way it was done didn't sit kindly on the other members of the stock exchange, other than one, the president, who was Andrew Young. Apparently the official receiver was involved in it somewhere along the line. They maintained that Bradman took over Hodgetts' clientele, which was an extensive clientele, and they said that it shouldn't have been done that way because virtually, from what I was told, it was only a matter of a few days before the name Hodgetts & Co. was taken down and the name Don Bradman & Co. was put on the building.

How did the members of the stock exchange let it be known that it didn't sit kindly with them?
I think it was just their attitude towards him. They seemed to think: 'Well who's this upstart who's now . . .' Because let's face it, the crowd who were members of the exchange then were the old school, fuddy-duddy type of people and if anybody did something wrong or hurt a client or not, according to what they thought was right, 'Oh no, he's not one of us'. And I suppose, from the time he was there he was never really received by the members of the exchange.

Andrew Young who was a fanatical cricket lover was about the only one that really supported him. When Bradman came back from England in 1948, Andrew Young arranged for a welcome home at the Stock Exchange Club and very few of the members turned up.

Of course everybody said Bradman did the wrong thing. I don't believe it (I may be wrong), but what he was supposed to have done seemed to be out of character. I believe that the person who the blame should be directed at or to was the official receiver. His name was Burns, I think and he was the one who obviously said you can do this and you can't do that.

It was generally felt that Bradman should have paid for the goodwill when he took over Hodgetts clientele, wasn't it? Was that the argument?
Oh yes, that's the thing. He just took it over. Whereas the other members said it should have been put up for tender.

So the creditors lost a lot of money.
Oh yes. Yep. It was done very quickly apparently, in 1945. Very quickly, very smoothly, but between who I don't know.

Did Don ever discuss it with you?
No, and I didn't ask. I certainly got a lot of information from Len Bullock. He was discharged from the services in about 1943, I think, through ill-health and he then became a member of the stock exchange. He was with Hodgetts and then when Hodgetts blew he just switched straight over. And I remember him telling me that it was the official receiver and that the members said it should have been put up for tender and it wasn't put up for tender. Therefore all of the people that Hodgetts owed money to, they just finished up getting nothing. And also a lot of clients who Hodgetts' office held their scrip and so forth, which he used to ease off his debt, they lost everything. He had a good clientele. He had the

Governor of South Australia and he had Lord Gowrie, they were both clients. The who's who in Adelaide were just about amongst his clientele.

So what did they do when they suddenly found themselves in this position?
Well, the clients couldn't do anything. They couldn't sue because he had nothing to sue and Bradman paid nothing for virtually the taking over of the business so there was no currency in the bucket for anybody. And that's where amongst the business fraternity Bradman's name was not exactly on the top line.

Did people take their business away?
Not a lot. When Bradman retired in '54 he had a very big clientele. When I first joined him quite a lot of the clients were still with him, or had switched over to him, put it that way.

When did you begin work with Hodgetts?
I was with Hodgetts until June 1941. Andrew Young was the Grandmaster of Freemasonry in South Australia and my father had a senior position in Freemasonry and so they were very close friends. It was virtually between Andrew Young and my father that I got involved in sharebroking.

I was only with Hodgetts for six months before I joined up and in that time Bradman was still in the services. He came in a couple of times on leave and I had met him as a youngster through my father, who was a mad cricket fanatic, with the secretary of the SACA, Bill Jeans. But other than then I hadn't met him until I went in to see him in late '46: 'Can I have a job Mister?' But no, he was very good to me. I've got no criticism of him at all.

What was your job?

I was originally the office manager and I was looking after the scrip side of it and ledgers and then when DG (that's Bradman), retired in '54, Len Bullock took over the whole caboose and I just kept on going with Len Bullock, right through.

How did Bradman fit the business in with his cricket?

He was a workaholic. And if he was playing cricket in Adelaide he'd get into the office about 7 o'clock in the morning. If there was a match starting at 11 o'clock he'd leave to go down to the oval around about half past nine, doing a couple of hours work just checking up and then when it came to lunchtime he'd ring up and see what was happening. And then at afternoon tea time we'd also get another ring and then of course after the match had finished at 6 o'clock he'd come up to the office at quarter to seven, 7 o'clock and probably work a couple of hours.

He was the sort of bloke that had to be involved in every aspect of the office. He wanted to have a stint on the operating, he wanted to do the ledgers and what we used to call our writing up of all the transactions during the day, and everything else. And we had to balance every day. Because of what had previously happened with Hodgetts we were subject to audit every day. That was the ruling that came in from the exchange. Everything had to be balanced off at the end of trading and the auditor could come in at 9 o'clock the next morning and go through your books, and if you weren't balanced off, well okay, you got reported to the exchange. But that meant it wasn't a nine till five job. One day you may get through about a quarter past five or something like that. And other days you may be working until quarter past six.

And of course when things went berserk when they found oil over at Exmouth, well then you were working quite often until midnight. And quite often in those times when we had to work very late, Bradman would take me out home to Holden Street and we'd have a meal out there and then come back to work.

He completely relaxed when he got out to Holden Street. Completely relaxed. We'd have a sherry and sometimes he'd play something on the piano, then we'd have a meal with Jessie and then he'd say, 'Well, we've got a half an hour before we go back, we'll have a game of billiards or a game of snooker.' I can remember one night we had a game of snooker and I never got to the table. He broke it up. He broke up the game and just went out and cleaned the table. I just stood there hanging onto the cue as much as to say: 'Why am I here?' Everything was a challenge. He was a good squash player, his golf, he got down to a scratch golfer, he could play the piano beautifully.

So it wasn't a matter of you'd whip out to Holden Street, have a quick sandwich and then rush back to work.
No. Jessie used to come and pick us up at around quarter past five, half past five and then we'd go back in about 8 o'clock and work until about 11 or so.

He looked after his few staff very, very well. I entered university to do a commerce course and he allowed me time off to get to lectures without any trouble at all. He worked hard – as I said he was a workaholic – but he expected his staff to be virtually on the same key as he was so you can't blame anybody for that. And he looked after us very well monetary wise too.

Did he want total control of the business or did he just like to keep an eye on things?
He wanted to know everything that was going on but I don't think you could say he was a standover bloke by any stretch of the imagination. Instead of just being the boss in the ivory tower and not knowing what happens in the scrip side of it and so forth, he made

sure that he was conversant with everything that went with share-broking from A to Z. And quite often when he was free and didn't have a client he'd come out and say, 'How are things going? What's happening here and what's happening there?' He was demanding, yes, but he didn't go overboard. You knew exactly where you stood.

He was a very considerate bloke and he did really look after his staff, because we had no turnover other than perhaps the office junior girls.

What happened when he was playing cricket in Sydney? Or in England?

There used to be a couple of telephone calls. I mean obviously he didn't play a lot of cricket. He gave it up after '48 and so you only had a couple of seasons really. I know he tossed up about going to England in '48 and I think Jessie was probably instrumental in saying yes, you go. And he spoke to all of us and said that he intended to go and he virtually asked us if we were quite happy to carry on the business while he was away. It did fall off a little bit, but not much. Not much. The clients used to say, 'Have you heard from DG?' We used to call him DG or Dadda.

Dadda?

The nickname Dadda came from Evelyn or Tim Wall. Tim Wall was a fast bowler and 'Evo', she used to work at the office and she called him Dadda, so we used to refer to him as Dadda behind his back. It was more Dadda in the office than DG really. Outside the office between other people it was DG but in the office it was Dadda. 'Who said that?' 'Dadda did.' (laughs)

Did he have problems with his health that you were aware of?

It was flat. Not that I'm any medico or anything, but he never appeared to me to be 100 per cent fit. And I think the pressures that he placed on himself towards when he retired in '54, I think that had just gradually caught up with him. Because he was a perfectionist and that must have put a lot of stress and strain on him during the time that he was running a business. And also he had his cricket interest, he had his boards that he was on and so forth and, as the saying goes, he had a full plate to occupy his time. And John's polio didn't help. And of course Shirley, the daughter, she was not a healthy little girl so all in all I think it just sort of caught up with him at the end.

Was he a conservative sharebroker?
I would say yes. He wasn't a gambler.

Was his integrity something he prized?
Oh yes. He was very cautious of everything, you know. I'd agree he was not a good mixer. You wouldn't call him a party man. Unless he was really surrounded by close friends. I mean we used to have some wonderful Christmas dinners. He was the life of the party. But otherwise he was very conservative and did the right thing. As far as I could gather, he never did anything wrong that somebody could turn around and point the bone at him saying, 'You did this'.

How did the winding up of the business come about in '54?
He told us that he was going to retire and apparently he had agreed with Len, who was a member of the stock exchange anyway, to take over the business. That was known to us for months before it actually happened. It was quite a smooth transition really. Just went from Bradman to Bullock.

He was only 46. Wasn't that quite young to retire?
Well he just said, putting it quite briefly, that he'd had enough. Had enough of the pressures and so forth. He just wanted to relax

and be himself. He had no problems financial-wise or anything like that. And also the problem with John and Shirley.

And then later in life of course John walked out and that was a big blow to him. I don't think he ever recovered on that one. You couldn't blame young John. John was a very good athlete. He was an excellent runner and he played cricket very well but any time he ever did anything, if he won an athletic event: '. . . the son of Sir Donald Bradman' and that got to young John. He went to England for treatment because he had polio and Gubby Allen took him under control and I think they finished up in Manchester or somewhere like that and the *Manchester Guardian* had a big heading: 'Bradman here again' with a photo of John. I think that was the crowning glory as far as John was concerned. You know, I'm going to be myself and so he changed his name. But I was very happy to see that they had a reconciliation in later life. That's one good thing.

Was there any feeling that Sir Donald was being forced out of stockbroking by the other members of the stock exchange?
I don't think so, no. I don't think that worried him at all. What other people think of Don Bradman, I would say, Don Bradman couldn't care two hoots.

He had two or three members of the exchange who were quite friendly. He used to play golf quite often with Keith Taylor from Taylor and Lang. I think that they played golf right up until Bradman was not able to play golf. So not everybody was agin him but at that time, I can well imagine the members who were the old-brigade type of people. Of course when the blokes came back from the war and took over the various firms, then the average age was a lot younger than it was during the war. I don't think anybody really worried about it after that because a new breed came in.

Adelaide was a hard place to break into then anyway, wasn't it?

Oh yes. You can't do anything in Adelaide without everybody else knowing about it just about, and particularly somebody in the limelight like Bradman. And that's why, to me it seemed he was always so careful in what he did and what he said and so forth. You know, he had the reputation of being rather aloof, but I can fully appreciate that because everybody was on his back. I mean even after the war, people used to just come in and: 'Could I see Don Bradman?' and the only reason why they wanted to see Don Bradman was to shake him by the hand, not to do business. And this went on for years.

And the mail that used to come in, there was buckets of mail, particularly from overseas people, people in India and people in Asia and also English people, from people wanting his autograph or wanting his advice on something. We used to talk about how we'd get a weekly laugh when he'd hand over a couple of letters for us to read. Some of them were amazing. Some of the demands and so forth, you know: 'And if I came over to Adelaide could I stay with you?' and things like this. Oh dear! But he answered them. He answered swags of them. I think people were jolly lucky to get a reply, to be quite honest.

Did you go on to work with Len Bullock after Sir Donald retired?

Len Bullock & Co. yes. Don offered a lot of help to Len when Len originally took over. He suggested Bob Pentilow who joined the company from the Commonwealth Bank. Then in the early 1960s, Len was killed after taking his son over to Geelong Grammar and Jimmy Tummel came in from the Commonwealth Bank and it became Pentilow, Tummel & Co. He was helpful to Bob Pentilow then too.

Did Sir Donald have an office within your office after he retired in 1954?

Yes he did, he had an office of his own. Even when we shifted he had access to an office to use virtually up until the time he pulled right out of it altogether. He used to come in pretty frequently during those days. He was always involved in shares and he continued right up until he was not well enough to transact business. He always used to hand over the jobs to me to follow up all his transactions to see that everything went right.

He had a mathematical brain. It was amazing. In those days if you wanted to add up things and your brain wasn't working too well, you used a machine and you'd pull the lever. And quite often he'd come in and he'd say, 'Do you want a hand?' and you'd say, 'Oh yes, righto, okay'. And he could run down a whole column, just go straight down like that and give you the answer.

He had an amazing knack of how to read a company's balance sheet. He admitted that he could not ever recommend a mining stock because their form of business was not a continuity type of thing. One year they could extract so many tons out, the next years so many tons less. But with an industrial company, he could assess the worth and value of the company. He had a wonderful brain on that.

You mentioned earlier that if you were working late, Jessie Bradman used to come in and pick you all up. Did she usually pick Sir Donald up from work?

Oh yes. She used to drive him in in the morning and drop him off. And then he'd ring her up, irrespective of what the time was, it could be quarter to six or something and he'd say 'I'll expect you' and he knew exactly how long it takes to come from Holden Street in Kensington Gardens out to Grenfell Street. More often than not she'd get caught in a traffic snarl somewhere and be five minutes late. There was no parking space outside the front of the office so she just blew the tooter and DG went down and if she was a bit late, it was: 'Where've you been? What have you been doing?' Oh dear. I can always remember the time when he came out and he said: 'Do you know what the excuse was? She said, "I'm cooking a roast, dear. What am I going to do with it? Could you wait a while and could I pick you up in a quarter of an hour or 20 minutes time?"' But oh no. If he reckoned that from the time he rang it was going to take 12 or 15 minutes, that was the time she had to be there. But it didn't worry her. It was just a bit of byplay really.

She was just fantastic. I do believe that a lot of his success was due to her support, because she was just an amazing person, Jessie Martha. She was a Rock of Gibraltar, the way she looked after him and the support she gave him. And those of us who knew him and worked for him, when she died the consensus of opinion was: we'll give him about six months and he'll just fade away. But anyway he didn't. Yes, everybody thought that, because they were such a wonderful couple and so dear and near to each other. He was amazing on the day that they had the service for Jessie at the cathedral. He was a pretty frail sort of a guy then but he stood up to it very well. And young John was very good to him.

It's amazing because as you say, his health was never up to much and yet he lived to 92.
Well, he'd be the sort of bloke who'd say, 'I'm not going to die'. You know? 'I'm not going to die'. That would be a challenge. That would be the way I'd look at it as far as he's concerned because everything was a jolly challenge anyway. I mean he wanted to be perfect in this and everything that he did. And let's face it, he didn't do too badly.

3

FOLLOWING THE GAME

When England's Daily Mail *invited Sir Donald to write about the 1953 Test series, the paper's cricket writer* **Alex Bannister,** *who was covering the series, was assigned the task of looking after him and his copy. A sprightly 87-year-old Alex Bannister met me at the Berkhamstead station to take me to his home with the comment: 'I hope you don't mind a walk. It's uphill.'*

ONE OF THE JOBS that was rather pleasant in the days when the Australians came by ship, was that the major newspapers sent their correspondents out to meet them en route. So I went to Port Said to meet them, to Malta, and on this occasion Marseilles. And next morning I was lining up at the purser's office and Lindsay Hassett was in front of me and he said, 'I'm surprised none of your papers have asked Don to come over.' I said, 'Is he available?' 'Yes,' he said, 'he's a bit disappointed nobody's approached him.' So I sent a cable and suggested we lap him up because it was the Coronation year and they'd asked for some good ideas to make the paper a lot more interesting for the year. And as a consequence, Don came over.

One of the older Australian players came to me and said, 'You know you won't remain friends with Don for long because he doesn't keep his friends.' Well, that I know to be completely wrong. He had a lot of friends, genuine friends. He was a bit suspicious of me at first because there'd been this story in one of the Australian papers that I resented his arrival, whereas I'd negotiated it. (laughs)

In 1953 I was responsible for everything he sent [to the newspaper]. I vetted anything and after I'd sent it, it was sacrosanct. It couldn't be altered. In one of his letters he referred to our association as one of his great partnerships, like the ones he had in the middle with Ponsford, you know, and that's a nice thing. We got on famously, we really did. I've got a bit of a sense of humour and if it got a bit dark we could always have a joke.

I had three great friends in my 32-year career with the *Mail* and that was Don, Alec Bedser and Len Hutton. All different people, with different characters and attitudes towards life.

Were you aware that Bradman had difficulties with members of the pre-war Australian team?
He couldn't work with two of them anyway: one was Fingleton and the other O'Reilly. It was a great tragedy, because they were very nice fellows, Fingleton and O'Reilly. But there was a lot of trouble going on in the team. You know the story of Fingleton's bat being sprinkled with holy water by the Catholic Bishop of Sydney before a Test match in Sydney in the Bodyline series, do you? And Jack was out in no time and Don had his bat on the massage table, and as Fingleton came in he picked his bat up and he said, 'Now we'll see what a dry bat will do.'

And I remember when Don was bowled second ball by a googly which he snicked on in his last Test innings in 1948, Jack in the press box roared with laughter. He only needed four to average 100 in Test matches. But I talked to Don about it and he told me, 'Well, you can't bat with tears in your eyes.' Because he was cheered all the way to the wicket and the England players gathered in a group and cheered him just as the Australians had done to Jack Hobbs in days gone by. But he later retracted that publicly. I think he did that because he didn't want to take any credit away from Eric Hollies, the bowler, and I think that was a generous act. But he didn't say it to me publicly, that was meant to be private. He played, he snicked a googly, and he said he didn't expect a googly with his second ball, which is logical enough and it was funny, he was cheered all the way back and Eric Hollies was a taciturn man with a great sense of humour. 'Look at them,' he said. 'All cheering for the batsman and not one for the bowler.' He was a lovely man, was Eric Hollies.

What did Bradman think of the result of the 1953 series?

The series in 1953 was a great boost for England and Don was a bit disappointed that Australia lost. But as far as our partnership was concerned, we grew to respect each other very much and became really good friends because we spent hours together in the car travelling around the country.

One time I was driving the car back from one of the northern places and Don was half asleep and we passed the outdoor zoo named Whipsnade. They used to have bison and kangaroos in the field by the road and we went about half a mile along and he said to me, 'It's amazing what goes through your mind when you're half-asleep. I could have sworn there were some kangaroos in the field there.' I said, 'Come on. Kangaroos in Bedfordshire?'

At Nottingham we sat apart and at lunchtime a big crowd gathered outside, you know, 'Oh look, there's Don Bradman', and Sid Barnes, who was engaged by the *Express* to counter Don which was all right as far as I was concerned (laughs), wrote that the big crowd gathered to see *him*. And at one or two other matches, it was just like royalty coming; people were in awe of him. And yet at Leeds where he'd scored these two great 300s and all the rest of it, we parked the car because we couldn't get into the official car park and walked half a mile down this lane. And there's this great man, you know, and nobody looked at him. He was greatly pleased.

He got absolutely sick and tired of people pestering. I've seen him and these obtrusive blokes that come up. One saw Don and he said, 'Oh, hello Don. You remember me?' and Don looked long and hard, and he said, 'Yes, I met you in 1930.' (laughs)

Another time we'd stayed at Harrogate for a Leeds Test match and he was driving and he came out of the hotel gates and went into the road before he should have done. There was a car coming and this chap went 'Grrrh' then he saw Don and he yelled, 'My fault!'

It was always funny to me. We'd be chattering in a restaurant, and the waiter would hover within earshot, hoping to hear something said. I walked down Piccadilly with him and nobody took any notice and another time, you know, they'd go, (whispers) 'Look, Bradman'. But you know what they said in Parliament when Italy surrendered? They said, 'Well, we've got rid of Ponsford, now we've got to get rid of Bradman.' (laughs)

What was his original copy like in 1953?
Good. Very painstaking. He used to have to do 1000 words a day and sometimes I'd happen to take a little bit out or put another word in. The one weakness he had which he probably shares with 90 per cent of professional journalists was the intro. We had our only discussions about the intro because he insisted on having one which started off like: 'The third Test began at so-and-so.' I said, 'Well, that won't do. No one wants that. Not even the *Telegraph* or the *Times* or the *Guardian*.' So he said, 'Well I think I'd like it.' Well, they came back to me as I knew they would and I prepared a new one. So I said, 'What about this?' 'Oh' he said, 'all right' and he let it go.

So what would your first paragraph have been?
Well you know, 'The hero of the day was Bedser' or whatever, you've got to go Bang! into it. But mentioning Alec, you know Alec

bowled Don for a duck at Adelaide. There's a funny little story behind that because it was towards the end of play on a Saturday evening and to avoid the rush, Jessie and John left early because John was only about seven. As they were leaving the ground this terrific roar went up and John said to his mother, 'I wonder what that's for?' and Jessie said, 'Oh that's probably your father hitting a boundary,' and he was on his way to the pavilion. (laughs)

But there was a great camaraderie between players in those days. They might have growled and bitten each other on the pitch but they were good mates afterwards and they liked to help each other's play and so on. Alec always said that he learned more from the advice given by Don, who was an opponent, than from his own captain Wally Hammond. Because Alec went to Australia in 1946 as a novice, he'd only had one year in English cricket.

The sequel to this was, in 1953, Alec took 14 wickets in the first Test at Trent Bridge and I was staying at the same hotel as Don and Alec and the first thing that Don said when we got back to the hotel, 'I must get in touch with Alec to congratulate him.' And the words he used, he said, 'I know you would never let me down.' And Alec afterwards said to me, 'Me letting him down,' he said, 'he's done everything to help me and I'm the one who's full of gratitude for what he's done.'

Another case. Denis Compton had a terrible Test run in 1950–51 and Don took him aside and tried to give him help. Compton thought that was wonderful and he told him the little things he was doing wrong. I found that although Don was fiercely Australian and I admire him for that, he was never, never short of being most kind to other players. He always was very willing to help anybody that was genuine.

I think he was a much more generous personality than people give him credit for, but others tried to manipulate him or take advantage of him and that made him a bit suspicious.

***What did you think of his analysis of the Tests, the matches that
you were working on with him?***

Well, I don't think anybody could have gone deeper into it and
been beyond criticism. His knowledge of the game was absolutely
extraordinary. I would fancy myself I knew a little bit about cricket
but I thought oh blimey, I don't know anything about it. (laughs)
But there was one occasion which puzzled him and that was in
1956 when Laker took 19 wickets at Old Trafford on a bad wicket,
and Locke, the left-arm spinner, only took one, and he couldn't
understand why. And it puzzled me a lot but I spoke to Laker afterwards and he said, 'It's quite simple. All you needed to do was to
bowl ordinarily, not get excited because it was a bad wicket, and let
the wicket do the rest. Tony just bowled too fast.' He got a bit
excited, you see, at the prospect and Jim being a bit more Yorkshire
and canny, he knew what to do. But normally Don could see the
tactics and the game plays so much clearer and earlier than anybody else. In his batting, I think he thought quicker and was
quicker on his feet and saw the ball longer before he made his
stroke than anybody I've remotely seen.

I went up to Derbyshire, where the great Wilfred Rhodes was
in retirement and he was blind then and we had a long conversation. And he said, 'You're a mate of Don's, how do you rate him?'
So I said, 'Well I reckon he's the best ever, by a very, very long distance.' He said, 'Well I bowled against W. G. Grace, C. B. Fry,
Ranijitsinghji, the lot, in my time and he was miles better than any
of those.' So he does stand apart. In what you might call splendid
isolation.

Was he a hard man as an observer?

Exacting I would call him because he had such high standards and
he was a bit intolerant if they kept on making the same mistake.

So that if they learnt, it was okay?

Yes. If they did their best and learnt from mistakes. I don't think there was anybody more loyal to Australia than Don. I had a little altercation with him at Lord's. I think it was Bailey made a great catch to dismiss Neil Harvey and Don wrote that Harvey would pay for that mistake. Then Benaud made a great catch off some-body-or-other and I said: 'Now you've got to write, Don, that the batsman (and I forget who it was) will pay for that.' Well he couldn't see that. But it went in the paper and quite a lot came in saying well, what's good for the goose is good for the gander. He was very fair. We had a little quarrel over whether one was out to a hook or a pull. So I said you'd better win that argument, I'm not game to (laughs), and everybody else described it as a hook so I won on unanimous approval. But he didn't say anything about that.

But the extraordinary thing is how meticulous this fellow was. A thousand words, right, each day. I used to go to collect him at his flat in Whitehall and he said, 'I see my stuff was cut this morning.' I said I didn't know that because I didn't read it through. Once it was in print, you know, I never did. I wouldn't dare to look at it. I'd look at the headlines and throw the paper in the fire or something. He said, 'It was 997.' So three words must have been missed some-where. (laughs)

We got him a flat in Whitehall which was a beautiful, beautiful flat I can tell you. It was all done up for him with a new carpet and you sank in it almost up to your knees, there was a drinks cabinet there full of stuff. And this was at a time when there were still shortages, but this was organised by Lord Rothermore, the propri-etor of the *Daily Mail*, so he was looked after very, very well. We got him a car, and he brought over Jessie and John and Shirley, so we went around to Test matches like a little charabanc. We had some great fun, you know. We got the children to put down the names of pubs they saw and it kept them quiet.

But often I went around with him alone and some of the things he told me I cherish, because he opened his heart on many occasions. I found Don a great friend and I used to stay with them in Adelaide. I was doing the washing-up with Jessie one night and she said, 'We're always pleased to see you because you're not overawed by Don, which he finds embarrassing at times and you're a great mate.' We had some real fun over there. On one visit to Australia we were in the middle of the Murray for two days and didn't even get a bite. (laughs) We went out in a little dinghy.

And he came down to my place and Jessie used to come. I lived with my parents until I was 43 and then I married, and then I went to a place called King's Langley. We had a huge garden and Jessie used to come down and take some plants which was totally illegal and when I went to their garden she'd say, 'A bit of King's Langley, a bit of Watford this one.'

We had a lovely relationship. I used to furnish Don with jokes for his after-dinner speeches because being in Fleet Street there were always jokes and most of them you could readapt if they were dirty. (laughs) But the last time I saw him in Australia would have been in 1978, something like that. I was almost on retirement but Jessie had been very ill. It was a very sad day to me when she wrote and told me she'd got cancer. But Don, the last letter he wrote to me was just before Christmas but one, and he'd fallen down the stairs and hurt himself. He'd got gout in his fingers and he was getting 500 and 600 letters a day, mainly from autograph hunters and so on and he said to me, 'Ninety-two,' he said, 'it isn't worth it.' And I wrote back and I said, 'Well the alternative isn't so hot.' And they were the last letters we sent. He died very shortly afterwards.

Did you work with Don on any occasion other than the 1953 tour?
Yes, he came over for the next tour in '56. He wasn't quite as good the second time. Probably he got too confident. (laughs)

Oh, by the way, the first tour that Don wrote for the *Daily Mail*, at the end of the series it was complimented as a 'force leader' in the *Times*, which is rather like getting a knighthood followed by, you know, a pension for life. So that was a great tribute to him.

Was it the 1953 tour that he was seated next to Jardine in the press box?

There's a story I can tell you behind that. I used to go up to the ground the day before because I had to do a story and I had a shrewd suspicion that a certain gentleman who organised the seating in the press box (this is the beauty of experience and knowing your enemy) might try some doddle-daggle with Jardine and Bradman. Sure enough they were put side-by-side, so I altered them discreetly so that Jardine was below Don. But the strange thing, I have seen in the paper both sitting together. Now I'm sure that was a put-together photograph because they certainly weren't sitting next to each other. As I say, I took good care that they weren't.

But there wouldn't have been any danger because by then Jardine was really a sick man and actually, although they didn't get on, Jardine greatly admired Don. But something had happened to Jardine off the field to really upset him when he was on tour in Australia in 1928–29 and he didn't like Australians. But I was in a brains trust with Jardine in 1955 or '56 (fancy me being in a brains trust!) and I drove him home. And I thought then, here was this man that terrorised the whole of Australia, I don't believe it, because he was mild, all the fire had gone out of him. He went on to die in Switzerland a year or two later.

Was there any aspect Don would have admired about Jardine and his tactics?

I don't think he admired them and I don't think 80 per cent of the cricketers at large did. Well it was banned but it was not thought up by Jardine, you know. It was thought up by some county captains. Mainly by Arthur Carr of North Nottinghamshire, that's the story anyway. But in a way it was a compliment of compliments to think up a series which could bring him down to a mere 50-odd average, you know. Other players would give everything they'd got, their soul and an audience with God in the next life, just to have an average of 50.

But the next series after the Bodyline in Australia, Gubby Allen was captain and I think they got on much better. But he and Allen came into conflict over certain changes to the law because Don was looking at this dragging law from the Australian conditions and Allen from English conditions.

He had one big advantage, Don, in that he was able to choose his tours because he only toured England and he only had 300 odd innings which was absolute chicken feed to people like Len Hutton who had to play every week. But Don never wanted to be called a professional, so he told me, and when he first started he had what he described to me as a fabulous offer to go into Lancashire League. But he was so concerned with getting a foothold in the stock exchange and so on. So he was a man of great purpose who really put his mind to something.

When he'd finished playing cricket Jessie told me she thought that she'd have more sleep, because he would keep her awake, but when he retired he started playing golf, for medals and so on, and before a tournament Jessie said he was worse than when he was playing in a Test match. A chap I know who wrote for the *Evening News*, a sister paper of the *Mail*, was a scratch golfer and he played one or two rounds with Don and he gave it up. He said, 'It's too much of a strain.' It was the impulse to win all the time.

How did you rate him as an administrator?

Well, he had a fine brain, there's no doubt about that. I think one of the reasons he was so out beyond anybody else was that he had a great brain and as Neville Cardus said, if he'd been a clergyman he would have been a bishop.

But when I was staying with him in Australia he'd come in at about 9 o'clock and he'd look washed out. It was very demanding, whatever he was doing, and I think he got a bit tired of doing the administrative work for cricket, locally anyway, although he would be very enthusiastic if a young player came along or something like that.

My mother made a shrewd remark to me after she'd met him for the first time. She said he 'hadn't any health to spare'. And that summed up a lot of his health problems. But he was thoughtful, you know. When he first went down to my mother and father, I was showing Shirley the canal that ran at the bottom of our garden, and he said to my father, 'Where does Alex keep his cricket books?' And he went upstairs and autographed his with a nice message inside. He didn't need to do that.

One story, while I remember it. Don went to England for an International Cricket Conference as Australia's representative about the throwing controversy. Cricket has never been able to find the proper words to define a throw; they've tried from 1903 onwards without success. And Don thought up a form of words which he thought might be appropriate. He was sitting in the conference and passed this suggestion across the table to Harry Altham, who was a former Winchester College school master and also a very valuable member of the English legislative of cricket and Don waited for him to cast his eye and give his verdict. He scribbled something on the bottom and passed it back, and Don read: 'There's a split infinitive in the second sentence.' (laughs)

Sir Donald was revered back home in South Australia, wasn't he?
Well, rightly so. W. G. Grace was a national icon in the Victorian age and Jack Hobbs was revered as well. I was having breakfast with

Don one morning and we watched Jack Hobbs walk across a square towards the station. And Don said, 'Now look at his graceful movements. He moves like an emperor.' He was genuinely admired.

And I'll tell you another little one. We were waiting for a taxi to go to the ground and a model came by. Graceful, you know. And he said to me, 'I'd give all my records and every run I've scored to see Shirley able to walk in front of me like that.'

You couldn't help but admire Jessie. She was a really lovely person. I don't think he could have carried on without a woman of Jessie's calibre and understanding. Because it was demanding of her, it really was, the people ringing up just to say they'd spoken to Bradman, you know the story.

Did you share any interests outside cricket with Sir Donald?
Yes, well, he was a great music man. I listened to him play the piano in hotels if I had the time. We'd listen to classical music and things like that and he was nice and relaxed because music was a solace for him.

What was Don's sense of humour like?
He had a great sense of humour. Very quick.

Keith Miller has described it as rather cruel.
Well, he didn't like Keith. During his testimonial match Keith bowled bumpers to him and he said Lindwall on the other hand told him when he was going to bowl a bumper, just for the mob. And there was the occasion at Lord's in the second Test match in '48 when he threw the ball to Keith to open the bowling and Keith said, 'Give it to somebody who's keen' or something like that. And as a result of that, I presume, Keith wasn't chosen to go to South Africa the next tour but somebody dropped out and they had to send him, so Keith won out in the end.

But Don could be a bit inconsistent. Because over bumping, Keith gave Len Hutton a real soaking at Trent Bridge in '48, when Don was captain and in bad light. Nowadays all four red lights would be up and they would have been off the field. It created quite a storm and as they were coming off Len, who'd got a half inch shorter left arm because of a war accident, protested to Don and Don said, 'Oh I used to love bumpers.' And Len said, 'You wouldn't have liked that lot.' That was a bit cruel really. It was hard, you know, relentless.

Was it true that the best chance you had was in the first few overs against Bradman?

I think that applies to most people. He was human after all. The best player in the world can miss a simple, straightforward ball that does nothing. That's happened many a time. But this ball that Alec Bedser bowled in Adelaide . . . did you see his big hands? They're twice as big as mine and he's got these long, strong fingers.

He was taught by an old pro how to stop the ball swinging. It was in the middle of this record-breaking stand between Bradman and Sid Barnes and he thought he'd try this. He bowled late inswings and to his amazement the ball was like a quick leg-break. Barnes said, 'What the bloody hell is going on here?' He was taken by surprise and so was Alec! So that was it. By a fluke he got this amazing leg-cutter they called it, which is really a fast leg-break. It had never been tried against Don but Alec got him out three times in a row doing the same thing.

Denis Compton described batting to Alec as a ball coming as straight as an arrow and ducking at the last moment. So what Alec did was to have a man at a 45-degree angle on the leg side and he bowled this late inswinger dead on the off stump so that you've got to play it with the bat otherwise you're lbw. And it worked three times straight to Hutton in his position, so he might have found a vulnerable chink in his great armour. But Don was 40 when this happened. Would he have fallen for it when he was 30 or 20?

The South Australian Cricket Association surgeon and keen cricketer **Dr Donald Beard** *had an association with Sir Donald that stretched back to 1946. We spoke at his home in Adelaide.*

YOU MIGHT SAY well why this man? He used to ask the question himself. Why? Many people around the world ask the question and when he died, I don't know whether you saw in your newspapers, but certainly here, many praised him but there were letters that said oh, but he's only a sportsman, what else has he done in life? Well, what he did, he did very quietly and that's why some people accused him of almost being a recluse. He did so much for the disabled and for other charities. I don't know how much he would have raised but it would go into millions. For instance, if you recall his albums that were published, there was the dinner for that. This is 10 to 15 years ago, it was at the Adelaide Oval and I think it was $200 a ticket and all the money went to the crippled children's home. But there was no fanfare and there was nothing published.

He also used to autograph bats and all sorts of other items which were either sold or auctioned for charity. He didn't get anything out of it. And finally, he went to things. For instance, the crippled children's home on Anzac Highway, every year there used to be a match of the press against the crippled children and he always went down there, year after year. Sometimes he would umpire, other times he would play. It was kept quiet. It was a time when people weren't hounded by photographers. He would appear at all sorts of functions quietly, he would speak at dinners. He was on a lot of boards of course, a great businessman, honest, ethical, and did a tremendous amount in the business world. He did a great deal for society. Add to that he was a friend to many, many people. There were some that felt he wasn't sufficiently outgoing. I mean, he wouldn't go into a pub with the boys and have a few drinks. That wasn't his life. But there were many functions that he went to where he did mix with everyone from top to bottom.

When did you meet him?

Came the war and I was a medical student and all first-class cricket stopped. Sir Donald was sick and he was discharged from the air force because of a chest complaint. He lived a very quiet, unobtrusive life because he wasn't well during those years. He improved towards the end of the war then started playing district cricket again. I was playing for University and I'd hoped that I would play against him, but every time University played Kensington, Sir Donald was away in a state team or something so I didn't ever play him. But in 1946 I was picked in the state squad. The Englishmen were coming out at the end of '46. Sir Donald was captain and a selector as well and I'd hoped to get a game against the Englishmen. At practice I used to bowl my hardest. One night he was batting and I was bowling in the same net and I thought, 'Oh, I'll get you', and probably foolishly I started to bowl short and as fast as I could. That's unwise in the nets. The coach Arthur Richardson came over to me and said, 'He wants some practice against some leg-spinners so would you move over to the next net?' Now I allowed my imagination to run riot. I thought, 'Oh, he's taking me off because I'm . . .' but of course it wasn't that at all. In addition the wicket was damp and it was getting dark. (laughs) So that was as close as I got to playing with him. Although I thought I'd get into the team, I didn't.

From those days onwards, I suppose the friendship started. I went away to the war in Japan and Korea as an army medical officer and when I came back from Korea in December 1951 I started playing with Sturt. I then went to England to do my surgical studies and I came back and I was appointed surgeon to the South Australian Cricket Association. I looked after cricketers because I loved the game and I think they deserve looking after. I was surgeon at SACA and for the visiting Test teams for 40 years. I was still playing cricket. By now he'd retired and he was chairman of selectors but of course I saw a great deal of him because I had to see all the injured players of the state side and the visiting Test teams that I looked after.

He would always be interested in the players and their injuries. Ashley Mallett, who was a Test off-spinner, injured his finger, which is important in a spinner, in the nets one night. Now Sir Donald was there at the practice. Selectors don't always go every night to cricket practice but he did and he'd be available for offering a word of advice here and there, and the players of course loved him. When Mallett was injured, by now it's evening, it's 7 o'clock, and Sir Donald rang me here at home and he said, 'I've got Mallett, he's injured his finger, can I bring him out to see you?' And he drove Mallett from cricket practice to here. Now anyone could have done it, but he chose to do it. He would do little things like that for anyone.

Sometimes for me it was difficult because I'd know the player, I'd know that he wanted to play but I'd also know that it was unwise for him to play or he wasn't fit to play. So I had to be honest and divulge that information. But Sir Donald was always sympathetic. He would always say to the player that he was sorry he was injured and therefore ineligible for selection. Whereas today you frequently read that a player learns that he's not been picked in the side and he reads it in the newspaper.

What brought you together as friends?
A great love of cricket, I suppose, number one. An interest in a lot of things apart from cricket, including music, reading, and a whole

range of things that perhaps he didn't get with some people. We were able to talk about all sorts of matters. His knowledge of cricket of course – I used to try and catch him out but never could – his knowledge of games in the past and the way cricket was going in the future. So we used to just sit and talk. Right to the very end he never forgot things. I would mention episodes from a game in the past, and he would pick me up as to the date, as to the runs that the batsman had scored, or the manner in which he got out.

I didn't agree with everything he had done as captain. I feel that there were some matches on the 1948 tour of England that were played too hard and that includes the match against Essex when they made 700 in a day. Why did he go on pounding a county that was not very strong? Keith Miller is a great friend (although he's very sick now), and he was very critical of that. He made statements that he really felt that the game should close and he threw his bat.

And Don remained bitter about Bodyline to the very end. When I would speak to him about it, he really wouldn't accept that they just had to do something about him because England just couldn't get him out, and he was going to make 200 whenever he went out to bat.

At the Adelaide Oval we would very frequently sit together up in the committee lounge at a match and talk. And he came here to dinner many times and I would often go up to Holden Street to see him, particularly in the latter years when he wasn't able to get out quite as much. I'd go up late in the afternoon and sit and talk and we became very close.

He would do little things, just out of the blue. I was in hospital a few years ago and feeling rotten. I'd had an operation and I just didn't do anything. Not cooperating. Doctors are bad patients. The sister came in with some cards and one of them said, 'Don. Sorry to hear you haven't been well. I suggest you put your pads on, go out into the middle, put your head down and play the innings of a lifetime. Donald Bradman.' Now to say that to me as an all-time No. 11 batsman really gave me a kick. But he wouldn't just send you an ordinary card, he'd put something like that in it.

Did Sir Donald talk to you about his golf?

One day I said, 'How did you go at golf yesterday?' 'Oh,' he said, 'I won the "B" grade championship.' He said, 'I went down to the lawn on the Sunday morning to get the *Sunday Mail* to have a look at the sports results but they didn't put it in the paper.' Now sometimes when he was a cricketer, the newspaper hoardings would only have two words: either 'Bradman in' or 'Bradman out', that's all. In huge letters. I can assure you the 'B' grade golf competition results are in very, very small print, but he was still interested enough to see if it was there. It's something all sportsmen do, particularly at club level – they open the paper to sport and they look at what has been said about them. And he was no bigger nor smaller than any of them. He said, 'But my name wasn't there.' I said, 'Oh, Sir Donald, why was that?' He said, 'I forgot to put my card in.' I think to make an admission like that, to admit that he'd go to get the paper to see the result and to admit that he'd forgotten to put his card in, is the mark of a big man.

Did you and Sir Donald share a love of music?

I listen to all sorts from jazz to opera. His love of music was very broad. And he loved the piano. That dates back from the days when he and Lady Bradman had moved to Sydney. They always went to the Menzies' (Lady Bradman's family) to Sunday tea and the whole family would stand around the piano. He used to tell me that those Sunday nights were some of the loveliest nights he remembered. He would play the piano, someone would play the violin, someone a clarinet, some would sing and they would have a Sunday night musical. He loved them.

He enjoyed light classical and lyrical things. Popular music – not the heavier classics. Chopin, he would play. He had an extensive collection of records and tapes and he would listen to music but I think he played the piano mainly because he enjoyed it himself.

What sort of books did he read?

History, I suppose was the most. Historical novels. He did quite a lot of reading when he couldn't do things with his hands and he couldn't play the piano.

He found it a little difficult to cope with age and the increasing infirmities. He loved golf and he felt very embarrassed when towards the end he had to use a motorised buggy. And then of course he got arthritis in the hand and that upset him. First of all he couldn't play golf, then he couldn't play the piano, then he couldn't play bridge, then he couldn't sign his name and things became very dark.

Did you share an interest in food and wine?

When I'd go up in the late afternoon to see him, we'd have a sherry together. At dinner he'd always enjoy a glass of white and a glass of red, he was never a big drinker but he loved it. He loved food. When he'd come here to dinner, he'd question my wife about it, though towards the end he lost his interest.

Can I tell you a little story about one dinner here? It would have been 1978. Australia was playing India. Amongst the guests were Jeff Thomson and Bishen Bedi, the Indian captain. Before dinner everyone went for a stroll around the garden. Now I've got a cricket pitch and practice nets in the backyard, my sons were playing at the time. Someone jokingly said, 'What about putting the pads on?' Well he did, and Jeff Thomson and my son bowled to him. Thommo of course didn't bowl fast but he didn't just roll the arm over. And the little dancing feet were still there. That was the last time that he ever put the pads on.

Did you ever see Sir Donald upset?
He used to get upset about misbehaviour on the field. He used to get upset in the 70s when sledging came in, when the umpire's decision was questioned. Behaviour in people – behaviour against their fellow man would upset him because he felt that everyone should help other people, particularly if they were less fortunate or disabled in any way. If people didn't do it when they were in a position to, that used to upset him.

Tell me about the charitable association, the Lord's Taverners?
The Lord's Taverners was formed here by Ian McLachlin and at the first open dinner we had Sir Donald spoke. He was the patron, he did it for Lord's Taverners because our aim is to assist young disadvantaged cricketers. Disadvantaged for any reason – whether it was physical, mental, geographic or financial or whatever. But he did a lot for us.

The Lord's Taverners arranged a testimonial cricket match for Les Favell, the ex-captain of South Australia, who was dying of cancer. We asked Sir Donald if he would be one of the captains so it was the Bradman XI versus the Favell XI. They were the two non-playing captains. We got all dressed up. Favell put his creams and his Australian cap on and out they went on the Adelaide Oval and tossed. And cricketers came from all over the world to play in it. There were storm clouds that would come up from the south-east – we could see them at the Adelaide Oval and we thought they're going to come over and drench the ground. They'd just get to the river and they'd back off and go back to the hills again. It was almost as if . . . you know. I don't know how many thousands of people went to that testimonial. Les Favell made it out to the middle, he tossed. He went home and had a rest in the afternoon and we had a dinner that night. I think about a month later he died. Bradman and Favell were great friends. He was a great respecter of Favell and the way he played.

I remember one time we were having a Lord's Taverners function and I asked Sir Donald if he would speak and he said, 'Don, you don't want me. I'm an old man. I can't do anything for cricket. You want a young man who can really do it,' and he suggested Barry Richards, who had just come here as coach. He said, 'I would do it but it's better to have a young man.' All the time he was trying to get the emphasis off him and onto younger people, younger cricketers. Sometimes he'd be accused of not being helpful but he said, 'Why do they keep on wanting me? I'm an old man and I can't do anything now.' I said, 'They still want you. They respect you and they love you.'

In particular of course he couldn't understand the absolute adulation from the Indians because he never played in India. He made a double century against the Indians at the Adelaide Oval in 1947, one year before he retired. He respected the players but he didn't have a great love of India. And of course he used to get more mail from India than any part of the world. Indians love him.

I've been up at Holden Street when the postman would arrive and he was still making a special delivery to Sir Donald Bradman, Holden Street, Kensington right up to his death, with a bag of mail just for Bradman. He used to say, 'I can't understand it.' And I said, 'Look, there are others who can't understand but you're a figure in this world that so many people have come to admire, to respect. There are all sorts of emotions that they feel that put you a class above so many.'

But I sensed that he enjoyed it. The best way to stop it was not to write back. Twelve months before he died, I said to him, 'Sir Donald, you've got to stop it, you've got to let me know you won't do any more,' but he continued. So I got the feeling that he protested but at the same time he appreciated it.

*The 17-year-old **Ian Craig** was touted as 'the next Bradman' when he made his first-class cricket debut in 1953. He went on to captain Australia, but retired from Test cricket at the age of 26. I spoke to him and his wife **Ros** at their home in Bowral, where he is chairman of the Bradman Museum.*

I MET SIR DONALD BRADMAN when we went to Adelaide in 1953. That was the year he stood down as chairman of selectors. It was the only year in 30 years that he hadn't been chairman. I think John had the polio so Phil Ridings came in from South Australia as a selector and then there was Jack Ryder and Bill Brown. I was only 17 at the time and had just come into the game.

You were proclaimed the next Bradman, weren't you?
I think I was realistic enough to know that I wasn't. In those days you used to very much just play the game. If you were good enough you kept being picked as you went up. You didn't make a conscious decision that you were going to be a cricketer or sign a contract with somebody to say you were going to do something, it just happened. I think I had my feet firmly on the ground as to my own ability and where I was going.

Did you discuss that title with Bradman?
No. He would never initiate any of those issues with you about anything personal. If you wanted to go and talk to him about something that you wanted him to assess, then he was very amenable to having a discussion with you, but if you were waiting for him to come to you and tell you that you were doing something the wrong way, he

wasn't like that. I think the only time I can ever recall him initiating anything was when he addressed the team in Brisbane before that Tied Test against the West Indies in 1960. He told the players they were looking for attractive players and that people who were going to be occupiers of the crease could forget about it. That's a time when he obviously came out and had a firm point of view but he did it to the team as opposed to doing it to individuals.

Did Sir Donald talk to you when you were appointed captain of Australia in 1956?

Bradman was a selector and he was on the Board of Control. After I'd been appointed, there was a game in Sydney and he had a long chat to me in the pavilion and I guess he really told me what the expectations were. But he wasn't telling me how to do the job or anything like that. I think it was just to bolster my concerns, especially as it was a fairly onerous task, at the age of 21. I think he just wanted to give me moral support and the expectations of standards – what they were looking for in a team and how they should behave and those sort of things – were discussed.

Were you surprised by the appointment?

Not so much the Australian one, the surprise one was when I was appointed captain of New South Wales when we came back from England in 1956. I certainly hadn't expected it. Richie Benaud was expected to be captain of New South Wales, Neil Harvey captain of Victoria and that was the shock, when they appointed me captain of New South Wales over Richie. Then it became a choice between Neil Harvey and myself for the Australian job. So when it's a choice of one out of two the surprise is not as great. But that first one, I had to sit down when they rang me to tell me. I'd captained schoolboy sides but that was about it. I was very much a junior boy in the team. I was the youngest player on both the tours of England and still a relatively young player in the New South Wales team. The secretary rang up and said, 'Are you sitting down? You've been made captain.' You obviously have that concern then, how are the other chaps going to react to it? Particularly Richie, he had reasonable justification to feel aggrieved, I suppose. And then when I was given the Australian job, I suppose Neil could have felt the same way. But to their credit they were both tremendously supportive in everything. Both in New South Wales and then on the Australian tours they were tremendously supportive, so that got rid of that problem really.

I hadn't got to see Bradman in the last year or so and I was disappointed that I hadn't had the chance to discuss the historical aspect of that appointment with Don, what had happened – why I was appointed ahead of these other fellows. Nobody's ever told me. I have a bit of an idea but I'd like to just have it confirmed. Just what the discussions were and why.

Didn't he discuss it with you at the time?
No, you wouldn't expect him to either. It's still a bit like all these Cabinet documents, isn't it? People will keep things quiet until it becomes a non-event except for a historian who is writing a retrospective of it. It would have been nice to have known.

Are there sides to Sir Donald that aren't so well known?
One of the things that I always admired about Don was his concern for people. On the 1956 tour of England, he was over there writing, and I got a stomach wog. I wasn't particularly sick, but rather than leave me in a hotel they shot me into St Thomas's Hospital for a few days to get over it. And he arrived one day to visit me when I was in hospital. I couldn't believe this. Here was this man and he had his family and was obviously pretty busy but to take time out to come to the hospital to see me, I shook my head. It was just the thought.

(laughs) I remember he was very chuffed. I think it was the day that Len Hutton's knighthood had been announced, so he was able to tell me that he was no longer the only cricket knight.

And then when I had hepatitis – this is after the South African tour in 1957–58 – I had just been diagnosed and I was in bed. In those days for hepatitis they kept you in bed for six weeks and isolated you and kept all the crockery isolated, sterilised and so on. And he arrived at our house in Mosman quite out of the blue. He'd just come to see how I was getting on. We were terrified he might get hepatitis, that I might give it to him. But once again, his compassion and general concern for people, I just found that quite remarkable for a man who obviously had so many other issues on his plate. He was obviously always focused on issues of great note in the cricket world and in his business world and just to take the time out on both of those occasions to say I must go and see Ian, it made me feel quite overwhelmed. I still remember both occasions very clearly. There was certainly an element of surprise for me that he would risk coming to see someone with hepatitis. You're not allowed to see anybody, and the chairman of selectors comes along. He was very considerate.

Was Sir Donald a presence in Sheffield Shield cricket?
Being an Australian selector, he was travelling around all the time to the state games. You used to see him quite regularly. He'd come to Sydney for a game or if you were playing Adelaide or it might be his turn to go to Perth when you were playing Western Australia. So yes, we certainly saw him, but he would never mix with the players. He'd come into the dressing room periodically and have a bit of a chat but it would never get to a personal level or to discussing the game except in the broad context of the way the game was being played these days rather than anything to do with the specific game being played. Changes in attitudes, maybe behaviour or something like that.

I think at that stage he was on the Australian Board of Control as well so I guess that caused him to keep a distance away from the players. There's always been that gap between the actual players and the administration of the game. I think they're trying to overcome that now by having player representatives on the Board. They've certainly done that in New South Wales, and they have meetings between the state captains and the Australian Board. Those things were unknown in my time. The Board administered the game and the players played it and that was it.

You made the decision to retire at the age of 26. Did you have contact with Sir Donald about this?

One of my treasured possessions is a letter from Sir Donald thanking me for the role that I played in Australian cricket. I guess it was an interesting period because we were going through the transition from the wartime and pre-war players to a totally new group of young players and all that maturity and experience of those older people had gone out of the team. The team had come through it and had played it with the right attitude and everything. He appreciated that I'd been involved in that. It was a very complimentary letter.

He didn't try and dissuade you?

No, I think he was aware of it. One of the things that happened at about that time, I had been on those two tours to England then I was sick [Craig had hepatitis in 1958] and then I came back and I was playing with New South Wales. But just about that time my boss said to me, 'Well, you know, it's about time you made up your mind as to what you're going to do, whether you want to push on with your cricket or have a career in the company.' That was at the beginning of the season when the West Indies were here (1960–61) and I thought about that and I thought, well, I've done the cricket thing, I've achieved all that, perhaps the time is now when I should be pursuing this career. So I went to the selectors and said, 'I'm not available for the 1961 tour of England. Forget me.' Well, of course then I started to score runs (laughs) and had the best season I've ever had. Late in the season I spoke to the boss again, I said, 'Look, you know, I would really like to do this tour if I get selected, so I think I'll just take my chances on the prospects with the company when I get back.' So I went back to the selectors and said, 'I've changed my mind, I'm now available' but I think in retrospect, Bill Lawry and I were then competing for the last batting and opening batting position and I think they realised at that stage that I was only a short-term prospect. It was the third position and they had two stable opening batsmen. They probably said let's give the young guy a chance and they chose Bill and of course it was the best decision they ever made, because he virtually won the series for them in England and I never regretted it as it transpired. The career I then had with the company was very rewarding and successful, so to some extent I have to thank Sir Donald and his co-selectors for not picking me. (laughs) But it would have been nice to have gone. I only played one more season after that.

What contact did you have with Sir Donald after cricket?
IAN CRAIG: He was at our wedding in Adelaide. He knew Ros's family.
ROS CRAIG: My father and he shared a floor. Dad was not a stockbroker, he was a chartered accountant, but they happened to share a floor in Pirie Street in the Epworth Building, so they saw each other on a just hello basis probably every day or every other day. And we lived in Kensington Gardens and he was Kensington Park. But they were just a lovely normal friendly family, and then I met Ian and it was quite a coincidence. Forty years ago last Sunday we were married.

IAN CRAIG: But then I used to see him at the cricket in Sydney just to say hello. The last time I had a long discussion with him really was when the Springbok rugby Test was on. He came over and I was on the Sydney Cricket Ground Trust at the time and virtually the only place in the ground that you could watch the game in comparative comfort on the day, because there were so many police and the devil knows what around, was in the trustees' box. So he came and sat there and watched the events unfold of this rugby match and the demonstrations and the police having to throw people in paddy wagons. At that stage the South African cricket team were due to come the following summer and he was chairman of the Board at the time and had to make some sort of decision as to whether the tour would go ahead.

We had three or four games and whilst the rugby went ahead and police were cheered and I think everybody was absolutely delighted the demonstrators were controlled and kept off the ground, Don realised that in a cricket match which goes over six hours there were other issues. They could be shining mirrors into the batsman's eye. He was thinking about all these prospective other things that you'd have to do in a cricket match as opposed to a rugby game.

I think he realised that just logistically it would have been impossible and he was a very, very pragmatic man. I sat next to him for quite a while and we talked about aspects of it, but I think he was just absorbing it as much as anything else. The police chiefs were in the box with us and he was able to ask questions of them as to how they had handled it and what would be the logistics of a cricket match as opposed to this sort of game.

How did you rate him as an administrator?
Oh, he was outstanding. His knowledge of the game, his analysis of the game was much greater than most administrators. Most have

not played the game at that higher level, or even at state level, so you have people who are competent administrators in a sense but without the in-depth knowledge of the game. He was such an analyst of the game as well as having the ability to have done it and then to apply that in an administrative sense.

My impression is that Don is a better analyst than most people I've ever met and he was able to apply this in his administrative knowledge and argue a very potent case, although he didn't necessarily get his own way. I think he was an outstanding man.

I think there was a streak of pessimism in Don. I think he probably tended to think the worst of things rather than the best of things. Always he was probably terribly cautious that people were trying to get at him. That was the make of the man. And that's where his wife Jessie was so good. Not that I knew her as well, but she was always just so charming and outgoing and pleasant. A great counterbalance to Don. I guess Don would get a bit cranky at things sometimes and she would smooth that over.

Did you ever play golf with him?

I had a game of golf with him and John one day. Whether it was with Richie or Bobby Simpson, I'm not sure. We had a four ball and I think it started off a very pleasant game, when Bobby and I or Richie and I were playing against the Bradmans. I think Don used to get very frustrated with John because John didn't have this same sense of application. They'd start off all right but by the fifth tee or something, they'd be barely talking. Don's expectations were of a standard. More that you apply yourself to it, I think. Okay, we're here to play golf, we give 100 per cent effort. I don't think Don could ever relax and say 'Oh, I'm just going to go out and have a walk around and belt a few balls'. That just wasn't The Don.

And that's the way I play my golf. I just enjoy it, a pleasant walk around. I played with Don on that one occasion and those who used to play with him say that he just wasn't a natural golfer, he didn't have a natural swing. And they said he was a relatively poor putter, which I was surprised about for a man with great ball skills, yet he still played down to scratch. Even when I applied myself, I couldn't get within 15 shots of that.

I find that amazing, that somebody can block everything else out of their mind and just go down that particular channel on that subject that's happening at the moment. It's a different talent. I don't think I ever met anyone in my life who seemingly could give so much attention and absorb all the detail and come to a conclusion so well. No doubt others can do it, but he was just quite remarkable. To me, that's what set him apart from other people. It wasn't just his natural ability as a cricketer that made him that much better.

Other players have had the ability and they'll go out and they'll get 100, then they'll throw it away, they've had their day's sport, but Don would just keep going on. He didn't have this sense that it was just a social event. He did to some extent but by and large he just was in a mode that he was going on and on and on. Even Steve Waugh throws it away if he's had enough for the day.

What is your role with the Bradman Museum?

I've been chairman the last couple of years. It's been very interesting. Don was obviously reluctant at the start of the museum project but once it got going he really did throw his weight behind it.

The first part of the museum was up and running before we came down to Bowral. I came on the board just about the time that we had virtually completed the new building but we didn't have any money to equip it. That's when the Ray Martin interview was organised with Kerry Packer.

***So was it the money that Sir Donald got from that interview that
went towards the next stage of the museum?***

Basically. We had some money but we wanted to do it well rather
than on the cheap. I guess you've been to plenty of country museums and they are always short of money so it's always a compromise.
We had this offer from Channel Nine to do this interview and they
guaranteed a million dollars and that was enough to equip the
museum to the standard we wanted.

Kerry Packer and Bob Mansfield, who was chairman of our
fundraising committee, had a meeting with Bradman and my
understanding of it is that Packer said to Bradman, you owe this to
the nation, and I will guarantee the million dollars. I think for all
his humility and shyness and privacy, Don was very conscious of
his place in society and I think when it was put to him on that sort
of basis he probably thought well, yes, I probably should do something like this.

His generosity was in always directing these things to the
museum. Potentially when you look at people selling Bradman
memorabilia, he could have made millions and millions out of the
stuff that he had or selling his autographs. He just wanted a level of
comfort in his own life and to see that his family were adequately
supported and cared for and that was it. He wasn't about greed and
grabbing the huge amounts of money which he could never spend
anyway.

What has happened in sport is that you've now got these managers who come between the celebrity and the public and they
make their living on doing that deal. I think that's a great disappointment in life. That's where I admire Bradman so much, that a
man who could have made so much capital out of his ability and
everything – he could have got $20 000 a night for a speaking
engagement – never did. He just wasn't materialistic in that sense.

*Australian all-rounder **Alan Davidson** dominated Test cricket during his 10-year career from 1953, and in the Tied Test in Brisbane in 1960–61 he entered the record books when he took 11 wickets and made 124 runs in the same Test. We spoke in Sydney.*

As a youngster I'd grown up with the knowledge that Sir Donald was our hero, our champion, and then I was selected for my first game for New South Wales in Adelaide, at the Adelaide Oval. And I never met the man right up until the toss or anything and I went out that morning and I took a wicket second ball and I got four wickets for 30 and went in and batted, and batted reasonably well. I took a couple of good catches and got a run-out when I threw the wicket down from square with the bloke coming back for his third run. I had one stump to throw at and I knocked the stump over and the fellow was run out. You know, I thought well gee, this is a good game. And still I haven't met him.

Then it would have been towards the end of the third day we were in the field and I bowled atrociously, that's the only way to describe it. None for 90 or something like that. Feeling very disconsolate, I felt the only way to do it was to come off last, and I've got the cap down over my head, not looking to either side as you walk up these steps to get up to the top. Up at the top there is a little gate that opens up and then you turn to your right and go down to the dressing room. But there's somebody holding the gate open and all I can see is two little tan shoes and all I got was this beautiful remark, 'Different game today, Alan, isn't it?' With the distinctive Don Bradman little twangy voice that he had. So that was my first meeting with the great man. (laughs)

Over the years the friendship just grew. It was just one of those things. I had a similar background to Bradman in many respects. He used a cricket stump and a golf ball against corrugated iron. I used to walk along the country road throwing stones in the air and hitting them with a gum stick. I'd run at the stone, pick it up and throw it at the post. That's where I developed my arm and accuracy with throwing. I was never coached a day in my life and I don't believe Don was either. So it was just natural talent of watching and observation.

I must say that at different times through your career, when you were talking with Don and you'd say, 'Oh gee Don, I don't know why I'm getting out. I'm seeing the ball well, I'm hitting the ball well,' and the squeaky voice would come back again, 'Well if you didn't hit in the air, you can't get caught,' or 'I can't see anything wrong with your game.' That reassurance. He was a one-liner in many respects. I think he just had that gorgeous gift. To have him in your presence was just inspirational, really. I come from fairly humble beginnings in the country and I suppose there's a certain amount of awe, even until the day he died. To talk to him I wondered whether I should be speaking to him, he was on that pedestal.

That remained right to the end, even though we became great friends. When I came to writing my autobiography, Don wrote the foreword. And funny enough, I believe mine is the only autobiography foreword to be written by Don.

He was a very understanding selector and chairman of the Board. He took a personal interest in the team. When for instance New South Wales went to Adelaide, our team was always invited out to his home, the whole team. We used to go over two nights, rather than the whole 12 going in one night. Richie and Neil Harvey and others would go one night and I was given the job of taking the kids out. I was the father confessor or something though I wasn't captain or vice-captain or anything like that. I used to enjoy that job actually.

And the homeliness of Bradman. He'd take us down into his den, and of course the young people could walk around and look at the things, the memorabilia he had in the room. You hear that he was always aloof, he was this and that and yet at the same time I was close enough to know of the enormous charity work he did, this openness with giving, giving, giving.

He never talked about himself. If you asked him questions he might say, 'Yeah, it was a pretty good dig, I think.' Something like that, but he never went on and said, 'Well I thrashed this fellow.' Never once did he ever speak about himself. He spoke about some of the great matches that he played in, but then he'd talk about some of the great things done by players, things like that. He had no hesitation about naming Bill O'Reilly as the greatest bowler he ever played with or against. That sort of openness was there, yet the humility and the modesty of the man were just unbelievable.

And Lady Bradman was just the most gorgeous lady, the most gracious lady who ever lived. She would bring down the sandwiches and pour the tea and young John was a young boy growing up at that time. So the family were shared by the cricket community. I sat through the whole of the last day of that Adelaide draw against the West Indies in 1960–61 with Shirley Bradman crying on my shoulder. 'They're not going to save it, are they Alan?' I said, 'Yes they are.' And that was one of the lovely things. Lindsay Kline and Kenny Mackay, they played out the last two hours and Shirley's there and of course, her emotions just overflowed, and my shirt was just saturated with tears. I've got my arm around her saying, 'Shirley, it's all right, we're going to make it.' I knew Slasher Mackay. Slasher was my roomy on two or three tours and while ever he was there, he would take the last ball in the centre of the chest, which he did, rather than play at it. He had that sort of courage.

Don was a very observant person. I remember playing in a game one day and the last ball for a session, I bowled the ball and took one more stride and I got – it wasn't a cramp but a little spasm in the back of the leg, and I might have skipped for one stride. As I came off the ground, there he was at the top of the steps again. He said, 'What happened on that last ball? Did you pull a muscle?'

I can always remember one day. Wally Grout was a bloke who never looked after money. Wally spent money, he was never rich, never would have been, but then again none of us were. But one day Don said, 'What's the time, Wally?' and Wally said, 'Oh, it's all right for those that have got watches.' And Don said, 'Has Wally not got a watch?' Then a couple of days later, a watch suddenly appeared, and it could have only come from one person. So it's the little things. You've got to understand the Bradman way of doing things.

Tell me about playing the Tied Test against the West Indies in Brisbane in 1960.

I got the 11 wickets for 120. I came to the end of the day and I was run out with seven minutes to go, seven runs required. If ever a match was thrown away! I was just so fed up, I was disgusted really. I took my pads off and I just sat there and watched the rest of it, it was a disaster, as I call it. In comes this little fellow with a smile on his face and says, 'Don't be disappointed, Alan, today you've made history.' At that stage the tie to me was a defeat and yet he said, 'It's the first Test that's ever been tied.'

Until he said it, my whole thinking and reaction was 'We've lost it, it's a disaster. We should have won it'. Don had seen past all that and said 'Today you've made history', because that just enveloped the whole world. That observation was so instantaneous. That was always that gift that he had. And looking at it in the sense of the whole series, well of course it was a tie, it was setting history, but in effect, it did more for the series and for cricket generally than an Australian win or even a West Indies win. It was a rejuvenation of Test cricket.

Do you recall Bradman speaking to the team beforehand?

Yes, he did actually speak. He asked us would we get on with the game and play it for cricket's sake and that sort of stuff. And it was easier to do that against these fellows. We all stayed at the same pub, there was only the one pub in Brisbane and we mixed together, we did things together after the day's play, yet the intensity on the field the next day was just as great as it would be in any case. But it was a great series, it evoked the spirit of cricket, and I think that's what Don was emphasising.

Did he offer any advice to you when you became an Australian selector?

About the only thing he said, 'Just make sure you pick the right team.' (laughs) No, he was very forthright. He said, 'Good luck' and just that whimsical thing, 'Make sure you pick the right team'. I'm the only New South Welsh selector, I think, that's ever picked an Australian side without a New South Welshman in it. That's a fair criterion.

Did you ever play golf with him?

No, but I played in a four behind him. I'm glad I wasn't playing in front of him (laughs) because he hates to be held up on a golf course. But he just amazes me, the scores that he made over all those years.

How did you rate him as an administrator?

Up with the very best because he had a compete understanding of the player and the administrator – it's give and take on both sides. I've been president of New South Wales for 32 years now, and I've learnt so much from him as an administrator, the balance of player and administrator.

What is your involvement with the Bradman Museum?

I've been on the Bradman Museum Foundation since its inception. It's been a long time but it's wonderful. Basically what he gave to me I've tried to put back into the museum. It's really been a devotion to duty on my part. He's an icon. Whilst he didn't want to be known as an icon, he is the greatest icon we've ever had in sport or in politics or anything. He was top of the tree for 70 years. He was always the top of the tree.

*Some things stand out in our memories. Canberra consultant **John Statton** can look back to the 1950s and still clearly remember one morning at the Kensington Cricket Club.*

I HAVE THIS VIVID recollection of Sir Donald cover driving in the nets. He was absolutely immaculate. He said it was no good hitting the shot if we couldn't hear the bottom of the bat pass through the grass. I think the bowler was an up-and-coming state fast bowler Alan Frost who was pretty slippery, and I can recall Sir Donald in the nets without pads, he had a pair of batting gloves on, just exhibiting the most – the kids would say 'awesome' – power. I've never seen defensive shots hit with such authority, with such perfection. And that's my memory of him, one of clinical perfection.

He took us for some skills coaching, as I suppose they call it these days. I was at school at Norwood, which was just down the track from Kensington, and in the summer holidays I was part of the Kensington Cricket Club schoolboys squad. From memory it was under 15s. There would have been 20-odd boys in the squad and we came from all the schools around the Kensington district.

He basically went through forward defensive shots and backward defensive shots. I can remember him very clearly telling us to keep heads still, to keep behind the ball. Basically it was footwork and still heads and just hitting this ball with the most incredible amount of power I've ever seen. I've never seen a defensive shot hit so attackingly. It was wonderful.

Did you realise how lucky you were?

I don't think we did. I guess when you're that young, you never appreciate things. From memory I just held him in awe. He was an Australian Test captain and something to be revered, you know. Boys Own Annual stuff I suppose, that's how I remember him.

Was he interested in you?

Oh yes. We were the Kensington schoolboys squad and he was Kensington and that was it. He was often around the club. But equally I think if the Port Adelaide Cricket Club had wanted him he would have responded appropriately there too, he was just quite generous with his time.

He had a great deal of genuine interest in kids. He was always in conversation with the group and he genuinely enjoyed that interaction, it was a sincere thing. By the same token, he had a certain stern facade. He wasn't one to be trifled with; he wasn't there for a laugh or to be a good bloke or anything like that, he was there to show us the skills as he knew them. He had that capacity that when he spoke everybody listened, like a good headmaster.

Lots of the 'A' grade Kensington players in those days used to help out with the schoolboy squad. But to have Sir Donald was just a little bit of something that nobody else had.

'Not close friends but regular acquaintances' is how former South Australian vice-captain **Dr John Lill** *describes his relationship with Sir Donald. Dr Lill was general secretary of the Melbourne Cricket Club from 1982 to 1999 and we spoke at his office in Melbourne.*

WHEN WE WERE LAUNCHING the Australian Hall of Fame, he was the number one inductee, and he came over for that of course and made the speech. I took him and Jessie back to the airport after that. There were all the greats of Australian sport there, and when I went to pick the Bradmans up at the hotel to take them to the airport, I ran into Reg Gasnier, who's a rugby league player, a great international player, out the front, and I said, 'Great day yesterday, wasn't it?' because it was a fantastic day. And he said, 'John, it was the greatest day of my life.' I said, 'That's fantastic, Reg.' He said, 'Yes, I met Sir Donald Bradman.' (laughs) But that was the esteem that he was regarded with in the sporting community.

*John Lill's wife **Rosie Lill** remembers Sir Donald dancing down the wicket in Dr Donald Beard's backyard one balmy Adelaide evening in the 1970s.*

DON BEARD, WHO is a great friend of ours, has a pitch wicket in his back garden. This is the wonderful days when they had the Test match in Adelaide in January on the Australia Day weekend and I was sitting next to Sir Donald at dinner. Don always invites a remarkable amount of different cricketing sort of people. Jeff Thomson, who was young then and the fastest bowler in the world, he was down from Queensland in the Test side, Les Favell who is since dead was at the dinner. He and John used to open the batting for South Australia and Les played cricket in England. Great hooker, he was. There were varying groups, about 12 or 14 of us and Sir Donald wanted to see Don Beard's wicket so out we went and the next minute Don Beard produces a bat. And he stands up the other end and Thomson and Les Favell tossed a few balls to him. Well, to see these little feet – I reckon Sir Donald must have been about 70 then – dance down the wicket, and go

'Bang'. It was extraordinary to see it, and he was thrilled to be doing it. Jessie was there watching. We were all standing out there in the twilight.

I've known Sir Donald Bradman since I was engaged to John and so I suppose I knew him for 46 years. He was always very amused at me because I'd get so uptight at the cricket, sitting there with my fingers crossed every time John went into bat and not moving until he was out.

Funnily enough, Sir Don was a great friend of John's engineering professor, Prof Spooner. This is going back to when John was doing his PhD at Adelaide Uni, we must have been engaged at that stage (I was married when I was 21 and John was 24) and Sir Donald used to see a lot of Prof Spooner and they had a food and wine society together. Prof Spooner is long since dead, but they used to go up to the Clare Valley to some of the wineries. Between them they decided that John Lill had to make up his mind whether he wanted to finish his PhD or concentrate on cricket, because at that stage I don't think he was doing either terribly well.

But then when we were eventually married we had our three sons and I had three boys under the age of three. He was always very amused because I'd arrive at the Adelaide Oval with these three little toddlers in tow. He'd almost say to them all in the dressing rooms, 'Lock up your things, here come the Lill boys.' (laughs)

I can remember sitting by him in the members' stands one day watching the cricket and being absolutely horrified. I could see my boys roaming, collecting everyone's empty bottles. I said to Sir Don, I said, 'Oh, I'm so embarrassed watching that.' He said, 'Rosie, don't even worry about it. I remember sitting up here one day watching John doing the same thing, horrified because he wasn't even letting the people finish their drinks. He was asking them could he have their bottle before they'd finished

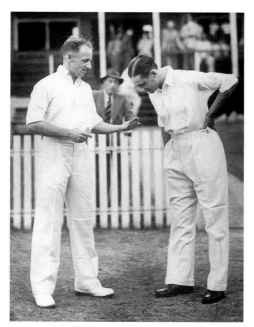

ABOVE: Don Bradman and Bill Brown resume Australia's innings, Leicester, England, 1934. (National Library of Australia)

LEFT: Don Bradman and MCC captain G. O. Allen toss the coin for the first Test in Brisbane, 1936–37. (National Library of Australia)

ABOVE: Don and Jessie Bradman seated between the English cricketer R. W. V. (Walter) Robins and his wife Kathleen at their home in Buckinghamshire in September 1938. (Bradman Foundation)

LEFT: The failed sharebroking business H. W. Hodgetts & Co. was closed in 1945 and reopened within days as Don Bradman & Co.

The Bedser twins, Eric and Alec, in their playing days.

OPPOSITE PAGE: Batting partners Don Bradman and Arthur Morris take to the field.

TOP: The 1948 Australian Test team arrives at Tilbury Docks on the *Strathaird*.

BOTTOM: Selectors (from left) Sir Donald Bradman, Dudley Seddon and Jack Ryder, 1958–59. (John Woodcock)

TOP: Sir Donald Bradman with the Australian captain Richie Benaud, 1958–59. (John Woodcock)

BOTTOM: Former schoolmaster and administrator Harry Altham, Sir Donald Bradman and G. O. Allen at the ICC meeting in 1960, when Sir Donald was flown to England in an effort to resolve the 'throwing crisis'.

TOP: Australian all-rounder Alan Davidson with Sir Donald Bradman and Dudley Seddon, 1962–63. (John Woodcock)

BOTTOM: Christmas Day, Adelaide, 1962. At the Kooyonga Golf Club, from left: journalist Crawford White, Ken Barrington, Billy Griffith (manager) John Woodcock, Tom Graveney, Sir Donald Bradman, Alec Bedser, Ted Dexter and Colin Cowdrey. (John Woodcock)

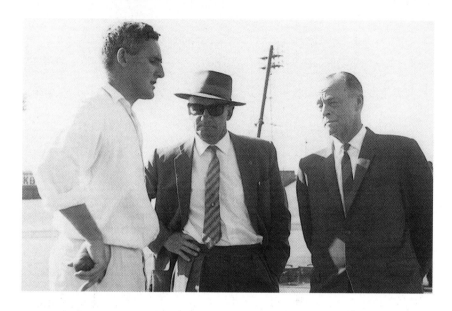

Sir Donald Bradman at the Kooyonga golf course. (John Woodcock)

their drink or before they'd even started it. And then he'd stand by until they did.'

He had a very probing mind. In fact, I'd think 'Ooh, he's going to ask me a heap of questions again that I won't be able to answer.' He'd ask me, say, 'Do you think they'll ever stop the smoking at the MCG, Rosie?' I mean, well, I'm not on the committee, I'm just John's wife. And I'd say, (laughs) 'Look, I don't know,' and he'd say 'Well, what do you think that would do to the sponsorship if they did stop smoking at the MCG?' And he'd say to me, 'What do you think they should do to get more people at the Shield games, Rosie?' And I'd think why doesn't he ask John these questions? I'm not the cricketer. He would ask about the ground, or about health, medicine, about eating habits, things like that. He had a thin reedy sort of voice and a very dry sense of humour. He wouldn't say I've got a good joke to tell you, but he was very quick on the uptake and he'd say something and cause us all to laugh.

Jessie was lovely. I'd have loved to have been like Jessie, I really would. She was my epitome of the perfect lady. She was super to look at – in fact, her granddaughter Greta is the image of her, and could have got her musical side from Don because he was a terrific pianist, he could sit there and just tinkle away. But Jessie was always so elegant, refined, knew exactly the right things to say. We didn't see them in recent years but before that we would catch up with them in Adelaide if we went across to the Tests or we were sitting next to them in a box at the cricket, and all that time she was sick, she still looked beautiful.

Australian Test batsman and wicketkeeper **Len Maddocks** *is one of the few players to have become a director of the Australian Cricket Board. Maddocks, who played seven Tests, was also an Australian selector (1981–82). We spoke in Melbourne.*

WHEN I WAS CAPTAINING the Victorian Shield side, Bradman used to come down to lunch at the Adelaide Oval and he sat the two captains on either side of him. At one stage I had just been made head office accountant for my company and Bradman of course was a stockbroker. My first impression of him was how meticulous he must have been as a stockbroker because here was me, the fairly newly appointed head office accountant of APM, a major company, sitting next to Bradman and he knew more about it than I did. And that was one company out of some hundreds. If my impression of Bradman was right, he would have known as much about every other company on the stock exchange.

Everything he did that I saw him involved in, he was a perfectionist. He wouldn't leave any stone unturned to master whatever the subject was. He was the world oracle on anything to do with cricket. His memory and his ability to analyse any situation just floored me.

In 1956 we went to England on an Ashes tour. We went by ship in those days so we had about four or five weeks on board and Bradman went to England in '56 as a journalist. He and Jess, his wife, and his little daughter Shirley were on the ship and we got to know them pretty well, day by day.

I was in my youth a pretty good billiard player and I was a pretty good table tennis player. I played Bradman at billiards and table tennis and it was like a champion versus a novice. It didn't matter what he did where there was a ball involved, it seemed to me he was brilliant at it straight away. He beat me at billiards so comprehensively I didn't like to talk to people about it. I was much better than average and he just wiped me off the table. I played a lot of table tennis on the ship with his little daughter. Shirley had cerebral palsy and she's been disadvantaged all of her life. When I was playing table tennis with her, she was maybe 13 or 14. She had this physical and a little bit of a mental handicap, but she was a lovely kid, you couldn't help loving her. Bradman came in one day while we were playing and decided he'd have a hit too. So he and I started playing and he just wiped me off the table again. It didn't matter what he did, he was good at it.

My relationship with Bradman was not really personal but comfortable. I never felt as if there was something I couldn't talk to him about. I had heard that when he was a player and captain there was some dissension in the team that I suspect was to do with religion. When I was a boy you were either Catholic or you weren't and I suspect that was carried over in that early stage, but that's just hearsay.

Bradman was never a wild drinker, or anything like that. He wasn't a wowser. To go home with him, he'd have a sherry and a glass of wine, but he was never one to stand up at a bar and drink 20 pots. And that was another thing I think that some of his team-mates couldn't handle. That he just didn't want to drink with them. He didn't want to drink full stop. Some of his team-mates were mad wild Irishmen, O'Reilly and Fingleton for a kick-off. They were on the ship going over to England in 1956 too. They used to have a party every night in their cabin. They had a cabin with portholes that lifted up and you hooked them up so you got the fresh air coming in. I was the smallest bloke in the team and at party time I'd be picked up by Bill O'Reilly, he'd stick me up on his shoulder and my job was to put the empty bottles up on the porthole, let go the clip on the top and shoot them out into the sea. (laughs) I was O'Reilly's gunner. This was when he was a journalist. I don't know what he was like as a player.

I was captaining Victoria in South Australia at the height of the throwing kerfuffle and in our team was Ian Meckiff who later was no-balled out of cricket for throwing. Bradman invited me to come to his place for dinner on the Saturday night and to bring Ian Meckiff with me and we sat down for some hours and Bradman ran film he had put together of all the fast bowlers, going back to the Bodyline series, to work out what caused a doubt about bowlers' actions. He had a theory about what caused the throwing controversy and the reason he wanted Ian Meckiff there with us that night was to discuss this with Ian and how it applied or didn't apply not only to Meckiff, but to all of the pace bowlers that Bradman had on this film. And surprisingly to me, just about every pace bowler that he had on the film threw at some stage. The impression that I got from watching the film was that the worst thrower of all time would have been Larwood in the Bodyline series. It was blatant.

How did you rate Sir Donald as an administrator?
Don was chairman when I first became a director of the Australian Cricket Board in 1972 and again he was meticulous. Everything was done perfectly. We had the six-monthly or annual board meetings and we'd be together for two or three days, the 10 of us. When he finished his term as chairman, Bob Parish took over. Bob was always a great administrator too, and he and Bradman developed a real affinity in that area, both as cricket administrators and as people.

Was Bradman demanding of those around him?
I don't know that demand is the right word but as I said, he was a perfectionist and I think that he acknowledged that everybody else wasn't perfect but he would like them to have been. (laughs) I've never heard him really shout at anybody but from time to time you could see that he wasn't happy with the standard of whatever it was that was being done. I suppose we're all like that at times.

You were managing Australia in England in 1977 when the World Series cricket furore erupted, weren't you?
At that time Bob Parish was chairman and Alan Barnes was secretary and any contact that I had from England was with one of those two.

What do you think of the suggestion that Sir Donald controlled Australian cricket?

I think that's probably true, with the qualification that he was always right. It's as simple as that. (laughs). There'd be some situation would crop up and he'd say whatever he'd say and I'd think, that's right.

In Sir Donald's last first-class match in Adelaide in 1949, he was dropped by the up-and-coming Victorian opener **Colin McDonald,** *who went on to play 44 Tests for Australia. We spoke at his home in Melbourne.*

MOST PEOPLE THINK his last first-class match was a testimonial match that they arranged for him after the 1948 tour. It wasn't. The following season he came back and he played one Sheffield Shield match. It was the very last match of the season and it was designated a testimonial match for a fellow called Arthur Richardson. Nothing to do with Victor Richardson. Arthur Richardson was the coach of South Australia and they designated a Sheffield match and Bradman agreed to play. He made a comeback. No practice, nothing, and he played in it. Neither Victoria nor South Australia could win the Sheffield Shield, we hadn't done well enough, but the match had to be played.

The only thing that was not fair dinkum in that match was the toss, the reason being that the whole point of the match was to get some money for this fellow Richardson so it was pretty important that Bradman bat on Saturday to get the crowd in. It was generally agreed that Victoria better bat on Friday so South Australia would probably bat on Saturday.

So Victoria batted on Friday and we proceeded to get out too quickly. We were all out by tea which was mid-afternoon on the first day and South Australia had to bat after tea. Then we started getting them out too quickly. There was four out and Bradman still hadn't batted because they were trying to keep him for Saturday. But eventually at about 20 to six – and 6 o'clock was stumps – he had to bat. We had a midfield conference, the Victorians, what the hell do we do now? Do we try to get him out or don't we? We weren't corrupt. We decided to try to get him out. (laughs) Pretty silly really. Bradman used to get out occasionally very close in, just behind square leg. Bedser, the English fast bowler, used to get him out occasionally there. About a metre and a half. And I was about there. And sure enough Bradman put one straight down my throat. And I dropped it. Not deliberately. I tried to catch it but I dropped it.

Thank goodness I did because he scratched around until 6 o'clock and he wasn't out. So he was batting the next day and about 10 000 people turned up, Arthur Richardson got a reasonable gate, Bradman made about 30 and that was the end of Bradman. He batted dreadfully. Don't misunderstand me. I know how great he was. But he'd had no practice, he was getting on in years. He sprained his ankle fielding and he didn't bat in the second innings. There wouldn't be very many people that realise that was his last match. Most think he retired – and he did really – a number of months before that.

This will give you some idea how good he was. A good friend of mine who's now dead was Ben Barnett, a Victorian captain and Australian wicketkeeper who went to England with the Australian team in 1938. Ben was keeping wickets in a Sheffield Shield match and Bradman had just come in to bat. Victoria had a bowler bowling in his first match, he bowled off-breaks. He was bowling to Don Bradman, the first time Bradman had ever seen him. Eight ball overs and he hit every ball in this over straight back to the bowler. Every ball. No runs at all. Bradman turned around to Barnett the wicketkeeper at the end of the over and said, 'Ben, he's slow and he's straight.' The next time he bowls to Bradman, Bradman hit him for eight fours. Took one look . . . (He mimes a stroke.)

Bradman wasn't a particularly good role model to follow as a batsman though he was a role model in most things. But he was so good that he could do things that were unorthodox and get away with it. Bradman always believed that his technique was perfect or very sound. Well, it was for him, but not for people who copied him. Bradman was perfect for his own ability which was so much greater than anyone else's that he could do things which were most productive but in the hands of lesser players would be very dangerous. Perhaps Bradman would say, 'Well, you ought to be copying my technique,' (laughs) but I don't think that's right.

He was once asked – because he averaged about 100 – 'How would you go against the current bowlers?' He said, 'Oh, I'd average about 60.' 'Only 60?' 'Yeah, but don't forget, I *am* 80 years old.'

What was your experience of Sir Donald as a selector?

I was captain of the Melbourne University Cricket Team when we went and played an intervarsity match in Adelaide against Adelaide University. John Lill who is the immediate past secretary manager of the Melbourne Cricket Club was captain of Adelaide University. I was just on the fringe of Test cricket. I was in the side, I think, but no certainty, and Melbourne University were batting on the Adelaide University Oval which is a lovely oval not far from the Adelaide Oval across through the parks there. I used to open so I was batting and Bradman walked into the ground. He was a Test selector at this stage. There wouldn't have been more than 30 or 40 people there so I saw him come in. And I made a hundred before lunch. After lunch Bradman was still there. In an intervarsity match, once you've made a hundred or so, that's enough. (laughs) But I thought I'm not getting out while he's here, so I made another hundred. At teatime I was 200 not out. We came out after tea and he's still there, so I made another hundred. I got 300. Adelaide University can thank Bradman for that.

My brother played 39 games for Victoria as wicketkeeper and he really retired early because he had to get on with his profession. He was a doctor. But he was not far off the Test side as a wicket-keeper in the early 50s. He got picked as wicketkeeper for an Australian XI team. His name was Ian – Ian McDonald – and there was another Ian McDonald at the time who was a journalist. (Until recently he was employed by the Australian Cricket Board as their media manager.) He was an outgoing character, a nice bloke, who in his journalistic days had written some fairly tough stuff about Bradman. Bradman had obviously read it. This would have been about 1960. I was captain of Victoria and Bradman was there as a selector. In those days the selectors didn't just walk into dressing rooms and he said to me, 'Colin, I haven't met a lot of your guys, could I meet them?' I said, 'Yes, come in.' So I intro-duced him to all of the fellows and Ian McDonald, the journalist – my brother had retired at this stage – happened to be in the room. He and I are good friends. I said, 'Don, have you met Ian McDon-ald?' 'Your brother?' 'No, no, Ian McDonald the journalist.' So I introduced Ian McDonald the journalist to Don Bradman. When it was all over he said, 'Colin, that was not your brother?' 'No, that was Ian McDonald the journalist. My brother is a doctor. He's retired, he was a wicketkeeper.' 'Yeah,' he said, 'I know he was a wicketkeeper. But,' he said 'that's not your brother?' I always ask the question did my brother suffer in selection because Bradman thought it was Ian McDonald the cricketer that was writing this stuff about him. (laughs) He probably wouldn't have got any fur-ther but you can always ask the question.

But as a selector, Bradman was perfectly approachable, not that many did. Everyone held him a bit in awe. But he was fine, he spoke to us all, he was helpful, and we liked to be in his company because whilst there's no such thing as a cricketing god, he was held a bit in that sort of esteem. The fellows who went away with him in '48 worshipped him. And the players since the war have had nothing but good to say about him. I'm included in that group.

The fellows who played before the war certainly had a different view. Bradman was very human and he's far from as perfect as he's been made out since his death. He knew that very well himself. He was a man of great integrity, but he didn't suffer fools. And in the earlier days of course, religion used to come into things much more than it does today. He had his enemies. And he was such a great player I think there were jealousies because Bradman used to get all the publicity. And sportsmen love publicity, whatever they may tell you, they love it. And there were other great players around in Bradman's day.

Did Sir Donald run Australian cricket?
No, he kept it on the rails, that's different to running it. He was a very good administrator, given an era that is totally different today. I think he'd be brilliant today. As a man of 50, not a man of 90. You'd never know what Bradman would know but once you questioned him you found out he knew almost everything about everything. (laughs)

What role did Sir Donald play during the throwing controversy in the later 50s and early 60s?
He was very effective in the 1961 tour of England in that there was a local rule as exists in golf for that tour. As I remember it, the umpires weren't to call the bowler, but if they had a doubt they were to immediately report him, not via the media, to the manager of the Australian cricket team and to the president of the Marylebone Cricket Club which in those days ran cricket in England. They would then confer. But there was no one who was suspect on that tour so it didn't happen. But Bradman, a very intelligent man,

got involved in that and it was very sensible and very intelligent, trying to cut out the furore that goes on, a lot of it uninformed.

What was it like playing in the Tied Test against the West Indies in Brisbane in 1960–61?

Bradman was involved with us in that one. Cricket had gone through a pretty dull period for a few years before that. A lot of it was the Englishmen's fault. They'd played some terribly boring cricket around the world. Some of it against us. In 1958 the Englishmen were out here and we batted all day one day and only made 203 runs. But they only bowled 50 overs to us. They should have bowled 70 or 80 overs and we'd have got 300, which is good going. But we got roundly abused for only getting 200 runs, at four runs an over which is above Test match average. But the perception out there was that cricket was becoming dreadfully boring.

Prior to this Test match against the West Indies, Bradman did call us together and he gave no instructions, he just said people playing more attractive cricket would be favourably looked upon. It was not even as hard as that, but the message was clear. Cricket's too good a game to be ruined, let's get on with it. That was the message that got through very well. Benaud, who was the captain, has reported on it. But here was Bradman – no threats, nothing nasty, very matter of fact and quite accurate. And yes, that was probably the greatest game ever played.

Sir Donald Bradman became a member of the Adelaide Rotary Club in April 1947. In those days the club had one person from each profession and Sir Donald was the club's stockbroker. Following his resignation in 1984, he was made an honorary member, which he remained until his death. Retired solicitor **Jim Mellor** *joined the club more than 40 years ago and was a member of the same district fellowship as Sir Donald.*

THE ROTARY CLUB of Adelaide was the city club and to become a member was something that had a bit of kudos. You were invited to join. He was in as the sharebroker. When I joined, it was as the solicitor. There was only one and that was quite an honour.

One aspect of Rotary was the fellowship of the club. Because the members were scattered throughout the metropolitan area, we had district fellowship groups of about 15 or 20 Rotarians. That gave us an opportunity to get to know the Rotarians and their wives in that group. He was a member of the Kensington group of which my father before me and I were members. We met on about a six-weekly basis and had a social evening at the homes of members.

Don played the piano occasionally when you attended at his home. Lady Jessie was there. She of course was a wonderful, charming person, an absolute gem. She was always Lady Jessie but it was Don in the group, because in Rotary we go by Christian names. He was always a very friendly person within that group. I think other people found him rather reserved but within that group he was just one of the Rotarians.

We were at his home on one occasion when he'd come back from England at the time of the throwing controversy for the fast bowlers. He had been to the BBC in England and come back with a whole collection of film of these bowlers. He got a small projector from the Education Department – one that you wound with your hand so that you could get frame-by-frame – and he was explaining what he believed to be the difference between a fast bowler and a thrower so that it could be properly defined.

The man I knew within the Rotary group was very friendly and generous with his time. I met Don one morning on the bus going into town. I asked him what was he doing, because he had retired at that time. He said he was going in to work in a sharebrokers where John was employed. John had become an athlete, a hurdler, and he was taking leave from the office where he was working as a clerk to go to Perth to compete. So Don went in to take his place and do the work while John was away so that they wouldn't be inconvenienced.

Later John did law and Don talked to me about his future. John wanted to be an academic but talking to Don I did persuade him that he should do his articles of association and become admitted so he would have the qualification to practise as a solicitor if he ever wanted to. He did that. John ultimately went off to England on an academic run and when he came back took a house up in the hills. The house was up above the water supply so that there wasn't reticulated water in that area. His parents used to go up and cart buckets of water to help the trees that he had planted become established. They would spend time doing that sort of thing.

Did Sir Donald have a favourite charity?
We've got a couple of tapes from addresses that he gave at the club and the proceeds of that go to the Crippled Children's Association. As they did originally. Rotary founded the Crippled Children's Association in South Australia pre-war and he was particularly interested in that.

Is Rotary a business aid?
It was not established as such, but it is a network. You don't join it for that but you get to know a lot of people and some of them come and do business with you because they know you. But it's designed as a charitable community international organisation.

Sir Donald and Jessie Bradman were close friends of the editor-in-chief of the News, *Rohan Rivett and his wife Nan. I spoke to* **Nan Rivett** *and her daughter* **Rhyll** *at their home in Melbourne and together they conjured up the world of parties and happy days at the Rivett household in Adelaide in the 1950s. The family returned to Melbourne in 1960.*

NAN RIVETT: Rohan was editor-in-chief of the *News* and he got Don to write for him on the paper. Don used to write about the cricket and it was in the *News* of course first and foremost and then he would sell it all over the world from there. That's when we first met him, and then Jessie. The children used to swim in their swimming pool. They were only little tackers then. Rhyll was a great swimmer in the swimming pool, weren't you?

RHYLL RIVETT: They have a very nice swimming pool. In those days there weren't many private ones around. Mum and Dad were inside but we used to stay outside. It was very good weather, and drinks and snacks would be brought out.

NAN RIVETT : It put me off having a swimming pool. Poor Jessie usually got left with all of the cleaning of the pool. (laughs)

RHYLL RIVETT: Yes, we used to go and enjoy it and leave it.

Did a friendship develop just from those early articles?

NAN RIVETT: We went out to dinners and we used to go to a lot of social functions, the same sort of things, then they'd be home to dinner and we'd be there to dinner and we'd see them for different occasions.

RHYLL RIVETT: Dad was mad on cricket so that was a great talking point. They were always getting into the cricket talk, weren't they?

NAN RIVETT: Rohan was not a player but he had a great knowledge of all the statistics and all this sort of thing and they'd both be vying, oh, how many runs he made at this match.

So he actually dared to challenge Sir Donald, did he?

RHYLL RIVETT: Oh, absolutely.

NAN RIVETT: He wouldn't worry about that.

RHYLL RIVETT: He had a very good memory.

NAN RIVETT: A very good memory. Don had too, but they appreciated that the other one had a big knowledge of the statistical side of it.

But Don wasn't always right?

NAN RIVETT: Oh, pretty often. He didn't make too many mistakes, did he?

RHYLL RIVETT: No, very good on facts.

NAN RIVETT: And figures. He was a sharebroker in Adelaide then and a very good sharebroker.

Did the relationship extend beyond the cricket?

NAN RIVETT: Oh, yes, they came out home a lot. They had to sit through some of our films when we'd been away on holiday. Don and I used to be nearly convulsed. My husband was very bright and very good but as for working a machine and the film staying in the right place, it was quite impossible, wasn't it?

RHYLL RIVETT: You know those old projectors that used to heat up violently? I don't think they were meant to but ours used to get absolutely molten. A grey thing. It used to have the big spools on it.

NAN RIVETT: And it used to twirl around.

RHYLL RIVETT: The film always got off the spools and was winding around chairs and things and Dad was merrily going on with the picture show and all the film. It was absolutely hilarious. And the films were not very good.

NAN RIVETT: No, they weren't very good.

RHYLL RIVETT: But he liked showing us the films and we always used to sit there . . .

NAN RIVETT: We'd have a picture night, oh, dear oh dear.

And was Sir Donald duly respectful?

NAN RIVETT: Oh no, we'd both be sort of almost behind the sofa. (laughs) I think Jessie was better at sitting up and saying the right thing. She was a very nice person, Jessie. Very sweet. She was very fond of Rhyll. She came over for the twins' 21st and stayed here and went to the party which was rather hilarious, with old and young and all sorts.

Don was away a lot of course with cricket. Jessie'd never be lost for something to do though. She was quite talented in her own right and she played a good game of golf, bowls, all those sorts of things. She could play some piano but Don played very well. He could sit down – he could read music very quickly and very well. He was very talented, he had many facets.

Did he play the piano for others?
Nan Rivett: Rohan was very active with the International Press Institute. He was later director of it but at this time he was just a member. And we had God knows how many Pakistanis and Indians out and we had them all to dinner. And they were in Adelaide and I don't think they could give a damn about the press and what was happening and the rest of it, all they wanted to do was meet Sir Donald Bradman. So after we had dinner and sat down in a room the piano was in, Rohan rang up Don and said, 'Oh, God, I'm sorry to do this to you but would you come round and meet these people? It's the only thing they want in Adelaide.' He very kindly came round. And he played all sorts of tunes to them, which was very kind. So he was a good friend. They were hysterical. It was beautiful.

Did he ever play just for you?
Nan Rivett: He has, but he wasn't that keen to show off or anything like that.

Did you share taste in music?
Nan Rivett: He was mad about *The Sound of Music*. I think my taste would probably have been a bit more upmarket.
Rhyll Rivett: He used to like the classics too, but he liked that sort of popular stuff as well.

Was it a close friendship?

NAN RIVETT: Oh, yes, we saw a lot of them. They came up to Canberra with us. Rohan was doing something up there and he introduced Don all round to different people. I can remember that trip. They drove with us, God help them, it must have driven Don mad because Rohan's driving wasn't the best. We stayed up in Canberra a few days and then came down again.

When we'd be living over here and after Rohan died, we'd still go back every year. On the holiday period and Christmas holidays we'd go back and stay in Adelaide for a while, because we had so many old friends over there and we'd always have dinner with them. Often at a restaurant.

The friendship is seen in some quarters as a fairly unlikely one.
The public perception of Don is of a fairly dour conservative . . .

NAN RIVETT: Yes, he was all that.

RHYLL RIVETT: And my Dad was the opposite, so he probably found it a refreshing change.

NAN RIVETT: Oh yes. It certainly loosened him up.

RHYLL RIVETT: He roared with laughter at times.

NAN RIVETT: Oh yes, we were always having good fun.

RHYLL RIVETT: There was a lot of humour in the meetings, it was very amusing – they were two very, very different people.

Did that lead to disputes?

NAN RIVETT: They might have had an argument about something but nothing worth really thinking about twice, was it?

RHYLL RIVETT: Dad used to get a bit angry if he didn't win a cricket bet, but not angry aggressive or anything, just sort of funny angry. A bit of a game going on. He used to just like stirring things up a bit.

Sir Donald too?

RHYLL RIVETT: Oh yes, he'd say things, but not really angry, just taking an attitude. You know, Don't you remember this? You haven't got the facts straight! Don't you remember the time . . .

NAN RIVETT: (laughs) Stirring the pot a bit.

Was he a man with a sense of humour?

RHYLL RIVETT: Very witty.

NAN RIVETT: He said some funny things, quite unforgettable things.

RHYLL RIVETT: Yes, very apt things.

NAN RIVETT: I don't think we'll repeat some of them about people.

Did he like to get the last word?

NAN: He wasn't dominating. About cricket he liked to think, I suppose, he knew better. But we'd have all sorts of people there at dinner parties; they wouldn't be necessarily cricket enthusiasts. So he'd just take his place with the rest of them and whatever they were talking about.

So did the Bradmans come to dinner parties with your friends?

NAN RIVETT: At our house? Oh, yes, yes. I always remember one dinner party, I could have killed him. I'd done the table I'd thought magnificently, with autumn leaves, because we used to make quite a thing of dinner parties in those days, and a great deal of trouble went into them. And he comes into the dining room and says, 'Oh Nan, for God's sake, I've just been sweeping all these bloody things up in the drive.' At which stage he was just about hit over the head.

RHYLL RIVETT: But I think he would have found our place a comfortable, civil –

NAN RIVETT: Well, it would be relaxing

RHYLL RIVETT: – sort of like going overseas without going overseas.

He never really liked going overseas much, unless the food was English, because he liked very conservative English-type meals.

NAN RIVETT: He liked lamb chops.

RHYLL RIVETT: Our place was always filled with a lot of multi-coloured multi-aged people from all over the world.

NAN RIVETT: They were interesting people from different areas of life. There'd be quite a few university people.

He left school at 14 so he had missed out on a formal education . . .

NAN RIVETT: No, his parents couldn't afford it. He said he'd like to have been a doctor. I would like to have been too but we had a very bad depression and they had a pretty bad depression and you couldn't go to the university unless your parents could pay for it, so that cut that out. And he was very good at his cricket. He must have read quite a terrific amount, I'd think.

He was a successful businessman, wasn't he?

NAN RIVETT: He was the director of quite a few companies and you would have been very glad to have him, I'm sure. Because he was so thorough, he wouldn't have been on a board without knowing what was going on.

A while before he had his stroke, he was terribly pleased one night, he was telling us that, oh yes, they could still use him at Argo, which he was occasionally consulted about after he left. He said he picked up one firm that he thought wasn't good for them to have on their listings. He said, 'The old man still knows something.'

RHYLL RIVETT: He had such a good mind, and his mind didn't deteriorate.

NAN RIVETT: Don was terribly good at doing things in the house too. He could paint awfully well or do anything that needed doing. Terribly handy, and do it beautifully.

So he and Rohan were very different men?

RHYLL RIVETT: Both very able but totally different personalities and focus. Dad was very outgoing . . .

NAN RIVETT: Had a very good knowledge of world affairs and what was going on in the world.

RHYLL RIVETT: I think Don loved hearing about all that. Don would be around the table and Dad would have other people who were from overseas who were interested in world events and Dad would talk his head off and serve the wine and all that.

NAN RIVETT: God yes, when the cricketers were over we used to have Arlott who would disappear at a stage and be asleep in the chair, and all this sort of thing. Wonderful people there.

RHYLL RIVETT: They were great parties. People would remember the parties they had.

NAN RIVETT: Wonderful parties.

RHYLL RIVETT: Mum cooked very well and Dad used to serve the wine.

NAN RIVETT: And there used to be a great deal of wine flowing in those days.

RHYLL RIVETT: And good talk, but the talk would peter out as the night went on. (laughs)

NAN RIVETT: It would get a bit a sillier.

Did Sir Donald know his wines?

NAN RIVETT: He did in the end but he didn't drink much at all at first, in his earlier days. Being in Adelaide, you had so much wine around you there, he probably decided it was a good thing to learn about it and get into it.

RHYLL RIVETT: Dad was much more random, he'd have good wines and he'd have not-so-good wines (laughs), whereas Don would have a lot of goodies.

NAN RIVETT: He'd know what you should have.

RHYLL RIVETT: I think he'd have read up intensely on anything and found out what he wanted to know. But I think Don liked listening to what Dad had to say about the world events and current affairs and other things, he loved all that.

NAN RIVETT: He was curious about things.

Was he also reserved?

NAN RIVETT: Basically I think so, yes. I don't think you'd say shy, I think reserved.

RHYLL RIVETT: Sort of the reserved country type. I don't know whether they exist any more, but that old-fashioned country type of person that's not wanting to talk too much but can enjoy different conversations. And a personal reserve too. He was a very private person.

Your dinner parties sound wonderful.

RHYLL RIVETT: Oh they were hilarious dinner parties. Very interesting.

NAN RIVETT: A good rounded picture of lots of things but of course in those days people drank a lot and there was none of this breathalysing or . . .

RHYLL RIVETT: They'd just steam off with their lead foot, you know, straight into the ether. There wasn't much to hit often, too. (laughs) You could go more or less in a straight line.

NAN RIVETT: Well, the traffic wasn't very great in that time.

RHYLL RIVETT: Oh dear, people used to drink an awful lot. Some people would get on to a little bit of soda or something. There was black coffee and that was it.

NAN RIVETT: Not like it is these days.

RHYLL RIVETT: As far as we know we didn't cause any deaths.

NAN RIVETT: I don't think so.

Who else would be invited?
NAN RIVETT: Oh, a mixture. They could be anything.
RHYLL RIVETT: Academics, journalists, writers, all sorts of artistic people, foreign correspondents.

And he fitted in there?
NAN RIVETT: Oh yes, yes.
RHYLL RIVETT: I think Mum and Dad had such an eclectic group of friends, they never felt much about it. They had such a variety of people. I think that was the great thing too. People were more hospitable in those days because dinner parties were in and cocktail parties and all that.
NAN RIVETT: We went to a lot of dinner parties, apart from giving them. It wasn't dull.

*Sir Donald Bradman turned to former Test captain **Bob Simpson** in 1977 when Australia needed an experienced captain in the face of the World Series breakaway. When we spoke at his home in Sydney, Simpson recalled the moment in 1954 when Keith Miller brought Sir Donald into the New South Wales dressing room.*

I WAS ABOUT 18. Obviously it was a bit overwhelming because I was pretty shy and just to see this great man. I was amazed how tiny he was. He had the stature of a different player yet he was so brilliant. Everyone was in awe of him. He was always very kind to me, I suppose coming in so young. When I was first playing there was still a lot of the '48 team around, so you had people like Lindwall and Morris still playing.

You were only 20 when you were first picked to play for Australia in 1957–58. Was it difficult representing Australia when you were so young?

I was very lucky because Ian Craig got in about 12 months before me, and he was just six months older than I was, so that made it easier. But they never made me feel anything else but a member of the team. I remember Arthur Morris when I first met him, turned me around and looked me up and down and said, 'Where are they?' and I said, 'What are you talking about Mr Morris?' (I called him Mister for two years at least) and he said, 'Oh your bloody nappies, you're so young.' And what was intriguing about that time – and I didn't think about it until later on – is that I was very seldom left alone in the dressing room. If I was watching cricket one of the experienced players invariably would sit next to me. So while we didn't have coaches, we probably had the best teachers in the world. That's where you sort of learnt all the folklore and the fundamentals of the game, and it was all done in that very casual but fairly structured way. I'm not sure they ever really thought about it either, but they just knew that was the right way to go.

What sort of contact did you have with Sir Donald?

Sir Donald was an Australian selector then, but often he'd come in before lunch or tea because he always wanted to make himself available if the captain wanted to speak to him, and when I was 12th man for Australia we'd just sit down and chat about anything. If you chose to ask him he always gave you a wonderful breakdown of the game, a balanced view of what was happening, but he would never be: boom, boom 'This is what we've got to do' or 'We've got to do that'.

He made himself available at every session. He was always on duty as chairman of selectors. When you came back off the field he would be there in the dressing room. He wouldn't come up to you.

If you felt you would like some advice he would be more than happy, yet he realised that if you didn't then that was all right too. He was very humble in that regard. He wasn't there to push his views. The captain is the captain.

I think the thing I appreciated even at a young age is how fair he was in the sense that he never knocked any era. You always felt that the era you got was the one we were privileged to watch so that was the best era and he was very, very objective. If you asked him a particular question about players or the past he always answered it with total honesty. Nothing on the personal side but the cricketing side, you know. It was always a really accurate assessment as far as he was concerned. That's what I've always tried to do when the players ask me, 'What about so-and-so?' I think he taught me not to live in the past. So some bloke might have had a big reputation and Sir Donald might say, 'Oh look, he's good at his business, but . . .' and give you his honest view about the man. Or someone might be underrated, or just pretty unlucky.

He knew I was reasonably good at golf and from when I was about 20, we played a bit of golf together, so we had another common interest. It's quite funny actually, we met one time in Adelaide more recently. I wanted to get some autographs from Bradman so I took my grandson Ash with me who was about six. And when we were going back in the car he said, 'Oh Poppa, was he the best golfer in the world?' because all we talked about was golf. So I suppose we had that double thing, with both sports, and golf in particular transcends all ages.

I remember writing to him once about the lbw law, which he was totally opposed to, and he just wrote back this five-page letter. And the same with the no-ball rule. Very much strongly felt. Still would be today, he'd be arguing with me about it. I was arguing that it must have been easier to get runs in the old days 'because the ball couldn't be pitched outside the off-stump' – in a very polite way. And he said, 'Yes that's good. It's nice to hear you talk about those sorts of things' and then he explained his side of it. That was the way he was. If you wrote a letter asking about something you'd get a four- or five-page typed reply. He was wonderful in that regard.

Did Sir Donald discuss the captaincy with you when you took over?

He knew that everyone has their individual style. When I got the captain's job I ended up giving up to 13 speeches in 10 days, sometimes two and three a day. The worst part about that is that you cannot use the same speech twice because a lot of the times it's the same people around.

Were you a natural public speaker?

No, I was a very shy person really. Every year at Rotary luncheons I'd get some practice in, and find out what it was like to be in the firing line. You had to work at it. Sir Donald had to work at it too. I was told an interesting story, I think it came originally from old Sidney Webb, that Bradman apparently used to get a new word every day. Whether it's true or not I'm not quite sure. And he'd use that word as much as he could that week to build up his vocabulary.

When did you first retire from Test cricket?

I retired in 1968 when I was 31 when I was at my absolute peak as a batsman. Runs were easy to get in Test cricket then, but it was time to get out and make some money and get into business. You used to have a drop-out time, but I loved the cricket and I wanted to put something back into it so I continued for another 10 years playing for Western Suburbs in club cricket, and I got more runs nearly every year than anyone else. By the mid-70s I was running my own sporting promotion and marketing company.

So what brought you back to the Test team in 1977?

I was still playing club cricket at that stage and out of the blue I got this call to see if I would be interested in coming back and captaining Australia. And my initial reaction, I wasn't that thrilled about the whole thing. But then I had lunch with Bradman and he persuaded me to do it. He explained the need for it more than anything. The fact that he still felt that I could do it because I was getting all the runs and I was 41 and I was still very fit, and above that he said, 'There's this great need. You're the person with the experience. You've got the experience as a cricketer and a captain. You've also got experience with the media.' And in the end it became a real media situation; there was probably as much media around then as there has ever been. I did think what the hell did I want to be involved for. Then it became a fascinating time for me.

Was Sir Donald very involved beyond that lunch?

No, not a lot, he just left it to me to get on with what was going on. I don't think he was selector then, but he was always there if I wanted him.

It must have been an emotional time.

I never felt that great passion about it. I thought that the players had every right to decide their own futures, so I never felt any real animosity towards them. I didn't think what they were doing was right, but they were doing what they wanted to do, I was doing what I wanted to do and let's get on and do it. The sadness of it all is that a lot of friends were never as friendly again. I think it affected the Packer players more than it did the traditional players, because my attitude always was they made their bed, they had to lie in it. They made the decision. I think they made it on the basis they could get both Packer's money and the Board's money, quite frankly. At least they believed there would be a compromise. And some of them seemed to have an axe to grind about the whole thing when in fact, you know, it was a revolution, but in the end it didn't go far enough. If you really look at it, the Board got what they wanted, control of the game, Packer got what he wanted, some of the senior players got what they wanted. But there were a lot of other blokes down the line on both sides who suddenly were saying, 'Hey, I thought we were going to get looked after'.

And they weren't?
Well, Packer certainly honoured all his contracts, but they thought it was a lifetime thing.

Was there a point in your relationship with Sir Donald where you felt you became friends?
Yes, I felt very comfortable in his company and we had no trouble communicating whatsoever. We used to get invitations to dinner and I played golf with him. My wife was particularly friendly with Jessie and that probably helped the whole thing, and with their daughter. So we were just as friendly with the family.

When you became coach for Australia, did Sir Donald express any ambivalence about there being a coach?
Not as such, I don't think. He was a great believer in you didn't need too much coaching. Well, I don't necessarily disagree with that. He did suggest that I could change the way people held the bat, and every bat, and I said, 'Well I'm working on it, I'm working on it.' So what he was suggesting were things that I had strong feelings for also. I think he was a bit worried we were getting away from the basic fundamentals a bit too much and fashion fads and theories were coming in, and this may not have been in the better interests of the style or the quality of the game. I think he would

have seen me as someone who probably would restore a few old-fashioned values.

I had him talk to the players. That was a wonderful night. I organised for him to come to the team dinner in Adelaide and the players wanted to meet him and I asked if he'd say a few words and he said he'd be happy to answer questions, he didn't want to make a speech. And I told the boys and they all had a question there, and he was just totally honest in his appraisal of the modern game in the last decade. He just blew the blokes away! There was no glossing over the past or shying away from anything he thought wasn't good in the modern game and they just appreciated that. And he said to them, 'I would just like to leave you with this thought. When you leave the game you should hope to leave it a better game for your presence.' He said, 'You've got to remember, you're just custodians of the game in the time you're there.' And that had a huge effect on them.

There was actually one time – it must have been when I was captain – I'd never seen him play and I asked him to come down to the nets and he was all set to do it, and it rained.

The Times *cricket correspondent and editor of* Wisden Cricketers' Almanack *(1980–86),* **John Woodcock** *had an association with Sir Donald which began in 1950. We spoke in his thatched cottage The Old Curacy in Longparish, Hampshire, with the black and white springer spaniel Googly adding an occasional affectionate contribution.*

I WAS ON MY first tour to Australia, which was in 1950–51, not long after he'd given up playing. He was still in his forties. I went out with our team as a freelance [journalist], doing bits and pieces and making among other things a film for BBC television. I took one of their cameras with me. Therefore I came into contact with Don when I was very young and needing all the help that I could get and I couldn't have found him friendlier. His wife Jessie, as everyone knows, was a very sweet person and she made life easy of course when I was with The Don. But I didn't see all that much of him.

Over the years I've been on all our tours to Australia since 1950, as well as one or two others involving West Indies, India and Pakistan. So I would have bumped into him quite often and I would have gone out to his home and that kind of thing, and had dinner with him occasionally. In 1950–51 I was doing a good deal of work for Jim Swanton, who was a great friend, and Jim had got to know Don well, so that was another contact. Of course over the years one got to know him, played golf with him a little bit, that sort of thing.

Throughout Sir Donald's life he was extremely wary of the press. In your opinion, had he good reason to be?
I think practically all sportsmen are wary of the press and I think they do have good reason to be wary, yes. I think that they pick out among the pressmen those they feel they can trust and those they're doubtful about. Journalists have to please their editors and different journalists, because of the papers they write for, approach their job in different ways and there are some whom the players feel are more trustworthy perhaps.

I can only speak as an English journalist, not at all as an Australian, and Don was always civil and helpful. But he was reticent too. I can remember once when I was in Australia, not with an England side, I tried very hard to get an interview with him. I wanted to fly over to Adelaide to see him, just to do a question and answer with him. He asked me to give him a ring back and when I did he said he'd rather not.

When I edited *Wisden Cricketers' Almanack* he was very nice when I asked him to write an article for us (for the 1986 edition) but it was hard work, getting him to do it. And when the piece came I suppose I thought it was a little bit bland. He didn't say very much in it. But by then he was more often than not non-committal. He was content to be in the background, playing golf two or three times a week with old non-cricket friends.

Obviously he had to give his opinions when he led the Australian Cricket Board. To my mind it's such a pity that he didn't speak out at the time of Packer. Over and over again he was asked what his view was on the Packer affair, but he wouldn't give one. He wasn't the chairman of the Board then and I think he felt that it was up to them to say what they felt and he didn't want in any way to compromise them. Bob Parish was chairman at the time. It was a painful time for many people. Many lasting friendships were broken up. It was an awful pity but there we are. It showed the very determined, resolute side of him that he kept so quiet. He took a stance and that was that; he wasn't to be shifted on speaking about it, though I know how very strongly he was opposed to it – to the Packer circus, that is.

Sir Donald came to England in 1953 and 1956 to cover the series for the Daily Mail. *How did you rate him as a journalist?*
He always did his own stuff. A lot of old players don't do their own stuff but he didn't have a ghost. He certainly didn't need one. I mean, he was so able that he could have turned his mind to anything, you know. He had such a good, sharp mind. He was analytical too.

Curiously enough when he came over here in 1953, Douglas Jardine had a press contract to write about the series, so they would both have been not exactly side-by-side but not far apart. They would certainly have been writing about the same match at the same time from the same place. Their relationship was more formal than friendly or frosty so far as I remember.

In your view, was Sir Donald a man who harboured grudges?

Sir Donald had every reason for never exactly forgiving MCC and England for bowling 'bodyline'. Personally I thought that was an indefensible method of attack, and it was much against the spirit of the game. But I wouldn't have thought that The Don was a man to harbour grievances.

On the other hand, there were certainly people who played with him who did, and obviously the two outstanding examples are Jack Fingleton and Bill O'Reilly. It's very difficult, Jack Fingleton was a great friend of mine and he used to stay here a lot. He wrote a lot of one of his books here, *Batting from Memory*, which I think was his last book, and Bradman was still a spectre. There were many things that went towards that I think. Whether the Catholicism had something to do with it I don't know, it may have done. Envy may have. At the same time, Fingo admired him for his genius.

There's the story of how when he got 309 in a day against England at Headingley in 1930 – whether this is apocryphal or not I don't know – when he got back to the Queens Hotel in Leeds, normally they would have said to someone who'd got 309 on the day, 'Come on boys, let's go to the bar and have a drink'. He said to the girl behind the counter, 'Send up a pot of tea to my room, will you?' That was The Don. That's him, that's fair enough.

I know he was a hard man, there's no doubt about that. Of course he was. He couldn't have played as he did but for that. He was also a very private man, a private man unable to live a private life because of his fame. He was an icon almost throughout his life but when he finished playing I think he made a point of being as private as he could. In those days he was so well known from having his pictures in the papers and so on, that he couldn't walk down Piccadilly without gathering a crowd around him. It would be even more intense now with television and so on. For someone like

Sachin Tendulkar, who is the nearest comparison to him today, there is no privacy at all in India, his native country.

Personally I feel that Tendulkar, who is a wonderful player of the modern game, is as good a batsman technically anyway, as The Don was. I think it's perfectly possible that he could have played the game that Bradman played much as Bradman played it. It would be absurd to say that anyone is or ever will be better but Bradman himself told me that he felt there were certainly other cricketers of his time who had as much ability as he had. They just didn't have his temperament. He was so insatiable. Jessie used to say that from the moment he woke in the morning, he started to concentrate on his innings if he had not been out overnight.

Was Sir Donald's friendship with Gubby Allen an important one?
Yes, unquestionably. They were both very much at the helm – simultaneously and for so long. For the great throwing controversy in the late 1950s, it was considered so important that they should get the law right that Don actually came over to England specially for a meeting of the ICC. It was still called the Imperial Cricket Conference then rather than the International Cricket Conference. There'd been a lot of trouble with throwers, particularly on the MCC tour to Australia in 1958–59, and Don's acute mind was invaluable in searching for a solution.

Gubby and Don would have met for the first time in 1930, and for the next time, more controversially on the Bodyline tour in 1932–33. Gubby was captain in 1936–37 and that was when they became close friends. They exchanged regular letters and became very good friends indeed. There's a letter that Don wrote to Jim Swanton after Gubby had died, in which he described Gubby's death as 'the end of an era'. He referred in that letter to 'an enduring friendship over 59 years which I valued so highly'.

Sir Donald appears to have had a number of close friends in England.

Yes, perhaps half a dozen people. Jim Swanton was one, Doug Insole another. Men he regarded highly. I'm Jim's literary executor and have just sent a lot of his Bradman letters to Lord's, to go into the archive there. Those particular ones are mostly on technical matters. There were various laws in the game on which Don had very strong views – the lbw law, for example, and the no-ball law to which he was bitterly opposed in its present form. He certainly didn't pull his punches when writing about them, being occasionally very critical on what he saw as a lack of foresight by the MCC. I thought it best that the letters should go to Lord's and be there for the use of future historians. Another of his closest friends was Walter Robins.

How important do you think Sir Donald was as an administrator in Australian cricket?

Hugely, of course. Whatever he said pretty well went. I am not saying he was surrounded by yes-men but he must have been a difficult man to stand up against. He loved cricket so much. In 1958–59 in Australia, England had played really rather poor cricket, so he was thrilled when Australia and the West Indians had that wonderful series in 1960–61; he thought it did the game so much good, and that was what mattered to him more than anything. He hated the sledging, he hated helmets, he hated endless intimidatory bowling, he even hated heavy bats. They were quite foreign to him and although he may have had a hard side to him he felt there was no need to play the game with wanton aggression.

Somebody once said he was a man with more admirers than friends. If so, it was of his own choosing.

What was Sir Donald like to play golf with?

Oh, pretty competitive but never disparaging. I've spent 16 Christmases, I think it is, in Australia and when we were in Adelaide for Christmas, we used to go to his course, Kooyonga, and hold a competition there among ourselves, with Don joining in and making us feel welcome. It was a lot of fun.

What was it that you liked most about the man?

I liked it that he was friendly and of course that he was a legend. One doesn't get to meet too many of those. I wasn't exactly a close friend, anywhere near, but I did feel a genuine affection for him and Jessie as well as admiration. I was honoured to know the old boy and dash it all, there's only one Bradman.

4

SENIOR SERVICE

Former managing director and chairman of the board of F. H. Faulding,
Bill Scammell, *had attended the funeral of Port Adelaide football great*
Fos Williams on the day we met. We spoke about Sir Donald Bradman,
we spoke about his own mother ('the most gregarious person I've met in
my whole life'), we spoke about how I had turned down one of the best
cups of coffee in Adelaide. After I returned to Melbourne, Bill
Scammell's son Anthony rang to tell me he had died later that day.

DON JOINED THE Faulding board in June 1959. He left in April
1966 and then he came on again in April 1972 until 1982. I was
managing director in that later period and I was chairman of the
board from about 1974.

I met him when I joined the board early in 1960. I was up in
Sydney with Faulding from 1948 until 1969 and I came down here
for board meetings. He was such a little chap. He had fairly big
forearms but little wrists and little tiny hands.

He treated me very nicely, Don. He was very kind to me. My
uncle was chairman of Faulding at that time and he and I didn't
see eye to eye on anything really (laughs) and a number of times
we'd have a box-on at a board meeting where he would challenge
anything I said. He always took the opposite view. But I'd come
home and there would be a message that Don had rung and I'd
ring him back and he'd say, 'Look, I just want to tell you, don't let
your uncle upset you, I think you were on course today, I think
you were spot on.' I must have had half a dozen calls like that from

him after board meetings. It didn't matter what I did, Old Alf would disagree. Old Alf Scammell was about six feet four and of course everybody in the company was totally sycophantic towards him.

I don't remember why – I think I had a few bob and I wanted to get a few investment tips – but I had lunch with Don on the day after John changed his name from Bradman to Bradsen and I was very impressed with the way he handled that. I couldn't have caught him at a more sensitive time, I don't think, but he was very sensible about it, flat-footed, and saw John's point of view. He chatted about it over lunch quite a bit. He wasn't a great chatter. And he told me the story about how he used to want to go and watch John play cricket and John run and hurdle and the things he did, but he found he had to get himself out of the road, otherwise he would attract all the attention from the crowd. And he hated it, he really did hate that, he didn't want that attention. He was very modest and a very shy man, I thought.

What was Sir Donald's contribution to Faulding as a director?
He made a very good contribution because of his investment knowledge through his connection with Argo Investments. And he was very solid and very accurate and very perspicacious in his studying of the figures. He could read a balance sheet and profit and loss accounts and he knew whether there was any nonsense in there or not. So the secretaries and the accountants wouldn't put anything over him.

He wasn't enormously innovative. He didn't set the world on fire with new ideas. He was very hard-working, he read all his papers and at the board meeting he was totally unpretentious. Of all the board members we had I don't think any of them would have studied the papers more closely than he did.

Is the fact that he studied his papers unusual?
Yes it is, I hate to harm the directors there, but it is. I think some of them open their papers when the chairman opens the meeting. Or did. I can't speak about today because I haven't been on a board for ten years.

Were there benefits in having Sir Donald on the board simply because of who he was?
No, I don't think so. And he didn't bring that about either. At annual general meetings he would just sit up there as another member of the board. Never sort of 'Look at me, I'm Don Bradman and I'm dancing'. None of that nonsense. (laughs)

Was he a conservative or progressive businessman?
Conservative. I think he was conservative financially and conservative in the attitude to strategy and policy. He came down to Adelaide before the war and then [the stockbroker] Harry Hodgetts blotted his copybook and went to jail for a bit. And people kept on saying Don should be up there with him. Knowing Don, I don't think he would cheat in a fit. But some of that rubbed off on Don. Oh, people were very nasty. People said he was in it but that he got out of it because he was Bradman. I don't give any credence to that at all. I don't think he let it dog him but I think it was very cruel.

Is it hard to become a director of companies?
Once you've got a start, it's a pushover. (laughs) Really the first one's the hard one, after that it's a piece of cake.

Was it a small group of men in Adelaide who were sat on most boards?
It was. It's better now, but it was terrible. Some of them would have had ten, twelve directorships which is outrageous, I think. Adelaide

in those days was really terribly small. It's much better now. Actually, there are hardly any companies here now, they've all gone to eastern states. And now Melbourne's going up to Sydney or going overseas.

Was there an element of the country boy still there in Sir Donald?
I thought so. I would sometimes call him the Cootamundra Kid. Don would say some rather naive things. I was having a chat to him one day at a time when people were getting hit in the face when they were hooking, and I said, 'What about this Don?' And he got a slide rule off my desk (in those days slide rules were used) and gave me a demonstration. You never get hit. You roll your head at the appropriate moment and you roll your wrist when you hit the ball, that way you hit it onto the ground and you don't get caught. But if he said that to a lot of people, they would say he's having us on. Of course if you hit it on the ground you don't get caught. They would think he was trying to take the mickey out of them and that was the last thing he would do. He was just clearly like that. I've never seen him trying to take the mickey out of anybody.

In my experience he treated everybody as an equal and at no time did he give me the opinion that he felt the slightest bit superior to anybody else. I went to a few Government House things with him, usually some sort of fund raising or an award function or something like that, and he probably played himself down more than anybody else did. A lot of people get to Government House and they really puff their chest out. His chest was the same size in Government House as it was out in King William Street. (laughs)

And another thing about him, he was very nice to the staff. To use an expression that you probably have never heard, he was never up himself. (laughs) And any of them could come up and talk to him and he'd chat away, one on one. They wouldn't let him be equal but he was trying to, doing his best to be on the same level as they were.

What do you mean they wouldn't let him be equal?

Of course they had him on a pedestal. They were determined to have him up there. He wanted to be talking more in tune, he didn't want to be elevated, but they did it because of their enormous admiration for him as a cricketer. He wanted to be Don, not Bradman, because it had cricket connotations. He just wanted to be Don, your mate, sort of thing. Although there are people who will argue with that because he was so reserved that people would misunderstand his reserve for being stuck up. He wasn't stuck up at all in my opinion, not at all. I think he was shy.

He was a meticulous man, in every sense of the word. With regard to facts and figures and with regards to ethics. That's why I can't think he'd ever have got involved with any naughty things that poor old Harry Hodgetts might have done. It just wasn't Don. Don was so ethical, so proper. He really was. He was very, very careful.

*F*ormer England vice-captain **Doug Insole** got to know Sir Donald Bradman through his role as cricket administrator. We spoke at his home overlooking the Epping Forest on the edge of London on a sunny winter's morning.

When you were playing for Essex in 1948, did you play against Sir Donald in the match at Southend when Australia scored more than 700 in the one day?

No I didn't. I was up at Cambridge at the time and I played with Cambridge in the previous match, which was against Australia, which Sir Don didn't play in. I was doing exams or whatever so I didn't come over and play for Essex. Trevor Bailey did. He was also playing for Cambridge at the time. He came over from Cambridge to play against Australia and got 1 for 120 and a broken finger for his efforts. I did meet The Don on that tour at Cambridge but that was really just a case of shaking hands.

So what were the circumstances of your next meeting?
In 1953 when he was over writing for the *Daily Mail*, Walter Robins was a great mate of his and he introduced me. I was young, and somebody must have thought a young, up-and-coming administrator, so we had dinner a couple of nights in Leeds, I remember, during a Test match. That was just 'young boy–great man' sort of thing, almost, but he was extremely chatty and friendly and full of advice.

But the first time I really had anything to do with him administratively was just after the big throwing controversy in '58 in Australia and he and Gubby Allen were going to try and sort something out. And Don came over, in the winter of 1960, prior to the 1961 tour to talk about the situation, which was getting a bit dodgy and on the verge of causing a bit of an upset. A meeting was organised by the president of the MCC, Hubert Ashton, who was the president of Essex, and I was captain of Essex, and he asked me if I'd attend. I suppose it was sort of comic relief really. I was a selector then. The other people there were the secretary of the MCC and Hubert Ashton himself and Don and Gubby Allen.

They had a three or four hour thrash in a club in London in St James Street about this throwing situation. They were both holding their national views if you like, but eventually came to the most sensible solution. They both agreed as chairmen of selectors that they wouldn't pick anybody who threw. They both knew, even if the umpires weren't calling them. But they also agreed to a change of wording in the law. Because it was perceived that in order for anybody who hadn't called people up till now to be able to call them, they needed some change of wording, so it would be, 'Ah well now, of course! If you'd said that before . . .' So that was eventually agreed, not without a lot of toing and froing of words like 'this' and 'that' and 'although' and 'but' and so on and so forth. But they eventually changed the wording, and in fact Col Egar no-balled Ian Meckiff immediately that wording was changed and it became law.

After this meeting I drove Don back to the Waldorf Hotel and we had a bit of a natter. He always stored all his information for years and years and eked it out as and when it was thought either necessary or appropriate. And I remember, I was on the selection committee at the time and so was Herbert Sutcliffe, who was one of England's openers in the Bodyline series. And he said, 'How's old Herbert?' And I said, 'Oh he's jollying along. In fact I see him quite regularly; he's on the selection committee.' 'Oh,' he said, 'I always thought he was far more involved with Bodyline than he ever let on. I remember I was out there once and Jardine said to him, "Sutcliffe, go to slip."' And impersonating a Yorkshireman with a plum in his mouth, The Don said, '"Which side of the wicket?" He knew bloody well which side,' he said. 'There was no question of his going on the off side. He was going leg slip which was where he fielded.' So this is 30 years on and he'd got it all sort of tucked away there about old Herbert and what he'd done or hadn't done.

But that was the first occasion that I saw him at work really as an administrator and I was impressed. He and Gubby Allen were two pretty strong single-minded obstinate characters and they both set their stalls out but in the end they both came to the conclusion: well the most sensible thing in our position is just not to pick anybody that's suspect. And that together with the change in the wording made the thing work.

Were there other instances when he particularly impressed you as an administrator?
When we were having the World Cup over here in 1975, which was the first World Cup, we had South Africa pencilled in as a

touring side and of course that was never going to happen. So effectively we had the World Cup here and nothing else in that summer. Well, the World Cup without a Test series was going to be a massive loss as far as we were concerned. So I went over with our chairman – I wasn't the chairman of the board, I was chairman of cricketers – to Australia to invite . . . to ask the Aussies to come here and play a Test series in that summer. This was in late '74.

What we were saying was that we were in big trouble with the TV people because they were offering peanuts and we were seriously thinking that if they didn't come up with something better we'd do without TV. All we needed to cover what they were offering was about 1000 people through the gates each day. And so we put the proposition to the Australian Board. We sat and made our plea and said to them, 'Would you be prepared to come and would you be prepared to come for so much money (whatever it was), bearing in mind that all your fares are going to be paid for by the World Cup?'

And when we finished I said, 'Well, I'm sure you'd like to talk about it so we'll go out.' And within two minutes we were back in and they said yes okay. And afterwards Ray Steele said to me, 'The Don said straight away, "These blokes need some help, you know. We ought to do it,"' which was extremely noble, extremely good. I mean there was a harder bargain to have been driven if they wanted to drive it, but in fact they were – and he in particular, according to Ray (obviously we weren't in the room) – they were saying well, let's give it a go. So that was something that he was happy to do.

You were the manager of the English team that toured Australia in 1978–79. Was that another tempestuous time?
Tempestuous for cricket but very harmonious between the England authorities and the Australian authorities. In 1977 when the

Packer court case was in England, I was chairman of our Board then and I spent four or five days in the dock. The Australians Ray Steele and Bob Parish came over to represent the Australian case as far as the ICC were concerned and I was representing England but with both the ICC hat and the Test and County Cricket Board hat, because we were taking separate action as it were. I thought the ICC action would succeed and it should have done, and it was a very poor judgement. I think it was proved to be nonsense within a very short time of being given. The judge said, 'Well, it's not going to change things. Test cricket's going to go on. People will be just as interested.' And of course they weren't. When England played Pakistan and Pakistan were without their Imran Kahn and all these people, people just didn't turn up. At that time in particular, the other countries were so dependent on gate receipts, television hadn't got then to the point it is now, and it was a massively difficult time for ICC. And the judge was very complimentary about understanding all the people were obviously doing what they thought was best for the game and were very honourable men blah, blah, blah . . . And then when it came to the domestic thing of course we've got exchange-of-trade laws here.

But The Don never really put his head above the parapet in the Packer thing. He was concerned, I think – well I don't think, I know – about possible legal action as a member of the Board and although he was massively, vitriolically against, he didn't actually say so publicly.

Was he realistically concerned about legal action?
I think he saw himself as the pivotal figure and that anything that he said would be massively more important than what anybody else said. There were writs flying all around the place at the time, from Packer to players and players to Packer. It was a very litigious period and I think he was just over-concerned that he might be

brought into the courts and that wouldn't be a very good idea. But he was writing to me some very, very long letters saying exactly what he thought and what he thought we ought to do about it, and some of it I was able to agree with and other bits I wasn't.

In 1978–79 we were in Australia and Packer was nibbling particularly at England and our players and I remember we started off in Adelaide. We made our base there for the start of the tour and so we were seeing a bit of Don early on. We were much less affected than Australia was. We had five of our players that Packer had taken over, Greig and Underwood and Knott and Snow and Woolmer . . .

What do you think Sir Donald's influence was on English cricket?

I would think that he was probably the most influential man around in the latter half of the 20th century. I think his effect on English cricket directly was minimal. But as a result of the part he was playing in the world administration of the game in terms of the formulation of laws and the build-up of international cricket generally, then obviously he had a big part to play and was listened to very earnestly by our administrators. It can easily be exaggerated but in the end he had a very good relationship with Gubby Allen and they became very good friends. They were the two strong men really of English and Australian cricket. And at that time and in fact up until 1989 England and Australia had a veto on things at ICC so provided they could develop things in unison, as it were, reasonably well agreeing, then they were able to shape the form of the game. And Don was a very sensible administrator and obviously he spoke well and he thought lucidly and his performance as a player made him extremely highly regarded.

He was never very anxious to be up-front as an administrator. He wasn't anxious to be getting publicity and he was not very keen on speaking at meetings and dinners. He prepared absolutely meticulously when he did speak but he did it so seldom, that he could. He was chairman of the Board on two occasions and he was chairman of selectors for a long time, but his administrative work was certainly much less up-front than his play on the field.

He had quite a few bees in his bonnet and he was very prickly – this is going back to as a player – that his authority might be being undermined. There are two or three tiny incidents. I mean in that match against Essex at Southend in 1948 when Australia scored 721, Keith Miller got a duck. He was out first ball. And to everybody else on the ground, including all our team and our wicketkeeper, he just let the ball go. He was bowled out. It took me about 40 years to get Keith to admit that that's what he did. But Don could never agree that he'd done it because he couldn't conceive that somebody would just go out and do it, particularly while he was at the wicket, you know.

I asked him in 1988 – 40 years on – to do a piece for the *Essex Year Book* about that game, and a good bit of the article was taken up with this scurrilous rumour that Keith Miller might have let the ball go, when in fact he was beaten by a perfectly good delivery by a Test match bowler. And he quotes all the figures of what all the bowlers had done in that year and in past years and who they'd played and got out. It was just something that he couldn't allow himself to believe, that Keith could have come out and said, 'What's the point? We've got hundreds of runs'. And actually what Keith said to me was that he was fed up because he hadn't had a knock in the previous game, which was against Cambridge and not much of one in the match before that, and there he was being sent on, down the order when the bowling was tamed and not being any sort of challenge and he thought, well, what's the point. It's amazing, it's a tiny incident, but The Don consistently refers to it. In his tapes he talks about it for five minutes. Amazing.

And we had a running argument. I've got some letters here, a lot of private ones from The Don. He writes endlessly about the front-foot rule. I was chairman of English cricket at the time and what he says is, 'If you could support what I'm saying then we'd have a chance of getting the thing altered.' And so I was saying to him, 'Yes I'd like to but I simply can't because if you were now starting writing the Laws of Cricket just like any other laws, like throwing the javelin or starting 100 metres, you've got to stay behind the line. You can't say because I'm seven foot I can put my foot four feet down the wicket whereas some bloke who's five feet three can't. And so, you know, logically I would have to say that I support the new ruling.'

Well, he went on and on and on, I mean page after page, with lots of good, practical arguments about the old days. It was something that he couldn't shake off and he kept on writing: '. . . and I've talked to all the Australian umpires and Richie Benaud and all these people and they are all in favour.' Well, the Australians were coming to Lord's, to the ICC, and voting in favour of the new rules for the front-foot law and saying, 'Our umpires association think it's far easier and far fairer to do it on the present basis.' But it was just something he wouldn't let go.

He also seems to have continued arguing against the accusation that he'd been afraid of the bouncers bowled during the Bodyline series.

Yes, but obviously Bodyline was aimed at Don. I've known very well a lot of the people that were on that tour: Gubby Allen, Bob Wyatt, Herbert Sutcliffe. The greatest pleasure I've had out of cricket really is getting to know people and I must have talked endlessly about those things to them. There was never any suggestion that Don was frightened of the ball. There was a suggestion that because of the way it was directed at him, he wouldn't be able to play it and therefore he might try and find other ways of playing it, which would get him out. But nobody in my hearing has ever suggested that he was frightened of it. And when that semi-inference was made he seems to have taken it on board and been absolutely paranoid about refuting it. But, yes, he's got lots of little things that remained there to be brought out again and again.

He had an extraordinary memory for details.
Yes, that was a sort of characteristic of that generation. I've heard Bob Wyatt, R. E. S. Wyatt, who was vice-captain on that Bodyline tour, talking about his first Test. And whether it's right and whether it's wrong, he described every ball that was bowled by Clarrie Grimmett, and what it was and whether there was a google on the topspinner or the leg-spinner. Sixty years on, you know, and how he played it and how he missed it and all this jazz. And he may have built it up in his mind over the years but it was so sharp, it wasn't true. Don was the same. He'd remember incidents, and of course being who he was, incidents got magnified, didn't they? You know, the '46 thing with Ikin catching him in the gully. I can still hear him talking about it now. It's just ridiculous. Any other batsman would say, 'So what?'

But it was also magnified throughout the cricketing world, wasn't it?
Yes, I think to be fair it was.

Did you consider your relationship with Sir Donald a friendship?
I would certainly regard him as a friend and I hope he did. We had a lot of correspondence. He was a paradox really. I lost a daughter in an air crash in 1979, and his letter's absolutely heartrending, you know. And then when my wife died, the same. He was extremely caring and he certainly opened his heart about his family affairs and those sorts of things in a way that one would hope a friend

might but one wouldn't expect of a general acquaintance. He seemed genuinely pleased to see me and I was certainly very pleased to see him. I think it may be true that he had as many genuine friends over here as he did in Australia. He was always quite wary of how Australians were going to use his company and his words, so I think he probably held back a bit. He was certainly very conscious of the reputation he had. I remember sitting next to him at the Centenary Test and he said to me, 'Change places quick. This so-and-so wants to sit next to me and I'm sure he wants to have his photograph taken and I can't stand him.' So we did a quick swap and I sat next to the particular guy up until lunch. And he seemed to think that if he sat next to the bloke and had his photograph taken then he might get tarred with a brush that he didn't want to be tarred with, as they say.

I've written to him about various people that have died over the years who have been, I thought, reasonably close to him and I said what my experience of them was, what decent people they were and their great sense of humour. And he'd write back and say, 'Well, not so sure about that. I mean he was all right but I wouldn't trust him as far as I could chuck him.' So I thought, oh well, you put your foot in it there, Insole.

What was it that you liked about Sir Donald?

I was obviously originally attracted to him because he was a tremendous performer in a game that I was mad on. And he was willing to be forthcoming and friendly about it. I mean I was 22 when I met him and then I was an administrator when I was 29, and he was always forthcoming and extremely frank and extremely open and there was no sort of hedging of opinions, no condescension whatsoever. That was a very attractive feature as far as I was concerned; he didn't say, 'Who is this young whippersnapper?'

And then subsequently he was always extremely frank and

forthcoming and he was always willing to spend time. He'd arrange to have a meal, you know, never a question of 'Sorry, I'm caught up, I can't manage it'. As far as I was concerned, he was friendly.

Was he a demanding friend in any way?
No. I mean, it wasn't a situation where he necessarily had things that he wanted from me, unless it was an opinion. And he did ask me about shades of opinion in England and how certain people were regarded and whatnot, but it was in an inquisitive sense. And we wrote letters very regularly over the years and he was a very good correspondent.

But it was an extremely straightforward relationship and I was hearing from various people that he wasn't the greatest thing since sliced bread but that wasn't my experience. I had a very good experience with him and although we had a lot of arguments – and about cricket you can have arguments that become quite heated and some of his language in his letters is a bit, you know, 'I cannot believe how anyone can be so bloody stupid as to think this' – it was totally forgotten once the door was closed as it were. So there was no ongoing friction or agro whatsoever. Which again is nice.

Mind you, I find that's a trait of Australians. I've been there a lot and know a lot of them and I like them very much. And one of the things is that you can have a bloody good argument and both be completely honest and forthright and then that's it, close the door, have a drink and nobody mentions it again. There's no sense of 'Oh, I don't want to see him again' or 'I'm not talking to him again'.

I get the impression that Sir Donald liked a good argument. Did he appreciate it when somebody put up an opposition to him and spelt out their views?
Yes. The last time I had a real discussion/argument with him was when Muralitharan was called for throwing at Adelaide. I'm on the

ICC throwing panel and I was the only one on the ICC throwing panel on the ground at that time. I didn't think they'd remember that but they did and I was asked to go along and say what the panel's view was with Muralitharan, bearing in mind that he had been called. And I told them exactly what our view was. The following day I went to see Don who said would I come up for morning tea. Well, it was a stately English occasion almost. And then we had a bit of an argument. No, argument would be wrong. We weren't really disagreeing but talking about throwing and the integrity of the umpire and how the umpire's situation mustn't be compromised, with which I was in total agreement. And then he was talking about past instances of throwing and arguing a case that you could sometimes agree with and sometimes not. On that day he appeared in a pair of carpet slippers, which was the first time I'd ever come across him in anything less than full attire, even an open-necked shirt. He'd got to the point where he was not feeling great obviously and was much more informal.

But yeah, he did like a good argument and he was very articulate and very forthright and quite obstinate. I suppose we all are in a way. Once you've got something in your mind you're not prepared to give way on then you argue the point and agree to differ. But there were a lot of points on which we did agree.

I also managed a tour in 1982–83 and there were some very contentious decisions, particularly run-out decisions. I spent hours talking with him about how the game could be helped by electronic or other aids and he was very forward-looking.

His whole attitude to the game was modern. He had a lot to say in favour of one-day cricket and he was very appreciative of people like Tendulkar and certain modern players. And his letters are full of assessments of modern-day players. There's one in there which says, 'I now think that Warne is the best spin bowler I've ever seen.' And then he says, 'I'm excluding O'Reilly from the spinning category and regarding him as a medium-pace cutter.' He's always said that Bill O'Reilly was the best bowler he had ever played with or against and he was obviously loath to back down from that, but then he was prepared to shift him into a different category and let Warne into the spin category.

Some very strange things have happened. They published an all-time XI that The Don picked. Well, over the years I've had endless conversations with him and I've got loads of letters from him saying who he thought was the best. Clarrie Grimmett was in that team as the best spin bowler. Well, he'd written to me a year previously and said that Warne was the best he'd ever seen. So how or why he changed his mind on that or if he did . . . I've always been a bit suspicious of that.

Did he discuss Bill O'Reilly with you on any other level?
I can tell you what he told me about the sort of animosity there was to him from Bill O'Reilly and Jack Fingleton and so forth, which he obviously felt very keenly. He always maintained, as I mentioned earlier, that Bill was the best bowler he ever played against, the best bowler the world had ever seen while he was around, even if he wasn't terribly keen on Bill in a personal sense. He put the group thing down to religion, and Jack Fingleton in particular. And he paid due regard to the fact that Bill's was partly religious but he maintained that the start of the whole thing was that in the first match he played against him in the grade, he hit him all over the ground. Bill was anti him from that time on.

Did you share interests outside cricket?
I'm involved with the English Football Association and he was always interested in that and the way the thing was moving and the way the professional contracts and arrangements were going and, you know, the standards now as against days of yore.

And families were a big mutual interest. He always liked talking about his family and he obviously had big problems as we all do with family but he was keen to talk about them. Not so much get it off his chest but at least to get another view on what was happening in their family, if you like. But we had the same sort of conversations one has with other blokes who are friends really.

I'm interested in what you said about him almost having more friends in England than in Australia.
I don't know whether what I'm saying is right or not but it's the distinct impression that I've got. I just think he was more inclined to be open and forthcoming with people like Alec Bedser and Colin Cowdrey. I know that when I used to go and talk to people in Australia who were reasonably close to him and said A, B and C, they said, 'What? I didn't know that.' He wrote long letters and he would spend a long time talking about quite personal things. The only reason I get that impression is that, as I mentioned before, sometimes when I've said: 'Oh so-and-so was a good bloke wasn't he?' – 'Ah, he was blah, blah, I don't know about that.' So one wonders how far they were indicating they were great mates with Don and Don wasn't terribly great mates with them, as it were.

I wonder if there was safety in having great mates that didn't live around the corner.
I think definitely yes. I think that was really almost the whole point of it. He was concerned that personal things that he was saying might get out into the public domain and he was obviously a very, very private person.

It's been said that he had a fairly cruel sense of humour.
Yes, I think that's not a bad description. My view is slightly milder than that, but he did laugh most heartily at misfortunes. His sense

of humour was fairly basic. In my opinion he laughed loudest at banana skins. I remember him telling me a story about a political figure who'd taken a trip to some island with a girl and expired while he was there with her. 'Oh, he died on the job', and he just roared with laughter and he must have roared about it 50 times previously but it so happened we were talking about politicians at the time and he was encapsulating his opinion of local politicians with this one incident. And he tended to roar when something fairly basic rather than fairly subtle was on board.

A very old friend of mine who has just died was keeping wicket for Essex in this match at Southend in 1948 and it was actually the first time he'd ever kept wicket for the Essex first team (he kept for the second team). And Don came in about half an hour before lunch and the last over before lunch our captain put on a leg spin bowler to rattle The Don, and he played the first ball and then he hit the next four for four, all to midwicket. And this guy Frank said to him, 'Excuse me Sir, have you got any other shots?' and he replied, 'Don't you worry. I'll show you a few after lunch.' And then the last ball came down and he hit that for four to midwicket as well and he tapped this fellow on the arm and said, 'I did say after lunch.'

Was Sir Donald a snob?

He wasn't inclined to be very forthcoming to many people, not because he mistrusted them specifically but because he was just generally wary about being misrepresented. And I can understand that people who might have been treated in that way could say that it was down to some form of snobbery.

But he wrote to me about his knighthood when Richard Hadlee was granted one. He said, 'I accepted mine because I felt it was a reward recognising the place of cricket in the community. As I have often said, life would be much simpler and easier without it. It's awfully embarrassing when long-time friends insist on calling

me Sir instead of just Don as they used to do because they think it's
protocol. There are so many other small ways in which it impinges
on one's life. I suppose my upbringing and background make me
question this business of honouring people. The last year I've
refused offers from two universities to make me an honorary doctor of laws. I refused on the basis I had no knowledge or
background to justify the receipt of same and was really very surprised that the offerers took a dim view of my refusal. But we all
have our viewpoints.'

My own experience was that I was a young guy of no particular
standing or reputation, who had never had anything by way of
condescension or anything like that and I've got to judge him on
that. He had no reason to be unduly pleasant or nice to me at all
but the fact that he was makes me feel that he hadn't got the pre-
tentiousness that other people ascribe to him. So basically you
speak as you find.

*Colin Egar umpired 29 Test matches during his 10-year career, 19 of
them with Lou Rowan and he went on to become a cricket administrator,
and chairman of the Australian Cricket Board from 1989 to 1992. We
spoke sitting at the boardroom table in the Bradman Room at the
Adelaide Oval.*

I UMPIRED GRADE cricket for two or three years and I used to umpire
Adelaide University and Melbourne University games. Bradman
then being an Australian selector and a South Australian selector
would attend matches anywhere and so the first one of these university games I umpired, I think it was probably 1953, he came over and
introduced himself to me. So I would have known him for nearly
50 years.

From those days on the university oval, I saw him mellow

tremendously. When I first met Don he was about 45 and he was a very strict type of person to speak to. He would ask you questions and, I'm talking cricket now, if you didn't give him the answer that he expected, he'd let you know and say, 'Well, I thought you might have had a different opinion to that', or 'Why don't you think this, that and something else?' He wouldn't ask you a question and say that's a good idea. He knew the answer to the question that he'd asked you already. That's the impression he gave you.

I only have hearsay of people that used to be under him, such as players, but he was a very strict disciplinarian. And I thought, he is a tough man. But from there on, I'd say from '53 to just prior to the time I started Test cricket in 1960, I could see him mellowing.

And later in life when we would be at functions together or we would be dining, he'd absolutely mellowed incredibly to the extent that his humour was really astounding. The storytelling he could handle and tell you. Mostly it was all about cricket – he never got onto sexy stories or anything like that but he wasn't frightened to laugh at them either. He had an incredible sense of humour, but in the close circles. And in his own private company with friends, he didn't dominate. He was an easygoing guy in the finish, a very down-to-earth bloke.

He was generally known as a tough taskmaster, yes, disciplinarian, yes, but also a wowser. But I knew him well enough to know that he was a connoisseur of wines, an absolute connoisseur. I met Max Schubert, the Grange man, at Penfolds through cricket, and on one occasion Max said, 'Right, I'll make sure we have a luncheon or two per year up at Penfolds.' It was up to me to do the organising. Don was about retiring so I'm talking back in the mid-80s and he couldn't get there quick enough. In fact, he would ring me if he hadn't heard to say 'Is there any news about when we're going to Penfolds? I was just thinking that I might have been forgotten.'

He and Max became very friendly. Don thought Max was the greatest thing on earth and of course Max reckoned that Don was, in their respective trades. Sherry was a very popular drink years ago but the market had decreased by 70 per cent. That meant that the only sherry you were going to get wasn't going to be the good stuff. On numerous occasions when we'd go up to these luncheons, Max would have a small box with string around it and it turns out he would make for Don a dozen bottles from the good old top sherry from after the vintage. Bradman would be in that committee room and you'd never see him have a glass of beer. But up in the little bar, there'd be a bottle of sherry tucked away. But he wasn't interested in beer, he didn't like it.

You started your career with the 1960 Tied Test against the West Indies in Brisbane. It was a remarkable Test to start with.
It was. I was at the bowler's end at the last over. I remember Don saying to me when we came off on the last day, 'You never umpired a football grand final as exciting as that.' I said, 'No.' I never had a draw, though they got close. But my feeling there was that I was very pleased in my inner mind to have been an Australian rules football umpire because I think it stood me in good stead. It was the experience in football of getting control of a situation that can be becoming a bit tight. I didn't have any nerves in that Test match at all, and I think that was only due to the fact that I'd been umpiring the grand finals in Australian rules football.

Oh, and Bradman was that excited about the whole thing too. The greatest thing to happen to cricket! That's all he could think of, what's good for cricket.

We just had a reunion of the Tied Test. I was a long way from being the oldest on the ground at that Test. I umpired Test cricket from the age of 32 to 42, when I retired for business reasons.

Tell me about Bradman the administrator.

Bradman was appointed to the Australian Cricket Board through South Australia, maybe prior even to him retiring from Test cricket in 1948. So he was full on, on Australian cricket and international cricket. He was very active in South Australia at the administration level right through but his commitments were first at the Australian level.

In those days administration was entirely different. One man could really be controlling overall. The finances were different. But he concentrated fully on that. In 1962 he became president here (SACA) and he kept the position going for ten years, but in that time he was still on the Australian Cricket Board. He didn't retire from the Board until 1980. I joined the Board in '81, just after he retired.

He continued on here as a trustee until well into the 1980s. Back in the late-70s or early-80s I was the first chairman of the Adelaide Oval Development Committee, and we had to do all this rewiring. It was going to cost an enormous amount and the then-secretary and I wrote this letter to the Adelaide City Council. Bradman was there and seeing he was a trustee, I said, 'Have a look at this letter.' He read it and said, 'Who wrote this?' I said I did. He just looked at me over the top of his glasses. He went away to the sideboard, and he got his pen and a piece of paper and he precised this letter and said, 'Is this what you're trying to say?' I said, 'Yeah, that's right. Exactly.'

When I was chairman of the ACB between 1989 and 1992, even though he had ceased to be a trustee of this association, we still used to converse. I used to ring him up or he'd ring me and I'd say, 'But you must have heard this?' And he'd say 'Colin, nobody rings me up and tells me what's going on these days. I finished in 1980 at the Australian Cricket Board, how would I know what to say?' I'd say, 'Well, okay, you've got a couple of other people there who you know.' 'No,' he said, 'I don't. That's why I want to have a chat with you, to keep my ear to the ground and see what's going on.' So even when I was going to the ICC meetings in 1989–92, and there were some changes taking place then due to slow cricket and the front-foot/back-foot law, he was still interested in what do they think about this? What do they think about that? I suppose he was a recluse to an extent, but he had plenty of contacts and he used to stop and think about the game right through.

What do you think of Sir Donald as an administrator?

Bradman was a brilliant administrator in relation to the laws of cricket and the playing of the game. He and Gubby Allen. Gubby Allen was the influential man in English cricket and Bradman was here.

To give you an idea of what their powers were, when I was umpiring a game, England must have been playing Australia, I remember Gubby asking me one day what did I think about this law of cricket? And I gave an answer that people were generally talking about, and Gubby said to me, 'Well I agree that we should do that as well but,' he said, 'we will have trouble getting it, because Don won't agree.'

So not long after, I was talking to Bradman and Don asked me the same question. So I gave the same answer. And Don said, 'Well I think it's a good idea, but we'll have trouble getting it through, because Gubby doesn't agree.' This was all within a month. A true story. (laughs)

Gubby and Don were friends, but they were the two hierarchies of their countries and they liked to be first in with the suggestion, otherwise, well, it wasn't my idea, bad luck. The Marylebone Cricket Club ran the law-making of cricket, it was all run from Lord's. If Australia suggested something to the MCC, it didn't necessarily mean that it was even going to get a hearing.

Don ran board meetings here. There wasn't much money

around then and Don was a conservative administrator in relation to financial expenses. Talking administration, I saw him thawing out over the years. Here at the Adelaide Oval when he was the kingpin, when he took over the administration of the SACA, in his mind his main purpose was to assist the SACA double the investments that they had. You see they were on Crown land, therefore there was no freehold. And he successfully did that, but by being involved in that type of administration with no money. 'Let's do this' or 'let's do that', he would not look favourably upon. Even to the extent that he might turn around, and he has at board meetings, and say that it's not only going to cost you x dollars but the interest rate that you're losing on it as well.

When I was chairman of the subcommittee for the indoor cricket centre, I had many phone calls from Don: 'Don't spend the money.' Phil Ridings was president after him, and a very good one, and he was different to Bradman in every aspect. Phil and I looked at some property for the indoor cricket centre just down on the western side of the city here and I would get a phone call from Don saying, 'Look, you are going about it the wrong way, it's going to be too costly, we've got to spend what we've got.'

But all of a sudden things changed, and he changed with it. In 1989 on his 80th birthday, DG said he agreed the players should be well rewarded. But he also said, 'However, the player must have an inner commitment, apart from the money. There is a great danger of the dollar being such a dominant factor that it erodes the underlying integrity and purpose of the sport. It behoves all of us to realise we are the custodians of the welfare of cricket and must guard its future even more zealously than its present.'

That's 12 years ago and none of this nonsense of game fixing really started popping up publicly until the mid-90s. So he could visualise the way the game was going.

Was he a delegator?

I would say, as I stop and think, yes. He was a delegator because when I was in Victoria at the Melbourne Cricket Ground one day with the South Australian team during the Packer problem, I recall saying to a Victorian representative about Bradman, 'I don't think he's enjoying the current situation with the Packer problem.' And the reply I got then was, 'No, he's asked us here to do this that and something else in relation to it.' I didn't know how to take that because it sounded to me – and I wasn't on the Board but I was close to it – as though he didn't want to do it, so *you* do it. So I'd have to say he delegated that pretty well.

Getting back to normal times, he'd have to have been a delegator because in those days the president of an association or the chairman of the board would direct and delegate the subcommittees and even the secretaries to do this and that. So yes, Bradman was a very good delegator and he had a very good team of operators around him in the other directors.

He was absolutely outstanding in relation to having discussions with the players and with other administrators. He never would say, 'No, I'm not available to talk about cricket to individuals'. He could sit in that grandstand up there. And it wasn't only players that Bradman was interested in, he thought umpiring was a very important part of the game. He was a qualified umpire himself; he did it when he was in New South Wales as a young fellow. That's the way he analysed the game. Lou Rowan and I umpired 19 Tests together and that was during Bradman's time. No other umpires have ever umpired 19 Tests together anywhere in the cricket world. So Lou and I had a rapport with Bradman. Lou's a very intelligent man; he was a detective sergeant of the drug squad up in Queensland and he and Bradman always handled one another very well. Bradman might walk past us and Lou would have a bit of a chiack.

I'd say that during that time, with Lou coming from a different state and Bradman getting to know him, all of a sudden I was getting a bit closer as well. And this build-up of friendship assisted me of course when I was put onto this board in January 1971 and then when I became chairman of the SACA and on the Australian Cricket Board in 1981 and chairman during that time. The fact of umpiring and being a friend of Bradman's, more than an acquaintance – bang, that's when it made it easier for me in being chairman of the ACB. Oh yes, all those things count in the long run. That's what they call experience.

Was Sir Donald interested in other sports?
He was very keen on watching Australian Rules football. He followed Norwood. He was the type of person who would analyse the football match. I think if he was watching the tennis next door at the Davis Cup, he'd analyse it too.

His golfing – he'd say to a fellow who'd just missed a putt, 'Now just remember when you're putting next time,' (particularly if it was his partner) 'the head of the putter must be moving at its maximum as you're going through the ball.' Who thinks of those things? He did.

Don was a fellow who – well, he didn't want to be known as Don Bradman the Great, which he was. He didn't like that. He'd come down to the golf club and he had a set group that he always played with and they were not Bradman buffs. They were just normal guys, a pharmacist and a media bloke and somebody else. Just nice fellows. He used to really enjoy his golf. He played competition golf. He was a great competitor and he used to hit the ball just down the centre, which made it look easy and never had a big back swing or anything like that. But he analysed all these things, same as when he was an administrator.

But everything seemed to be in sections. He had his cricket, then he had his golf. That was the type of person he was. He seemed to be a freak person. I've never known anyone like him from the point of view of efficiency. Everything was done just to perfection. He was an amazing man.

Did you find yourself defending him at times?

When I was 20 years younger and that wartime group were around, you were always being asked to answer questions on his behalf. And you'd say you didn't know and they'd say, 'Oh, you don't want to tell us but you mix with him.' I never knew what his illnesses were, I didn't want to know. You see after the war, he very seldom played for South Australia. He wasn't that fit but he'd always be eligible for international matches. One game here in 1947–48, Amarnath brought the last combined India team together, that was before partition, India and Pakistan, and Bradman came out here to bat. I can see him now, he came out to bat at 20 past four and at 6 o'clock, 100 minutes later, he was 102 not out. People used to say, but he's not well, he's not supposed to do this and he's not supposed to do that. Why doesn't he play for South Australia? Ah God. Well, he did play for South Australia that day. They were playing India. That was the first time the Indians had seen him play. They saw it all right. I think his reputation suffered here and I don't think it was warranted. And then to come out and play Test cricket in '48 . . .

Was Sir Donald a snob?

No. I've got to stop and think of this. Along the line of who did he mix with? When you get back to his playing days, O'Reilly, McCabe, Fingleton – particularly O'Reilly and Fingleton used to talk against him in regards to his anti-Catholic situation. I'm a Catholic. And on one occasion, around 1989–92 again, I was getting ready to leave home to go to the airport for a board meeting starting on the Monday. He rang me and I thought, oh well, he's got something. He was always putting good ideas into your mind or asking you what you thought of this or that. Turned out he said, 'Did you read the *Advertiser* (the morning paper) yesterday?' It was a big centre spread written by Bill O'Reilly or somebody writing for him, I'm not sure that Bill was alive at the time. Anyway it got back to the O'Reilly story and Bradman the anti-Catholic and all this stuff. And he said, 'I just want to let you know, it's an absolute pack of rubbish.' I said, 'Well, I believe what you're saying.' Because I knew what O'Reilly was like.

How did you get on with Bill O'Reilly?

I could tell you how I got on with O'Reilly. One day all of a sudden Bill O'Reilly started talking to me. He's an old man, I'm a young man but I've been umpiring, I'm an administrator by this time and you know, we'd say 'G'day, how are you going?' but we'd never discuss cricket. And on this particular day, O'Reilly has started to talk to me. I thought, 'Gee, this is rather strange'. And what I didn't know at the time was that somebody had told Bill O'Reilly that Egar is a Christian Brothers old collegian. The person who had told him came to me later and said, 'How are you getting on with O'Reilly?' Because it was a Catholic who told him. I said, 'Did you tell him that?' I said, 'It just goes to prove doesn't it?' Now that's a true story.

Bradman knew I was a Catholic right from the word go. He knew everything about me in every aspect. He knew that I was a Catholic before I became a cricket umpire, and he knew that I was a Catholic before I was put on the Board. There weren't too many Catholics down here, I doubt there were any before me. I can't remember any of them.

So to start with, I can't say in my time that he was an anti-Catholic man. I can't say that I know too many people he mixed with outside of cricket who didn't go to colleges. He mixed with businessmen, that type of thing. He wasn't a snob but he was a man who due to the misfortune of having the name of Don Bradman, he didn't mix much at all.

He used to play golf with a fellow by the name of Sylv Phelan. Now Sylv was a bit of a rugged sort of a diamond. He and Don got on famously. They'd go down and play golf together at least once a week, just the pair of them. So I think that would probably answer your question, along the line that no, there was nothing in his make up which said I can't mix with those people. No.

Did Lady Bradman ever come to the Adelaide Oval to watch the cricket without Sir Donald?
That is absolutely correct. He got to the stage eventually Jessie would come on her own because he'd be at golf. But there'd be days when he wasn't playing golf and he came down one day and I said to him, 'You haven't been coming down much lately. Just sick and tired of it or can't be bothered?' 'Oh, no,' he said, 'I can be bothered. I'm following everything that's going on. But I sit up here' (he was talking about the Adelaide Oval) 'and I can be talking to you and all of a sudden somebody comes in and says, "Oh, Don, so and so would like to see you for a minute." I'm absolutely sick and tired of that.' And that's why he wouldn't come.

Did you ever visit him at home?
I would call in to Holden Street with former Test players. I'd ring him up and say so and so's in town. Oh, bring them around. And as soon as you'd get there, the first thing he'd say is, 'Who's having a beer?' He'd have beer in the fridge and that sort of stuff. On this particular occasion, very early doors, he sat down at this grand piano – I don't know who was there, it might only have been two or three of us – and he's playing by ear all this classical

music. He was astounding. What I know about classical music is nothing, but I love to see people playing the piano. He was spot on there.

But you'd never ever know he could play a note. He never mentioned anything. Virtually you wouldn't know what Bradman did at home. Unless you went in and he'll have his gardening clothes on and you'd say, 'What? Gardener not here today?' Or something a bit cheeky. And he'd say, 'I can't afford a gardener.' He used to always talk that way. I can't afford this, I can't afford that. He had a Rover car once, he liked all the English type of thing. If you were there for a dinner when he was much younger they had a housekeeper there who used to work during the day. They'd do the cooking, but Don would carve at the table. He'd do everything right there with the right wines and all that sort of stuff.

But people he just knocked around with wouldn't have any idea what his lifestyle was. He built a swimming pool. I remember him grizzling about that. He said, 'I suppose it's done its job but I think I'll have to do something with it.' He only built it for John when he had polio, you see, but he hated swimming pools.

He was a very good family man. He was very good to Jessie. But on the other hand, by gee, Jessie was a sensational woman. An absolute bomb of a woman. She was so outgoing and what have you. She was such a personality he just seemed that he was the little husband tagging along. Lovely lady. I used to have a lot of fun with her. She'd be at a dinner and he'd say something and she'd look at him and say, 'Don, you don't even believe that.'

Was chucking something you discussed with Sir Donald?
In 1962–63 the Australian Cricket Board had a problem around the table in relation to illegal bowlers and there were quite a few around. And all of a sudden the Board decided that one representative from each state would call a meeting. I'll talk Adelaide now.

Bradman, one of the three on the Board from Adelaide, would call a meeting in Adelaide in say March '63. He would call a meeting of the grade captains, the state team including the captain, some of the SACA administrators and all the umpires who were umpiring second grade, first grade district cricket and the Shield umpires. So there was a group of us in this room and I think from memory it was down in what they call the Ridings Room. And there at that meeting Bradman, the same as all the other administrators had to do in their states, explained to us the problem that was in cricket. And the administration wanted the help of all concerned to try and eradicate it. So that was the first time that I knew of it.

I'm listening to all this and here we are in '63, just finished the 1962–63 season, I've umpired nine Test matches, Lou Rowan has umpired two, Bill Smyth has umpired two from Victoria, the others had umpired one. So all of a sudden I realise, where are all the other guys? All the responsible blokes had retired, see. I think the time was getting a bit hot for them, they knew what was going on in 1961–62. So that was the start of the whole discussion.

And I made up my mind that okay, it's either the game of cricket or it's me. Where do I go in all this? It wasn't as if somebody had umpired 15 Test matches or as if somebody had even umpired six. There was a difference between nine and two, so where's the experience? To be quite honest with you, I thought to myself, oh well, here we go. I knew there were illegal bowlers around but like everyone else I left it to everybody else. Leave it to the administrators, leave it to somebody else. But those on the administration table are arguing amongst themselves, naming people – you got 'em in your state, you got 'em, you got 'em. Too hard, you see. So they said righto, let's go and tell the players and the umpires they've got to do something about it. Not the administrators. When I look back on it, that's been the story right through.

Anyway from there, the discussions took place about illegal bowlers, oh yes. There were rumours and stories around, and still are, it doesn't run away, that Bradman, Benaud and Egar were involved in this illegal bowling in relation to Ian Meckiff because it was in a Test match. Nobody said anything about the other five or six or seven I called in Sheffield Shield cricket. Nobody said anything about me being invited to South Africa to work on them over there as well. I got invited because I started calling them in grade cricket, in Shield cricket.

Now with Mecko, down here I was umpiring with a fellow name of Jack Keiss, a former state player. He wasn't much off Test cricket, he was much older than myself. Now he called Ian Meckiff for illegal bowling on this ground. Only on the one occasion. That night after it happened, Mecko and I went out and had a meal up in Rundle Street. People said why didn't I call him? He bowled from my end both innings. People just try to concoct the story that Bradman the administrator instructed us what we had to do. It's just absolute rubbish. But nevertheless, that's the way it pointed. I've heard people say, 'Oh well, when DG dies we'll probably hear about it.' I'm still waiting for people to get on the bandwagon. I don't know where Richie fits into all this because Richie and I have never ever discussed it in our lives. Not even discussed it the night after the incident. Because that night after it happened there was Richie Benaud, Ian Meckiff, Normie O'Neill, myself and Barry Gibbs, as soon as we came off the ground, we went out and had a few drinks and what have you. So if there was any nonsense going on anywhere, you wouldn't have had Benaud and I and Meckiff together anyway. Amazing things. But just let the public go and let them think – who cares.

But the fact was that Bradman was a very, very tough administrator in relation to illegal bowling. Very much so. In other words, if an umpire did something due to the fact that this is what the cricket board wanted to do, okay, that's no problem. Now the boot's on the other foot. I've been through it with the number of illegal bowlers I had to call – and I didn't call them all. I should have. What I used to do in Shield cricket and grade cricket was to go and talk to the captains and say, 'Now listen, it's going to happen. I've been watching him and if he keeps this up . . .' I mean, he could change his action. Very fortunately in those days, the captains used to say, 'Oh okay, let him finish his over and go.' Richie virtually did that at the Brisbane game. Today – oh, jeez, you call an illegal bowler, you've got all the players against you, you've got the administration against you. See, it's money, money, money.

When I started, you virtually had to pay to play. Now of course you get paid to play.

Former Test umpire and Queensland police officer **Lou Rowan** *describes himself as 'a non-entity who attended school at Ewingsdale, Byron Bay and Wilson's Creek, unheard of by almost everyone'. He cherished his friendship with Sir Donald which grew over a period of 40 years.*

THERE WAS SIMPLY nothing about the game of cricket Sir Donald didn't understand. He was completely at ease discussing rules and intricate points of law and he was always ready and willing to assist at all levels of the game.

He was also the only administrator in my time who made himself available under any circumstances to discuss matters of concern. He always did his utmost to make it easier for umpires in the administration of the laws of the game and I had a number of discussions with him. He never assumed any hint of superiority and he always listened intently to other points of view. And if a point of view put forward seemed flawed to him, he would carefully and courteously demonstrate where he disagreed and why.

I first met Sir Donald at the 'Gabba during the first Test of the 1962–63 series when I was the 'standby' umpire and he was so easy to sit and talk to over a cup of tea. During the 1963–64 series when Australia played South Africa, Colin Egar and I officiated at all five Tests and I met him on a number of occasions. Our friendship seemed to develop during that season. I was invited to his home in Adelaide for a delightful dinner, the first of a number of memorable visits to 2 Holden Street. We were already corresponding and this continued until it became impossible for him to maintain such contact. He had given me his unlisted phone number and I was able to keep in touch with him until only weeks before his passing.

Right to the end of his days, Sir Donald sought to have the administrators of cricket revert to the previous 'front-foot rule'. Colin Egar, Sheffield Shield umpire Bill Priem and I totally opposed the new rule which was introduced to curtail the drag of some fast bowlers. It always seemed to me that some cricket administrators believed they'd secured a victory over Sir Donald in defeating him on this point.

Sir George (Gubby) Allen was the el-supremo of England cricket for a time and he and Sir Donald were firm friends. At Sir Donald's invitation, Test umpire Tom Brooks and I met with these two to discuss the front-foot rule at a dinner during a Test at Sydney in the 1970–71 series. England was then a force in world cricket. It was a most enjoyable dinner but it was a waste of time as far as discussing the front-foot rule went because Gubby had made up his mind and had a non-negotiable stance on the issue.

Sir Donald was a meticulous man. But those of us who knew him had the advantage of knowing he was indeed a man apart. He had a delightful sense of humour, coupled with great humility. To sit and listen to him as he dealt with a variety of subjects and expressed his points of view was in itself an education.

I had the honour of dining with Sir Donald and Lady Jessie on many occasions, sometimes with my wife Isabel. On those occasions you saw the real man, fiercely determined to enjoy his privacy and obviously comfortable that his chosen friends would never betray the trust he placed in them. I'm sure he felt that in the past some had been less than honest with him despite all he did for them.

At the game between Australia and the Rest of the World at Adelaide at the end of the 1971–72 series, Sir Donald called at the umpires' room for a breezy 'good morning' and a wish of good luck, as he often did, and I told him of my decision to make that game my last. When I told him my decision was final, he simply said, 'Well I'm very sorry, but I can accept your decision.' He was generous to me in his public comments at the end of the match.

Colin Egar and I stood in 19 Tests together. We were opposites in many views but we did develop a great understanding. I had worked for many years as a detective and knew the value of team-work and I am not critical of others, but that partnership understanding was missing when Egar retired. Sir Donald understood the partnership we had developed.

Sir Donald took me to a Rotary lunch the day after my final game. To have such a great man stand and introduce me to the gathering is another cherished memory. Without the friendship extended to me by Sir Donald, much of my involvement in cricket would have meant so much less.

I joined Phil and Joan Ridings on occasions with the Bradmans on visits to Adelaide as years went by, dining with such people as the Bedser twins, Alec and Eric, and with Peter Burge. What great human beings.

Peter Burge, John McKnoulty and I took Sir Donald to dinner one night during the Centenary Test. It was a great night, and typical of him, Sir Donald phoned me at our motel at 7 a.m. next morning to thank me.

I believe I saw the true Bradman in the almost 40 years I knew him. I knew him as he handled some most difficult personal problems and I knew him in his roles as one of the greatest administrators sport has known.

He told me once he envied me in my lifestyle when, after retiring from the Police Force, I again became a banana grower and a small-crops farmer on a property on the Gold Coast hinterland called 'Stumps'. He said he always loved the country and would have remained there except that fate had decreed otherwise. We must remain grateful for that twist of fate.

Australia left-arm fast bowler **Ian Meckiff** *played 18 Test matches before he was controversially no-balled for throwing by umpire Colin Egar in the first Test against South Africa in 1963–64. When we spoke in Melbourne he looked back on that incident and recalled Sir Donald's generosity when he began his career with Victoria.*

I WAS PLAYING in a Sheffield Shield game in Melbourne in 1956, I was about 21 years of age and Sam Loxton who was then our captain, came to me and said, 'The little fellow wants to talk to you down in the dressing room.' He and Sam were great mates. So he took me down and we had a long conversation over what he thought I should do bowling-wise. He'd gone to a lot of trouble to work out the best way he could explain to me where I should pitch the ball so I could get the most benefit out of what I was doing. He'd worked it out on graphs. When I bowled, being left-handed, he said that's where you should be trying to pitch it, and he had a line which would more or less go where the ball should go. So I spent quite a bit of time with him. We must have been batting (laughs) so I had plenty of time seeing I was at the end. I think that pointed to me the sort of guy that he was. That everything he did was done spot on, that he went into great detail about doing it. A lot of other guys would take you out to the nets and say this is where you should be pitching it and how you should do it, where he actually had this graph drawn out. I thought that was something pretty special. I was very raw and to have Sir Donald doing that and knowing full well that he is Mr Cricket and all that sort of thing, it was fascinating that he had gone to that sort of trouble.

Did he see in you a potential Test bowler?

I suppose any 21 year old that was playing in Sheffield Shield cricket had to be a potential Test player. Plus the fact that they'd just come back from England and Keith Miller had retired, Pat Crawford had retired, Ray Lindwall would have been about 35 and Ron Archer had done his knee on the matting in Pakistan on the way back from England. So there weren't a lot of other players around.

What did you think of his advice?

It was spot on. It was logical. If you're bowling left-arm over the wicket to a right-hand batsman, you try to bowl at off stump, but I was very erratic. What he was trying to do was make me look at a focus point on the pitch which would roughly be a certain line or pick out a spot and that's where you had to bowl. By putting it in lines on a piece of paper, you could see exactly what he was trying to tell you to do.

I think his whole history of cricket and everything he did, he studied. Everything was done in a way where he wanted to make sure everything was spot on and that he knew everything about the game. He was a brilliant fieldsman, so it would be easy for him to teach fielding. But from a bowling point of view – well, he spent a lot of time out in the middle facing up to a lot of people, I suppose.

What was Sir Donald's relationship with the Australian team?

Most players sit down at the end of the day and you have a beer, whether it be with your opposition or just your own team players. And other selectors would come in and have a drink with you and have a chat with you but if he came into the dressing rooms he never had a beer with you. Quite often Bradman wouldn't so much come in after the game as during the game because I think he'd prefer to sit down with the captain. So he would sit down with Richie Benaud and they would sit slightly apart just chatting about what was going on. They would be working tactics and things like that out.

He wasn't really a mixing-type person, I think everybody knows that. He was very much a loner but he still did so many good things for so many people. As I said, he came to me right at the beginning of my career and said 'This is how you should do it.' And there's no doubt he did that with a lot of batting guys and a lot of bowling guys. I think he enjoyed being with the players and he could have a chat to them if he wanted to or if somebody wanted to chat to him. Maybe he preferred to be there rather than being with the establishment where you'd be pestered by every Tom, Dick and Harry. But he was never pushy, in any shape or form.

To what extent do you think he controlled Australian cricket?

I don't think he said to Benaud you've got to do this, you've got to do that. Richie was, I think, the best captain that we've had, in more ways than one – and that includes your current ones. He was very fortunate that he had a vice-captain in Neil Harvey who had most likely as good a cricket brain if not better than Benaud's, and the two of them combined were a great pair. Wally Grout was a great tactician as a wicketkeeper, Ken Mackay was a great tactician. I think that was one of the beauties of the Australian team, that they had so many guys that were very good tactical people. If Bradman had said, you've got to do it, I think Benaud would have argued.

What was Bradman's response to the tie in Brisbane, which was the conclusion of the 1961 Test against the West Indies?
I think he'd have most likely been delighted that I was run out because it changed the whole game. We've just had our reunion which was fantastic, a lot of fun, a lot of truths and untruths but who really cares (laughs), that really wasn't the point of it all. I made the comment that if I had got in, we wouldn't have been having the reunion. Which is very true. What it did, it really made the whole series and it really was a very exciting series of cricket, in more ways than one. There were some great performances.

Richie has made the comment that Bradman said he would only look at players that were attacking. I don't remember that coming out before but there is no doubt it was attacking cricket. Frank Worrell got most of the credit but if anything I believe that Richie was more responsible for it by taking it back to the West Indians rather than just letting it happen. There's no doubt that Bradman applauded that. He knew that cricket was at a bit of a crossroads and we'd played a Test match against England two years prior, 1958–59, and they scored 108 runs in a day. Remembering there were only five hours in a day (they used to play six-day Test matches in that series) they scored 108 in a day and they got 15 off one over from Jim Burke near the end of the day. So you can imagine, it really was dreadful cricket. When you start looking at that there's no doubt that Bradman said we can't afford to have another series like that, we've just got to play attractive cricket.

Your cricket career ended when you were no-balled for throwing by Colin Egar in the first Test match against South Africa in Brisbane in 1963. What can you tell me about the throwing controversy?
It goes over a long period of time and it's still going on. But nobody's game enough to do anything now because of the legal ramifications where you're taking away the livelihood of a player.

That's why they try and rectify it. Nobody ever really told me to change my action. Sir Donald was very heavily involved in it. He wasn't chairman of the Board, but he and Bill Dowling went to England in 1960 to put the Australian case against what was going on in England. Bradman went to the BBC and he looked at old footage of players going back to the 1930s. He had Larwood on film and he actually had it reversed and made Larwood bowl left-handed. This is the sort of man he was, he went through it all.

Sam Loxton told the story only recently that he actually said to Gubby Allen, 'Well, who's that bowling?' and Gubby Allen said, 'That's Meckiff or it's another one of your Australians.' And he said, 'Gubby, can you tell me who the batsman is at the other end?' and Gubby said, 'I don't care, that's Meckiff bowling, that's one of your mob.' And he said to Gubby, 'That's me, and I don't think it's Meckiff bowling.'

Did you have any contact with Sir Donald leading up to the incident?

He showed me the film he'd reversed when I went to dinner at his place with Len Maddocks, who was the captain of Victoria and the team manager, and basically it was identical to my action. But that was the only thing. He never really said anything about you've got to change your action otherwise you can't play or that sort of thing, no. Nobody ever did say that.

I know that Bill Dowling was a great supporter of mine. The Victorian selector Jack Ryder was a great supporter of mine and I'm sure that in their opinion they could not see anything that was wrong. Ryder saw me bowl often enough; he used to always be at the nets for practice.

There was a lot of talk about me changing my action, especially against the West Indians where I wasn't very successful and only played two Tests. But I actually had an Achilles tendon problem so I couldn't bowl at flat out and that's one of the reasons why I was dropped from the second Test match. And then I did my back in the third Test so that was more or less the end. That's one of the reasons why I didn't go to England in 1961, because I couldn't prove that I was fit, and that was the tour when they'd more or less made agreements that nobody would be called in the games building up to the Test match, the umpires would say if anyone had suspicious actions, and they wouldn't play in the Tests. So I missed that.

Bradman and I never really spoke about it after it all happened. I think it was a case that he didn't believe it, at the time anyway, otherwise he'd never have selected me, I'm sure of that. But when I was selected to play in my last Test match, there were members of the Board who complained and said I shouldn't be selected. But when Tests are in Australia the Board cannot have anything to do with the team selections on cricketing ability, only on personality or the behaviour of players. That was the reason why I was selected. Because I'd taken a lot of wickets, Alan Davidson had retired and there was no one else around that was any better than I was at the time.

Did you have any contact with Sir Donald after you were no-balled?
Yes, I actually asked for a meeting that night with him. I sat down for about an hour and had a conversation with him on the basis of not so much why, but just to more or less talk about it. There were a lot of things that I have never told anyone, and I won't tell them because he more or less said it's between you and me. There was nothing to do with the bowling side of it, it was more the personality side and what life's about and things like that. And I must admit that he was fantastic, he really was. He made me feel a lot better, he put me a little bit more at rest.

How did the incident affect you?

Cricket had been my life. Up to all this, I'd more or less set myself on going to England in 1964. I had left one job I'd been in for 11 years when they came to me and more or less said it's either your job or you play cricket. The ultimate to me was playing a Test match against England on the MCG, which I'd done, and then to tour England, because that's what you all think about. But to have that taken away and all of a sudden!

So this is why when I sat down with him and had this fantastic conversation about life and all that sort of thing, I came out of it feeling a lot better. I could have been a bit drunk at the time too, I can't remember that far. It hadn't really sunk in I suppose that I'd never be able to play again. It wasn't until a couple of days later that I was informed that I'd be able to play Shield cricket for Victoria in Melbourne only. I wouldn't be able to play interstate, because there'd be other umpires. Jack Ryder was very supportive of me and he was very upset about the whole thing. He did say, 'Look if you want to play for Victoria, that's fine. We won't pick you in the next one, you tell us what you want to do,' and that's when I decided I'd retire, it was just silly to stay. Because there really wasn't a future and as much as I loved playing cricket, I didn't want to have to go through being called by a district umpire or by some woody who'd get his name in the paper. That wasn't the way it was going to be.

Did you have further contact with Sir Donald?

Oh yes, I go to nearly every Test match in Adelaide and I always used to have a bit of a chat to him. He always had his own little seat which was at the back, right next to the aisle, where he could disappear quickly if he wanted to, I suppose. It was more or less the prime seat. And Lady Jessie of course was always at the cricket. She was just a charming lady. In Adelaide they have a ladies' room and a men's room and she used to always sit in the ladies' room. She used to look after all the wives. My wife got on very well with her. Everyone got on well with Lady Jessie.

But mostly Sir Donald would only go for a couple of days, he would never go for the five days of a Test. Lady Jessie was there every day. Whether he would have always gone one day or two days on his own bat I'm not sure, but I know (I was told) that Lady Jessie more or less said, 'Well, you are going today' on the days he did. He wanted to go and have a game of golf. She preferred watching the cricket.

I think he was a bit like most sportsmen, they prefer to do rather than to watch. He'd been so involved. And he loved his golf. Even though he used a cart in the end, he would prefer to be doing that than watching somebody play cricket.

Did you ever play golf with him?

I actually played with him one day with Sam Loxton. He was on a plus handicap at golf. I mean it is quite extraordinary, because I don't think he took it on until he retired. With cricket, everything was natural, but when he got to golf, everything was done by the book because that was the way he could teach himself to do it. I remember we had a very good game and I was playing against him and I think we were all square with two to go or something. Sam Loxton chiacked him a little bit and instead of hitting it straight down the middle as he had done all day, he duck-hooked it into the trees, we won the hole and that was more or less the end of the match. Because he was taught by the book, when a bit of pressure was put on him in golf, he faltered a little bit. Well, this is what I found. It would be one of the few sports it would ever happen to him because he was a great tennis player I believe, as well. But golf is very different because it's a stationary ball and I think even though he mastered it, I don't think he ever really mastered it.

Did you ever feel that you were a sacrificial lamb in the throwing incident?
Ah yeah, I think the longer it goes, and the more people talk to you. Little things come out every now and then and you've more or less got to say that yeah, I was. Yep. It was a set-up thing, but until someone turns around and tells me that it was, I'm still not going to say Richie Benaud set it up, or Bradman set it up or anyone. I think it will come out eventually. It may come out a lot sooner now that he has died. I'm pretty sure that it was a deal that was done with the English cricket board, with Gubby Allen, because of the tour coming up, and most of the so-called suspect action players like myself had retired. But I'm not going to say I was completely because I really don't know.

You don't seem bitter towards Sir Donald, even if he was involved.
No, life's too short. I got a lot out of cricket and I still get a lot out of cricket because I go to all the Test matches in Australia. It's part of my job here, we're involved in all the signage and the big video screens and things like that. So I still go and I still meet all the guys that I've been meeting for years. The reunion of the Tied Test was fantastic. So I don't have any really bitter feelings about it at all.

A lot of people say do you get bitter now when you look at the money they're earning, but it's all relative. It's completely different. I've enjoyed every bit. In fact, I think if you've played one Test match for Australia you should be very happy, and I was lucky enough to play 18.

Sir Donald Bradman played his last competitive game of cricket in 1963 when he captained Sir Robert Menzies' Prime Minister's XI against the English touring team at the Manuka Oval in Canberra.

*The young Liberal Member of Parliament **Don Chipp** found himself amidst the team of Australian greats.*

Sir Robert Menzies, while prime minister of Australia, developed a custom of having a Prime Minister's XI versus a visiting Test team, whether it be England, the West Indies or whoever. In 1963 I received a telegram from him saying, 'I'd be pleased if you'd play in my XI against Ted Dexter's visiting XI in February', I think it was. I was just a backbencher then and I'd only been one for 18 months. I couldn't believe my luck because cricket was a religion more than a game to me so to be given that opportunity of playing with the Prime Minister's XI against the Duke of Norfolk, who was the manager of the English team's XI, was almost beyond contemplation.

Menzies was very serious about his cricket. The year before, Lindsay Hassett captained the Menzies XI and in typical Hassett style, fooled around a bit and they had a bit to drink on the day. Menzies didn't appreciate mixing that behaviour with his lovely game of cricket and he asked this time that it be deadly serious, which it was.

The Australian team was Neil Harvey, Sam Loxton, Richie Benaud, Ray Flockton, Slasher Mackay, Rob Guest, Bob Cowper, Wally Grout, one Canberra player, a bloke called Don Chipp, and also a bloke called Don Bradman who came out of retirement to captain the team.

It was a brilliant day in Canberra. The ground was absolutely packed full, we had 12 000 people there. The English team was captained by Ted Dexter and had notables like Freddy Trueman, Brian Statham, Alec Bedser, Tom Graveney, the Reverend David Sheppard playing for it.

The night before we all participated in the famous dinner at the Lodge which Menzies traditionally put on. A good night was had by all. If Menzies hadn't been a famous politician he would have made a fortune being a cocktail mixer. His cocktails were quite lethal.

Bradman spoke on behalf of the Australian team and as usual he was laconic. His wit was acerbic I suppose you'd say. But very pleasant, very smart and very funny. It was a wonderful night. Almost one of those nights you dream about with the sort of notables that were there. Freddy Trueman distinguished himself by telling a couple of ribald stories, which Menzies seemed to adore.

When the day came, the Englishmen batted first. Bradman put me at deep extra cover which was right on the boundary and they had some good hitters in that team with Colin Cowdrey and a few others so I had to do a fair bit of fielding. I was fairly fit then. I remember Harold Holt who was treasurer then came to the match and he said, 'Chippy, you looked like everyone else,' which I suppose was a compliment. I don't remember the scores but it was fair dinkum, there was no funny business.

When we turned out to bat, Bradman said to me, 'Oh, young fellow' (I was only about 35 then), 'where do you normally bat?' I said about number four. He said, 'Right, you'll go in number five.'

I went in number five and Neil Harvey was number four and he was batting with me. Harvey went out and I looked at the scoreboard at the Manuka Oval and I still see it to this day. It had 'Present batsmen: Chipp, D. L. 4 not out, Incoming batsman: Bradman, D. G.' This was a big international headline that Bradman was going to bat and I was out there batting with him. It was unbelievable.

Now what's not generally known, there was a conspiracy afoot. The Brits had conspired that Bradman would make 50 runs. He didn't know about it, he was never in on the joke. He wouldn't have been in it if he had known. But every catch was to be dropped, lbw appeal was verboten, run-outs were unthinkable and so on.

Graveney bowled the first ball to Bradman which he made a full toss by dancing down the wicket and straight drove for four. Then it was my turn to face the other end and it was Brian Statham. I'd been used to facing quick bowling but Statham was bowling like lightening. I hardly saw the ball. To be honest I don't think I did see it and he was probably only bowling three-quarter pace. So I went through the motions of a straight drive and to my joy it was a beautiful straight drive through the covers for three. That left Bradman to face Statham. The first ball he faced was dutifully six inches outside of the off stump as had been arranged so Bradman could make 50. He shuffled across in true classic style, played a perfectly straight bat and then the ball did an extraordinary thing. It hit the bottom of the bat, trickled against the laws of gravity upwards on the bat and lodged in his pad. He shuffled his bum and the ball dropped out and then trickled inexorably towards the base of the off stump. No one could stop it. It hit the base of the off stump very slowly and dislodged the bail.

Bradman's action then reminded me of another time, when he went out for a duck to Bill Bowes in 1932. He just threw his head back and walked straight towards the pavilion. Alan Davidson, the former champion Australian cricketer, was umpire at the time at the bowler's end and I said to Davo, 'For heaven's sake Davo, call a no-ball.' But as with most of my bright ideas during my career, it was about 20 seconds too late. By which time Bradman was passing the square leg umpire on the way to the pavilion. It was a deep disappointment to the whole ground and to the Poms. They would have loved to have let him make 50. I don't know whether he knew about it at all. But that was the story. A wonderful day.

It was a wonderful experience. I can't even remember who won. I think the Prime Minister's XI won but it didn't really matter because of the spirit in which it was played. Sam Loxton of course was one of the great characters of the time and still is a great character. He was cracking jokes all the time and there was the odd bit of good-humoured sledging.

And what was your impression of Bradman?

He was a very quiet man in many respects. He wouldn't be a good fellow to have a drink with because he couldn't bear small talk. Not that he was a bore, on the contrary. Everything he ever said meant something, he always chose words carefully and used them well. He was perfectly relaxed with the boys on the field although you always felt, whether he aimed for this or not I don't know, he was a level above you. Well he was, in many respects. But what did Kipling say? He could walk with kings and keep his virtue and talk with crowds and not lose the common touch? I suppose that aptly describes Bradman.

He had the sort of wit that fitted beautifully into an after-dinner speech at an important occasion. He did Australia proud in that way because it's a pretty difficult audience, the cricket audience. They don't suffer fools gladly, particularly over in England when the Australians visit, because they still have a view that there's a colonial brush about the Australians. Don't trust them with the silver, sort of thing, though not quite that bad. And Bradman always filled that role of leader of Australia with incredible dignity and won so much respect.

We had a couple of chats about politics and little things in the dressing room during the match. He was quite interested in politics and politicians. Why I did it, what the life was like, what I hoped to get out of it, that sort of stuff. Incredible fellow. I was pretty much of a nonentity in that game, looking at all the cricketing greats there. A few heavyweights there. Richie Benaud, Alec Bedser, Neil Harvey, Wally Grout, a legend in himself. Throw in the Duke of Norfolk for good measure and the Prime Minister. I felt very unimportant, which of course I was.

*Former stockbroker and president of the South Australian Stock Exchange, **Jim Tummel** knew Sir Donald in a commercial capacity. The stockbroking company Don Bradman & Co. was a precursor to Pentilow, Tummel and Co. We spoke at his home in Adelaide.*

MY UNDERSTANDING IS that Sir Donald only ever wanted to be a sole proprietor in Don Bradman & Co. He believed the responsibility and the liability should be all his. But he did have Len Bullock who was a member of the exchange working for the company as a broker so it was ready-made when Don decided to get out of business in 1954. He just said to Len, do you want the business, because it's all yours. I think Len rushed and got some letterheads and some contra notes printed and the business became Len Bullock & Co. Len, who was quite well known as a broker, ran the business as a sole proprietor and later invited Bob Pentilow, who'd worked in the Commonwealth Bank, into partnership with him. Not long after that in 1964 Len took his son back to Geelong Grammar and was killed in a car accident returning to Adelaide. I was in the Commonwealth Bank at that stage and Bob Pentilow rang me that night and said Len had been killed. He asked me if I was interested in coming into sharebroking.

Before I left the bank, Bob Pentilow took me to lunch with Don Bradman. Bob wanted Don to tell me about the sharebroking industry. I always remember one thing he said to me that day. He said if somebody asks you a question and you don't know the answer, never guess it. Because if you do that, you'll be out of business before you know it. Tell them you'll find out, then do the research and let them know.

I joined and bought the seat on the stock exchange from the estate of Len Bullock and we formed Pentilow, Tummel and Co. I remember the very day I started in sharebroking, he walked in and said, 'Lad, I want you to sell some shares for me.' And it was a line of shares in a company called Farmout Drillers. I said, 'Could you spell that?' And he said, 'Don't you know?' (laughs) So he put me to the test. He was a great one to put you to the test.

Don was an enormous help to Bob after Len's death in terms of advice on shares and portfolios. In those years Bob would put a portfolio together, and need to write his comment and he'd always give Don his draft copy and Don would have a look at it, and say, 'Bob, I think you could add this' or 'I don't think you're quite right there'. So he helped to vet things. But it was all done without reward, freely and voluntarily; he never had any financial or direct interest in the company.

His son John was our trading floor operator for a short period and it was from our office that John one day decided he was going to do law in the university. I always remember him saying to me, 'People will not be able to say that my father was a better solicitor than I am. They've been telling me that my father was a much better cricketer, much better sharebroker.' People would come to the office and say, 'John, if you are ten per cent as good a sharebroker as your father, you'll be all right by us.' I think John could have been very successful if he had decided to use his father's good reputation for himself but he decided the better choice was to do something that John Bradman should do, not to ride along on the name of Bradman.

We always provided Don with an office within our office and he used that as his headquarters. He was on the boards of a number of Adelaide-based companies: Kelvinator, Clarksons which was the old glass company, he was the chairman of Rigby the book people, and he was on the boards of the investment companies, Argo, Bounty, Wakefield. He was on SA Rubber, which became Uniroyal and now it's Bridgestone. He was also on the South Australian Board of Advice of the City Mutual and Mutual Acceptance (City Mutual being an assurance company and Mutual Acceptance being a finance company). So he had the office to enable him to pursue those commercial activities and he would come almost every day, unless he was away with the cricket or the Board of Control. He would always call into our office because it was just down the passage and if Bob had five or six queries, Don would sit down and talk to him and give him advice.

Was it an advantage to you that Sir Donald maintained an interest in the company?

Oh yes, I think very much so. Firstly he was a great studier. He read all the reports that he would get. Argo Investments used to get circulars from all the broking houses in Australia and as a director Don used to take those home and read them from cover to cover. And he had a jolly good memory of course, so that he really did understand companies and he knew their profit history and he knew who the directors were. He was very helpful. But he did it because he had a great interest in the broking business having been one, and an interest in the performance of companies.

It was a reciprocal arrangement. I mean the fact that we provided him with an office, we'd keep telephone messages, we'd collect his mail from the GPO and if he wanted some secretarial work done, there was always one of the girls to help him with that. I remember one speech he wrote and we had it typed in our office for him. And retyped and retyped. Because he was so meticulous in getting it right. He was probably Australia's greatest authority on all the cricket history but he always had to be very accurate.

His mind and his brain when it came to figures and retaining information were terrific. We were back in the pounds, shillings and pence days and if you bought 400 shares at £2.13.4, he knew automatically what that was. And with a foolscap page of figures – pounds, shillings and pence – he'd run his finger up and down and he'd have the total at the bottom within 30 seconds. I'd never seen anybody do that. I think John Bradman was very good at that also.

Don was a very meticulous person in relation to his directorships. Other brokers believed that we got some advantage because of these. That was not true; we didn't at all. Never at any stage. He was a director of Kelvinator and if Kelvinator made some decision on a share placement or a share issue, he was very careful never to tell us any more than anybody else knew. People also believe that we got quite a lot of share business because of his directorships on Argo and Bounty and Wakefield but he was once again very careful not to put his favours in other directions. He was a very fair person. He was a very ethical man.

Were there advantages just in him being Don Bradman in having him around?

Oh yes, I guess to the extent that a number of people that were clients of Don Bradman & Co. and then became clients of Len Bullock were very happy to stay with Pentilow, Tummel and Co. We were Johnny-come-latelys at that stage, because Bob and I had both come out of the Commonwealth Bank. John Parsons joined us subsequently and he was also from the Commonwealth, so we almost put an elephant above the door, Get with the Strength. But a lot of the clients felt relaxed because often they'd be in our waiting room and Don would step out of the lift to go to his little office. (laughs) But once again, we didn't use that connection. We didn't go out and advertise or boast about it because he wouldn't have wanted us to do that. We wouldn't have ever suggested to him that in our letterheads we put Pentilow, Tummel, successor to Don Bradman & Co. We would never have suggested that because it would have offended him to have said no.

Did his name help him?

When he was in business as a sharebroker he had a very busy business simply because his name was Don Bradman. People wanted to do business with him. Often Don would ring Jessie at half past six and say, 'We'll be there in half an hour, have the meal ready,' and he'd take his staff out and they'd have a meal, then back to the office again. So he did work long hours.

When did he give up the office?

We moved several times [the company merged and was sold], and he came with us. But when he eventually decided he would give up his city office, he would have been at least 80 years of age. By then he didn't have any boards left, so there was no need. But once he had given up the office, he usually came into our office one day a week for that hour or two, because we had a little anteroom and people used to leave cricket bats and Bradman books. He used to come in and autograph those, and then he used to go down to the Adelaide Oval of course and autograph things down there.

Was signing a huge part of his life throughout the time you knew him?

Yes, it was. People used to ring from interstate and say if they sent a book over, would he autograph it, and with some of them it was for commercial reasons and he would say, 'Yes, but you'll need to make a donation of $200 to the spastic centre.' And he raised a lot of money for the spastic centre through that, because as you know his daughter Shirley had cerebral palsy. There were a lot of things like that he did, which people didn't ever know about. But he never wanted people to mention them, he just did them.

When he and Jessie went overseas, I think it was probably the last trip he made to England and that would have been 20 years ago I guess, he said would I mind looking after his mail for him.

I used to call into his home in Holden Street to collect the mail, and bearing in mind in his heyday he had a four gallon round drum to house his mail, even 20 years ago there was a lot of mail each day, particularly from India. I used to take all this to his office and if it was about cricket, I'd do a brief acknowledgment and say Sir Donald was overseas and that he would attend to it on his return. I used to sort out the dividends, write those up in the cashbook and deposit them and if any bills came in, I paid the bills. When he came back, he went through it all, and he said, 'Thank you, I've balanced all of that. Thank you, you've done a very good job. I appreciate that. But,' he said, 'there's only one thing you didn't do.' I said, 'What was that?' He said, 'You didn't lodge a claim with the health fund for the medical bill you paid for Shirley, my daughter.' It was inevitable that he was always going find one thing that he felt he should just pick me up on.

Why was that?
Firstly he was meticulous on things that have to be done. But also he never wanted to give one person 100 per cent. You'd never get a hundred out of a hundred. You might get 99 out of a hundred, but not a hundred, (laughs) and I think that was just part of the system.

So was he a demanding man?
He was a person that if there was a job to be done, he didn't want excuses for not doing it. He was demanding to that extent. I suppose it was related to him being so meticulous in everything he wanted to do and to achieve.

But he did have concern for other people. Broking had a number of years of fairly tough times, times of credit squeeze. Don and Jessie did their business with us, of course, and I'm quite sure that there were times when he was so concerned about the level of business, he used to ring and either sell some shares or buy some shares when he didn't really have to do it. He would never have admitted to that, but when he would ring and sell some shares in Argo Investments, a company he had such a long association with, and then perhaps buy them back a month later, it always seems to me that he was concerned for Bob Pentilow and me because business was tough. I think he just wanted to help us along. He would want to help other people but he didn't want it blown up in lights.

Did he have empathy for others?

Oh yes, and there are things which Don Bradman did that nobody ever would have known or acknowledged. For instance, when he was away overseas and I was collecting his mail, a letter came in from a country town to thank him. What had transpired was this person had written to him to say that he had a son of 13 or 14 who was mad on cricket, who wouldn't study. He was letting himself down at school because he was so preoccupied and he had wondered whether Don might be able to write to the boy to help him get it into perspective.

But what Don did, he nominated a day at a Sheffield Shield game at the Adelaide Oval and said, 'Send him down, he can sit with me in the stand for that day and we will watch the cricket together and I'll talk to him.' The letter that I received when he was away was to thank him and say that his lad was now balancing his cricket against his study. So some people said he may have been selfish in promoting things that were for Don Bradman, but I don't agree with that at all.

Was he a busy man?

Yes, but he was a pretty good organiser of his time. He was on those boards, he was very strongly involved with cricket, he had his love for golf at that stage, of course, and he spent time when he could with his daughter, Shirley. Because while Shirley lived away from Holden Street, she invariably went there most days, this is particularly when Jessie was alive and Don spent a great deal of time being concerned about the welfare of his daughter and also establishing her own financial independence.

Did the sharebroker Harry Hodgetts' arrest for fraud in 1945 affect Sir Donald?

Some sharebrokers used it as an excuse to denigrate him and I believe some of those stories were more manufactured than real. It was a form of jealousy among the brokers. My understanding was that he was brought from Sydney, he worked for Harry, he was never a partner, he never had any authority in running the business. A number of people would say that yes, he did know that Harry Hodgetts was getting himself into trouble, but Harry Hodgetts got into trouble and Don started his own business. I think he had no responsibility for the Hodgetts business because he was not a partner.

Did it hurt him?

Don didn't ever talk to me about it because it happened before I really knew him. I would never have asked him, because I think it was past history for him. When I was on the stock exchange committee for a number of years, there were one or two brokers that couldn't help but have a dig at Don Bradman, but I think that was a professional jealousy. That's what I always believed, anyway.

Did it mean he wasn't asked to join the Adelaide Club?

I'm not sure, but I think he was invited to join and then was told that he shouldn't proceed because there was a number of people who were going to oppose his membership. So I think once he turned his back on that, he just got on with life. I don't think that it really worried him, because he was not a great clubman at any event, not a social clubman. Don was self-made in everything he did.

What was his contribution as a board member?

Most people, his fellow directors, would all agree that he was a great contributor because he studied the reports. He would never ever accept a position on the board of a company unless it was a full bottle, unless he understood what he was going for. He would never have sat on a board just to lend his name to it and when he was on a board he wanted that company to be successful.

He was on the Faulding board for many years. When I was chairman of the Adelaide Exchange, the phone rang one Sunday morning and it was Don. He said, 'Can you come over home? I've got some of the directors of Fauldings here, we want to talk to you.' I said, 'I'm just finishing a set of tennis.' He said, 'You can do that anytime, could you come over here please?' (laughs) So I went over and at that stage Fauldings were under a takeover from Nicholas Kiwi and he'd arranged an informal board meeting, a gathering at his place, and they wanted to talk to me. They talked to me about a placement of shares, which was quite legitimate. And of course the chairman of Nicholas Kiwi accused me of getting on the side of Don Bradman and the directors of Faulding.

So he was a key player.

Yes he was, absolutely.

Was Sir Donald extravagant in anyway?

(laughs) No, he was not extravagant. He never went out and bought expensive motor cars, he bought Mitsubishi cars, I think he had a Magna, but he had the normal Australian-produced vehicles. He didn't ever want to own a beach house or a holiday house.

Was he conservative?

He had a conservative view. It was no good talking to him about mining companies. He wasn't very interested in the speculative companies. He was conservative in his view on tipping in relation to investments because he hated to see people lose their money, so conservatism was also on the side of safety. He always lived in the one house, he never had a second house, and he was not one that threw the dollars up in the air but then he didn't expect people to throw the dollars at him either.

Was his health a problem?

If he came into the office and say you'd broken your wrist and had it in plaster, but he'd been pruning the roses and he'd got a thorn, he'd say, 'What's the matter with you, lad? You break your arm or something? Have a look at this finger.' He would bypass your problem and exaggerate his. He was a little bit of a sook, I reckon, (laughs) when it came to his own little injuries or health.

Was he also a lover of good food and wine?

I think you will find that in the eyes of the public, if he was at a function, as say the guest speaker, they used to put orange juice out for him. That wasn't meant to be deceptive, that meant that he always maintained his faculties. But in his own home yes, he did enjoy good red wines. In fact, he had an investment company he set up quite some years ago for the benefit of his two children John and Shirley, and I was a director of that company because he needed a second director. Each year for my director's fees, he would ring Penfolds and say, 'Would you deliver Jim Tummel a dozen St Henri?' And he was quite friendly with Max Schubert who was the then-maker of Grange Hermitage so that yes, he had some good wines in his home and did enjoy them but never – not that I used to go there for dinner every day – ever to excess. He always kept control.

When I used to call in if he had rung me to say would I drop a prospectus in on the way home, he'd say, 'Oh you'd better come in and have a drink.' He had the three crystal decanters for the brandy, whisky and gin with the little silver tags around them, it was probably a presentation he would have received somewhere along the line, and he'd say, 'Well I'm going to have a sherry, would you want a whisky?' And Jessie came in one day and said, 'Don, you're such a mean pourer.' She'd get the decanter and say, 'Give Jim a decent one.' (laughs) So he always said, 'We'll have a drink,' but it was always a moderate drink.

I must say that apart from having been invited to a few meals at the Bradmans, I'd call in there to drop something off, so it was mostly a business association, although I think I was regarded as a friend to the extent that I could call in home. But I didn't call in there every week or every fortnight.

I must also say he had a great sense of humour. He could always tell a good story or a good joke. In the eyes of the public he controlled the things he did; he was always very disciplined. But if you had him in his own home, he loved to tell a joke and then he'd rock back on the two back legs of the chair and he'd roar with laughter with you.

Did he achieve a certain anonymity in the business world?
The name Bradman was almost a magical name, wasn't it? But I think as far as I could observe, he didn't want the companies of which he was a director to use his name, he was a director along with everybody else, it was all on equal terms. He didn't ever want anybody to take advantage of that good name commercially. He used to come into the office and everyone on the staff really did like him. He was friendly, he was never aloof and I don't think he ever saw himself being set aside as a more important person than anybody else.

Bob Parish served on the Australian Cricket Board with Sir Donald for 30 years, having joined as a representative of Victoria in 1950 while it was still the Board of Control for International Cricket, and together they weathered a number of international controversies. Parish didn't mince words. 'I would like to say I support him 100 per cent,' he said when we met at the Melbourne headquarters of the ACB.

THE FIRST TIME I really got to know him was in 1965 when I applied for the position as manager of the Australian team to the West Indies. I was elected by the Board and I was a member of the Board so I could vote for myself in substance. (laughs) Very useful. After the meeting he asked if I wanted some advice and not being a complete fool I quickly said yes. And the only advice he gave me was six words: 'Don't lose your sense of humour'. And that is the best advice ever given to a cricket administrator. Don't lose your sense of humour because it's awfully easy to lose. (laughs) And I did lose it a few times (laughs) but I kept my cool the majority of times. And that was the beginning.

Did he have a sense of humour himself?
He had a very good dry sense of humour because we had some pretty rough times. He could find the humour in anything really.

How often did the Board meet?
When Bradman was a member of the Board, the big meeting was the annual meeting in September at which office bearers and the selectors and everybody were chosen. Other than that, we'd meet probably only twice. In those days it was called the Board of Control for International Cricket, it was not until 1973 that it became the Australian Cricket Board. That's when it moved down here to Melbourne. But the Board meeting would last sometimes two days, sometimes a day. It would cover everything that happened

but it was purely cricket. We were not a promotional board. It was a much easier job than it is today. Don had two three-year terms as chairman.

Was he involved with you during the World Series cricket furore?
I was chairman of the Board during the World Series Cricket period and thank God he was on the Board and part of the emergency committee that handled the whole thing. My emergency committee comprised Don from South Australia and Tim Caldwell from New South Wales. You got an immediate reply from Don if you put something up to him. He saw what was going to happen much better than anybody did, he had foresight in these sort of things, and he gave me one hundred per cent support. He insisted that I should carry on past the three years and I had a five-year term during that. (To let me go on we had to move an amendment to the constitution clause year-by-year.) Don believed I should have continuance. I appreciated his confidence and as it turned out it worked out. That three-year restriction has since been taken out.

When we did reach the stage of looking at a compromise, Mr Packer went across to Adelaide and spent about an hour with Don. When he came back I saw him and he had a definite view that the Australian Cricket Board should control the game, provided he could get an agreement in regard to television. And not only television, he also got an agreement through PBL to promote the game, and that's when the game changed.

Don supported that. He believed it would be much better for cricket and he was right, as usual. When we drew up the basic peace treaty, as they called it, the contract between PBL and the Australian Cricket Board, I took the draft over to him and when he came to things like coloured clothing he just turned the page. I said, 'You've got no worries about coloured clothing?' And that's when he said that wonderful remark: 'Why should I? The pinks played the blues in Sydney in 1892.' Whether you went out on the field in a white uniform or coloured didn't mean a thing to him. His thought always was for the benefit and the welfare of the game of cricket. And white balls. We had a great deal of bother with England to get them to accept white balls and coloured clothing. Strangely enough they didn't like one-day games and yet I firmly believe that the one-day game was the saviour of the game of cricket.

Don always said that we've got to live with the times and in his opinion the young of that era wanted immediate results. They didn't want a five-day drawn-out match. And also, as he often reminded me, we were no longer an Anglo-Saxon country. In 1945–46, there were roughly six million, that's all there were, and 95 per cent of those were Anglo-Saxon, all raised in the game of cricket. You look today, what have we got? Nineteen million, of which at least 40 per cent were born in different countries or raised in different cultures and not brought up in the game of cricket. They wanted immediate results and this is what the one-day game gave them. It also gave them razzamatazz and clash but you've got to put up with that. And you've got to live in the year 2001 and not back in the year when cricket really started, which is back in the early 1600s. There are very few people that are not hidebound to the past in some way, but Don was not. He may have been 92 when he died but he had a young brain. He lived on that day and that's the way he thought.

Did you ever see him angry during the Packer negotiations?
No, not particularly. We discussed everything as a trio, Don, Tim Caldwell and myself, and we went into every meeting that we had to go to. But there weren't too many, because it was pretty quick. I don't think that I ever saw him lose his cool.

As far as the game of cricket was concerned, he knew more

than the rest of us put together, not only the ability to play it but he knew the laws, he knew the rules.

He worked hard on everything, he didn't go into anything not prepared. That's the sort of man he was. We asked him to propose the toast to cricket for the Centenary Test match in Melbourne and I've never heard a more brilliant speech. He traced the history of cricket and he had the background of every one of the Test players, all 250 of them, that were in the room and he knew them back to front, upside down. You couldn't fuss him in any way whatsoever, because his homework was immaculate.

Did you always agree?

He listened to what you had to say, and he came up with an opinion, but he was not always right. Jessie said that he and I fought like a pair of cats. But we respected each other and the result is that he listened to what I had to say and I listened to what he had to say. But our differences were basically on laws and rules of the game. I couldn't make him see quickly that he had to listen to what other countries were saying. This was particularly over the front-foot law.

Don has always maintained that the front-foot decision was wrong. What made him change his mind was that every country in the world started to support the front-foot rule and Don, I think being a very able administrator, saw it was a waste of time and so he supported it then. One of the things that convinced Don that he had to change was sitting in the stands at the Adelaide Oval watching a bowler run up to bowl. We were right opposite to the creases, their members' stand is side on and you could see them perfectly. And we watched this fellow land, slide and before the front foot hit the ground, his front foot was way over the popping crease. If you slide, you're going to hold on to the ball, and that's where the danger of throwing the ball comes in. And Freddie Brown, manager of the England team, went around the schools, and he told us that players in the schools were practising sliding. So he changed and he supported the front-foot law, again showing that he was amenable to reason and had sense. I could understand him. I think if there was an alternative . . . But the moment way back in the past they allowed overarm bowling, this problem of being able to watch the foot and the arm together grew into the game.

Did you have a relationship outside the Board?
I used to go over to Adelaide once a month, nothing to do with cricket, and in those days I knew Jessie well, I knew the children. There's been a wonderful friendship. I won't have a bad word said about him.

We had the first of the Bradman Orations at the Australian Club last year. John came over to read the piece that Don had written. Don wouldn't come. I tried to get him to come, then I tried to get him to agree to record on tape. We'd send over cameramen and the rest of it and we'd record it on tape. He said no, he wouldn't do it. Then I asked him would you write something? He turned England down on that but fortunately, I think I was a good friend. He agreed to do that so he wrote it and John agreed to come over and read it. He read it beautifully, he's a very nice young man. It was a wonderful evening at the Australian Club, all televised back to Don.

*The State Library of South Australia's collection of Bradman papers and memorabilia is available in the Mortlock Library. The donation of the material was negotiated by Sir Donald's Rotary colleague, the state librarian **Hedley Brideson**, who was in his 92nd year when I spoke to him in Adelaide.*

BRADMAN WAS A fine gentlemen in every way and I well remember the first time he spoke to me. I'd been speaker at a Rotary Club luncheon and it would be two weeks later, I was walking Gawler Place, going back to North Terrace to my office. The place was crowded. Suddenly there was a chap on my arm and he went, 'Hello Mr Brideson'. I thought crikey, I think that's Bradman. It's true of course that I was up on the podium speaking and he was one of about 140 people there but it surprised me that his memory was so good. I was doing some night lecturing at the Institute of Technology and I used to tell them that people like to have their names remembered. A couple of weeks later, I wanted to buy some shares and I rang Don Bradman. Not that I was big in shares, but I used to dabble and he'd give me a hand.

I didn't become a member of Rotary for another few years but once I did he was one of the first to come up and welcome me into the club. We shook hands and he said, 'I'm glad to see you've come in with us.' We were supposed to mix a lot but I think Don did a bit of wangling and we often used to sit together after that. We spoke on general things, not necessarily cricket. We'd discuss things of the day. He would generally be interested in whatever was happening in the city, as I was.

He was proud of what he did in cricket. At lunch we'd talk about cricket and I said, 'Oh I watched you make 199 not out against South Africa on the Adelaide Oval.' '299,' he said. (laughs) Probably joking, I don't know, but he wanted me to know. I said, 'Well I sat out in the outer and watched you play.' That was before I became a member and sat in the members' stand.

Were you involved in the donation of Sir Donald's material to the State Library?

I was the one who got it for the State Library. We used to sit at lunch and often I'd come around to Don, 'What's happening to all your papers? You must have an enormous amount of interesting stuff.' 'Oh,' he'd say, 'Mum looks after that.' His mother looked after cuttings and so on.

I said, 'Look, someday you're going to pass on and all of a sudden somebody will say "What's this bloody rubbish?" and throw it out.' I'd seen it happen. 'Oh,' he said, 'it's only cricket.' And finally one day he said about it being just cricket, I said, 'But Don, you are cricket.' And that apparently struck him. He looked at me and for quite a time he never said anything. Then he said, 'All right, you can have it. When do we start?' As quick as that.

I said, 'Tomorrow, the next day, whenever you're ready.' One of my board members used to drive me out to the luncheon at the Australia Hotel, in North Adelaide, and coming back he must have wondered what was wrong with me because I didn't say anything. I was thinking who the hell am I going to put onto all this Bradman stuff?

When I got back I sent for Jill Wallis. She was one of my secretaries. This is not boasting but I had a secretary and in the outer office there were two more girls to do extra typing and Jill was one of them. I reckoned she'd be right and I called her in and told her. I think she was scared stiff. She knew nothing about cricket and she was scared of Sir Donald Bradman. I said, 'Oh, you'll find you make him feel at ease.' I think it was the next day he came down with a suitcase, and I called her and introduced them and she took him to the side room and there they went off. I think he appreciated Jill. I gave Don my car park (I didn't drive) right at the back door of the library and he used to come around there and up in through the back door and up to Jill's room one or two days every week. After five years, 52 volumes were ready.

Earlier in the library there had been a little bit of casting out of some material of value by one chap. I didn't agree with what he was doing, but I suppose every library does it at times. I told Don, we'll fix that. We'll store it in such a way that nobody would dream of throwing anything away, it will be bound in leather. It's 52 volumes bound in leather.

Were you surprised at the amount of material?
No, I can't say I was surprised, I was delighted. I thought he would have a lot. After all, he was the head of cricket here for a long time. People from all over the world would be writing to him on cricket.

And are the books, **The Bradman Albums,** *from the collection?*
Yes, that was all from there, there were two volumes, done by Rigby. You see Don was a director of Rigby.

Did you consider Sir Donald a friend?
Oh yes. He was approachable. I could ask him anything. When I was ill in hospital Don came to see me. He said, 'Before I came, I got in touch with the Adelaide Oval. Only one more needs to drop out,' he said, 'and you're a member.' I thought what a kindly thing to do, he was a busy man. He was very, very nice, put his arm around my shoulder and said, 'Come on, buck up.' He'd been ill a couple of times, he told me. 'I touched the bottom of the bucket a couple of times,' he said and Jessie, his wife, had kept the broking firm going.

He played the cards pretty close to his chest. It was Don Bradman and Jessie, they were very close. Jessie was a very nice and very fine woman. Not that he said very much, but the little he did say, you could see he thought the world of Jessie.

Was he accepted by the establishment of Adelaide?
I don't think he was. Don wasn't a member of the Adelaide Club. The Adelaide Club was *the* establishment. I don't know whether he was ever approached to join, I don't think he was. I think there were too many in the Adelaide Club who remembered the sharebroking

business at the beginning and therefore they didn't want him, but I'm guessing.

Was Adelaide shaken in 1945 when Don Bradman's employer, the stockbroker Harry Hodgetts, was declared bankrupt and convicted of fraud?

Terribly. I didn't know Hodgetts but he was a society sharebroker. The governor and all those people, all dealt with Harry Hodgetts. And Harry was one of their mainstays in cricket, one of the top boys. What he did I suppose probably didn't seem to him to be terribly bad but he used people's scrip which had been left in his office to cover his own borrowings with the bank. That's where he went wrong. What was worse, I believe, the governor lost a lot of money over it, and I believe some charitable organisations lost money also.

How did the affair affect Don Bradman?

He became the sharebroker, nothing happened. I was going home one night, it was 6 o'clock and Hodgetts was the name on the sharebrokers. At 9 o'clock the next morning I came back the other way to the office and Don Bradman & Co. was up. He worked very fast. Harry Hodgetts was a sort of second father to him, he brought him over from Sydney. It must have hurt Don. I don't think he was implicated but there would be people who would say snide things to him, I'm sure. They said it to me: 'Oh Bradman knew what was going on, he was up to his neck.'

Adelaide is a small place.

Yep. You know everybody. Everybody who matters knows who matters, as they say. (laughs) There wasn't even a million people yet in Adelaide back in the days when Bradman started as a sharebroker. And the number of people who would be dealing in shares was very small.

Joan Ridings met Sir Donald fleetingly pre-war when she was 19, before she was married. 'I was interested in cricket then,' she said, 'but it was never to the proportion it got to through life.' Her husband Phil Ridings, a postwar captain of South Australia, went on to become a state and national selector, chairman of Australian selectors, SACA president, delegate to the Australian Cricket Board for 21 years and chairman of the ACB from 1980 to 1984. He died in 1998.

ACTUALLY MY HUSBAND captained South Australia when Don was playing still. Don stepped down and Phil took over but he was still in the team. But it was only for one game.

Did your husband Phil's career follow Don's?
It followed in his footsteps really. And we became involved socially. We became very compatible over a long period when he was president of the South Australian Cricket Association and Phil was vice-president under him. But socially Jessie and I would do things without the men, we'd meet socially, she and I.

What drew you to the Bradmans as people?
We just kind of gelled. It was just a lovely combining of four people, socially as well as cricket, because the Bradmans were great friends of my neighbours over the road and they met socially a lot, these people. And then there was bowling, and she and I played bowls together over the road, and then it's just been, just like topsy really. To begin with it was because I was a young person that just became involved.

Is that one of the good sides of cricket?
It is. Still is. The number of people that ring me still that were friends of Phil, players with Phil and they ring to see how I am and things like that, which is lovely.

Did Sir Donald's fame affect his life?

The hero worship has only gathered in the last 10 or 15 years. I'm saying worship because it's got bigger as he's got older. Because he was in business like my husband was in business, he had to go to work. They played cricket and worked in those days, whereas now it's more just cricket. It was a different life completely.

It did affect his life. And of course more so since she went. She would have shielded him a lot from the intrusion of people. And people did intrude.

It seems to have been an extraordinary marriage.

Wonderful really. People lived a different life from what they do nowadays. It was the same with us, you know what I mean? It was 55 years for us and it was just gone so quickly.

Were they a contrasting couple?

They were in a way. She was full of compassion in every way, she was just a wonderful person because it was a hard time for her, a terribly hard time for her, because she had a young family and of course one child was spastic that she had to cope with. It was tough.

So people intruded more as he got older?

Oh, they'd go to the home, knocking on the door, which is wrong. It's just not on. Especially people coming from overseas. It wouldn't be people he'd know. I'm picking out Indians for one, they'd go knocking on the door. Because they just idolise Bradman over there, they really do. More so than England, than anywhere. They were just fanatical about him.

So fame did get in the way?

It did. It intruded terribly, but even when he first played cricket, people would be on the station waiting for him to go through on the train, just to see him. I'm talking about my husband's experience of being in the same team as him before the war. Phil was only a junior player in those days and people in these country towns would be on the platform waiting to see if they could see him go past. Fancy going to the station to watch someone go through. Although I did as a little child when the Duke and Duchess of York visited – I can see myself now and there she is, going to be 101 next week. (laughs)

But I think in their later years it became more intrusive than ever. But he would be protected. Even when we'd go to the Oval for an ordinary proper cricket match, Phil and the committee would protect him from people, wanting to get autographs mainly.

You'd be also very protective of him by whom you had at your table when you invited them for lunch too, because people can be very pushy and demand his attention. I thought it was cruel. I don't think people should be put through that.

Your husband became chairman of the Australian Cricket Board in 1980.

When Don was chairman, the board meetings were always in Sydney because that's where the head office was in those days. Then when Phil took over they moved to Melbourne and he had to set it all up afresh, because they had new staff and that, you know.

Was your husband very involved during the World Series Cricket business?

It was a difficult time. It broke up a lot of friendships. They went their own way and that was it. Don was at the tail-end of his time and he was there at the very beginning of it. He and Packer got together at some stage. I'm not privy to that at all but I'm pretty sure that it happened. But it was after that that Phil was involved.

When Sir Donald retired, did he remain interested?
Oh gosh, yes. What did you do that for? What are you doing this for?

Did cricket play a positive role in your lives?
Oh, definitely.

Are there any particular times with the Bradmans that you remember?
Our luncheons. We used to mainly have Sunday luncheons so they took all the afternoon. They were always so good. It was as though at least the day was never wasted, that you had perhaps learnt something, or me anyhow, listening. Both of them always had something to offer.

An average Sunday lunch would end when?
Do I have to tell you? (laughs) Late. They went home for tea, yes, but they could have stayed.

That happened I suppose three or four times a year. I'd make a decision, oh, it's time we had them for lunch. That's how it went. It was the same with them. If they had any English visitors, they'd ask us to join them to help things along.

Did Sir Donald have an enthusiasm for good food and good wine?
Oh yes, he acquired that over the years actually because he was a person who didn't drink. He learnt. Because Jessie did. As a person he was very knowledgeable about his wine, and his food, but that came later. At restaurants he would know what he wanted in the wine department and order accordingly, especially if he was host. But at one another's homes he and my husband would try to outdo one another. We mainly did our entertaining in our own homes. It was only later for them that we stopped and went to restaurants, so she didn't have to cope with it.

Who won in the wine stakes?

Well, I think it was a bit even Stephens. I wouldn't like to say. (laughs)

Were you aware of Sir Donald's love of music?

Oh yes, I knew about that and I heard him play the piano at home. Just as in, 'Yeah, all right, I will, but that's all', sort of thing. It was just part of our togetherness that it happened. But he didn't play very often. We never got around to music playing when they came to dinner, the conversation was too intense.

Was the conversation cricket based?

Yes and no. Because Sir Donald was in finance really, like in the share market, and my husband was in finance too you see, so we had a pretty broad range of subjects actually.

They had different views on finance?

Oh yes, they did on cricket too. It was all fun in the end. (laughs) We didn't agree, that's all.

Did they discuss, or lay down the law?

I'd sit and listen and it was a bit of both, but a lot of fun too.

Did you ever see Sir Donald angry?

No, not in my presence. I wouldn't say that.

Did your husband get angry with Sir Donald?

Not in front of him. He might have said something afterwards. (laughs) Not really, no. They had a friendly animosity in a way because they agreed to disagree over certain things. Which is fair enough, you've all got your own opinions. They let one another know if they didn't agree with whatever, they really did. But it was good. Don wasn't always right. Phil wasn't always right.

What made him laugh?
What made him laugh? (laughs) When people were wrong. I don't
know how to say this in a nice way. He was a very sarcastic man
over a lot of things, possibly just to get his point across. But he had
a wonderful sense of humour. Very dry.

Was that something he shared with your husband?
Yes very, because my husband was one of those one-liners, you know.

*Did your husband and Sir Donald have administrative
differences of opinion?*
We're talking about building the Bradman Stand, I suppose, are
we? Well, you see he wasn't on the committee then but he couldn't
see how that should happen but they had to do it because it became
a fire hazard for one thing.

Was he conservative?
Very very conservative. In everything.

He gained a reputation for being forward-thinking.
Forward-thinking in playing conditions and things like that, yes,
but in the material things I suppose (whispers) he didn't like to
spend the money.

Was Sir Donald one of Phil's closest friends?
One of his many friends, I wouldn't say he was closest. They
played golf together occasionally, not a lot.

*Sir Donald seems to have had friends he played golf with, his
cricket friends . . .*
And then there were his bridge friends. They had a wonderful
friendship with another Test cricketer and his wife, 'Tim' Wall,

who was one of our masters at St Peter's College here. He was in the 1948 side with Don and they were great friends. He died many years ago and I think that was a big loss to Don. He was a bit of a loner then. You see, Don didn't really have many close friends. He wasn't the type to go and say, 'How about if I come and pick you up and we'll go and have a drink?' He was not the outgoing type. But they had certain sets of friends.

When I had them here, I was very careful as to whom I had. I mainly kept it to people he knew. In fact, I don't know whether I did have anybody here that he didn't know. The daughters from these people over the road, I'd get them and their husbands to come. When their mother and father had passed away, they'd be here for him to still keep up with them, and catch up with them. And whenever we had overseas people whom he knew, yes.

So you treated him differently to the way you would treat other people?
Oh yes. Because he could sit back and just not open his mouth if he didn't want to, let me put it. It could happen with him, I can tell you. And if he was not in the mood – you'd be constantly pushing the conversation.

Was he perhaps more involved with his family than most?
Mother was. She was wonderful. She was a saint, truly. She was a beautiful person.

I've heard that you and Lady Jessie were fixtures in the Ladies' Stand at the Adelaide Oval when there was cricket played.
That's right. (laughs) I still am.

And sometimes Lady Jessie would be there and Sir Donald wouldn't.

Oh yes, many times. Phil played golf too, and both of them would be playing golf. I think they got a bit tired of it all. They'd get mad at things that go wrong out there. That's what their problem was. Whereas we wouldn't know what was going on out there probably. Okay, they're bowling, they're batting, they're fielding, they're whatever, you know. We knew the finer points but we didn't know *the* finer points like the men do.

Was it partly that people who 'do' don't want to watch?

That's right. They play and they think oh, what do I want to watch this for, you know. When we'd sit together and watch it when it was interstate on the television, ooh, I'd think, I'm not going to sit and listen to you.

Is that why you and Jessie preferred to sit in the Ladies' Lounge?

Yes. She and I didn't want to sit with the men. Heaven's above, we sit with them all day at home; we don't want to be with them when we're at the cricket.

Alison Steele [wife of ACB treasurer Ray Steele] mentioned Jessie knitting in the Ladies' Lounge . . .

We used to all knit. Oh, the women from Melbourne. Talk about Alison Steele, her crowd would come from Melbourne and they'd all be knitting up there, the whole lot of them, as well as us. (laughs) One thing that Jessie used to do a lot of was knit socks. She used to give them to the St Vincent de Paul and whatever. I'd like a dollar for every ball of wool I knitted too. But most of us used to bring knitting. Alison's right, I'd forgotten about that. (laughs)

Tell me about the Ladies' Lounge.

It's just a lounge at the back of the stand. I still prefer to sit there because it's the best viewing spot. The Men's Lounge is not nearly as good. The men say to me, 'Why don't you come down with us?' and I say 'No, you come in here, it's better here than it is up there.' That's only because it is a better view, I'm not just being stand-offish or anything.

When we were up north in Cairns in the 1980s and Phil wasn't at the meeting, they passed this vote that the women could join the men in the Men's Lounge. Because some of the women objected to it you see. And that's all right, that's fair enough, they can go. But I'm quite happy to sit there, which I still do until the stand gets pulled apart and then I won't be able to sit there. Then I'll have to do what I'm told. And yet the women just love it now. 'Oh, I'm so happy to be able to sit with my husband, praise be', you know. (laughs) It's nothing to do with me, I'm not in it any more.

But you must be so much a part of it still.

I am. I'm dying for the cricket to start again. In Adelaide a wife can take up a membership and when Phil died I was given the honour of having his honorary life membership. It was wonderful.

Was Lady Bradman sick for a long time?

It's four years this September [2001] since she died. It would be about two years before that. When she was well enough, she'd still come to the cricket. But we'd talk on the phone a lot. Especially when they'd gone to golf on the Saturday. (laughs)

Saturday and Wednesday?

Yes, Phil played Fridays too. I'm glad he did, too. Though on Friday they only played nine holes; it was just to get out and do a bit of exercise, that was all. Phil was captain of Kooyonga at one stage.

Was Jessie one of your closest friends?
Oh yes, and I think we became closer as I got older. I suppose at one stage she thought, 'Oh well, she's only young', which I was. But as we got older and in later years, yes, definitely more so. We'd had different interests when I was younger but then our grandies are virtually the same age. I'd say later in life the friendship was more then than ever before.

I've heard a lot about Sir Donald's curiosity, that he would bombard people with questions.
Oh yes. But I think that that's also a feature of a bit of shyness. My husband, I would say, was shy too. It took him a while to make up his mind. I think probably what you say is curiosity, I think is a bit of shyness.

Were there aspects of Sir Donald's personality that were formed by his being Don Bradman?
I think so. His aloofness. He put a shield around himself a bit, you know. Don was a great one for summing up. I think he was the type of person – and I might be wrong here – he either liked you or he thought, 'No, I can't be bothered with you'. I don't think he'd give you a second chance. Actually (laughs) I'm looking at it from a different angle. I didn't find that myself, but yeah, I reckon.

He doesn't seem to have needed a lot of people in his life.
No. Of course, mind you, it's the people that have made him become a private person. Lady Jessie would protect him too, especially if it was a stranger, a person they didn't know.

Did he still have influence after his retirement?
Oh yes, he still had so much to offer.

Did Phil and Sir Donald come into conflict as state selectors?
I was never privy to their meetings. Probably they had a fair bit of
sorting out to do, knowing the two of them. One wouldn't be trod-
den on, I can tell you. I'd love to have been a fly on the wall, quite a
few times actually.

It must have been interesting at lunch.
Yes it was. There was a clash of personalities, actually. That's why
Jessie and I used to laugh. 'Oh well, we'll be having some arguments
today.' Yes. (laughs) They were more discussions than they were
arguments, really. But they had their own opinions, you see.

The way you describe it they seem unlikely friends
Yeah, they were a bit opposite.

But they had cricket in common.
Yes, sure.

Whereas you and Jessie didn't seem to need that.
No, we didn't have to. We just fell in.

*Retired company executive **Mal MacPherson** describes his relationship
with Sir Donald as a 'man-to-man golfing friendship' which developed
over a period of 30 years, and he still treasures the scorecards which Sir
Donald signed over the years – 'He'd kill me if he knew'. We spoke at his
home in Melbourne.*

WHEN I WAS TRANSFERRED to Adelaide in 1968, Shell used to
sponsor the junior cricket and Sir Donald was the president of the
South Australian Cricket Association so I met him in Shell's
boardroom first. He'd always been a bit of a hero, of course. We

were both members of the Kooyonga Golf Club and he used to say to me, 'Oh what about a game next week?' We played and we got on very well. We were both playing off about five at that stage.

Then I used to play with him once a month, I suppose. Sir Donald was a bloke that always had a partner. In the early days he played golf with a bloke called Sylv Phelan, who used to write for the *Advertiser*. He and Sylv played every week and in Kooyonga you play in threes. They'd put their name on the time sheet and if you wanted to have a game, you'd just put your name down with him. I used to do that at fairly regular intervals, just to keep things rolling, and we enjoyed the game.

There were quite a few 36-hole events in those days and I happened to draw him a few times, so we played together a fair bit. Then I got on the committee at Kooyonga and I was the bloke he used to ring up to whinge about what was going on. I was receptive and we had developed a bit of a relationship in that respect. He used to trust me because he knew that I wouldn't let any secrets out of the bag. If you want to be a friend of Sir Donald's, you've got to be pretty good with your integrity.

When I was transferred back to Melbourne in 1980, I used to go over to Adelaide every October and we just maintained this annual game. We used to correspond a bit. It developed into more of a friendship, rather than the hero worship thing. I got to know him as a bloke.

He's actually 20 years older than me and when he'd reach a milestone, like when he was 70, I was 50. So we'd know how we're going. I've seen his golf over many years. When you get older, your game deteriorates and I've seen him hurt by that. But it wasn't too bad, I can tell you. I remember playing with him one day and we came up the ninth hole and he said, 'Oh, I don't know, I'm playing so poorly.' I said, 'You know Sir Donald, I know exactly how old you are and if I can play as well as you can when I'm your age, I'll be

pretty pleased.' 'Ooh,' he says, 'that's one of the nicest things anyone's ever said to me.' (laughs) 'What are you doing next week?' So
we had that sort of rapport.

Was golf his passion?
I don't think I've ever played with a bloke who enjoyed the game
more. He was absolutely completely and utterly involved with the
game once he started. Almost parochially so. His concentration
and dedication to the competitive side was really something to see.
If we were waiting on a tee for some blokes to finish, there might
be a five-minute delay, and then he would tell a few stories or a
joke or two.

He's been criticised all his life because he's not a social animal
and when we finished, he didn't ever go in and get on the turps
with all the boys. But he used to come in with me and he'd have
two orange juices and a dry sherry. And then off. And that's fair
enough. And he was very social and extremely intelligent. He used
to probe you with all the political questions about the place, what's
happening in Victoria? He was very interested in politics because
he was pretty close to a lot of politicians. Not to say that he was all
that much in favour.

It was more a man-to-man golfing friendship that we developed. He used to be very interested in my golf. He'd say, 'You're
hitting the ball really good, some of those shots you've got to control,' etcetera, and I'd talk about his game. I might say, 'Gee, you
haven't lost any length off the tee.' And he might say, 'Yeah, but
I'm putting so poorly.' We'd discuss these things.

Was he self-taught?
I'd think so. He had a variety of grips. (laughs) He'd have the standard Vardon grip but every now and again, particularly if he
wanted to get a bit of power in the right hand, he used to grip it

with an ordinary two-handed grip. I remember one day onto the 15th hole, it was a long par three, he hit this beautiful shot and I said, 'Oh, great shot Sir Donald,' and he said, 'Well, I hit it with my two hands because I get a bit more power into the wind.' He said, 'Furthermore, the ball hit the hole.' He reckoned that he could see the ball actually hit the hole, and when we got up there it looked as if it had, so he obviously had darn good eyesight.

When you're a cricketer and you play golf, you've either got the natural ability or you haven't. And he had a hell of a lot of natural ability. But he was never a classical player. He had a short backswing. Very consistent, but not a classical sort of swing like you see in these young blokes today. I think he was mainly self-taught, but you've got to remember, he'd played golf with Gary Player and a few of those notable fellows and he would have picked up an awful lot of advice around the traps. I can imagine him sitting down talking to these guys but I don't think he was a technician. His basic principle would be to take it back and hit it square and go through it, you know? The same as he played cricket.

Whilst he was a fine golfer, played off scratch and all that, played pennant, you couldn't put him in the top class in the golfing circle. He would never in his wildest dreams have thought about pro golf. But you could say that he was a well above average pennant player. The first time I played with him, which would have been when he was 60 years of age, he led the qualifiers in the club championship, that's how well he was playing. At 60 he was still able to play off three or four.

I last saw him at lunch in 1998 when he'd become too ill to play. He said, 'I can't play any more. I feel very old and too weak.' It was quite an emotional discussion we had because I knew I was never going to play with him any more. He couldn't play and that must have hurt him.

Prior to that, he had a stroke and he couldn't play one year.

The next year, he was in a cart and we shared the cart together and he paid for it (laughs) which was an incredible situation, I tell you. Well, he hasn't got the reputation for being overgenerous.

He got old gracefully really. When he had the stroke, they gave him a 27 handicap. This time I played with him, he had exactly 100 off the stick. Less the 27 gave him a net 73 and won him the 'C' Grade Medal. So I said to him, 'Gee, that's the best 100 you've ever made.'

When Sylvie Phelan passed away, Bruce Ewing became his partner. He played with him every week, and sometimes twice a week. He was a very good friend of mine too, so when we used to play it was Bruce and Don and I. We never ever played for any money. Never. But I'm sure he was very competitive against Bruce. (laughs) I think he wanted to beat Bruce because they were about the same mark. I was sort of the intruder. He used to say to me, 'I like playing this annual game because you can tell me whether I'm slipping or not.' He used to say, 'Well, see you again next year,' and I'd say, 'Yeah' and he'd say, 'Just keep your eye on the press in case there's anything goes wrong.' (laughs)

Did you share interests outside golf?
Not a great deal, because he wasn't prepared to talk cricket much, nor did I wish to ask him a great deal. I'm very interested in cricket. We were playing one day and it was a 36-hole event and we were having lunch. That morning in the press it was reported that Gary Sobers had just hit 6 successive sixes in the county game in England, so I just said to him, 'Gee that was a pretty good effort by Sobers.' And his reply to that was, 'Oh yeah, but they're very short boundaries over there.' He wasn't prepared to concede.

I thought I'd better counter this, so I said, 'I don't think anyone will ever come close to your record of making 100 off three overs in Bowral when you were a young bloke.' He said, 'Actually I made 101 and I lost the strike twice.' (laughs) So that really fixed me up.

What contact did you have in your role of committeeman?

He used to complain to me a bit. I'd have to say he upset a few blokes, he used to complain a lot about various aspects of things. There was one incident apparently when he went into the bar when he wasn't correctly attired. At Kooyonga at that stage you could go into the Swing Bar in your golf clothes but you couldn't go into the main bar. Hence all the blokes are crowded into the Swing Bar and there's no one in the main bar. He saw it as just ridiculous, which it was, so he went into the bar without his collar and tie on and got asked to leave. Oh boy, that really upset him. I was instrumental in having that rule changed. They were so traditionalist over there in South Australia that it took a while to break it through. And he wouldn't go in anywhere, he'd just go home, until the thing was changed. He was pretty strongly principled in that respect. But while logically he was correct, he was against the club rules.

His principles were very high and he would allow that to impair his enjoyment. He didn't accept it. If it was logical, he would have accepted it. He used to ring me up too and complain about certain aspects of the course and usually I'd listen very carefully and he'd have a point. He wouldn't be ringing me irrelevantly.

Was there still something of the country bloke in Sir Donald?

I can accept that. Certainly he was never a high-flyer, you only had to look at him. He used to wear the same sort of daggy golf clothes every time he played and his golf clubs were shockers. I can't remember him ever changing his clubs in all the time I played with him and he pretty well wore the same. An old pair of suit pants – he didn't really go out to look the part. That's his style.

He used to ring up occasionally here and I've got a few letters that he's written. He had time for people. I was only an associate who played golf with him but if I was out somewhere and he saw me, he'd come across, it would be just like old home week. There was no aloofness in any shape or form.

I was playing one day with Sylvie Phelan, and we got to the ninth green and all of a sudden, this fellow comes charging across, obviously an outsider, a little tubby bloke, and he spoke with an English accent. He said, 'Which is Sir Donald Bradman?' I said, 'That's him over there.' So the next thing, we putted out and we walked across to the 10th tee to hit off and this bloke's deep in Bradman's ear. Sylvie looks at me, and I look at him, who is this? He won't put up with this. So we hit off, and we walk all the way down the 10th and this bloke walked all the way down talking to Bradman. Sylv and I are nonplussed about this. Bradman, I might tell you, had a double bogie six on that hole, so we walked across the 11th and he walked the whole 11th hole with him. And then we putted out and Bradman's had another double bogie six and we thought he'd be absolutely furious and this bloke's now gone. So Sylv knew Bradman pretty well and he said, 'What was all that about, Don?' He said, 'Well look, that bloke's a Yorkshireman, and he rode his bike 50 miles to watch me make that 300 at Leeds in 1930 and he's wanted to meet me ever since. I could hardly deny him the privilege of walking two holes of golf, could I?'

Was it true that he'd prefer to play golf than go and sit and watch the cricket when you knew him?
I'm sure that would be the case. He liked the activity of the golf and the challenge of it. Cricket he had by the throat. But I'm sure he never ever got that feeling about golf. Golf was a hell of a challenge to him so he was going to try and beat it. But he's like all of us, you just can't. It's too hard a game. (laughs)

Australian batsman **Paul Sheahan** *played 31 Tests before he retired in 1973–74 at the age of 27. He has been principal of Melbourne Grammar School since 1996 and we spoke in his office.*

I ATTENDED AN award dinner in Adelaide when I was 19, I'm a bit embarrassed to say this, but it was the Golden Peanut Award (laughs) which was offered by I think the Kingaroy Co-operative for the person they regarded as the best young cricketer in Australia. I was asked to go to the dinner in Adelaide and be presented with a blazer and a bat that had been signed by Sir Donald. He was obviously a very astute man. He was a great analyst of the game of cricket and knew every player and what their performances were, and so on. And he knew who I was and what I was doing. It wasn't long after that that I was selected to play for Australia.

But I must confess that I was rather taken aback with his lack of height. I didn't realise he was so small in stature and when I reflected on that, I wondered why on earth he'd been able to generate such a sort of presence. But then I suppose you look at people like Churchhill and Montgomery of El Alamein, and Mahatma Ghandi for that matter. They were all short and they all had that sort of indefinable something that Bradman had that made people stop and listen whenever he spoke and sent a buzz around a room whenever he walked in.

So there was something about the man himself?
Oh, there was no doubt about that. Obviously an aura builds around a person because of their achievements and his quite astonishing achievements as a batsman gave him a status that was so infinitely superior to everyone else who's ever played the game. But he did just have a measured air about him that made you want to listen to what he was going to say. He never wasted a word and he didn't speak a lot. I guess in my whole cricketing career I'd have

had at most half a dozen conversations with him and even then they were only fleeting ones.

He never, for instance, when he was chairman of selectors, offered you any advice about technical flaws in your batting or how you might eliminate means of getting out if you were showing some sort of deficiency. You tended to have to go to him; he didn't impose himself on you, but you were always aware when Bradman was around.

Jack Ryder, who was the chairman of selectors for Victoria and a co-selector with Sir Donald when I first started playing for Australia, had a similar presence in Victoria and yet he was a giant of a man and had that sort of rather imperial look about him and an aquiline nose. He was not dissimilar to De Gaulle in visage.

What was Sir Donald like as a national selector?

He didn't waste words whenever he spoke. He had a sharp wit. Sometimes you might have suggested he had a sharp tongue. I do recall, and I'm not sure whether this was embellished or manufactured, that when Bill Lawry returned from the tour of England in 1961 having made over 2000 runs on the tour – which is a remarkable achievement for a young batsman on his first tour of England – when he first met Sir Donald, I think Sir Donald's opening gambit was, 'How on earth could you make 2000 runs on a tour of England with feet that big?' Which is rather off-putting, I guess. But I'm led to believe that that was the sort of person he was. Just a little sharp comment here and there, but an incredibly astute cricket brain.

How did you rate him as an administrator?

I think people respected every single thing that Bradman ever said about cricket. And it was extraordinary that in the days of some of the controversial areas in cricket – the throwing controversy came to the fore, the lbw rule came to the fore, the no-ball rule came to the fore – nobody would say anything until they'd heard what Sir Donald Bradman in Australia and Gubby Allen in England had said. They had enormous influence over the way in which the game developed. Some would say they had too much influence, that everyone was frightened to say anything for fear that the 'great men' would demur, but there's no doubt that everyone pretty well hung on everything that Bradman and Allen said.

I think he had an enormous influence over the way the game evolved. It's hard to be definitive about these things but I think most people had such respect for him as a person and what he represented to cricket that it dictated the sort of behaviour they exhibited on the playing field too. But I suppose you'd say the Chappell era came pretty hard on the heels of Bradman and that marked quite a distinctive change in the way players behaved.

I just have the highest admiration for the man. I thought he behaved impeccably as an administrator of the game, I thought he set the highest possible ethical standards for anyone to model themselves on and he was somebody who people in Australia really looked up to. And we don't do that readily in this country. I know at times we tend to perhaps laud our sporting heroes but a lot of that is transient and once they've stopped playing, that's the end of them, and we move on to the next lot. But Bradman won such an affection in people's hearts for a whole complex web of reasons that meant he was almost revered in this country. But in some ways I reckon he would have hated the thought of being revered, because he wasn't that sort of person.

Bradman distinguished himself with so many wise things that he said that it wasn't just the fact that he was Sir Donald Bradman and finished with a Test average of 99.94 that made people want to take notice of him. It was also the fact that he had a very nimble mind, he was articulate, even if he wasn't easy to listen to, and you wanted to know what his thinking was on various issues.

As a fellow company board member, **Brian Cole** *knew Sir Donald Bradman the businessman and admired his zeal as a director.*

LET ME EXPLAIN the extent of my connection. I was on the boards of the three investment companies which made up Argo Investments. I was the chairman of Wakefield for five or six years, I was also on the board of Argo and Bounty. Bounty and Wakefield have since merged with Argo, so we only have the one company, Argo, which has about 30 000 shareholders, so it's a reasonable size. It's a pretty compact little organisation, Argo. They run it with less than 10 staff, dealing with over a billion dollars in assets.

I was a director of those companies for a number of years and for quite a bit of that time Sir Donald was a director or perhaps chairman too, so I got to know him. In fact, he didn't retire from the Argo companies until he was 75, which was in accordance with a contract that the directors had with the company. After he retired, he was so highly regarded he continued as a consultant to the board until he was about 80 and he was still sharp as a tack.

An outsider might see joining a few boards as a fairly non-participatory sort of role.

And the fact that his name was there was good for the company and that sort of thing. But no, it was far more than that. As a consultant he'd come in weekly and see the CEO Rob Patterson and he'd take away a lot of stuff to read from brokers and new issues and share placements and so on and he'd make his recommendations and talk to Rob about them. Not bad when the fellow is in his late 70s. Most people have had enough by then.

Did he stand alone on issues on the board?

No, he didn't work that way. He'd discuss things before they came up at the meeting and he'd make sure that he and Rob Patterson were thinking along the same lines.

Was Argo one of his major directorships?

I believe it was his love in that area. He was involved very closely. As a director he gave 101 per cent of his time to it. This is his real interest, in stockbroking and investments and so on, apart from cricket.

How did you come to meet him?

He was a director of Kelvinator and I looked after the books of the Kelvinator superannuation fund. Years ago I had something for him to sign in respect to Kelvinator and I went out to his home at Holden Street and Lady Bradman came to the door and said, 'Oh hello Brian, Don's up on the roof doing a bit of painting, I'll call out to him.' He'd have been in his late 70s, or 80. He'd still do these kind of things.

Which was his first directorship?

Clarksons was his first, I believe. He gave them credit for that fact. For anyone to break in being a company director, the first one's the hardest to get and the Clarksons were very keen on cricket, Len Clarkson and so on.

Tell me, what sort of a board member was he?

Oh, tops. He had a very keen brain and mind and he'd get straight to the point, but more particularly he'd do his homework, better than probably anyone I've known connected with boards or committees. He did a lot of reading. Company reports. Brokers' recommendations. Those sorts of things.

What would you consider his real strengths as a board director?

His memory was very sharp. He was so complete and thorough in all that he did, I suppose. He wouldn't take a position on a board unless he felt he could make a contribution. He wasn't a qualified accountant but he had an excellent knowledge of financial matters and so on. He could follow anything that was brought to the table at a board meeting. And his connections. If he needed to get to one of these guys – the commissioner of tax, the treasurer and so on – then they'd see him or hear him. He'd correspond from time to time with those sorts of people

Was he demanding of others?

Yes, he didn't want to spend time with anything that was irrelevant, he just wanted to deal with the point at issue and so on and he expected others to act the same way. He got his way in his own way. He had a very analytical mind. I think this probably comes out as you may well find in sport and cricket, business and whatever.

Did you consider him very intelligent?

Very much so. You're dealing with a very special person here. He really was quite an incredible man.

Jill Gauvin spoke at Sir Donald's memorial service. She ponders her friendship with the man who invited himself to dinner only weeks after they'd started work on a project at the State Library of South Australia when she was 25 years old. I spoke to her at her home in the Adelaide hills.

I was working in the State Library and I had to leave when Rob and I married in 1966 because they didn't employ married women. The State Librarian, Hedley Brideson, had set up a special collections area and I knew that just before I got married he was trying very hard to get Sir Donald's collection. He would see him at Rotary every week and Don of course had all of these scrapbooks at home. He also had the Warwick vase and the Worcester vase and a lovely hand that had been sculpted of his.

I went back about six weeks after I got married and I was working part time on a myriad of things in this special collections area and Hedley said, 'I've finally got Sir Donald to agree to bring his scrapbooks in. Would you like to do it?' Well, I was absolutely terrified, because he was this famous cricketer and I knew nothing about cricket, just nothing. He was the age I am now, he was 59 and I was just 25. But I really wanted to keep working, so I said yes. I couldn't say no really. So he said, 'Well, what if you just meet him? Come in and we'll get together.'

Well, my dear, I couldn't believe it, this wonderful man who walked in and said, 'Hello Jill.' (laughs) I was so stunned because he was so normal. I was not worldly. I was not used to meeting people like him and it was just like he'd known me forever. I thought why am I being so nervous? We just clicked. I can't explain it. It worked from the moment we met.

Anyway, we talked about the project for a while and there was lots of laughter and lots of fun, and he said he could help with it. And goodness me, I wouldn't have been able to do it without him. The scrapbooks came and I was quite appalled when I saw them, they were just bits of newspaper cuttings that people had stuck in albums with glue. (laughs) Half of them were not even identified. And I knew so little about cricket. I thought, how am I going to work out which match this cutting applies to?

His memory was just amazing. He could look at a cutting just an inch by an inch and it would say 'And Don Bradman made 3 before tea.' (This is hypothetically I'm talking.) And he'd say, 'I know where that was. That was when we played at Gladesville and . . .' (laughs) What we'd do, we'd get all the papers from the newspaper reading room, and we'd go through them, and he'd just place the cuttings. So we had all of these concertina files, we had all of the matches, and as we'd find a piece, we'd put it in. We did a copy for him and a copy for the library. I think his copy is in the National Library. So that's how it all came about.

It was going so well. I thought I'm really going to enjoy this, this is going to be great fun. I'd been working on it for about six weeks and the phone went one night. Rob answered and called me to the phone. And I'll never forget it, he said, 'Jill, it's Don Bradman here. Can I come down for dinner tonight? Jessie's gone overseas. I'll bring a bottle of wine.' I didn't even drink in those days. So down he came, casually dressed. 'Oh, this is lovely,' he said, and we had the best night. We didn't talk about cricket, just about life in general. And that's how it all started.

I would never ever have asked him for dinner. Never. And I am still astounded about it. I've thought about this a lot since he died and I wonder if he thought I was just so unworldly. I think he knew that I was almost scared of letting him down and I just wonder if he got that feeling that I think this friendship would be all right. I'm still amazed because he really was very wary about people. I don't know. I didn't even think about it until he died.

We really didn't talk much about cricket. If he was up here, Rob might say, 'How do you think the West Indians will go, Don?' And I really couldn't have cared less about how the West Indians went. Do you know what I mean? (laughs) And I still wouldn't know where silly mid-on is, or any of that. And I think he quite liked this in me. He thought I should know a bit about it, but okay, so you're not with it, all right.

The one thing I am very proud of, as I said in my memorial eulogy, is he trusted me. And I live by that. I often think about it. The things he told us. It wasn't just me, it was Rob, too. But he knew that we would never take advantage of it. We never talked about it. I've got friends who didn't even know that we knew him. He used to give me things, like he'd say 'Would you like that type-writer?' The typewriter he did all his journalistic stuff on. And I thought what am I going to do with a typewriter, but anyway he said, 'I'd like you to have it.' Of course when the library started this memorabilia collection, I just gave all of these things back.

He once said to me, 'I'm never sure if people want to speak to me because I'm Sir Donald Bradman, or if they like me as a person.' And that's a fairly large cross to bear, isn't it? Because there were a lot of people in his life who just wanted to dine out on the fact that they knew him or that they did this, that or the other with him. And he knew who they were. He could pick them a mile off. And I think that's why he didn't allow himself to get close to a lot of people.

Did you just have him to dinner that one night?
Oh no, my dear, that was it. Say that was a Wednesday, 'Well now, what are you doing on Saturday night? I might come down again on Saturday night.' Because he could avoid the phone. And then he'd come for dinner a couple of nights the next week, and then he thought well, if we weren't doing anything on Saturday, maybe we'd go out and have a bite to eat. And if he stayed over . . . and it was just amazing. He just slotted into that house as if he'd been doing it for years. I couldn't believe it. He said to us the first night he came down, 'Now I really appreciate the fact that you are call-ing me Sir Donald, but I'd really rather you called me Don.' He said, 'Please don't call me Sir Don.' He didn't like being called Sir Don at all.

And all this time, we hadn't met Jessie. She was away for a cou-ple of months, I think. He used to talk about her all the time. He'd say, 'You wait until you meet her, she's just going to be so different from what you expect.' He said, 'You know she wears lisle stock-ings, don't you? And she wears this flowered hat all the time. It's really embarrassing. And,' he said, 'if I don't watch it, she wears odd shoes.' (laughs) He got us to the stage where we didn't really know if he was serious or not. Anyway, in the week after she came home, she invited us to dinner, and that was the first time I'd been to their house. Well, she was just stunning. And she was not only gorgeous to look at, she was a gorgeous person. She had the best eyes. She'd look at you and she'd talk to you about the most insignificant thing and you'd feel that you were the only person in the world that mattered.

And she didn't wear lisle stockings?

(laughs) No, and she didn't have the flowered hat either. We told her and we used to laugh about it. He had this wonderful sense of humour and people didn't see that side of him. He had this fantastic belly laugh. I'd just laugh at him, I wouldn't even know what he was laughing about but I'd have to laugh.

Jessie and Don were just amazing. Don would start a sentence and Jessie would finish it, it was that sort of relationship. It wasn't perfect and sugary, but it was lovely and solid. They were meant to be together, do you know what I mean? They went to primary school together. I can remember Don talking about when Jessie went and stayed with him. That was when he reckoned he fell in love with her, when he was about 12 or 13. She knocked the alarm clock off the bedside table where she was sleeping. He came from a very frugal family, he said, 'Oh, that's not very good, you've knocked that off.' 'Oh well,' she said, 'it won't be the first bump it's had.' It was along those lines. She was just so unfussed by everything.

Did you ever see Sir Donald angry?

I didn't ever see him spit the dummy. I have never seen him furious. I have seen him disappointed or upset, but I've never seen him rant or rave. And unless he's repeated something that someone's told him, or a joke, I don't think I've ever heard him swear. He was very controlled. I don't think he ever told me, except when we were playing bridge (laughs), that he was very disappointed in me. Because my attention span for playing bridge was about nil and I'd always think of something to say. He was very competitive. He taught us to play and Jessie would play with Rob. And Jessie used to play a lot of bridge, she played with her friends during the week and she used to do all sorts of wonderful finessing things, and give Rob clues as to what he should do. That used to really upset Don. He'd say, 'If you're going to give him information, then I just don't think we should play.' He'd get upset, too, if I started to talk in the middle of a rubber. I mean, that was fair enough. (laughs) He played right up to three or four months before he died. And he was as astute then as he ever was. I didn't play with him then but he loved playing his bridge, he said it used to keep his mind going.

He seems to have spent a huge amount of time in those last years responding to requests for autographs.
He was so conscientious about all of this signing business. You should have seen what used to come into that house every week. He had a den, it had a big desk in it and two comfortable chairs and book cases all the way round with *Wisden* in it and there were days I'd go down there and you couldn't move for parcels and bats and books and plates and stumps and balls and posters. I'd undo all of this stuff for him because he got to the stage he couldn't undo it and parcel it all up again. He would sit at his desk, sometimes for five or six hours at a stretch. He'd have his lunch in between and he would sit there and I'd say, 'Come on, dear, don't do any more.' He was having trouble writing because he'd use these big texta colours to sign. 'No,' he said, 'I've got to do it.'

A lot of people wouldn't send postage and he was spending a lot of money on return postage. I used to have my car and the boot would be full, I would have the back seat full, and I would bring it up here to post it because I could park outside the post office. In the end I said, 'Look, you're not to pay all this money and if people don't send return postage, it goes back COD.' 'Oh no, sweetie, we can't do that. That's not on.' In the end he gave in because I just thought that's really abusing his generosity. I think people forgot that he was 92.

Did you and Rob take holidays with the Bradmans?
The four of us would go away fishing together to lots of different places. To friends' shacks. He loved it to be really casual, uninterrupted, where he could be totally himself. If he wanted to have a nap in the afternoon, he'd just have a nap, if he wanted to sit down and read a book or talk or do nothing or go for a walk, it could all just happen.

Like everything else, it just evolved. It was, 'Oh what a good idea, let's do that'. We were playing bridge one night and Jessie said, 'Let's go on a houseboat, wouldn't that be nice darling?' 'Oh, I'll go on a houseboat,' he said. 'No one will know me. I'll do that.' I think we must have had three or four holidays on the River Murray. Don just loved it. It was safe up there. There we'd be in our tracksuits and we'd catch catfish and we'd cook a barbecue. We'd tie the boat up and put the rods out and we'd play bridge. And all of a sudden a reel would go, and it would be, 'Oh, we've caught a fish'. We had a few episodes where people recognised him. I would go stiff with fright. They'd say, 'Oh you look like Don Bradman,' and he'd say, 'So they tell me,' and he'd just wander off. And there I'd be, speechless and my heart would be pumping and I'd be thinking I don't want him to have to go through this and he'd just go back on the boat and he would have hysterics about it all. It was so much fun.

Did his need for anonymity influence his holiday destinations?
Well, yes. You see, Jessie loved to go to England. They had a lot of
friends in England and he loved her to go but he said that if he hit
England, he wouldn't be able to have a holiday because he'd be
having to be out every night, being entertained. He'd be recognised, he'd have to do this, that and the other. And it's true. Even
when he was 91 he'd get invitations to go to England to do things.

He really did hate to be in the public eye, it was not like he was
putting on a turn. That was very genuine. He would just say,
'Look, I'd love to do that but you know what would happen if I do
that. I will just be hounded to death.' And he just couldn't cope
with it. And as he got older, it just didn't ever decrease.

I think he'd just had enough. He'd spent an incredible amount
of time away from his family. And in those days, it was not like you
get on a plane and you're there in 24 hours. It was a month over on
a boat. And he'd say he'd get seasick going down Port Road. He
used to get airsick. He hated flying. I mean, he'd do it. He was a
selector. He was constantly travelling around. Jessie would sit here
having dinner and she'd say, 'Now what are you doing for the next
three weeks, dear?' 'Oh well, I've got to go to Queensland because
there's a match, then I've got to go to Perth.' He'd come home in
between because he had board meetings or something like that.
He was full-on and he loved to be full-on.

Were food and wine important to Sir Donald?
They would have a sherry before dinner. I'd come from this family
that didn't have alcohol in the house and I can remember him saying to me, 'Why don't you have a sherry?' I said, 'Now look, I can
remember going to a ball and I had a little sip of sweet sherry and
it was foul,' and he said, 'Oh but you don't drink sweet sherry, that's
for cooking. You drink dry sherry. You just taste this.' And he gave
me this little glass of Grandfiesta, it was a beautiful sherry. Well,

I got hooked on this stuff. (laughs) He said, 'Maybe you should have a little glass of wine as well.' This was just after he'd started coming down. Rob drank.

We'd go out to this Italian restaurant, it was our restaurant, and we took him along. We always sat pretty much in the same position. He'd sit with his back to the door and we'd sit either side of him. Occasionally people might recognise him but nothing was said and for three years this restaurateur thought his name was Fred. (laughs) This guy had several restaurants around Adelaide over the years, and when Don and Jessie entertained, they'd always go to his restaurant so they kept up the relationship. When Don was 90, we took him out to a restaurant owned by that guy. He provided a little private room for us but we had to walk through the main dining room. You should have seen him skittle through that room, he took off like a rocket. Don was quite nervous about going out that night. It was a night or two after his birthday. He was just wonderful.

Was he a painstaking man?
Rob showed him the Internet once, he said, 'Look, there's about 300 pages about you on this, come up and have a look.' So he set him down and pulled it all up and Don read the first two pages, and said, 'Well, I've found five mistakes in the first two pages, so I don't want to read any more.' And he just got up and walked off. (laughs)

And if you saw Don's desk when he was here and working, he would have everything beautifully laid out. The pencils would all be here, and if I used his pair of scissors and left it on the desk, he'd put it back in the drawer. Everything was in its place. I am very much like that as well.

Is it fair to say his life was very much like that?
Probably. And I think my life is like that too. And I think that's why I found it so easy to have our life with him and Jessie and not to

involve them in everything. I didn't feel I had to tell my friends about it. There were a few people that we used to talk about a lot to them and Don would say, 'Oh, he sounds interesting, I wouldn't mind meeting him.' And it would always be him who'd say it. I would never suggest it.

Was a love of music something you shared?
Oh yes. From day one. I played the piano myself and I love all sorts of music. I love classical music. Chopin and Liszt were his favourites. He was a magnificent pianist himself. Absolutely extraordinary pianist.

He made a record when he was 25 I think. He used to play beautiful classical music but this is actually the record he made in 1930. (She plays a tape of the 1930 gramophone record on which he played 'Old Fashioned Locket' and 'Bungalow of Dreams'.) He'd sit at his grand piano and play this right up until he was 80.

If you look at Sir Donald's family life, he had some deep sadnesses, didn't he?
I don't think anybody has everything. If you just look at Don as Sir Donald Bradman, you think god, wouldn't that just be fantastic. All of that talent, all of that notoriety. But he lost his first child, he had John and John was all right, then he had Shirley with cerebral palsy. Shirley copes very well and she copes very well because Don has enabled her to cope well. He's been a wonderful father. They've allowed her to live independently, and I think he tried to make up for what she couldn't have. Then John gets polio, and Don actually gave up a season of cricket to look after John.

Don actually stayed with us the weekend that John's change of surname was made public and as disappointing as that was for Don, he understood. Jessie went to Sydney to visit her family on a trip that had been organised long before. He didn't want to be hounded by the press. He knew the article John wrote was going to be in the paper that Saturday and he said, 'I'm going to go and play golf but can I come and stay with you over the weekend and I'll go back home on Monday morning, because then Jessie will be back.'

Jessie was upset too but it didn't impact on her in quite the same way that it impacted on Don. And I can remember when John changed his name back, Don said to me when it was going to happen, 'John is going to change his name back.' And he said, 'I'm really pleased about it but I want him to do it because he wants to do it. It's not going to make any difference to me.' He was still really very generous about it. He said, 'I don't want him to do it just on my account, just because I'm getting old.'

When he turned 90 I think if he had one birthday card he must have had 15 million. I wanted to put them around the house, but there was no way that was going to happen. He read them and they would be deposited in the wastepaper basket. They came in sacks. I actually almost got RSI slitting the envelopes and I said to him, 'Gosh darling, what's going to happen when you die?' He said, 'Well, it's not going to worry me, I'm not going to be around.' (laughs) He used to make me laugh. I said, 'What about the state funeral?' He said, 'I won't be having a state funeral. I've never wanted a state funeral and it won't be happening. Actually,' he said, 'I've discussed it with John. There's going to be a few surprises about my funeral and,' he said, 'I think you'll probably get one of the biggest surprises.' I thought oh my gosh, I wonder what's going to happen, it's going to be totally private, for family only. I thought I'm not going to pursue this. John says he has never known anyone who could say the things to him that I said and get away with it. But I really did know my limit, so I didn't pursue it any more. So when John asked me to speak at the memorial service, I thought so that was that.

The attention I've experienced since I spoke at the memorial service, it hasn't been unpleasant but it's made me very aware what it must be like to live in the public eye. He couldn't walk down the street without someone going 'Hi Don'. In restaurants people were always sort of looking and whispering. We've been out to dinner and he'd have people at his elbow and they'd get him to sign anything at all. And he'd be so nice. They'd say, 'I haven't got anything to sign, would you send me a photograph?' He'd take their name and he'd send it. He was so good. He might cut loose a bit about it on the way home, say, 'I don't know why I've got to put up with this', but he did it. I really respected him so much for that because he could have just forgotten it. He always felt an obligation to put up with it. It was as if he needed to honour the position he'd found himself in. I don't think he ever regretted being who he was or having done what he did. I think it was what went with it that he found uncomfortable.

We would be out to dinner with him and if he was getting a little bit of interest shown in him, he'd stop drinking the red wine and go onto orange juice. And he was wonderful with kids. They'd come to the front door and bring a Mars Bar to give him energy when he was sick. It's lovely stuff. (laughs)

Did you ever play golf with Sir Donald?
Oh, golf! I said I'd never played and he said, 'Look I think you should play golf.' He really did take over a little bit. He'd just say 'I think you should do this'. I think he knew that I'd come from this rather – it was a good family, but it wasn't the sort of family that went off and played golf, and he thought I should, so he would teach me to play golf.

He and Rob and I would play. Jessie would be off doing something – Jessie was always busy. 'Oh, what a good idea, darling,' she'd say. 'What a good idea. Now you take Jill to play golf, now if Rob could pick me up . . .' (laughs) 'That's fantastic.'

So these golf lessons started. Well! He was so patient, he was just amazing, but the competitive side of him always showed. You had to do it properly, there was none of this hit and giggle stuff. I would be absolutely in hysterics. He could see the funny side of it because by the time I'd get my head straight and my feet in the right position, I had forgotten what I had to do with this arm or the other or whatever.

Eventually, I can remember playing up here at Mount Osmond. Rob was a member up here and Don and Rob and I played one day. By this stage he'd taught me to really hit the ball well, and Rob's golf had improved no end too. And off we went and I hit this cracking drive. And when I did, I absolutely pulled a muscle in my back. I could hardly get back to the car, I could hardly move, and he came back and he said to me (laughs), 'Oh, I wouldn't have let a little muscle worry me. That was the best drive you've ever done.' (laughs) I was just lying there prostrate on my back, I could hardly move, and he just couldn't understand why I'd let this little muscle thing bother me. Oh dear. I said, 'I think you're my second-best friend at the moment.'

He got close to a few golf mates and as they died . . . It must be awful to get to that age and be so wonderful, and to have friends who have maybe got around that age, who don't cope as well. He had this wonderful old golfing friend called Bruce and when Bruce died, Don said to me, 'You know, I will miss Bruce so much.' He was so upset and he said, 'Do you know, there's nothing worth living for now.' And I say this really unreservedly, and I've said this to John, when Bruce died, Don dropped his bundle. It was as if he didn't want to live any more either. He'd lost Jessie, and losing Jessie was like losing half. He struggled on with it, he was good but it wasn't the same.

Jessie was such a large character, she made everything all right. He would get upset about people coming to the door to have things signed, because, he said, the house isn't his own, there's always someone at the door wanting something. And it's true, I've experienced it, and Jessie would just go to the door and say, 'Oh good afternoon, how are you?' She'd be so lovely. 'Oh look, I'm sorry, he's not here at the moment but if you'd just like to leave it maybe if you call back next week, I'll see if he can sign it for you.' She'd bring it inside and then when she felt he was receptive, she'd say, 'Oh by the way, darling, there's a bat down there, I don't suppose you would just sign it quickly, would you?'

And he didn't have that any more. He said to me one day when I was there helping him with this signing stuff, 'Do you have to rush away?' Someone was coming and he was afraid he wouldn't be able to get rid of them. He didn't like to be rude. He didn't like to say that's enough. It was those little things that Jessie had done all his life. I think he was quite sensitive to people's feelings.

So do you think Jessie shielded him?

I suppose you could call it that. She just made life a little bit easier. She was really just being a good wife, do you know what I mean? But she had her own life because she'd had to have her own life. He was a really busy man. He went every day to the office, he played golf, he'd go to a board meeting or go into the library. Sundays would be about the only day that he didn't do very much at all. Then he might plaster a bit around the house or something.

He wasn't a great gardener but he used to love doing things. He bought John a little hobby farm up here on Waverley Ridge and they used to go up there and clear the African daisy and stuff like that and they used to love coming here and pulling out the blackberries before we built the house. When the house was put in, he said to Rob, 'I reckon we could put in those storm water drains, you know.' Rob said, 'Oh', because Rob doesn't care for digging ditches, I might tell you. I can see Don saying it, 'Look, it will be a soda. I'd love to do that. All that exercising.' It was like he needed to have this exercise all that time.

Seven o'clock we hear clunk clunk clunk, he's out there digging ditches. I didn't even know they had a 7 o'clock in the morning. I said, 'God, Rob, he's out there already.' (laughs) We were exhausted at the end of it all. Absolutely exhausted. He was as fresh as a daisy. He would have been 64 or 65. There was no holding him back. Had the best day! He went home, 'Oh, I had a lovely day. I feel so good.'

Even the last months of his life, he was incredibly strong. The muscle power in his legs was amazing, and yet he was very thin. I think that's why he lived as long as he did, he just had this incredible strength. Strength of character and strength of body.

When Sir Donald met 27-year-old **Bob Radford** *in 1970, he recognised another committed cricket administrator. Radford was assistant secretary to the Australian Cricket Board (1970–76), and subsequently secretary and chief executive of the New South Wales Cricket Association. He was a trustee of the Bradman Museum and Bradman Foundation from 1988 to 1997. We spoke at his home in Sydney.*

I THOUGHT I'D BE overawed when I met him but I wasn't. He put me right at ease; he was a very relaxing fellow. He never spoke down to me, ever, in all the 31 years that I knew him. We just became friends straight off. For me it was, this guy's up on a pedestal and I'm just a little clerk, and he was the chairman of the Board then, and here he is treating me as an equal and I admired him very much for that. And I later found out he admired my love for the game and the fact that I wanted to see the right thing done by the game. And when he knew that I wasn't just one of these fly-by-night administrators to be there for 10 minutes and gone, when he knew that it was my career and I had the game at heart, he became even more open and warm towards me.

And then of course when I ended up on the Bradman Foundation and then became chairman of it, we became even closer in a different context. That was more of a business type context than administrative.

You worked with him in two different fields. Was he a demanding man to work with?

I think he expected people to do the right thing and to do their best, while underneath I think he always knew that people didn't have his natural intelligence. I think he always made a secret and private allowance for the fact that whoever he was talking to about cricket didn't know quite as much as he did. But he was never overwhelming.

He was very, very efficient but here again I think he realised that everyone couldn't be quite as efficient or as forward-looking as he was. You see, he had to make allowances for the fact that he was highly intelligent. Though he never, ever said it to anyone, how intelligent he was.

It's the same with him playing. I don't think he ever realised quite how good a player he was, he just couldn't understand how other people couldn't play as well as he could. It was a real conundrum, I think, and similarly with his intelligence, he couldn't understand why people didn't grasp a point as quickly as he would grasp it, because his intellect was so enormous.

I've met a lot of very intelligent people in all walks of life in my life. In 1962 I met Lord Bertrand Russell, perhaps the greatest philosopher of the 20th century and I left his home in awe, thinking I'd never again be in the company of true genius. But I was wrong because Don Bradman was a genius.

And I've never had to concentrate as much on anyone as I had to with Don Bradman. His brain was two or three times ahead. He could ask a question having a third question in mind down the track. You just could not put a foot wrong with him; he'd pick you up just like that. He wouldn't be critical, he'd just point out that he didn't think you were right – and then he'd give you reasons why he didn't think what you'd said was exactly correct. It might be only one or two words out, but he'd pick them up. That's why you had to concentrate absolutely in his company if you were talking seriously with him. You were a wreck when you got through talking to him because it was gruelling.

But he could be very relaxing and very funny privately, and over a bottle of wine to go out to lunch, which we often did, it was different then. He'd laugh and a lot of the pressure would go off. But I always felt I still had to be very much on the ball because I respected his brain so much and so I never wanted to say anything to him that might have the least semblance of appearing stupid. I wasn't terrified; I was just on my guard all the time, whether socially or in business. I had enormous respect for him.

You speak about him as a person of almost overriding intelligence. Was he someone who wanted his own way?
I don't think he was dogmatic, if that answers the question. I think he liked to see done what he thought should be done because he was invariably right. But in administration, a lot of people reckon for many, many years that Don Bradman absolutely ran Australian cricket. They said forget the Australian Cricket Board, they were numbers, that Australian cricket was him. It's not true. As the chairman of the Australian Cricket Board, he was unfailingly fair. He didn't run Australian cricket, he advised Australian cricket and if you didn't take his advice you were silly. He'd advise the Board of what he thought but he wouldn't thump the table and say that's what's got to happen. And invariably the Board would come around to his way of thinking because it was logically sensible.

Sir Donald Bradman competing in the Kooyonga Golf Club Championship, watched by Lady Jessie and daughter Shirley in July 1961. (Bradman Foundation)

TOP: Sir Donald Bradman with Colin Cowdrey at the Prime Minister's XI versus England match in 1963. (John Woodcock)

BOTTOM: Leading out the team at the Manuka Oval, Canberra, for the Prime Minister's XI, 1963. (John Woodcock)

LEFT: Sir Donald finishes his breakfast at the Windsor Hotel, Melbourne, as he speaks with journalist Graham Eccles on New Year's Day 1971.
(The *Herald & Weekly Times* Photographic Collection)

BOTTOM: Sir Donald Bradman greets the Rest of the World XI at the Adelaide Airport in 1971. Left to right: Clive Lloyd, Bill Jacobs, Sir Donald Bradman, Tony Greig (behind Sir Donald), Rohan Kanhai, Richard Hutton, Sunil Gavaskar, Hylton Ackerman (behind Sunil), Asif Masood, Bob Cunis, Norman Gifford, Intikhab Alam, Farookh Engineer, Gary Sobers, Zaheer Abbas, Bob Taylor, Bishen Bedi.

TOP: Sir Donald enjoys a joke at the Windsor Hotel, Melbourne, during the Rest of the World XI tour, 1971–72. From left: Bill Jacobs, Sir Donald, Gary Sobers, Ian Chappell.

BOTTOM: In 1974, English administrators Doug Insole and Cecil Paris approached the Australian Cricket Board to request a Test series be played in England in 1975. From left: Tim Caldwell, Ray Steele, Sir Donald Bradman, Cecil Paris, Bob Parish, Doug Insole, Alan Barnes, Mel McInnes.

TOP: Sir Donald, *Wisden* in hand, chats with cricket writer David Frith.

LEFT: Sir Donald and Greg Chappell shake on it at the Adelaide reception for Greg on his retirement from cricket in 1984.

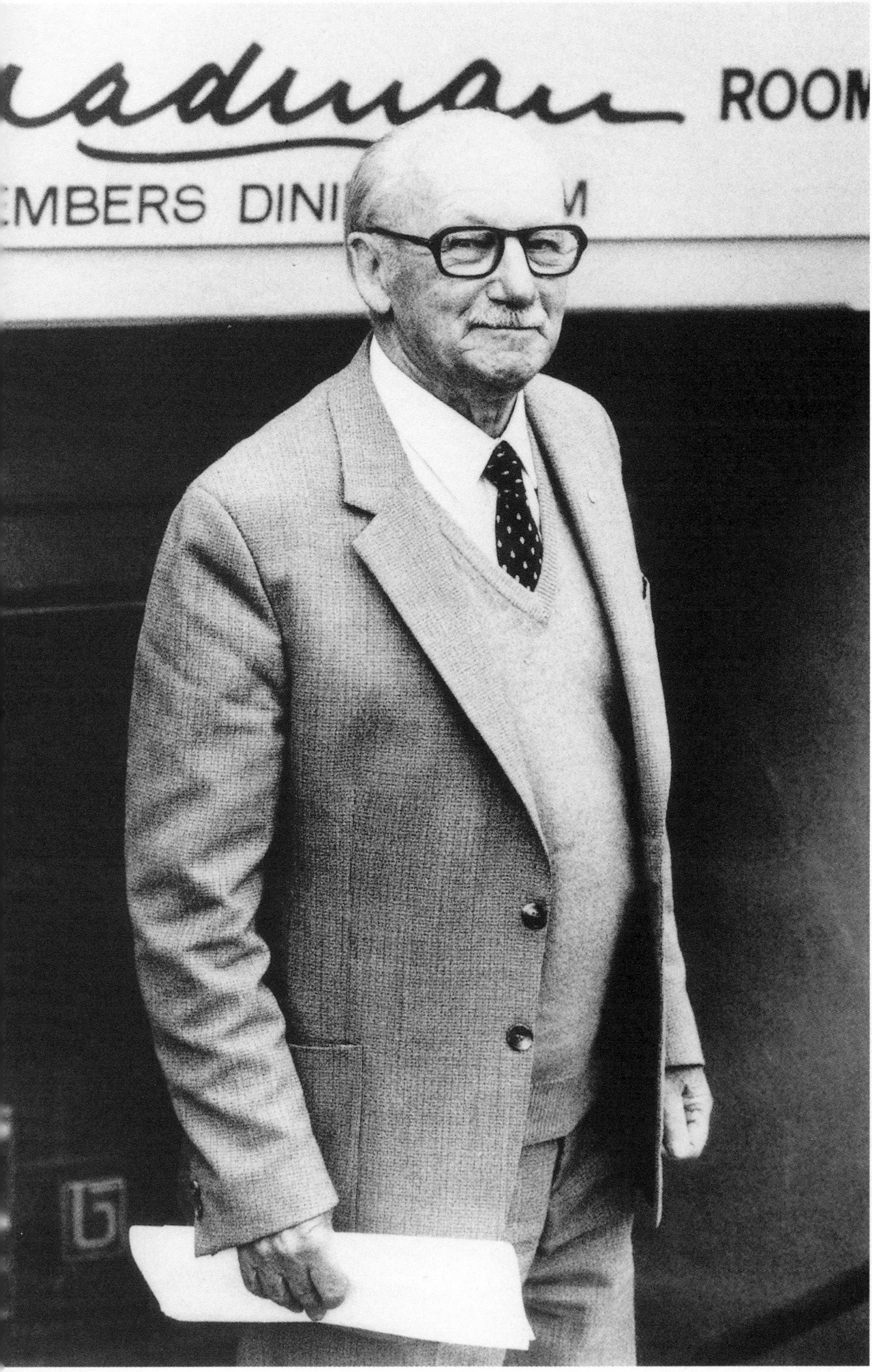
ROOM
EMBERS DINI

OPPOSITE PAGE: Sir Donald Bradman leaves his last cricket committee meeting, the South Australian Cricket Association's ground and finance committee, in July 1986. (National Library of Australia)

RIGHT: The HMY *Britannia* menu that Sir Donald signed for Lord Moore in 1986. (Courtesy Lord Moore)

BOTTOM: At the Lord's Taverners Testimonial for South Australian great, Les Favell, from left: Sir Donald, Dr Don Beard, Les Favell.

E II R

H.M.Y. BRITANNIA

MENU

Salade de Fruits de Mer

———

Caneton Bigarrade
Petits Pois au Beurre
Céleris Braisés
Pommes Fondantes

———

Salade

———

Mousse au Café

LUNDI, LE 10 MARS, 1986   PORT ADELAIDE

TOP: Sir Donald faces Norman May over the microphone during the 1988 taping of *The Life and Times of Don Bradman*. (Courtesy Australian Broadcasting Corporation)

BOTTOM: Sir Donald Bradman and his fellow cricket administrator Bob Radford.

Some very controversial events occurred in Australian cricket while Sir Donald was involved. As chairman of the Australian Board of Control, how did Sir Donald come to the decision to cancel the 1971–72 South African tour?

He agonised over it. He agonised over it terribly. He handled it brilliantly. Because it was such a hot potato, it wasn't just in cricket, it was in politics and we were being inundated. This was all happening in Sydney at the Board's meeting and they were literally wheeling mailbags on trolleys down the corridor to our office. They were all over the place, from the archbishops and all these people who were getting involved and saying yes, the tour should happen, no, it shouldn't happen. It was a huge social thing. The politics of it overrode the sport and that's where Don handled it absolutely masterfully.

He seems to have canvassed widely for opinions.

He did. You see, the terrible problem about it was that it was a huge issue and Don didn't want cricket to be the scapegoat or the fall-guy. But the government didn't want to be the scapegoat either. Don spoke to the prime minister hoping he would say call it off, and then he of course would go to the Australian Cricket Board and say the Australian prime minister says call it off. But the prime minister was too smart to get involved and he put the acid on the Board to call it off. It just happened that Don was chairman at the time. It was dreadful, not just for him but for the Board, but he was the bunny. He was the spokesman. Whoever was chairman would have copped a heap but because it was Bradman of course he copped more. But he was a wonderful diplomat. It broke Don's heart because he was very fond of the South Africans. He was absolutely thrilled when they came back into the play in 1992.

Another hot issue in the late 1970s was World Series Cricket.
Sir Donald was on the Board of Control's emergency committee
at that time.

We always had an emergency committee of the Board. We thought the word emergency was a bit silly, but what it meant was we had one director each from three states. So if something happened in between ACB meetings, the emergency committee would get on the phone and sort it out and they'd report back to the next Board meeting. That committee had been in place for 60 or 70 years then all of a sudden we did have an emergency (laughs) – and how. So yes, Don was part of that, but only because he was the senior representative from South Australia. Bob Parish was the bloke from Melbourne and I'd toss a coin as to who was the better chairman of the ACB out of Parish and Bradman, that's how good Parish was. He was outstanding. And then there was a bloke called Tim Caldwell from New South Wales. They were really the big three in Australian cricket.

Don was very, very disturbed, obviously, about World Series Cricket. He could see it was threatening the fabric of the game. Anybody who was slightly interested in the wellbeing and welfare of the game was very concerned about it; the only ones who weren't were the players and Kerry Packer. The players got more dough and Kerry got the TV rights, that's what it was all about. But we could see that it was a threat to take over the running of the game. Whereas in fact as it turned out Packer didn't do that. Once he got the TV rights he was happy and then we were able to come to an arrangement whereby we did the controlling of the game and he had the TV, which is all he was after in the first place, which is fine. (It's an interesting comparison. Murdoch bought the rugby league for his television as well, but he won't give it back. That's the difference. (laughs) Kerry gave the cricket back but Rupert's kept the football.)

Parish was chairman then and he's the one who was able to smooth it over. Don of course was of tremendous use. For example, it was Don who convinced Bob Simpson to come back as captain after an absence of 10 years and we needed him because we'd lost all our senior players, all our experience had gone. That's the sort of thing that Don did behind the scenes. But Parish was the one who really carried the can on that and did it brilliantly. Absolutely.

The two greatest crises in cricket in my time were the South Africa question, when Don was in the chair so he copped the flak, and the World Series, which was Parish in the chair. And they were probably the two greatest crises we ever had in Australian cricket.

And it survived.
It's come out of them all damned well. It has. Unbelievable. So as long as Test cricket retained its place, that's all that Don and people wanted, for Test cricket not to be overshadowed by the one-day form of the game. And that's what's come to pass, so everyone's happy. It was quite a fun time, I can tell you.

Was his resignation as a selector in 1972 a surprise to the Board?
No. He'd foreshadowed it. He always foreshadowed things like that. Same as when he was chairman of the Board in 1969–72. He announced at the start of the meeting when he was re-elected that it would be his last time. And he always liked to set up some sort of succession. He never thumped the table and said I don't agree with this, I've had it and I'm walking out the door.

So did you ever see him angry?
I saw him have plenty of reason to be and I saw him upset, I saw him disappointed, but I never, ever saw him angry. And there's only one occasion on which I can recall him swearing and that was

in a letter in response to some accounts I had sent him from the Bradman Foundation in 1991 which indicated some fathers had reneged on paying for their sons' cricket coaching. I'll read you what he said: 'I was annoyed to see that cheques for the coaching classes to the value of $640 had bounced. Evidently there are still some bastards around.' I remember that because it was so out of the ordinary. But I've never heard anyone say, 'Oh, Don lost his temper about this or that.' Remarkable. Considering the enormous pressures he was under. I mean his whole life was just lived in the public glare.

What influence did you feel that public glare had on his life?
I think Don was able to handle it because of his intellect. He never let anything overshadow the fact that he was basically just a country boy and all these things had happened to him that he didn't sort of ask for, they just happened because he was so damn good. That's the only way he was able to survive. He could turn off by listening to music or playing his piano or playing bridge or going out to dinner with friends and having a nice glass of red wine. They were his escape hatches. He didn't have time to go away and have a nice holiday, for example. He lived his whole life under an absolute magnifying glass. And I don't care what anyone tells you, it's hard to find how he ever put a foot wrong.

I'm talking about him like he's some sort of a god, but the fact is that you can't find where he ever got drunk and fell over and abused someone or walked out on someone's function or . . . you just can't find those things, they just didn't happen in his life. He was an extraordinary man.

With an extraordinary degree of self-control.
Absolutely. That's what made him so unique.

Was there anything of the country boy left?

Well, he used to like to think so. He always considered himself the boy from Bowral. He didn't rave on about the fact that he knew royalty etcetera. I took him to lunch one day and the next day he was invited to lunch at the Governor-General's place where Prince Charles was the guest of honour. Don didn't actually want to go but his wife Jessie wanted to so . . . I caught him on the way through. And he remarked completely off the cuff that he reckoned he was the only Australian alive who would have met George V, George VI, Elizabeth II and now Charles. Then he just kept on talking. He didn't think it was a big deal at all. That's an amazing thing.

His accent remained strongly Australian, didn't it?

Very. That's where the boy from Bowral stayed there. He was always very well aware of his humble beginnings. He had a difficult time in that his family wasn't rich, and then the Depression came and unemployment was rife and for everyone who came through that Depression, a quid was a quid. Nowadays a quid, you go and whack it through the poker machines and you laugh about it. But they were brought up in a different way. A quid was six loaves of bread and some milk to feed the family. And that never left those people, none of them. So when he was playing Don was always looking to the future after cricket to make money. He wasn't a greedy avaricious person but he realised that money was important to bring up your family.

But in later life he knocked back that many offers of money from people that it was just amazing. He could have been a very, very rich man. So he didn't chase money, he just knew that it was pretty essential in life. When he signed over the rights of his name and everything to the Bradman Foundation, that was a huge gesture, because that was really the family legacy that he signed over.

But he was comfortable enough and he provided very well for his daughter, who has cerebral palsy. His son was a lawyer so he could look after himself, so it wasn't as though the family was going to struggle.

Did you consider yourselves friends?

I was very proud to have called him a friend. We hit it off well back in 1970, and our mutual respect grew over the years. Especially in 1993 when I became chairman of the Bradman Foundation we were in quite a bit of financial trouble and I was able to guide us out of that. Don loved that because he never sought that museum at all and frankly he never thought it was going to work. I know that because he told me. He used to call it a pipe dream or words to that effect and of course when we finally did it and it was so magnificent he just couldn't believe what we had been able to achieve. When things were hard for the museum I spent a lot of time with Don going back and forth to Adelaide and a lot of time on the phone to him. I always wanted to keep him informed. He used to say, 'I don't want to know anything about the museum, Bob, that's your job, but . . .' and then two hours later . . . He wanted to know all right.

Don and Jessie seem to have had an amazing relationship.

I never saw two people so much in love as those two. Never. Jessie was a magnificent woman. Wonderful. Getting back to the time he was going to have lunch at Government House with Prince Charles, he said, 'You know, as much as I love Jessie, she loves two things that I can't stand.' I said, 'What's that?' And he said, 'Meeting people and travelling.' (laughs) And Don couldn't stand either of them. And here he was going to Government House, driving from Adelaide, so that Jessie could be part of the party.

Jessie visited England without Sir Donald, didn't she?
She travelled with her sister, because she just loved England. You see, whenever Don went there it was impossible, it was no fun for Jessie at all. What's she going to do? Sit in a hotel room at night while Don's out being entertained? And Don hated cocktail parties and all those things. He and Jessie both loved England. In 1934, when Don was recuperating after he'd been desperately ill, someone loaned him a car. They reckoned it was about the best two or three weeks they ever had in their lives, they just drove all over England, to all these little out of the way places. No one knew they were coming, they'd just turn up and check in to a little hotel. They had a lovely time because they could be anonymous and do their own thing.

Don was offered the presidency of the MCC at Lord's on at least two occasions. I'm talking about the real MCC – the Maryle-bone Cricket Club, not the Melbourne Cricket Club. He was the only non-Englishman ever offered the presidency and he declined on both occasions. I think he thought it was a silly thing to be president there and living here. So he was very keen on England but he certainly wasn't going to move over there.

Was Sir Donald a man with any small talk or was small talk something he didn't like?
Hated it! Absolutely hated it! But you know he would always do the right thing. That's the sort of manners he had. Everything was proper. But that didn't mean he couldn't think like a young bloke. And he didn't mind one-day cricket and coloured clothing. People like Bill O'Reilly and Sir Roden Cutler just to name two wouldn't go anywhere near it. Don didn't go back to that stage of tradition.

What was he like to watch cricket with?
It was very difficult at the cricket because he didn't want to be dis-turbed. And the reason I often sat next to him was because he knew

that I wouldn't earbash him. So I would take up a seat and hope-fully no one would sit on the other side, thinking that we were talking about the Bradman Foundation or something. We were in the private committee room, but there's always a thrasher and of course he was the bunny to be thrashed.

He enjoyed my company because he knew, a) I wasn't going to talk nonsense, and b) if necessary I wouldn't talk at all. And when we did talk watching cricket matches, we very rarely talked about the cricket. We'd talk about the stock market or something, not why did Joe Blow play such a stupid shot. We didn't analyse the actual match.

Did he have any extravagances?
His one extravagance, if he had one, would be red wine. He was very particular about his wine. In the days he played he didn't drink. The Bill O'Reillys and the Lindwalls and all that mob, they drank their heads off like the current mob do. Like most sportsmen do, it's not just cricketers. Over the years they always have – let's go to the bar and have a beer. And that was a good thing because it got the teams to fraternise, not only with each other but with the opposi-tion, which is what the game is supposed to be all about. But Don didn't like that. He didn't drink, he'd have a soft drink.

Later on in life, he discovered the pleasure of the South Aus-tralian vineyards. We had some mutual friends down there, and we'd always go up to Yalumba when the Test match was on in Ade-laide. Don knew his wines, and he got to meet the Henschke family, a magnificent red wine mob. But he'd have two or three glasses of red at lunch or at dinner; he wasn't a bloke who would sit in a corner and guzzle a bottle of wine. He knew his wines and he loved red wines, really good wines, he loved them. And sherry. Sherry before dinner.

And was he a food buff?

Nah, I don't think he could care less. I remember when he was chairman of the Board, the Board always had a dinner, and Alan Barnes, my predecessor, would consult him as a matter of courtesy and say, 'What would you like?' And Don would say, 'Send me the wine list and you organise the rest.' He didn't care, he wasn't into food.

Was he a workaholic?

Absolutely. He received hundreds of letters a week and replied to every one of them. Some he'd reply two pages, some he'd reply one paragraph. One sentence. That was an enormous job and that was work. He was always whingeing about it. He always wanted a whinge. You never quite knew what he was going to whinge about but you had to be prepared for a whinge. Nothing was ever perfect.

And then of course Jessie got ill, and when he got rheumatism later and had to give up his golf – golf and Jessie were two great outlets towards the very end of his life and he lost them both. And then he'd get more cranky. It got to a stage when you got the feeling that he really didn't want to hang on much longer. And he'd whinge about all the autograph requests and so on. People would send him bats and he'd sign them and then he'd go down to the post office and then he'd get in the queue and he'd have to post all these bats. What it must have cost him in postage over the years I've no idea. I offered him secretarial assistance that the Bradman Foundation would have paid for. Nup. He had to do everything himself, wouldn't let anyone do it.

When we had big functions here, he would sign the menus prior to the function. Say there were a thousand people coming to a big black-tie dinner at the Regent Hotel which we did have for the Bradman Foundation, you'd drop a thousand menus around to his hotel and he'd sign the whole lot. So the MC would then get up and say, 'Please do not interrupt Sir Donald through his meal. On your table you have your menu autographed by him.' He would say, 'Are we going to have a glossy menu or are we going to have a board type menu? What quality paper because the ink doesn't take so well on the glossy but it will take much better on the board.' He knew all these things.

Eventually I got some kids from the coaching classes in Adelaide (the academy, they call it) at the SACA office and they'd go up to his place once a week and pick up all the bats and take them all down to the post office to save him doing it. At least he relented that much. And then of course it got to the stage where the amount of stuff coming to his house was just ridiculous so it all went to Adelaide Oval. They had a special room there and Don would come down when it mounted up and he'd spend three hours signing a whole room full of stuff and he used to say, 'I'm just not going to Adelaide Oval any more, I just can't stand it.'

So he did it all the time but he complained.
All the time. He always had to have something to complain about. And it was usually this autograph stuff which would drive any human mad.

I think most of us would stop doing it.
Many of them do. A lot of them say no more. But Don thought it was his responsibility. He had this fantastic sense of responsibility about the game and doing the right thing by the fans and by the people that made up the game. So he felt it was irresponsible to throw away someone's letter, however stupid it was.

When he was chairman of the Board of Control, was he able to delegate or did he want to do it all himself?
The secretary Alan Barnes was a very good administrator. In fact Barnes was a workaholic but he wasn't nearly as efficient as Bradman

and Bradman admired efficiency. He'd get onto Barnes about things like the minutes. 'Where the hell are the minutes?' Barnes would say, 'Oh they're coming, they'll be here.' And Don had virtually taken his own minutes at the meetings so he'd compare them with whatever came out.

He had his own funny little loose-leaf book he designed himself. He'd get the agenda and he'd cut out the heading and put it on a page. There might be 100 items on the agenda, and he had 100 pages in his book. At the meeting he'd write the resolution underneath that heading and turn the page and there was the next item on the agenda, and that was his next minute, and so it went on. So then if he told Barnes and myself we were wrong, then we were wrong, because he'd put down exactly what the resolution was, word for word. I never saw anyone else do it, ever. Other people would just scribble something or other on the margin of the agenda, but he had it all worked out.

Everything in Don's life was meticulously worked out. Everything. As Bill O'Reilly said, even in his cradle, Don Bradman wouldn't have done anything that wasn't thought out. It's so true. All his life, everything was planned. He never did anything off a whim. Ever. That's just the way his mind worked.

Was he a reader?

No. He didn't have time. He certainly wasn't well read, as they say. People would send him cricket books and he'd read them. People like me, I suppose. He'd find 50 errors and write back to the bloke and point out all the errors. Then they'd write and they'd want him to write a foreword and he got so sick and tired of writing forewords. He just said no to all forewords near the end, he just couldn't do it. Then he was asked one day to do an epilogue. He'd never been asked to do an epilogue in his life and he thought that was rather interesting, so he did that.

I remember once the Cricket Club in New South Wales were

going over to India and they asked me if I'd ask Don to do a foreword
to their tour book and I said, 'No, Don won't do it, he's told me he's
sick of forewords.' They kept at me and at me so I wrote the foreword
and I sent it to Don and I said, 'To save you the time and the trouble,
here's what I think you might like to write.' And he changed about six
words in it and thanked me very much. He said, 'I've changed a little
to make it a little more Bradman-esque.' So they got their foreword
and they put it in their tour book and they went away happy.

I did a lot of that for him. I'd give him the background to
speeches and things like that because it was just ridiculous what he
tried to do. If he made a speech at an important function, he knew
exactly how long he was to speak for, he'd tell the MC, I'm going
for eight minutes, or twelve and a half minutes. He'd do his speech
and he'd play it to himself on the tape recorder at home and time it
and change it and time it. So when he actually got to do the speech
it was perfect as far as he was concerned and he knew exactly to the
second how long it went. Other blokes just get up and make a
speech and sit down. Not Don.

When we had the big dinner at the Regent Hotel when we
started the Bradman Foundation off, he wanted a lectern and a
glass of water. And I said, 'Look, this is a five star hotel, they'll
know how to set things up.' He said, 'I'm leaving it to you. I want a
lectern and a glass of water.' And he wrote me a letter later on and
he thanked me for organising the lectern and the glass of water.
That's the sort of bloke he was. Amazing.

*One of the few interviews Sir Donald Bradman granted to print
journalists during his career, he conducted in his pyjamas and dressing
gown early on New Year's Day in 1971. Thirty years on,* Herald
journalist **Graham Eccles** *spoke of it at his home in Melbourne as one
of the highlights in his 40-year career.*

IT WAS 1971 DURING the Test match that got washed out in Melbourne. Totally washed out, there wasn't a ball bowled, and I tried to get him because we needed something on cricket. I asked twice in two days for an interview and he was really adamant that he wasn't going to be in it. At this stage he was chairman of the Board and a Test selector. I tried the day before and he said, 'Absolutely no, no, no, I won't be in it, Graham. No interviews, no.' I thought gosh, you know, there was no play that day. So later that afternoon before I went home I rang again, to see if I persisted he might just give in.

He wasn't there but Lady Jessie was, and oh gosh, she was just a beautiful lady, just like your grandma, she was a wonderful human person. She said, 'Oh, Graham, I know what he's like, he doesn't like doing these things. But leave it with me and I'll try and talk him into it. We'll get back to you.' But I didn't get a call.

Anyway, the next morning, I was desperate because this was the big column piece run on page two we used to call 'On the Spot', and it was every day. This was it. The first day when he knocked me back I was able to get out of it because I had something else. But this time I was pinning everything on it.

I didn't want to try him much before 8 o'clock because (laughs) it's not a good time to get people out of bed. Anyway, I rang through from downstairs in the lobby and he answered the phone. We went through the spiel again. You know: 'I think it's appropriate with the Test being washed out,' dum de dum de dum and he said 'No, Graham, I told you, I don't want to do it, really, I've got nothing to say.' I said, 'Oh, I really do think you have. Apart from that, I'm in real trouble, I've got nothing else to fill this column.' There was silence for a minute and then he said grumpily, 'Oh, all right, come up.'

I slammed down the phone quickly and I said to Ken Rainsbury, the photographer, 'Boy, we're in,' and I said, 'This is going to be tricky and touchy, he sounds very grumpy, so just sit there and we'll get a good pic when it's all over.'

Anyway, I went up there and I gingerly knocked on the door, and there he was in his pyjamas and his dressing gown. And he had a beaming smile. 'Come in, Graham.' Shook my hand. Lady Jessie was in the other single bed – I always remember her, she was reading a Taylor Caldwell novel and she said, 'Don't take any notice of me, Graham,' which was rather difficult. And he said, 'Do you mind if I finish my prunes?' And I said, 'Yeah fine.'

So he got back on the bed and finished his prunes and away we went and it was just the easiest interview I've conducted in 40 years. He was forthright, answered everything, he was great. It was so intimate I couldn't believe it. I just felt like I was a member of the family sitting on the end of the bed, it was like coming in and having a chat with your parents.

I suppose I had about 40 minutes with him and this was for the *Herald* which was an afternoon paper. I interviewed him at about 8 o'clock and I had to get back to write it for the first edition. It had to be all finished by about 10.30, quarter to 11 at the absolute latest. It was an extraordinary situation, the editor was hanging over my shoulder, and they were ripping each page out of my typewriter to get it into the paper. It was the biggest thing we'd done in ages. We'd got The Don!

The Don says in the interview that he was always open for anyone to speak to him, but really, you couldn't get to him. Simply, very few people would ask him in the media because they felt it wasn't the right thing to do. Sir Donald was just up there on another level. You'd see him in the grounds and he'd be sitting up there just near the players, he'd generally be sitting outside. The first time I met him, he said, 'Good morning, Graham.' I'd never been introduced to him, but he knew who was around and who was doing what, and you'd say, 'Good morning, Sir Donald.' I'd never really

had any conversation or been in company with him. I would have
felt out of place and I think most cricket writers would have. Perhaps
with somebody like Ray Robinson it might have been different,
because Ray was from his era. But when I started cricket writing in
1961, I was only 23, I was a baby, so you had to feel your way.

The other selectors never said anything. Dudley Seddon from
New South Wales was a little nondescript bloke who didn't really
like the press, and the other one was Jack Ryder, the famous Victorian and Australian batsman. Jack was a lovely fellow. I knew Jack
reasonably well but he'd never tell you anything. You could ask
him but he'd just give you this enigmatic smile and that was as far
as it went.

Everyone wanted Bradman to talk. Anything that he would say
would be picked up – and I think this is why he kept away from a lot
of media people. I talked about it in the interview. I asked him,
'Why don't you talk about cricket? Everyone wants to know what
you're saying.' Everyone wanted him constantly. Why was this man
so quiet? He's the leading figure in the game, he should have been
talking about all sorts of things. But he felt it was up to the players
to do their thing and that the administrators who ran the various
states should be taking a front line. It shouldn't be just him imposing his views on cricket simply because of who he was.

It was an extraordinary interview. It was one of the great thrills
in my career. We'd got Bradman, it was such a rarity.

Meredith Burgmann *was the 20-year-old co-convenor of the Anti-
Apartheid Movement in Sydney in the midst of a campaign against the
South African Springboks rugby tour in 1971 when a letter arrived out
of the blue from Sir Donald Bradman. We spoke in Parliament House
in Sydney where Dr Burgmann is President of the New South Wales
Legislative Council.*

WE WERE PROBABLY the major group running the anti-Springbok campaign which was aimed at the South African rugby team, the Springboks' visit in June and July, but more importantly at stopping the South African cricket tour altogether six months later in December–January.

Bradman was chair of the Australian Cricket Board when that decision was being made and blow me down, before the footballers come, he writes to me, right address and everything. Goodness knows how he found me. He writes to me basically saying why are you doing this? You shouldn't mix sport and politics.

I, of course, being a 20-year-old think it quite normal that an icon writes to me and I write back with all my arguments, very politely because I'm a big cricket fan – a big cricket fan. I write back and say it's the South Africans that are mixing sport and politics, they're the ones who are refusing to let black South Africans try out for the team. All that sort of thing. This goes backwards and forwards for quite some time and I realise that he's querying. It's not an outraged person; it's someone who's trying to find out what the issues are. He's actually trying to find out!

In one of his letters, he says, 'When I was very young, I did certain things which in the fullness of time I now see were unreasonable. Now that I am an old man I see more clearly that there are usually two sides to any case; that the problem is to get at the rationale of the viewpoints.' And in my notes for my reply, against his comment about his age I write, 'I'm not that young myself.'

In September when they announce that the cricketers aren't coming, we had expected them to say, 'We can't guarantee their safety so they can't come,' but Sir Donald doesn't do that. Instead the *Sydney Morning Herald* reported, 'Sir Donald said that his board had faced every aspect of the unenviable problem and had weighed carefully the views expressed by responsible authorities including churchmen and police. It had decided with great regret that it would have to advise the South Africans that in the present atmosphere the invitations would have to be withdrawn . . . the Board said it hoped that the South African government would in the near future so relax its apartheid laws that cricketers of South Africa would once again take their place as full participants in the international field.'

He actually says until they stop the system of apartheid, we won't play them, which was quite remarkable. That announcement that he made was basically the beginning of the cutting of sporting contact with South Africa. We didn't expect that because cricket was pretty traditional and conservative and him saying that was quite remarkable.

Had you felt with your letters that you were getting somewhere?
Absolutely. It wasn't an outraged cranky old man writing to me, it was someone questing for more knowledge and wanting to know what our motives were. The arguments sort of change as he goes along. And then there's my favourite one of the lot, where he's cranky that I haven't written back and he says, 'Dear Miss Burgmann, I had been hoping to receive a reply to my letter but none has arrived,' so he's waiting for the next instalment. And then just at the end, about six months after it was all over he sent me a cutting about some multi-racial games in South Africa and writes, 'Dear Miss Burgmann, is this what you were wanting?' And I write back and say, 'No, it's got to be non-racial. Because multi-racial games is when Indians play Africans play whites, whereas non-racial games is where everyone plays in together.' So he was still thinking about it well after the Springboks had been and gone.

But he really grapples with the issues. He keeps talking about things, good things that have happened there where Africans have been advanced and everything. I knew a lot about it at the time. He talks about allowing black golfers, and I say, 'Yes, but when Papwe

Segolum won, they had to hand his trophy through the window because he wasn't allowed into the clubhouse to receive it,' really offensive stuff like that.

He kept sending me things. He was basically saying that racism's everywhere so why are we picking on South Africa. And of course my answer to that is apartheid is the only case of a country institutionalising racism. Of course those terrible things occur. He talks about Zambia and one of his arguments is South Africa is more civilised than these other countries. He wrote about Russia. He absolutely believed that if you were opposing the Raj you were probably a communist. But then everyone did in those days. When we opposed the Vietnam War everyone immediately thought we were communists. If you questioned the status quo, they thought you were a communist.

In one of the letters in response to my mention of an 'ideal situation', he wrote: 'I could say to you "thank heaven for the optimism of youth", or I could say "Meredith – when will you grow up?" There can never be an ideal situation.' In that same letter (it was three closely typed pages) he wrote of Australia's own history: 'And if you'll pardon me for saying so – how did you come to get a chance of a university education? It was made possible because your forebears and mine plundered this country, murdered Aborigines etc. etc. and took over the land. Our ancestors evidently did things as bad or worse than the South African whites have done.'

He wrote to quite a few people – I think Peter McGregor, another of the local organisers was writing back too. And he wrote to Peter Hain, the British organiser of the Anti-Apartheid Movement, who is now a senior minister in the Blair Government.

And his letters are long and they're detailed and he obviously loved an argument. I felt by the end that he was fond of me. And I grew fond of him. I certainly felt that they were very civilised letters we were having and that he was changing his view, which of course he was, because by September he cancelled the tour. What was very clear to them was if you can stop a football match, you can stop a cricket match. Because mirrors in the crowd, anything, it's really easy to stop a cricket match, even just a little bit of yahooing can be very distracting, so I think he just realised it was going to be impossible.

Don't forget at the same time the international pressure would have been coming on. I think he was too practical a man. He realised that he couldn't stand out against what was coming. And he saved Australian cricket from being the centre of a nasty division within the Australian community. It was a really sensible decision and I think the issue of principle clinched it for him.

*When the Australian Cricket Board fielded the Rest of the World XI in place of the cancelled South African tour in 1971–72, Board chairman Sir Donald Bradman called on Test team manager and sports commentator **Bill Jacobs** to manage the visiting team. A spirited 83, the former Victorian player, administrator and selector remembered Sir Donald with great affection.*

IN 1960, I WAS president of the Fitzroy Cricket Club and the club controlled the old Brunswick Street ground, the bowling green and the tennis courts. And Bill Dowling, the president of the Victorian Cricket Association, told me that Sir Donald and Lady Jessie were coming over and they wanted to see the Fitzroy versus Melbourne football game. Mainly because Rohan Rivett and his wife Nan were coming across. They were very good friends, those two. Rivett was a rabid Australian Rules and staunch Fitzroy man and they wanted to come and watch the battle of the Smith brothers, Lenny with Fitzroy and Norm with Melbourne. So Bill asked me if I could get a seat for them. I said sure. And the president's reserve accommodated about 12 people so I had to kick four of my mates out to get them in.

It was a great experience. Prior to the match Bradman asked me if it would be possible to hear one of the Smith brothers address the team. I knew it would be futile approaching Norm, so I went to Lenny and Lenny said, yeah, that's all right. Bradman and I are making our way from the old stand – you can visualise a crowd at the football – he was about the same height as me, both little fellows, pushing our way through the crowds to get to the door of the football room. Nobody recognised him. When the doorman let us in, he just looked at him and didn't take much notice. So I took him in and he heard the team addressed and at the end of the speech proper in the main body of the room, Len took the team into the committee room for a final briefing. It was just the two of us sitting there and Lenny talking to the team out in front of us. It was really something. And he didn't say anything at all to Sir Donald. Exept at the finish he said something like, 'Well now boys, I want an extra special effort from you today, to give pleasure to a man who's given me a lot of pleasure during my lifetime. Sir Donald Bradman', and shook his hand and walked out.

Did Sir Donald have any sympathy for Australian Rules?
I'll tell you how much interest he had. In 1969 I interviewed him at my home in Pascoe Vale and afterwards I drove him into the Windsor. On the way he told me that one of the things he was going to do in Melbourne was to speak to Sir Albert Chadwick [president of the MCC] about the possibility of forming a southern states football league, comprising ten teams from Victoria, two from WA and two from South Australia. A 14-team southern states football competition. So he was miles ahead. He later told me that Sir Albert wasn't all that pleased about it because it would mean losing Victorian teams. But that's how keen he was on Australian Rules. That was 1969 and South Melbourne went to

Sydney in 1982, that was the start of the national competition. So he was at least 13 years ahead of it, but he was like that in a lot of things.

Tell me about that interview.
I wanted to get the interview for 3AW; we had a Sunday show called *Sportlight*. Nobody had interviewed him, not a soul, and I said to Sam Loxton, do you think Sir Donald would be receptive to an interview? He said, 'Well it bloody well depends who does it.' I said, 'Well, I'm going to do it.' He said, 'Oh well, why don't you write to him?' And that's how it came about. So I wrote to him asking for an interview and I included a set of questions that I'd like to ask him.

It was only a 30-minute show and that included commercials and it went for about ten minutes. So the other interview we had planned went by the board. It took up one-third of the program.

He rarely gave interviews, did he?
He had two reasons, I think. A lot of the people who possibly asked him, he didn't feel inclined to trust them. And I think a lot of people were afraid to ask him. That's only my assessment of it. I didn't ask him face to face.

I remember I asked him about sponsored cricket, which wasn't about then, and his view then was he hoped cricket could continue the way it had, but if sponsored cricket came along then okay, accept it. Now unbeknownst to him or anybody else, it was only two or three years after that that we had a sponsored tour. When South Africa couldn't come here, at his instigation a Rest of the World XI team toured. It was sponsored by the *Herald & Weekly Times* for I think $70 000 and he asked me to manage it.

What was it like to manage the Rest of the World XI in the 1971–72 series?

That was one of the greatest experiences I've ever had in my life. I'd had the experience of four and a half months in South Africa managing the Australian team in 1966–67. I'd done a bit of travelling overseas with Norman Banks a couple of times, ex-3AW. But I was quite surprised when Bradman asked me to manage the team.

In the December of the tour we had a little seven-day war between India and Pakistan. I had three Indians and three Pakistanis in the team. I got them together and I said, 'What's the situation here, what are the problems as far as you blokes are concerned?' And they were terrific fellows. There was Sunil Gavaskar, Farookh Engineer and Bishen Bedi from India, and from Pakistan Intikhab Alam, Asif Masood and Zaheer Abbas. All different temperaments and personalities and I just said, 'How does it affect you?' They were all very friendly and they said, 'As long as we don't get our photos taken together,' because if the photos were beamed back, it would be rough for their relatives. So we had to play ducks and drakes, and by some means ensure that their photos weren't taken together. The war lasted about a week. So we'd have Sunil walking out behind Gary Sobers and three back would be a Pakistani. (laughs) It was good. It was terrific.

I had quite a bit to do with Sir Donald during the tour. He and everybody else were pretty worried about the 1971–72 series because it commenced in an atmosphere of uncertainty. The tour of Australia by the South African team had to be cancelled at the eleventh hour because tremendous pressures had been brought to bear by various sections of the community and finally the Australian Board of Control was faced with the unenviable task of having to make the final decision.

The Rest of the World XI played with only moderate success in the early stages of the tour. Drawn games against Victoria and New South Wales did not excite much interest but a win against

Queensland kicked things along a little. Then a high-scoring draw in the International against Australia did nothing but boost the averages of a few individuals. The World XI defeated Western Australia but were thrashed in the second International in Perth. When we got to Adelaide, South Australia beat us inside of two days, which was a hell of a wake-up. At the end of the second day they were packing their bags and I was absolutely furious about it all and I told them not to bother to pack their bags, they'd be practising the next morning. They weren't too impressed with me about that.

And of course Clive Lloyd had hurt his back and I'd rung Sir Donald. We had to talk about a replacement for Cunis who was going back in January anyway, and we obviously had to talk about one for Clive. And he said, 'Well, could I see you tomorrow morning?' I said, 'Yes, we'll be practising.' He said, 'Practising?' I said, 'Yes, we'll be practising.' So he agreed to come down at practice and I told the team with a few epithets thrown in, what I thought of them, and told them that Bradman was coming to have a look at them. Sobey and Bradman and I sat behind the nets in Adelaide in three deckchairs and you've never seen a practice like it. They thought he was watching them. And he said to me, 'My word, you've got them steamed up this morning, Bill,' and I told him what I'd said to them. He thought it was terrific.

But from Melbourne on, when Sobers made his 254, the thing picked up and they actually won the series. But the Australian selectors were altering the team a bit, using players with a view to the tour of England in '72 so players were being omitted not because of poor form.

But on the other hand our team did lift and they did lift particularly after Sobers' 254. Sir Donald said it was the best innings he'd seen played in Australia and it was really something out of the box. Cricketers have got these phobias and superstitions of not moving from one place to another when an innings is in progress and all that. Nobody moved for about three hours. It was a wonderful innings.

At the end of the World XI tour, I organised a dinner for the team and I asked Sir Donald to come along as our one and only guest. So he came along and there were a couple of speeches. I remember saying something about it wasn't to be a night of speeches but I spoke to the team and the team made a presentation to me and he just touched me on the arm and said, 'I want to say a few words.' And he got up and he said, 'Bill said it wasn't to be a night of speeches but I want to say to you how much I've appreciated you being here.' And then he went around every member of the team about their performance on the tour. And then he arrived at Richard Hutton, who was the son of Sir Leonard Hutton. Richard had had just a very ordinary tour and he said, 'Richard, better things will come your way', something like that. And he said, 'I have an appreciation of what it must be like to be the son of a famous father because I can tell you that in the space of the next few days my son is changing his name by deed poll.' That was in February 1972. He wasn't critical or cynical or anything like that. He mentioned it simply because he was talking about Richard Hutton and his famous father. He understood fully.

He certainly enjoyed himself that night. They were a mix – we had three West Indians, three Pakistanis, three Indians, one New Zealander, three Poms – Richard Hutton, Norman Gifford and Bobby Taylor who were fantastic, and by that time four South Africans, Tony Greig and Hylton Ackerman who were there all along, and Peter and Graeme Pollock who joined us late. They were a mixed mob, I can tell you.

During the course of the night, I knew a bit of Afrikaans from touring South Africa and the Indians taught me a bit of Urdu and this that and the other and I made a little speech using different languages, just very brief, and Bradman asked me what I'd said. Intikhab told him and he said, 'That is not very becoming of an Australian manager.' (laughs)

Just as an aside, they got $200 a week, $150 plus a $50 allowance, for the World XI tour and when I told them that they were going to receive $200 a week (I got the same), they were rapt. They were all pros and they thought $200 a week was terrific.

During that World XI tour I felt that I got to know Sir Donald pretty well. Some people have said that he was a bit shy and I think that there was quite a bit of that about him and the other thing, he didn't intrude on other people. And also he'd been overwhelmed all his life with people breaking their necks to see him and to talk to him and get his autograph and all that. As a consequence I think that he hadn't exactly put up a wall but he didn't push himself onto people. I found him easy to talk to at that stage.

You had managed the Australian tour of South Africa in 1966–67?

When I was appointed as manager for that tour at the Victorian Cricket Association lunch Sir Donald came from one end of the room to the other to say hello and congratulate me and wish me well, and I had quite a bit of contact with him on our return home. The bushfires were bad at that time and the Board of Control organised a Bushfire Test, as it was called, between the team that toured South Africa and an Australian team that had toured New Zealand. They had the game at Melbourne and I spent about three or four days talking to him there.

Some 18 months after the tour of South Africa I was in Adelaide and he invited me home, and Rohan Rivett and his wife were his other guests that night. At dinner they were discussing a subject, it was something that Bradman and Gubby Allen had discussed. They were great friends, Allen and Bradman, and Bradman said to

Rivett, 'You're wrong,' and Rohan Rivett said, 'No, you're wrong and I'm right', and all that sort of thing. And Rivett said, 'Look, do you want to have a case of red on this?' Bradman said, 'Righto.'

So he went out to his study – he took me out and showed me his study – he had all these filing cabinets with all his letters filed and he plucked out a letter he wrote to Allen and a copy of the reply and he put it on the table and he said, 'There you are, you owe me a case of red.' As good as that. So you didn't argue with him. I remember he laughed his head off that night.

I remember another occasion when he had invited me to his home for dinner and drove me from Adelaide Oval to his home in Kensington. He mentioned that he objected to wearing a seat belt, that he felt that they restrained him too much. Obviously like everyone else he had to continue wearing them but he was his own man and I really don't think he liked being told that he had to wear them.

You worked on the early commercial television cricket coverage. What did that involve?

In 1962–63 Tony Charlton got this idea of covering the Test matches for Channel Nine. Of course, until then the ABC had had exclusive coverage. A mere pittance, they used to pay. Anyhow, Charlton got permission to cover the two Test matches in Melbourne and Adelaide. Bear in mind this is January 1963. The Adelaide Test was always played over the Australia Day weekend. It was an earth-shattering moment. To get the signal to Sydney – it sounds stupid now (laughs) – we set up in Adelaide and ten minutes before play started an aircraft would take off from Nhill and circle. And we'd bounce the signal from Adelaide to the aircraft to Melbourne and up the coaxial cable to Sydney. That's how the picture got to Sydney. It's like winding a television set up, isn't it? But that's what it was.

I don't know whether the pilot ever got dizzy flying around. He flew for two hours before lunch then he'd go down and have a drink and go up again. Something like that.

Tony wanted to interview Sir Donald on this occasion, and he said to me, 'You know him a bit, you go and ask him.' So I fronted up and told him what it was all about and he said, 'Yes, that'll be okay providing the ABC get it as well.' And that was no problem, because we were using ABC cameras. So out of loyalty to the ABC that was the stipulation and Tony interviewed him.

5

Out of the Limelight

*An Australian Test captain and grandson of Australian Test captain and Bradman team-mate Vic Richardson, **Greg Chappell** encountered Sir Donald in his role as administrator and selector at both state and national levels. He had returned to his home state to coach South Australia, and we spoke in his office at the South Australian Cricket Association.*

I'D HAVE BEEN A teenager before I first met him. I think it was when I first started playing cricket for South Australia in 1966 when I was just out of school. He used to come into the dressing room every morning and have a cup of tea with Les Favell, our captain and Phil Ridings, who was the other selector at the time, and the three of them would chat about whatever they had to chat about. Sir Donald wasn't particularly outgoing. He was chairman of selectors but he never spoke to me when I was first chosen for the South Australian team.

Did you ever feel that his relationship with your grandfather set you apart?
From what I understand the relationship between him and my grandfather wasn't particularly close so whether that made it difficult for him, I don't know. I was never really conscious of it then because he wasn't particularly communicative with the other guys. Some of the senior players he would speak to because obviously he'd seen them around for a lot longer.

Later I approached him as Australian captain via a mutual friend to attend one of our team dinners, not to do anything other than just be there and be an inspiration and speak if he felt like speaking. But he declined on the basis that he didn't do that sort of thing and yet he did it on a number of occasions after I asked him. Little things like that happened that made you feel that the relationship between my grandfather and Sir Donald had strained any relationship between any of us.

What was your first significant contact with him?
I can remember the one conversation that I had with him early in my career, the only conversation that I had with him during my playing career with South Australia pretty much. One morning he was in the dressing room. As usual, he hadn't communicated with anyone other than those that he had come in to talk to, and he was walking out and I just happened to be near the door. And I don't know what made me speak to him because I'd never been moved to do it before but probably the fact that he was as close as we are now, I felt . . . I don't remember to be honest whether I felt I should do it or whether it was almost a bit of 'well, I'll force him to say something'.

But I just said, 'Good morning, Sir Donald'. And I was standing there with a cricket bat in my hand and bear in mind that I'd played a full season the year before. He stopped, almost surprised and said, 'Oh, good morning. By the way, I'd change that grip if I were you.' Which then sort of put me on the back foot and I can't believe that I had the presence of mind to say, 'Well, what would you suggest?' because I wasn't a particularly outgoing person myself at that stage. And he said, 'Well the one I used worked pretty well.' And not having really seen him play I said, 'Well, what grip was that?'

He said, 'Well, you can see it in my coaching book but I actually held the bat with the V between the thumb and the forefinger on both hands straight down the bat.' Whereas I had my top hand more around to the off side, (he demonstrates) which as you can see is quite uncomfortable. It didn't seem uncomfortable to me because that's what I'd always used but it made it very restrictive for me to hit the ball on the off side, much easier for me to hit the ball on the leg side and that was the comment that he made. He said, 'You'll find that it will widen your range of shots, and help you to hit the ball on the off side.' And he said, 'It'll take you a few weeks to get comfortable with it but I suggest that you persevere because I think it will help you a great deal.' He started to walk away and he stopped and turned back and said, 'By the way, I've given this advice to one other player. He didn't take it, and he's no longer in the team,' and with that he turned on his heel and walked out the door.

Was he being funny?
I don't think so. I didn't get that.

You took it as a serious comment.
Yes. As I say I was staggered that he spoke, staggered that he offered this advice just . . . It was obviously something that he'd been aware of and I got the feeling that if I'd never said hello to him he would never have mentioned it to me. But it was obviously fairly uppermost in his mind for it to be the first thing he thought of. Anyway, we were batting that day and we'd already been down in the nets. I went back down and I tried the grip there and then. Sir Donald had said that it would probably take about six weeks to get use to it, but in fact I found it totally comfortable, very natural, and I used it that day and used it for the rest of my career and it was a very important piece of advice. But it was interesting that it happened that way, and the tone in which he gave me the advice was most unusual. But I think very typical of Sir Donald.

So the follow-up to that story was that at the end of the day we were standing around having a chat and a few beers and I told the story of what Sir Donald had done, and everyone sort of said, 'Oh yeah, fair enough'. But there was a fellow called Alan Shiell who had played cricket for South Australia and he was now a cricket writer for the *News*, and as I wandered away he sidled up alongside me and he said, 'Do you know who the other player was?' I said, 'No, he didn't mention it.' And he said, 'It was me. He gave me the same advice and I didn't take it because it just didn't feel comfortable and I didn't persevere with it. So he was right. I was no longer in the side.' He'd been dropped the season before.

Your grandfather Vic Richardson died in 1969 when you were 21. Had you been close?

Not overly close. I think it was a lot to do with the era, men weren't particularly close with men. And Vic, I think, had made a very conscious decision and because he knew that our father had our cricket careers under control, he tended to sit in the background. But I was aware of him, often. A number of times at cricket matches I played at school, I'd look up and see Vic's car parked way down the road and look around and find him hiding behind a tree somewhere or standing in amongst the trees. He never came into the school grounds and made his presence felt and I can understand that because he probably would have felt it was intruding. But if we had a particularly good day often we'd get a phone call at night at home. Mum would come in and say, 'Your grandfather's on the phone' and you'd say 'G'day' and he'd say, 'Well done today. Keep it up.' Clunk. That would be the end of the conversation.

Ian, being five years older, was much closer. I can remember sitting at his feet one day, probably a few years before he died, at our home down at North Glenelg and Ian pumping him about players and matches and countries and so on and Vic answering all of these questions. I was an interested spectator. Ian has always had more of a feel for the history and knew the records of players that had gone before. He was able to ask Vic, 'Well, what about Trumper?' and 'What about this guy and that guy?'

I was probably about four years of age when Trevor was born and I stayed at Vic's home while Mum was in hospital for a few days. And I can remember dragging Vic out into the backyard at his place and I had all the kit on – the pads and the gloves and the bat and so on – and Vic had a practice wicket in his backyard and I said, 'Come on, Pop. Come and throw some balls to me.' And I get the impression that it was a fairly reluctant grandfather that came out and did it, that it wasn't something that he was particularly relishing. Apart from that we hardly talked cricket at all. But I always looked upon Vic as more of an inspiration just from the fact that we knew what he'd done.

What was your father Martin's relationship with Sir Donald?
Oh, he was a team-mate. My father played his early cricket with Kensington up until 1948. Sir Donald wasn't particularly close with any of the players. I can remember my mother telling stories of Lady Bradman coming to team barbecues and things like that but Don never turning up. He wasn't a particularly sociable person; he didn't really enjoy those sorts of thing. Lady Bradman used to turn up and apologise for him. And she had a good time and was very well liked and loved by a lot of the ladies there because she was so open and outgoing.

I think she was a human face of Sir Donald because it was something that he wasn't very comfortable with. During my playing career whenever I was at Government House and other social functions, Sir Donald never approached anyone but always Lady Bradman made a point of going around, particularly with the cricket people, and talking to them. She was very, very generous and very pleasant and she was the real strength behind the throne, I think.

Did your father play for South Australia?

Oh no, but he was in the state squad for a number of years. He would have loved to have played state cricket and in hindsight – I was never aware of it and he never talked about it – I think there's a fair bit of frustration there, unfulfilled dreams and a lot of that energy was put into us, I'm sure.

What was behind your move to the Queensland team in 1973?

It was an opportunity to captain a first-class team. Ian was captain here and would have been as long as he kept playing, so if I was going to get any experience I really had to go elsewhere. When I got approached to go to Queensland it was as much a surprise to me as anyone else because I'd never thought about it. In fact, I had expected to finish my career here in South Australia and finish my life here, for that matter.

How did Sir Donald respond to your move from South Australia?

I didn't get any feeling from the discussion over lunch that I had with Sir Donald and Phil Ridings that there was any real understanding at all. I got the feeling that they were offended more than encouraging or understanding of the reason why. It was 'what have we done wrong?' And it was nothing to do with that at all. It was just an opportunity. I was newly married, so from a family point of view it was a chance for us to strike out on our own. And it was an opportunity for me to strike out on my own and create a reputation for myself, rather than being the 'grandson of . . .' and 'the brother of . . .' That wasn't a big thing but I just felt that I perhaps had a chance to stand in the sun myself for a while.

Out of courtesy to the South Australian Cricket Association I went and said, 'Look, I've had this offer. I'm considering it. I just want you to know.' I didn't go with any intention to try and extract a better deal out of them. There were no deals in those days, I mean we were getting paid five dollars a day for goodness sake. What were we going to get? Ten dollars a day? But I think they may have taken it as that because I remember Sir Donald saying over lunch, 'Look we can't set a precedent by doing something special for you to keep you here,' and I said, 'I fully understand that. I don't expect anything. I'm just informing you.' And that's when he set about trying to enlighten me as to what I was getting myself into and he took offence at me mentioning that sometime later.

These were his comments critical of the administration of Queensland cricket that you revealed in the press during the World Series furore in 1977, is that right?
Yes.

1977 must have been a rough time for cricketers.
Yes, very sad. It was difficult in the sense that it sort of polarised everybody and put friend against friend and all that sort of stuff. It was like a civil war really. I mean that's what it was. We were the anarchists. And you know it was totally against everything that we'd all grown up with. I mean we were as much traditionalists as anybody – we as in Ian and I – and we were heavily involved and obviously had weighed it all up.

And it was very uncomfortable leading up to it. We the players were given no credit for having any insight into what was good for the game and what was good for us as players. All we wanted was a say in anything that affected us, basically. We'd been to the Australian Cricket Board on a couple of occasions looking at ways of improving the financial lot of players.

Ian as captain of Australia had a meeting with the Board at which Sir Donald was chairman, and had talked about a retirement fund and Sir Donald said, 'We don't have the money to do that so we can't do it.'

A couple of years later I was captain and I made a presentation to the Board. At this stage Sir Donald wasn't chairman but he may as well have been. The meeting was at the Queensland Cricket Association at the 'Gabba and Phil Ridings and Bob Parish were the heads of the Australian Cricket Board at that stage. I sat up one end of the table with them and the other Board members sat down the side and Sir Donald was right down the end. And the first half of it was playing conditions and tour stuff and other sort of house-keeping things and Sir Donald just sat back through all of that with his arms folded. Never said a word. It was Parish and Ridings and Caldwell and other members of the Board that responded to any comments that I made there.

As soon as we got to the financial side of it, Sir Donald sat for-ward with his arms on the table and the others all sat back with their arms folded. It was a prearranged thing. I mean: you blokes talk about the other stuff and as soon as he gets to the finances, leave it to me. It was just as though someone had pushed a button and he very aggressively sat forward and shot down everything that I brought up. You know: can't do it, can't do it, can't do it. I said, 'But surely you can . . . We're not asking for very much. We're not asking for the world. We're basically asking for a fair share.' We could see there was a lot of money coming into the game and we were getting a pittance. We were getting $200 a game each, so there's 11–12 players, $2400 was going into the players and they'd just had a million-dollar gate at the MCG, they'd had a $750 000 gate at the Sydney Cricket Ground. We felt that we were getting the raw end of the pineapple.

What we were talking about here is not paying exorbitant

sums to the guys that are playing, but making sure those that make a significant contribution to Australian cricket at least have got something at the end of it that says: 'Well, thank you very much and well done and this is what you've got to go off with as a retirement fund'. And we'd have been talking about a few thousand dollars. We wouldn't have been talking about hundreds of thousands of dollars, or anything like that. It wasn't a significant amount.

And Sir Donald basically said, 'Well, we can't do it.' His argument was that we can't do that because we don't keep the money, it goes back into cricket. And I said, 'Well at least if you could give us a one-page print-out of what comes in and what goes out. If we can see that we're getting a fair share of what's in the tin, you'll never have a problem from us. But we get the feeling at the moment that we're getting ripped off.' So he said, 'Well, all that information is available to you. You can get each state association's annual report. You know, the ACB is made up of the states. All the money goes back to the states. We don't keep any of the money. It's all there for you to see.'

And I said, 'Well look, Sir Donald, that begs a couple of things – first of all that I want to take the effort to get hold of all of them, and then that I can read it and understand it, and that what's in it's the whole story.'

And he said, 'Oh, that's the whole story. We don't have any money. The ACB doesn't keep money. It all goes back to the states and it all goes back into cricket.' Then 12 months later World Series Cricket happened and it came out that there was a million-dollar slush fund that the ACB had, so he hadn't been entirely honest in what he told me. So that left a bit of a sour taste.

Then when World Series Cricket happened, we were outcasts and a lot of pressure was put on the individuals. The touring team was in England at the time and our management was dividing the thing down the middle and getting the blokes who weren't involved and saying, 'Well, you're our friends, you stick with us and you'll be right. Those blokes, they're never going to play cricket again.' And so for a few of the younger blokes who had signed for World Series Cricket, all of a sudden they're thinking, hang on a sec, we're never going to be able to play cricket again.

It was a very difficult time because none of us really knew what was in front of us. We'd gone in on a wing and a prayer and a promise that Kerry Packer was going to be there at the end of the day to organise cricket for us. But the fact of the matter was that 50-odd guys had been approached world-wide, and 52 finished up playing in World Series Cricket. From the Australian signings point of view, we'd all been approached separately, we all agreed to sign separately, and we never discussed it. It was an unspoken commitment and unity in the whole thing.

In the meantime I tried to contact Sir Donald Bradman and I tried to speak to Bob Parish, who snubbed me at the team hotel. I approached him in the foyer the day after it had broken and said, 'Look, we need to sit down and talk' and he just turned on his heels and said, 'We've got nothing to talk about' and got in the lift and left us standing there.

And you wrote to Sir Donald?
I wrote to Sir Donald and I never got a response. His response years later was, 'Well, I wasn't chairman of the Board, Bob Parish was looking after that. I didn't need to respond.' Well, fair enough. But I wrote to him only on the basis that I felt that we needed to have a discussion, particularly for the younger blokes. It didn't matter for Rod Marsh and myself, the senior players. If I never played Test cricket or any other form of cricket after that it didn't matter, because I'd probably played about 50 Test matches at that stage. That was a career for most people anyway. But I was concerned

about the younger blokes. You know, surely we should be sitting down and talking.

Because you have to understand the history that there had been other approaches prior to that and we'd done the right thing and said, 'Look, you'd better go and talk to the Australian Cricket Board' and the Australian Cricket Board just sent them on their way. So when we explained that to John Cornell when he first brought up the idea, even before Kerry Packer's name was mentioned, we said, 'This is the previous history. You'd better go off and talk to the Australian Cricket Board but this is what's happened before.' And he went away and thought about it and thought well, that's obviously no good, so he went and talked to Kerry Packer instead. And that's when Kerry Packer said, 'You go and get the players and I'll bankroll it'.

So obviously it had been devious in the sense that we hadn't gone and sat down with the Australian Cricket Board, but I felt that the Board had a very head-in-the-sand approach. Any approach that we'd made as players we'd just been turned away and treated with disdain and as I've said on many occasions, like second-class citizens: 'You've got nothing to offer us but your ability to play cricket so just bugger off and go and play cricket', which didn't sit well with us. I mean, we were reasonably intelligent people. We could see what was going on. This was a business, and we were part of it and we felt we should have been treated better.

A lot of people were disappointed that Bradman didn't speak out on that issue.
It was not his style. He did it in other ways. He had his network of people around the world that he used to write to and communicate with and he did it all through that network. He was never one that came up front and did it out in the open. He was always doing it behind the scenes and pushing others forward to speak out.

Are you thinking of him and England's Gubby Allen? That sort of relationship?

It was a real cartel. Gubby Allen, Joe Pamensky in South Africa and all those sort of guys. And in Gubby Allen's case he played the game with him and against him so there was that sort of relationship. But the other people who were in administrative roles around the world, he cultivated the association because it gave him the inside knowledge and the background information that he needed to keep his foot on it all.

He knew about what was going on around the world long before the Internet. He had his network and they'd keep him informed of who was who and what was what. Even in the days when Sri Lanka was Ceylon and they weren't involved in world cricket, I know people who'd been writing to Sir Donald for 50 or 60 years.

They obviously had high regard for Sir Donald and his brain and his knowledge and all those sort of things and you can't deny it but he used it in a strange way. He used it in a controlling way, it wasn't ever in a collective situation. It was always we are the bosses and we will do it this way and you will do as you're told.

And yet in 1977 he doesn't appear to have seen it coming.

I think because he was instrumental in causing it, he didn't see it coming. Because I think he felt that they were impregnable. He knew what was going on around the world so this couldn't happen.

I held all the traditions of the game as highly as anyone else did. But I could also see the game was sliding backwards and that if something wasn't done, if we didn't drag it into the 20th century, the game could have just evaporated. And I think there was a very real danger of that. Like there is today. If the rest of the world don't get their act together like Australia's got their act together, we'll have no one to play against, and the game will disintegrate through a lack of interest. And that was what was happening.

Test cricket was boring. I mean it was bloody awful, and mainly because of the way England were going about playing it and basically they were the only ones we played. The West Indies we played occasionally and India and Pakistan almost never. South Africa were out of it altogether at that stage and the Poms were strangling the game. And with all his prescience and all his awareness, I don't know whether Sir Donald saw that.

Now I'm sure he was needling Gubby Allen and others to come on, you guys have got to get your act together and sort this out. But the main thing that Sir Donald and others would have been worried about was that if England paid their Test players too much then the pressure would be on them. You know: 'Don't pay your blokes any more than we pay our blokes otherwise our blokes will want to get more money' and this was all going on behind the scenes.

What about the rapprochement in 1979? Did that resolve the problems?

No, far from it. There are residual problems to this day. There are people who have never forgiven and forgotten, probably on both sides but particularly on the traditional side. The relationship between the players and the Board now is much better than it's ever been. In fact I think the players have almost got the upper hand, certainly from a financial point of view, almost to the detriment of the development of the game at the moment.

What prompted the rapprochement?

The fact was that the members of the Australian Cricket Board were going to be held personally liable for any debts and that was when the message came down – you'd better talk to Kerry Packer and sort this out. Because there was one bloke in particular who had quite a lot to lose. And unfortunately we, the Australian players, were over in the West Indies at the time that they decided to 'get married' and we weren't invited to the wedding. And there were a lot of things that were left unsaid, a lot of things that were left undone. We still had the same problems but all of a sudden with a different programming. It took us years to work out the programming problems. You know, we had two touring teams, Test matches and one-dayers. And we'd have two Test series going concurrently. We played the first Test against West Indies and then the first Test against England. And so on. I mean, it was just horrendous.

And everything that was wrong with it impacted on us, the Australian team. We played every double-header of the one-dayers, every weekend we played Saturday and Sunday, it was just killing us. And again the administrators just turned their backs on us. And it's documented, the under-arm incident was a direct result of my frustration with the fact that we hadn't got anywhere. We'd gone through all this ruction of World Series Cricket and they still weren't listening to us.

You've talked about the under-arm incident and said it was at least partly due to tiredness.
Oh, I was exhausted. I mean I was going from on the field to meetings off the field almost every day, to try and solve some of these problems. You know: you blokes have got to listen to us. You've got to hear our arguments. And it was: Oh look, we've got enough problems. And they did have enough problems. They were struggling with the new world as well and they didn't have the answers and they were struggling to keep up. Again we were down the food chain and didn't get a look in.

In spite of all that, do you think that overall Sir Donald had a positive influence on Australian cricket?
Well, he obviously was positive. There were a lot of positive things but I think you can't escape from the fact that even when he wasn't

chairman of the Board, he was still pulling the strings. And there were only a few people, like Phil Ridings, who really were prepared to stand up and argue with Sir Donald over things. With most others, whatever Sir Donald said, went.

He and Phil Ridings had disputes about financial matters, didn't they?

Yes. Phil is the only one in my memory who ever really stood up to Sir Donald over certain issues. And they were generally on financial things because Sir Donald was very controlling of that as well. I can remember discussions here years ago, in the late 60s about the South Australian Cricket Association. I was part of a player group that was involved in a discussion about a cricketers' club being built in the premises here somewhere. And there was discussion about getting control of grounds on the four sides of Adelaide and the SACA building premises that clubs could use rather than each having to fund their own individual clubhouse and inadequate facilities. And again, that got knocked over for financial reasons. You know: 'that's not our role'. I don't remember the full argument but it was really about not opening the purse strings to allow these things to go ahead.

So he was very conservative financially?

I believe so. A product of the Depression and all that sort of stuff, and I think the thinking of the time was very much conservative. Inflation wasn't around until the 60s probably and up until that stage having your funds sitting in the bank earning two or three per cent was pretty prudent. But after that it became less prudent.

Is it fair to say he was surrounded by yes-men at the Adelaide Oval?

Look, I think most of the people that came into his orbit were in awe of the man. He was an awesome person. You know, as a personal presence in the room, there was just something about him that was very dominant. Even though he was a small man, he stood out in a crowd. Now that was partly because of the legend, but he had a presence about him and a strong aura. It was like he was surrounded by this invisible shield and it didn't encourage people to come through it. And it was only those that were able to be in a working environment with him who were able to get very close with him and it was those people who became his – not friends, I don't think so much, but they were the people that he had a social contact with and some sort of social intercourse with. And I mean they were all just hanging off each word that he spoke. Most of them were younger people who had been kids when he was playing cricket and so they tended to sit back and say nothing and agree with anything that Sir Donald said. And that's not necessarily a criticism. I mean that was just the way it usually was.

He was also very sharp.
You can't escape the fact that he had a very sharp mind and was a very clever individual. And he was a very skilful person, not only from a physical point of view, but mentally he was very skilful and if he wanted to dominate someone he could do it very well. And I think he enjoyed doing that at times. I mean, it was a game also.

It's interesting that when Sir Donald was involved as an Australian selector, as chairman of the Australian Cricket Board that he made a point – early mornings, late nights, he'd lob up at Adelaide Airport when visiting teams would arrive. And there's the great story of when the 'Rest of the World' team arrived here in the early 70s, it was either very early in the morning or very late at night, I can't remember which, and Sir Donald went down there, as was his wont. You know, probably had a cardigan and open-necked shirt, slacks and whatnot and just went down there as part of the greeting group. He helped throw a few bags onto a trolley and I think it was Hylton Ackerman, one of the South African players, who saw this elderly gentleman. 'Are you involved with cricket?' 'Oh yes I'm involved with the South Australian Cricket Association.' 'Did you play the game at all?' So when he wanted to be he could be very nondescript and hide in the background and not push himself forward. But in a situation like in a meeting where he was in charge, he would certainly make his presence felt.

Was his approach to cricket progressive?
He was very progressive in terms of cricket, yes. I think that was one of the great strengths, certainly outwardly. He never criticised players or the game. He always saw the positive things. All the comments that have been attributed to him about one-day cricket have been very positive and I have no doubt that he did enjoy it. He would have loved it himself. But he spoke very positively.

You were the first Australian batsman to pass 7000 runs. Did you get any response from Sir Donald about that?
I got a telegram from Sir Donald congratulating me on the milestone and the fact that I was very generous to him in my comments about having batted twice as often as he did. I mean obviously it was a product of playing more often than anything else so, yes, I don't remember the exact words but it was congratulations and thanks very much for your generosity in your comments sort of thing and that was it.

You became a member of the Australian Cricket Board in 1984. Was that another occasion for a congratulatory note?
No. Apart from a couple of occasions, the exchanges were really only if I'd done something or said something that offended him directly. Then I'd get a letter from him. That was basically the communication. I'd get a page or two.

But certainly the last few meetings that I had with him, social occasions, he was much more relaxed and much more outgoing and had, I think, mellowed quite considerably.

Tell me about those last social meetings.
I had a little more social contact with him probably after I finished playing cricket than I had at any stage during my cricket career. In my final season, even though I was still playing for Queensland, the SACA were very kind to put on a cocktail party in the Bradman Room at Adelaide Oval in my last game here and Sir Donald was present for that. I remember being in a group of people and we were just talking, and Sir Donald had a moustache, which I'd never seen before. Anyway, I observed, 'It's interesting Sir Donald that you've got a moustache. I didn't think you were all that happy about moustaches and things like that.' And he said, 'Well it was recommended by my doctor.' He'd had some sun problems with his bottom lip and the doctor suggested that would help to protect it a little bit more.

And because I'd had a few sunspots burnt off my arm and face and hands I asked him, 'Have you ever had any problems with sunspots, skin cancers or anything like that from your playing days?' And he said, 'Yes, well interestingly enough I had a few spots burnt off the left side of my face,' which was the side that would have been exposed when he was batting. And I sort of flippantly said, 'Well that will teach you for batting so long,' and he said, 'Ah, it wasn't that long you know.' So he didn't ever miss an opportunity just to let you know that when he batted he got his runs pretty quickly. (laughs) That was a hobbyhorse of his. He detested slow cricket and boring cricket.

And there was a centenary of Test cricket at the Adelaide Oval in 1984 and all the captains who had captained their country in Test matches at the Adelaide Oval were invited to come back for this celebration. So a number of us were in a procession in open cars around the Adelaide Oval, and I noticed that Sir Donald was wearing a Greg Chappell hat, which staggered me. I'd designed this hat, which we were distributing in conjunction with Albion Hat and Cap Company. And with the previous history I thought he would not want to wear a Chappell hat.

Anyway I thanked him for his promotion and said, 'Oh, I'll send you one,' which he laughed at. I sent him a new hat and subsequently he just wrote a little thank-you note and it was probably the friendliest exchange that we'd ever had.

Former Test bowler, commentator and AIS Cricket Academy coach **Terry Jenner** *spoke to me in Adelaide while he was coaching, the interview interrupted every now and then with shouts of encouragement or advice to the young bowler in the nets. 'That's great,' he said after one particular ball towards the end of the interview. 'Now that is sensational. And my question is, why don't you do that all the time, Brian?'*

WHEN THE DECISION came to move to South Australia in 1967, the consideration was a second chance. In Western Australia my cricket was just about shot to bits and I needed another start and when Ashley Mallett looked to come as well, we'd played a lot of our cricket together so it was easy then for both of us to come.

As it unfolded, you were sitting there one day in the dressing room after a day in the field and you'd feel a hand on your shoulder, and there'd be 'Well done today, young Terry', and you'd think gosh, thank you Sir Donald. Not that you would ever take anything like that for granted but we did become a little bit blasé in the end. In fact probably in the end if you'd had a good day you were kind of hoping he'd walk through the door. So that was a huge bonus.

But he also went into the opposition rooms, so it wasn't as if he just hung around his own players, he would wander next door and a lot of guys would get the bonus of feeling the hand of Sir Donald on the shoulder.

That was really my first real knowledge of him and the closeness of him. I think I was probably a bit brash, and I dared to ask him things and sometimes he'd sort of smile. For example, I remember one day at the Prospect Cricket Club and I said, 'Sir Donald, we've been having a debate. Should a batsman start an initial movement back and across or forward with the front foot?' And he said, 'I don't think either, but if there was to be one, I imagine it would be back and across.' Those sort of things. Other people didn't want to ask him questions because he was Sir Donald Bradman.

I know the pressure of when you went to the nets, practising for South Australia and there was Sir Donald standing behind your net. Pressure. Wondering what he was thinking of you. Also uplifting, because you'd probably try to produce a bit extra while he was watching you.

He was an Australian selector when I got my first crack in 1970. Coming back from Melbourne, the paper was shoved under our door on the train and there was a photo on the front page with Greg Chappell saying that we'd made the test side. I was 12th man in the second test in Perth and then omitted, but prior to being omitted, Sir Donald came and told me that I was being left out. He just walked up to me and said, 'We don't think you are perhaps bowling quite as well as you were at the start of the summer. Perhaps some wickets in the next game or two will see you right and you'll end up back in the side.'

I was out for most of the summer and then the last Test, which happened to be his last as a selector as well, the seventh Test of that series against England, I came back into the side and Sir Donald resigned. And Bill Lawry lost the captaincy, if you remember, and his position in the team.

After that I was left out of the side numerous times, but no selector ever told me. He did. And as I reflect on my life, it was good that he was able to do that and not let me read it in the paper. He made the moment to tell me.

Tell me about the incident in 1974–75 when you were asked to offer an explanation to the Australian Cricket Board.
I made 74 in Adelaide against England and I got an important wicket, I got Fred Titmus. For the first time ever, I felt like I belonged, I really felt that I was in the Test side. We were heading to Melbourne and for once, as Phil Ridings said to me, instead of having a seat in the middle or on the aisle, you've actually got a window seat. He was a selector and I felt really good about that. (Just bear with me for one second – Brian, your front foot's now going square with the crease. You've got to open it up, that's it.)

So we arrive in Melbourne and I've helped Australia win a Test match and I'm feeling pretty pleased with myself. We go to the nets on the morning of the game, having a bowl, and probably it's the only time ever I've just relaxed. Ashley Mallett and I were bowling together and I said, 'Have you heard who's 12th?' He said, 'No, I haven't.' Obviously it wasn't going to be him, because he hadn't heard. And obviously it wasn't going to be me because I hadn't heard. Which I thought was fair, I thought it must be Ross Edwards again and I was waiting for the announcement.

Anyway they said team photos over near the stand, and we head over towards the photo and as I'm walking over, Ian [Chappell] walks past me and says, 'TJ, you've got it.' Just like that. I said, 'Oh, bullshit.' And he said, 'I don't pick 'em, I only tell 'em.'

I was livid. And after the photo, we went into the room and I was a bit silly, I kicked a bit of furniture, I just really couldn't believe it. Because after that was the team for England and the World Cup. And I was feeling that my hard-hitting 74 would help me into the World Cup squad. It didn't make sense to me. Especially later when I missed the side and they replaced me with Jim Higgs who was never ever going to play in the World Cup, and it was the same squad.

Anyway, when I was made 12th man, Ian comes up to me, and I think maybe in front of Neil Harvey I might have made a bit of a fool of myself, slammed a locker and a few things like that. And Ian sat down with me afterwards and said, 'I can't believe, TJ, that you're so uptight,' he said. 'You can't fail.' And I said, 'Ian, I can't succeed either, and I figure that this is the reason I'm not in the side.'

And seriously, Ian Chappell never had a say in selection in those days. So I told him, I said, 'I know, I'm feeling it.' My perception was the reason that I wasn't in the side was because if I was successful, they would have to have taken me. If I came out on a plum Melbourne deck and made another 50 or whatever and picked up three or four wickets. Ian said, 'TJ, yep.' (– You've done it every ball actually, you haven't once got it around there a bit so go and stand in your delivery stride position to do it. This is back to the old rubbish.)

So Ian said to me then, 'If you don't make this side, for once in your life I give you permission to open your mouth.' Words to that effect. So sure enough, I don't make that side, and sure enough, I said a bit. There were a lot of people disappointed for me. I'd been battling for 11 or 12 years and I just looked like I was a chance, and at the top of my form, I couldn't get chosen.

So I made a statement to the press, 'Obviously the selectors don't think I can bowl. Well, if I can't bowl, there must be 280 batsmen who can't bat.' I figured I'd had that many wickets.

So I got a consolation prize of a trip to South Africa with the Derek Robins XI. Max Walker, a guy called Malcolm Franke from Queensland, we were the three Australians. It was breaking down the shackles – it had coloured, blacks and we all played as one team. That was trying to break down that apartheid thing. They would get honorary white status because otherwise they couldn't have stayed in our hotel.

Whilst I was in South Africa a letter arrived in the post from the Australian Cricket Board. I opened it up quite excited, thinking perhaps someone is injured, or I could be on standby for the World Cup or something. It just said, 'You've breached the player/writer rule,' which was pretty much in vogue in those days, 'please explain by return post.' I was so angry, I just chucked it in the bin. I just couldn't believe that I could cop it.

Anyway I came home, went back to work for Coca-Cola, life just moved along. I think I might have got a second letter as a reminder. I got back to work one day and there was a message on my desk, Please ring Don Bradman. And I said, 'Oh yeah, and please ring Mr Lyon at the Zoo, Mr Fowler at the chicken yard.' After a while I looked at the number. It was a city number. So I thought I'll ring it and at the very worst, just hang up.

Anyway I rang it, and the voice at the other end – no message banks in those days – was unmistakably Sir Donald's. He asked me if I felt I could take the time out to come and see him in his office. I said sure. I wasn't really sure what it was about. So when I got there, he told me that he was aware of the fact that I'd received a couple of letters from the Australian Cricket Board re breaching the player/writer rule and he told me then that he thought it was a little bit harsh. There were others that had breached it during the summer and they were in fact on the trip, and he cited those couple of examples. And he said, 'I've taken the liberty of typing up a letter for you, would you care to read it?' So I read it. And it was quite clearly outlining that I felt as though I was harshly treated – his words for me. That there were other players that had in fact committed similar breaches and they were actually going with the team while I, the one that was left out who probably had every right to be disappointed, was the one being charged. Etcetera etcetera. He said, 'Now if you were to send that letter to the Australian Cricket Board, I'm sure it will be dealt with appropriately. A further suggestion is that if you'd like to send it after the first (or whatever) of June, the chairman of the Board (I think it was Tim Caldwell) will be attending a conference at Lord's. I'll be acting chairman and I will receive that correspondence and ensure that it is properly dealt with.' In other words, he knew that if it was to be a fair hearing then he was going to have to follow it through.

You couldn't dream of Sir Donald Bradman doing that, as I said, for an average cricketer, for a guy that – I hadn't done anything that I thought would prompt him to say 'I'll give this young kid a bit of a crack'. I was probably stupid, do you know what I mean? I'd probably had my car repossessed on the way to the cricket. That sat with me all these years and the only sadness for me is that the one time I went bankrupt they changed the keys on the place and took all my memorabilia, and that letter was there. That letter is somewhere. Of course, it is not written by Don Bradman, it's written by Terry Jenner.

You organised the 1948 reunion in Adelaide in 1998, didn't you?
Yeah. Because I'd been doing functions for charity for a few years, and you've always got to think ahead of what might be coming up, anniversaries. And we did an anniversary of the 1972–73 side and it was extremely successful, but I was part of that, they were my team-mates. And we'd done a couple of football ones. So this was upcoming, and the decision was let's have a dip at doing something for the '48 side here in Adelaide.

I sent correspondence to Sir Donald Bradman knowing that he hadn't done anything or been anywhere for a long time, so I gave him three options. I invited him to the dinner as our first preference, the cocktail party and Government House. I hadn't heard anything back and I just naturally assumed he wasn't coming. At that stage Keith Miller was definitely coming and then Keith couldn't come. Just as I was feeling on a downer about Keith not being able to come, I got a message through from Barry Gibbs who was then the CEO of the SACA, to tell me that Sir Donald asked him to convey the message that he would be delighted to meet the boys at Government House. That was a huge fillip. Some of those guys hadn't seen The Don for 20 years or more so it was a terrific moment.

He was 90 years old. He drove himself there and stayed there for a few hours and took time out with each of the guys. I identified that day how frail he was. I went to shake his hand – it reminded me of my dad's hands. They looked very arthritic. He was fantastic that day. He signed everything that we required from him for the dinner. As it would happen, we ended up doing a second one in Queensland, because everyone had such great fun. Which meant going to Sir Donald and asking him to sign another 48 of these Invincibles photos which he did again, and of course he couldn't attend, but he sent a personal message. In that message there was something about his fallibility again, him saying no one lives forever, and that type of thing. There was a sadness when it was read out. And then that function went so well, that at the wind-up night where we said thanks to everybody, Sam Loxton got up and he said, 'You know there's about six Victorians in that side and nothing's happening for us in Victoria,' so I said 'I've only got two months, but do you want to have a try?' So we had a try and then we did it in Melbourne and the Don signed another batch for that. He signed and signed and signed, but I will tell you, when he signed the last one, he said, 'Tell Terry Jenner I've just signed my last one for him.' Because he'd signed about 180 of these things.

So that was the last time I saw him, at that Invincibles lunch. I don't say he did that for me personally, he also did it for his team-mates, and he did it for the charities that we were involved with. But in there somewhere I know that The Don was doing it for me, which I'm very humbled about.

The Anglo-Australian cricket writer and collector **David Frith** *developed a friendship with Sir Donald over a period of 30 years. As we spoke at his home in Guildford, Surrey, he nursed a folder containing 119 letters from Sir Donald.*

ALL OF US CAN quote his scores and his averages straight off, schoolboys can do that. But what sort of bloke was he? Well I've got my view of the man and it was quite a stirring view because he used to let loose with me, in letters and when we were together, which was a privilege. No guarded comments. He let his guard down and in the letters he'd have a good old go about the plumber who hadn't turned up or the electrician who'd overcharged, and he had to do this about the house and of course repeatedly the deep concern about Jessie. Towards the end the letters were loaded with worry about her next operation and her condition and massive admiration for her bravery and the way she carried on as if there were nothing wrong with her and then his own little illnesses and worries which fortunately turned out to be nothing more than worrisome.

My first contact with Sir Donald was a letter written in April 1970, I think it was, with an instant reply. That was the nature of the man and we quickly got onto first-name terms. But he came to England in 1974 for the last time and addressed the Lord's Taverners, brought the house down, 800 or so people there and I'd arranged by letter to meet him in London at the Lord's Taverners office to get some books signed. I took about 26 of them up there and he gladly signed them. So the correspondence then intensified because we'd met. In fact for that event, knowing of my cricket collection, he said: 'Well, I'll find something for you' and he brought over a pair of batting gloves in a brown paper bag. And I'm sitting in the midst of all the splendour and glamour of the Hilton Hotel on this gala occasion, sitting on a pair of Don Bradman's gloves, still wrapped in brown paper.

The letters then began to accelerate back and forth and they were equally long and detailed and the friendship really was warm from the start. I think first and foremost he detected my commitment to cricket and real love for it. I was already editor of the *Cricketer* in 1974 but then I started *Wisden Cricket Monthly* in 1979. I'd send the magazine to him every month of course but he probably felt it was a good idea to feed me with ideas and opinions and objections and suggestions. I got him to write once or twice which was a coup because he didn't write for anybody.

The first really long session I had with him was during the Centenary Test in Melbourne in 1977. He rang me at the motel because he wanted to check something out for the speech he was making, and I said, 'Oh look, it's my fortieth birthday on the third day of the match.' I said, 'Love to see you that day. Can we go out with you and Jessie?' and he said, 'Oh we've booked that evening. I'll come back to you.' And sure enough he did. He said, 'We're staying at the Windsor. Come and have breakfast with us on the way to the match.' What a delightful way to start a man's fortieth birthday. Breakfast with the Bradmans.

I thanked him for that because they didn't have to do it. But he said: 'We'll have a chat later,' and we met up back of the pavilion, probably the fourth day, and we sat out on the seats there watching – one eye on the play – and just having a heart-to-heart chat and this time it was all about the economy and finance in general. This was a stockbroker speaking, really serious stuff. Had a trilby hat on and he looked the businessman, you wouldn't have thought he'd ever picked up a bat in his life.

We fell out over the no-ball law. He was very keen that I should support his view that they should go back to the back-foot law. His argument was probably one quarter acceptable to me and that was on the count that umpires now have to stay watching the crease a little bit longer so when they look up the ball's already down there and it probably results in a few more bad decisions. But I didn't think that outweighed the other reasons for sticking with the front-foot law. He got really agitated about this as the years went by. He wanted me to support him and I just stoutly refused. I said, 'I can't. I don't believe in it.'

So I'm sitting with him on one occasion in his dining room with Jessie and we're having lunch and he brought it up again. He was flushed with emotion at this point and so was I, and he said in exasperation, 'And so you think you know better than Denis Lillee and the Chappell brothers and Richie Benaud and me?' There's not a great deal you can say to that so I just said, 'I just know what I know.' And Jessie, as she must have done so many times, came in at that stage and changed the subject and she said, 'David, have you written Don's obituary yet?' (laughs) I had to think fast again and I said, 'Well, no. Firstly, I'm not that well organised and anyway, he's going to live to 100, isn't he?' And that was it.

But I did give him space in the magazine to air his point of view. I couldn't have been fairer to the man. To be honest, he was so used to having people fall into line with his wisdom because he was thought to be just about infallible in matters of cricket judgement and assessment. But I just couldn't fall in line with that one, which probably caused him a certain amount of surprise but it didn't ruin the friendship, thank goodness.

What came close to ruining it was a couple of years later, when I was offered the Bill O'Reilly tapes shortly after Tiger died. They were in the oral history collection at the Australian National Library, and O'Reilly as you know disliked Bradman the person.

They were so different. Not just their religions – their temperaments, their attitudes – but he respected him highly, as did Don
Bill, for their cricketing ability. But he had a few pings at him during his lifetime and then out came another ping after he died in the
form of this interview, which included a reference to a Shield
match in the late-30s when Don was accused of cowardice by Clarrie Grimmett. I've since found other references to it, in 1950 in
Keith Miller's book with Dick Whitington, so it's not a totally
unknown story.

But when he saw it echoed in the magazine under 'The
O'Reilly Tapes' he was quite furious and sent me two letters, one
personal in which he is saying, 'I don't know how you can do this to
your old mate and it's untrue.' But they were all dead, bar him, by
this stage. He did have the generosity to acknowledge that as an
editor and journalist myself I felt the need to give this space. I published his 'letter for publication' in which he denied this and I
really thought that was the end. But it wasn't. We carried on corresponding and then ill-health was overtaking him so the letters got
shakier and less frequent. I think he forgave me on the surface but
underneath he was hurt and I didn't wish to hurt him and I was a
bit sorry about the whole business then. But I'm essentially interested in history, in what happened.

Did he have an obsessive streak?
Obsessive, that's a word I don't like because it's applied to me quite
often, and to others. I've used it myself. Maybe a cleaner word is
dedicated and with the determination to see something through,
whether it's an argument or some sort of physical objective. That
was the key to the man, that he was used to getting his own way at
the crease, over bowlers and fielders and captains, and he was
fiercely determined and there's no comparison with anyone else in
batting history. He had the technique to do it but a lot of people

have good techniques but they don't have that mental capacity and it showed in everything he ever did or said.

Once, no sooner had I entered Holden Street than he sat me down and produced a bit of paper from his pocket and he said, 'Now this book you've written (it's called *The Slow Men: A history of slow bowling*) you say in page 193 (or whatever it was) that I bowled Wally Hammond out with a full toss in Adelaide.' He said, 'That's not so.' And I said, 'Well I've read five or six accounts, even Hammond's, and they all say it was a full toss.' He said, 'It was not a full toss.' And I said, 'Well there's surely nothing to be ashamed about, Don? Arthur Mailey bowled them as a hobby. He got Jack Hobbs out at least twice with a full toss.' He said, 'It was not a full toss.' And I thought, goodness me! It's as if I'd accused him of burglary or murder or something like that.

I go on seeing references to that ball and it definitely came through about waist high; it brushed his arm and hit the stumps on the full. But he was very agitated about that. He was a man concerned with detail who was never wrong and I was glad when the subject moved on to something else and it was good to see him nodding in agreement with anything.

He believed in getting his own way. I'm of that disposition because my dad was too, and probably most men are. Perhaps he actually appreciated my forthright approach to things, allied I hope, to a certain politeness and respect. But there were too many yes-men around him, as with all figures of power. They're surrounded by people: yes, yes, yes and he had such integrity that I think he felt deep down it would be refreshing to have the odd little argument, as long as it didn't get ugly.

Of course he had plenty of enemies. The suggestion has been made he didn't have many friends. He had friends in a social setting but I think he was very hard to live with on the cricket field. He was so good, he was self-enclosed, but as far as I know there was quite a range of friends, from Archie Jackson through to Ben Barnett and Ron Hamence, Charlie Walker. Now I knew several of those and they were probably the sort of gentle friends that he wanted around him. They knew what to say and when to say it and they were good fun to be with and they were nice men, but if there was any suggestion of combat, verbal combat, I think away from the necessities of life, he didn't want any more of that than he had to put up with.

Sir Donald was very suspicious of the media. Did he extend that suspicion to the cricket press?
I was a bit different in that I wasn't a regular newspaper writer, I was a magazine editor, and I think he probably sussed me out before he committed himself to a friendship. What sort of stuff does this bloke write? Well he's obviously interested in history, perhaps above all, and what he writes about the contemporary game is meant to be constructive, so I think he probably felt safe with me.

I'd been knocking out these books and he responded to them by giving me the foreword to a big pictorial history of England v Australia, and then for one on the history of cricket, called *Pageant of Cricket*, which was in 1987, a huge book. And I was struck then by his humility. He not only agreed straight off to do it, he didn't enquire about money and when I brought that up he said, 'Oh well look, don't worry. Maybe you can do me a favour one day.' And he did a good job on both the forewords, as you'd expect. Both beautifully typed. He said at the time, 'If you don't approve of them send them back.' And he didn't deal in platitudes. He meant that. Some people say that and they don't mean it. He never said anything he didn't mean, he was a very direct person.

One thing that comes through clearly is that he was an extremely meticulous man in everything. Was he a demanding friend? Was he a demanding correspondent?

Yes, he loved to pick up little errors, (laughs) which helped me because I believe in being meticulous as an editor. I used to be reading page proofs at midnight, red eyed the next day but at least I'd done the best I could, and perhaps he appreciated that, in the books and magazines that went his way from my stable.

Being meticulous, as I've discovered, can really irritate people and I'm sure that he irritated a lot of people because he was never prepared to say, 'Oh, that's near enough. That'll do.' And that maybe was one of the reasons why we clicked. It must have been, because if you were sloppy with the facts, even if he thought you'd been and you hadn't been, you'd simply disagreed with him, he was onto you like a fox. Maybe that's not about being meticulous, it's about getting the story the way you want it and he's talking to a bloke younger than himself and therefore felt that I was controllable.

Do you think he would on occasions attempt to rewrite history?

Gee, that's a big question. I have the feeling that he wanted his own way so much that there might have been times when he'd even convinced himself that things were a certain way and unless you were there with him on that distant occasion you were in a fairly weak position to argue. This hardly ever happened, but when it did it was electrifying when he's saying one thing and I believe another and it's up to me to say, 'Oh okay' or 'Well hang on'. And I would prefer to say 'hang on' because I'm not the submissive type, even in his presence and I was just wanting always to get at the truth. That's my job in life, is to find out what really happened, even if it was long ago, and it was great to be talking to someone who was there. But with him it never got angry, we never suspended relations over anything. Maybe deep down it was fun having an argument, because not many people argued with him. I mean: Yes Don, No Don, three bags full. Yes, it was fun to have a slight disagreement – so long as Jessie was there. (laughs)

Was he a man who bore a grudge?
I think the way he handled the problems with Bill O'Reilly suggests that he wasn't a grudge-bearer because for many years he had to put up with this and I know that Bill overdid it. He just overdid it. If I can just try and encapsulate it in one minute, Jock Livingston, the old New South Wales and Northlands player, was a great friend of mine and we used to go up the Noble Stand at Sydney and he'd sit down in his regular spot and I'd go in the press box. He played his first Shield match in 1940 under Bill O'Reilly's captaincy and there was Bill sitting there and he said, 'Hello, Bill' and Bill knew that Jock Livingston idolised Don Bradman because he used to be one of the kids in F. J. Palmer's coaching school and they corresponded and all he could say to Jock was, 'Been to Bowral lately?' And it just shows you the depth to which Bill continued to seethe about the 'little fella' as he always called him. And I was sad about that because Bill was good company on other matters. Just ask about Stan McCabe or anything else and away he'd go.

But you didn't get retaliation, not that I was aware of anyway, from DGB. He's gone public on acknowledging that O'Reilly was the greatest bowler he ever saw and Bill would say that Bradman was the greatest batsman he ever saw. That's the standard issue, but what went beneath that, well, with Bradman on O'Reilly there was never any 'but'. And in private, I don't recall there was any feeling of grievance there. Maybe sadness.

*Growing up as a child in South Africa, former South African captain
and administrator* **Dr Ali Bacher** *idolised Sir Donald Bradman. He
met his hero for the first time in Adelaide when South Africa rejoined
world cricket for the World Cup in 1992.*

IN THE 1970S I was in general practice and on a one-page letterhead
of Dr Ali Bacher, medical practitioner, I took the liberty of writing
to him, asking him for answers to certain questions, for example the
eight-ball over against the six-ball over. It was a one-pager, I wasn't
certain whether he would respond. Within two or three weeks I got
about a ten-page letter typed out, an extraordinary letter, going
through all the statistics and why the eight-ball over was better than
the six-ball over, relating to what happened in 1902, in 1920 – it was
just unbelievable. And the terrible part about it is I never kept that
letter. You know when you're young, it doesn't hit you, you read the
letter and it goes into the rubbish bin. But I couldn't believe it. From
that moment on, we had a little bit of correspondence. I would write
to him and he would always immediately reply.

And then when South Africa came back into the world of
cricket for the World Cup, I don't know whether I phoned him or
wrote to him, but he said, 'Now you must come and spend an
evening with me in Adelaide.' It was the first time I'd been to Adelaide and he took my wife and myself out to dinner with his wife
and he had a very close friend who I met in Adelaide, a surgeon, Dr
Don Beard. He came with his wife. First we came to his house and
we spent about an hour and a half and he was just talking to me
about South African cricket. He knew more than I knew. I remember there was a lot of political discussion. He was very intrigued
about the politics of the African National Congress because that
was a time of the emergence of the ANC as the legitimate political
player in South African politics. He was asking me a lot of questions about Chief Buthelezi, who was head of the Inkatha Party

and still is, about the ANC. He knew exactly what was happening in the political arena of the early-90s, he knew everything.

Then he got his car, my wife in the front seat, he opened the door for her, he drove us to a restaurant, we had some good wine and went on to about 11 o'clock in the evening. I would say that off the field of play, that evening has got to be the most memorable in my cricketing history. His mind was still so incisive and logical and he just had fact after fact. We spoke about South African players, great players that he'd played against. But cricket-wise and outside of cricket, he had an extraordinary intellect, even though he was a very humble man.

I asked him about Graeme Pollock, how good he was. He said to me, 'The best left-hand batsman of all time.' I said, 'Better than Sir Garfield Sobers?' He said, 'Marginally, although Gary was the best all-rounder of all time.' So then I asked him about Barry Richards and he said to me he was as good as Sir Jack Hobbs and Sir Leonard Hutton. Extraordinary praise. I have told the whole world this because I'm so proud of those two cricketers, what he said about them.

But it was an extraordinary evening. He just made me feel very, very welcome there. I didn't know how you should respond to the great Sir Donald but he made me feel very welcome in his house and he was delighted to meet me and just talk about South African politics and cricket.

*Ray Steele was president of the Victorian Cricket Association and treasurer of the Australian Cricket Board, and in 1977 received an OBE for his services to cricket. He died in 1993. I spoke briefly to his wife **Alison Steele** about Sir Donald and Lady Bradman and her husband's role in cricket.*

Jessie used to come to the cricket an awful lot and she always used to bring her knitting. She always was knitting socks. She'd knit them and then she'd say, 'It'll be the same as usual. One's always longer than the other.' So she'd have to undo them and she'd start again. Sometimes Shirley would come. She was quite keen on cricket. She and Jessie got on very well together.

Would Sir Donald chat with you?
Not if there were men around, he wouldn't. He wouldn't come and chat to the women especially. He was always polite but he didn't come and chat like that because he didn't have to, Jessie would do it. She was the one. She was really a very, very nice woman. I thought he'd have been lost without her. She was pretty sick in the last few years. Gorgeous looking. Lovely face. Lovely woman.

Did your husband enjoy his time on the Australian Cricket Board?
Cricket was a lot of work, especially in the latter days when he was doing the money side of things. Nobody pushed him; he took it on himself. He went through the ropes and got there, but I don't think he enjoyed it a lot. There were always a few disputes. The men were always having rows about something. Kerry Packer – that was a dirty word at those stages. He used to come quite often and I thought he was always quite nice but he was a very shrewd man. Actually Don was a very shrewd man, very intelligent and a very good businessman. But he wouldn't give in to things, you know, he'd make them all a bit cross at meetings sometimes. Sort of pig-headed in a way, I suppose you could say. They all liked him very much and respected him. He probably didn't give much away about himself, he played down his successes on the cricket ground. The Packer business and that was all a pain in the neck. They were all pretty crabby at that time, trying to work that one out. It wasn't funny. Still, that's something they found their way through.

Sir Donald rated South African batsman **Graeme Pollock** *amongst the best he had ever seen. We spoke in Melbourne at breakfast during South Africa's 2001–02 Test series.*

I WAS 19 YEARS OLD on my first trip and when we arrived in Perth on our tour in 1963, Sir Donald came across just to say hello and welcome to Australia, can I help you with your bags? That type of thing. And then we met him through the tour at various times. He was very approachable. The manager of that 1963 side, Ken Viljoen, had in fact played against Sir Don in the 1930s and he was a personal friend.

Then in 1971 when I was playing for the Rest of the World side, my brother Peter, Tony Greig, Hylton Ackerman and I went to his house for supper in Adelaide during the Test. It was a very interesting night. He was just going through various stages of his career and what had happened and he had some videos which we had a look at of some of the Tests he'd played in. We saw his 100th first-class 100, I can remember, it was against India. We saw quite a few videos and he would pass comments that might have been of interest as to what you were watching at the time. He had a good collection and they were fantastic to see. A fantastic night.

Was he concerned for South African cricket after the cancelling of the South African tour of Australia in 1971–72?
Ya, I think he was, but he realised that you could never maintain security and to play five days of cricket would have been absolutely impossible. But I'm sure he was disappointed, I think he was a great friend of South Africa. He'd played against South Africa, but it was one of those things. Looking back, I'm sure it was the right decision.

I think he always tried his best to support South Africa through some difficult times. With all the world opinion and everything that was against South Africa I don't think it was easy to be seen to be blatantly in favour but he obviously was looking at it from a cricketing point of view and had enjoyed playing against South Africa.

Sir Donald rated you as possibly the finest left-handed batsmen he'd seen.

He did say after I got a hundred in the first game in Perth in 1963, 'If you are going to play like that let me know, I'd love to be around to watch it.' It was great to have someone of that calibre pass those type of remarks.

Did you ever play golf with him?

I actually had one game with him at Royal Adelaide with Barry Richards many years ago on one of my trips to Australia. He was still obviously a fine golfer but he was getting on at that stage. But he loved his golf. I remember that he didn't hit the ball all that far but he hit it very straight and obviously around the greens his short game was excellent, he scored well. You could just see from him there, the basic great control that he had when he had something in his hands. And he always knew what he wanted to do and how far you'd hit a club.

Are cricketers drawn to golf?

I enjoy it whenever I get the opportunity. I think a lot of cricketers once they get out of the game try and play as much golf. I think it's quite relaxing and on the off days of the Test, you'd be able to go along and have a game of golf.

Do you take your golf seriously?

He did. I think everybody, if you play sport at a level, no way are you going to go out there and treat it as a joke and just sort of hack around. No, no, no, like any ex-cricketer, it's critical that you are a reasonable golfer. Absolutely. I wouldn't like to say I played good cricket and I'm an 18 handicap golfer. A lot of cricketers, you'll find they play off six, seven, eight or nine, round about that figure. If you've got ball sense, it's not a problem hitting the ball, all it is really is the finer points of the game and your short game I think is probably the hardest to adapt to. If ex-cricketers play off higher handicaps it's probably because their short game is not as good as the professionals. But it's never a problem to hit the ball; if you have the ability or ball sense, that's pretty normal.

The CEO of Argo Investments **Rob Patterson** *valued Sir Donald as a commercial consultant until he was into his 80s. We spoke at Argo's office in Adelaide.*

I JOINED THE COMPANY in 1969 as company secretary and Sir Donald was chairman of Wakefield Investments, the smallest of our three listed companies, and a director of Argo and Bounty which were the other two larger companies. They were identical board memberships and the group had a policy of having a different chairman for each of the three listed companies, so he got Wakefield.

I became CEO of the group, which was the whole three, in 1982 and Sir Donald became chairman of the main company Argo in 1982 for two years. Then he had to retire having reached the age of 75. There was an agreement between the company and each of the directors to retire at 75. He wouldn't have got a retiring payment if he hadn't.

I enjoyed those two years. I'd been working under the founder of the company and it was quite interesting the different approach Sir Donald had. I've had three chairmen since and none of them has had that level of enthusiasm for the position that he had. I found that he was like that in anything; if he was involved in something, he was very dedicated to it. I guess his cricket was an example.

Sir Donald was the first what we might say non-executive chairman from my point of view. He used to come in at least once a week for quite a long chat about what had happened the week before and whether I needed any help with anything, and what were the issues, the major developments in the stock market from that previous week.

And when he retired in 1984 from the board, we retained him as a consultant for some years afterwards, right through until about 1992. He was a very, very good sounding board. I know he had a very close connection with the local manager of the Reserve Bank, so he kept up with the economic happenings, and he was very interested in politics. His addresses to the shareholders when he was chairman of Wakefield and also for those two years of Argo, always delved into politics. One of his pet hatreds was inflation and he was always at the government to do away with inflation. He thought that was very bad for society and the country generally so he'd be very pleased in recent times that inflation has been slain. (laughs)

Was he financially conservative?
Oh, very. Very conservative, but quite willing to embrace risk if a proper analysis had been done of a proposal. But he was very much a stickler for detail. Sometimes that's frustrating for a chief executive but it's also (laughs) a good protection against getting into trouble. He liked everything to be done properly.

Was it basically his stockbroking background he was drawing on?
Yes, and I think the company was drawing on that skill. And in fact he was appointed a director almost immediately when he sold out of his stockbroking business. The company has always had a policy

of not having a practising stockbroker on the board because we felt and we still feel that it would just limit the support we get from other brokers. He's been the only retired stockbroker that has been on the board. We tend to have more the accounting and legal and straight industrial-type commercial background people that have been involved in their own business. The board's fairly stable, we don't have a lot of movement until retirement.

How did he come to be on the board?
I think the founder Alf Adamson must have been impressed with his meetings with him as a stockbroker. And I think he considered that he could be helpful to the company as soon as that stockbroking connection had ceased. He was a director of other companies so I imagine he was partially appointed because of his corporate involvements as well. He had some very, very good business contacts, what with Fauldings, Kelvinator and Uniroyal, and they were all operating internationally or had international connections which helped.

Were there benefits to having Sir Donald on the board simply because of who he was?
Oh, absolutely. But that certainly was not why he was appointed. No question that he was appointed for his knowledge of the stock market and his corporate background, corporate involvements and I think the fact that he was who he was from a cricketing sense was just a bonus really.

Did he ever use the contacts he had in high circles for the benefit of the company?
Oh, he may have, but not to any large extent. It wasn't really necessary. Put it this way, we've gone on and prospered without him. I don't think those contacts were essential but it would have made it easier to communicate with some people in high places.

When I started running the company in 1982 he had some very useful UK business contacts. Quite a number of his age group of cricketers went on to become serious businessmen in the UK and he'd obviously had relations with them. They were more helpful in keeping track of the outlook for markets or the economy than specific company matters. It was that sort of big picture involvement that was very helpful. In those days globalisation hadn't taken hold and it was harder to get good information from overseas.

We'd also get interstate people coming over who'd want to take Sir Donald to lunch or dinner. So they'd pick up the bill but we'd arrange it at his favourite restaurant and we'd attend as well.

So was that an advantage of having him on the board?
Well, I guess so. It was certainly part of a networking business advantage. He was pretty comfortable with that because he did enjoy eating and good wine, as I do. But we'd use it for genuine business purposes and he was very interested in those sorts of groups. Normally they were pretty interesting people that were involved in those lunches.

How did you utilise him as a consultant after he'd resigned as a director?
He would continue to have this weekly meeting with me. He'd come in for a couple of hours and he would collect the stock-broking research that I'd looked at over the previous week. In fact, we'd provide a space here for him and he would sit down and he'd either take it away and absorb it or sit down and actually physically read it, and then come and have a chat to me. So anything that came out of that from his point of view he'd raise with me, and I'd normally have a list of things I'd raise with him. And if there were any new investment opportunities, I'd quite often pick up the

phone and ring him and ask him his advice and perhaps even get him to check it out from his other contacts if there was a reason for doing that. You know, if it was an industry that he'd been involved with or we knew he had a connection with.

He must have stayed very involved in the business.
Oh he did, very much so. I think it was '92 that we ceased that arrangement. By this time Sir Donald had become a bit more remote from business activities and probably even felt himself that he was offering less to us.

He'd always maintained an office at his old sharebroking firm, right through until he stopped coming into the city, I believe. And he'd come here as well. We talked about providing an office when we talked about this consultancy but he said there's no real need because he's got the existing one and it was just across the road so he used to just go in there and then he'd walk across here and sometimes he'd take the reading back there.

Was it important for him to maintain an involvement?
He was quite happy to continue to be involved. Very happy. (laughs) We paid him a pittance for this consultancy; it was something he wanted to do. Certainly for me, having only been CEO for two years when he retired in '84, I felt it was necessary. Most of the other members of the board were not actively involved in the stock market so his skills were much more valuable to me. It was early days for me of running the show so I found it very important.

I think he enjoyed it and I think it enabled him to keep his business connections up. Because of the wide range of people that he knew, I think he wanted to make sure he'd kept his knowledge base up. That was important to him. And he still undertook some personal transactions in the stock market post his retirement and I guess it would have helped him in that connection.

Was he a workaholic?

I think so. He used to, as you know, answer every letter that he got, a huge number and he used to type them away on this terrible old typewriter. He used to type letters to me on that. Some of these new investment opportunities, I'd send him a copy of the prospectus which we'd been looking at and he would take it home and then it would come back with a couple of pages of typed notes on his thoughts and views.

Having said that, he still played his golf regularly at least one day a week, I suspect at the weekend as well. And he played the piano of course. He knew a lot about music – I recall him talking about it and he knew a lot more than me. Serious music.

Did H. W. Hodgetts' bankrupcy and conviction for fraud have a lasting effect on Sir Donald's business career?

He always expressed it to me as if it was something that happened before he came onto the scene and he worked extremely hard to clean up the mess and keep the business together. That's how I was told the story.

It's funny you know, but he wasn't strictly speaking establishment. He was never a member of the Adelaide Club and he tended to shun the establishment a bit. I think he probably held some of those people responsible for trying to sheet home some of H. W. Hodgetts' blame to him. But I certainly don't think there was any lasting stigma in the business community. There might have been a pool of those old stalwarts that have long passed that had a view about it but it's not been an issue since I've been involved. And it wasn't an issue with him as a director of our company to my knowledge.

Was there a point at which you became friends?

It would have been in that '82 to '84 period. You can imagine from my point of view going from company secretary to the chief executive of the company, it was quite a leap and he was very supportive. In fact, I imagine he had a lot to do with me being appointed. From '82 to '92, those 10 years he was pretty important. I used to go to his home quite regularly to get things signed and I obviously got to know his wife, Jessie, reasonably well. We'd all go out to business dinners together. In fact, I'm one of the executors of his estate.

Did you share other interests outside the company?
Not really, no. The business consumes me actually, and he was very consumed in the business in those years.

The cricket writer **Mike Coward** *met Sir Donald when he began writing for the* News *and* Sunday Mail *in Adelaide in the 1960s. Over the years they developed a rapport and mutual respect. We spoke during the second Test against South Africa in Melbourne in 2001.*

THE THING THAT ALWAYS frustrated me with Sir Donald (and I'm speaking very much as a journalist) is that everything seemed to have been done on his terms. I mean he was an incredibly powerful and persuasive man. I got the only interview with him at the time of the 50th anniversary of Bodyline in 1982–83 for the *Age* after the editor Creighton Burns guaranteed that Bradman would see the copy before it was published. And that was an understandable decision by an editor.

To get an interview with Bradman at any time was a compliment, be it to the journalist or the paper or whatever. But there were always conditions attached. And certainly to an extent you felt used, although at one level, it was a tremendous privilege to be speaking to him, both from the cricketing point of view and to get a special insight into a remarkable period in our sporting and social history.

He was very sensitive to any discussion of Bodyline. I think that goes back to 1930 and the last Test at the Oval when he and Archie Jackson both scored heavily and there were a lot of people who thought Jackson was going to be as good as Bradman. He died very young, sadly, just into 1933, of consumption. He was only 23. But he was an exceptional player. Anyway, both of them faced a barrage of short-pitch bowling. Bradman ducked and weaved and got a century, Jackson stood up and got hit a lot and got all the kudos for showing the courage to stand up to this relentless attack, etcetera, etcetera. Whereas of course Bradman said if you had the skill to duck and weave, why wouldn't you do it?

And I think there was a perception that he was afraid and I don't think that he ever, in his mind, fully convinced his critics that on that particular occasion he did have courage. And he used this interview I did 50 years on in 1982–83 to again reassert his position. He didn't lack courage but he had a good enough technique not to be hit. He was still proving that point right through the years and I think even to the end. There is correspondence about that article now in the Bradman Museum. He'd sent the story that I'd written to Gubby Allen, to spell it out again. It is extraordinary. I don't think he ever really fully came to terms with that.

But he really could be intimidating on cricket matters (and probably on other matters) and of course he was a pedant of the first order, which just drove everybody to the point of distraction, myself included. In a classic case, in that piece that I did in 1982–83, I made a reference to a bar that he'd been presented, and I got a very firm note in the notes on the proofs that it was a 'drinks cabinet', not a bar. See, that was a connotation which was unacceptable. Which was interesting. I mean, I didn't give it a thought when I was writing it because it was clearly a bar. But no, it was a drinks cabinet.

But he was very gracious. On this specific occasion he drove me back into town. He had just fitted those automatic controls to operate the garage doors and he was like a kid with a new toy. And Lady Bradman had produced the morning tea. I mean the civilities were always there. He was very gracious and always polite.

Do you think his attitude to the press was grounded in his experience?

If you sit down and go through *The Bradman Albums* in the National Library (or the State Library of South Australia), it's hard to believe that he could have ever been antagonistic towards the media. The press that he had was always pretty well totally supportive. He was just lauded really, from the time he began to the time he concluded. From a journalistic point of view, and particularly from a cricket writer's point of view, our predecessors didn't serve us particularly well. There was so little criticism of him, and so little analysis.

We do have to certainly see him in terms of what he represented to the people, and that he really did represent hope at a time of hopelessness, in terms of the Depression, in terms of a world war. Looking back, I can understand the way the community and even the writers felt about that. But there was so little analysis. I mean, you saw the other day in the *Australian* magazine, (David) Nason's piece about the difficult days he had in Adelaide business-wise. A couple of people within the cricket community have said, 'Oh that was interesting' but the overwhelming reaction was the impertinence of that being done. What right to question, you know? But I often found his attitude towards the press very irritating, for a press that historically had been very good for him and to him.

The media changed so much in his time. When I started on the *News* in 1963, he was such a powerful figure in Adelaide he would often be rung by an editor when something of significance was breaking in the community. I think this relationship encouraged him to believe that the media should be cricket's public relations arm.

But as the game changed and as the nature of media changed, there was more discussion, there was more analysis, there was more editorialising, and I think his unease or discomfort probably coincided with the quite dramatic change in the way the media fulfilled its roles. And that, of course, had a lot to do with the explosion of the electronic media. And it was only as an administrator he had to deal with that. And characteristically of course, he developed fairly impressive skills to deal with that too. His presentation on radio and television was always pretty good. He could look gun-barrel down a camera. He was a very adaptable man.

He took great pride, I think, in being a perfectionist, to a point that, for us mere mortals, was pretty unsettling. I mean, at Government House in Adelaide he argued with the Queen about a match. She erred on something. It was the Tied Test I think, in 1960–61 at Brisbane. She erred on some observation and he would not even let his monarch off without some sort of reprimand. Extraordinary stuff. It is said by just about everybody I knew connected with him that Lady Jessie was the only one who could ever say: 'Oh, don't be silly, Don.' She was clearly his muse, his everything. She was the most powerful figure and she was the one who put people at ease. That was always very evident.

6

TOWARDS A CENTURY

I MET HIM, NOT surprisingly at the cricket, at the members' stand at the Adelaide Cricket Ground in 1985 when I was the leader of the opposition. He would have been about 75. He was a great presence and because I obviously knew who he was and he knew who I was, we sort of fell into easy conversation. I met him a few times after that and more frequently after I became prime minister. I found him very affable and he was a person who was incredibly interested in any current affairs. He would talk about issues and he took a lively and critical interest.

We had a very memorable lunch in the early 90s when a mutual friend invited me to lunch in Adelaide and Don was there with the late Max Schubert who ran Penfold Wines. We talked about cricket and wine and it was very pleasant. We were still in opposition then and we said we were going to introduce a GST and I remember him saying, 'Oh, that's a very good idea but,' he said, 'you're going to have a lot of trouble selling it.' He was dead right! (laughs) Of course that was later on.

Janette and I visited the home in Kensington Park, Holden Street, on a couple of occasions. Just after I became prime minister we went out after the Test in Adelaide which was then still being held on the Australia Day weekend. It would have been early in

1997. We saw both Don and Jessie – Jessie was still alive then – and we had a very pleasant yarn. It was really very pleasant to open a bottle of champagne and we had a drink and it was just terrific to have a talk.

Jessie was a marvellous person, as everybody attested. One of the things that Janette and I both used to talk to her about, I think her mother's maiden name had been Kell which was the same as my mother's maiden name and there was a distant sort of association there. But we would just talk about cricket and world affairs and you talk a bit about your families. He talked about his children and grandchildren and I met his two grandchildren on a number of occasions. And Jessie and Janette would talk about those things as well. It was the sort of conversation you have with so many people where you have a common interest but it was largely cricket. He was interested in politics, not in any partisan sense, but the politics of contemporary issues. And I mentioned to you about the GST. He mentioned that a couple of times in letters he wrote to me. So it was a very lively mind.

You never got the impression that Don had stopped doing everything right. He never seemed to be disinterested or just coasting along. If you said anything to him he would always analyse it and give you a very considered, precise answer. He was a very deliberate person in anything he said and whenever he talked about some cricketing feat or some innings or bowling feat or victory he'd always have every last run correct and he'd always have the location and the atmospheric absolutely correct. And he would have been a perfectionist in everything he did, I imagine.

One of the last conversations I had with him, we talked about one-day cricket and he told me what a good game he thought it was and how entertaining and how much he enjoyed it. He was not a person who, in the discussions I had with him about cricket, said look, it's not what it was. He was a person who would have given plenty of credit to current players, and he did, people like Tendulkar and Warne. He was very contemporary and fair-minded and he was remarkably alert until he got very ill right at the end, remarkably alert.

Did you correspond at all?

Occasionally. He was a very good correspondent. He was quite amazing. We didn't do it on a regular basis. I would ring him occasionally, particularly after I became prime minister, and just chat to him for a while. If I was in Adelaide I'd see him. I didn't see him every month or anything, but I kept in touch. He was a courteous correspondent and he would be doing 30 or 40 letters a day, right up until just before the end. It was amazing.

He belonged to a generation when people wrote. People don't write very much now. They use telephone and of course e-mails or mobile phones, it's just all different. But I remember once I did something for the Bradman Trust, the Bradman Museum, some promotion they had in South Africa and I just wrote a little foreword for it. This would be three years ago, and he wrote me a nice letter out of the blue saying thank you for doing it. It was very courteous of him. But he was like that.

Would you describe your relationship as a friendship?

Because of who he was, you hesitate to make claims. I thought we had a friendly relationship and I was particularly keen to help in any way. I felt particularly after I became prime minister it was important that I keep in touch with him because I was doing that for the Australian people, not that they wanted me to. And because I got to know him before I became prime minister it was a very easy and welcome thing to do.

Have you had anything to do with the Bradman Museum?
Yes, I opened the second stage in '96. I managed to twist the arm of
the Treasury to provide a contribution to it and Channel Nine ran
a telethon for it.

***Sir Donald was also a friend of Sir Robert Menzies, wasn't he?
Did you ever discuss that?***
A little bit but Don was not the sort of person to keep talking about
something like that because that would have given the impression
that they were the good old days. Although so much of what he
achieved was achieved decades ago, the really good and positive
thing about him, and perhaps one of the reasons why he remained
such a dominant figure, is that he kept himself contemporary. He
always had something relevant and contemporary to say about the
game and the way it was being administered, right to the end. And
although he talked a little about Menzies when we were together,
he didn't dwell on it. He would never have given the impression
that that was the only association with a prime minister that he
thought was worthwhile having.

When was the last time you saw him?
I saw him about a week or ten days before he died. One Friday
afternoon in February last year, I went to see him. I knew through
his son and a friend of his that he was pretty ill.

   I was very pleased that I went to see him. That year we struck
an Australian sports medal to mark the centenary of federation.
He'd had many awards and many trophies and there was something
like 3000 or 4000 of these medals distributed, but he was obviously
entitled to one. I thought it would be a nice gesture to present him
with a medal and I was able to do that. It was just obviously a private
call. A few of the media found out about it and I confirmed that I
had been there but that was the last time I saw him.

Tell me about the legislation to protect the . . .

Oh, to protect the Bradman name, yes. That was an approach that was made to me by his family and it was pretty unusual but I just felt given the special place he occupied it was . . . Some people were a bit critical of it but the Labor Party supported it and I needed the support of two state premiers to get it through. I rang up John Olsen, the South Australian Premier, and Bob Carr, so I got one from each side, and they agreed. We made the amendment to the Companies Act which really protected the name 'Bradman'. We thought it was going to be subject to enormous commercialisation and I guess in retrospect it was a valuable thing to have done for the family and for the Bradman Trust. So much of the money from the Bradman Trust will go to helping junior cricket and helping indigenous cricket, it seemed to be worthwhile doing.

Does that make the Bradman name unique in Australia?

It really puts it in the same category as words like Olympic and Anzac and so forth, so yes, maybe. I don't know whether there are any other individual names like that but I have no difficulty defending that. It's quite easy to defend because of the unique place he occupied in our history.

He was really the first great celebrity in this country. He still remains the greatest celebrity Australia has had. And it came so early. His fame predated television and it goes back to the late-20s and early-30s. And his fame and achievements were not diminished and denigrated as the years went by.

And he wasn't just a great sportsman, he was a cultural figure and a person who gave a lot of hope and inspiration to the country in the worst days of the Depression. It's very easy to forget that. He gave people a lot of hope.

Lord Philip Moore was private secretary to the Queen and keeper of the Queen's Archives when, after a wait of 55 years, he finally got Sir Donald Bradman's autograph. Lord Moore of Wolvercote is now a Lord-in-Waiting to the Queen and I spoke to him in a tiny interview room in the House of Lords.

I FIRST SAW Don Bradman when I was nine in 1930, in the first of his great tours to this country. We lived in Tunbridge, which is a few miles from Canterbury in Kent and the Australians' fixture against Kent was right at the end of the season in August after the Test matches had taken place. And Bradman had made this huge impact of course on the cricket public in this country.

Canterbury is a very lovely cricket ground and my father took me and we sat on the grass and Bradman was by then the great hero of all the schoolboys of course. And he came out to bat and Kent had a slow bowler, a googly bowler called Titch Freeman – he was a very small man – who used to take 300 wickets in the season in county cricket but the English selectors always reckoned that he was too slow through the air and that good batsmen would use their feet and murder him. And the whole of that summer they didn't play him once for England. And Bradman came in. Either Woodfull or Ponsford was out quite early and he'd scored 17 when Freeman bowled him three leg-breaks which Bradman left and they turned outside the off stump. Then he bowled him a topspinner and Bradman was lbw. And I was heartbroken. It was ghastly. Although Kent was my county and Titch Freeman a great hero, golly, my father was devastated. Anyway, we small boys ran on to the field as he made his way back to the pavilion, all trying to get his autograph which he'd been very good about during the summer. But he was angry and he waved us away with his bat. None of us got his autograph. That was 1930.

By 1934 my parents were living in Oxford and I was a boy at the

Dragon School in Oxford, a very well-known preparatory school in this country. Our cricket master took us to see the Australians and of course everyone wanted to see Bradman. It was quite early in the season – the Test series hadn't started. It was on the Christchurch ground at Oxford and once again I was disappointed. Oxford had a fairly ordinary seamer called Evans, and Bradman having made about 50, I forget what it was, tried to turn him off the leg stump and was lbw again. Could you believe it? A second time I was frustrated. It was slightly compensated by the most lovely hundred from Lindsay Hassett. But not a real consolation.

In 1938 I didn't see him and the war came, we all went to the war, and I went to see him when he brought over the great Australian side of 1948 at Lord's. My memory's not frightfully good on this. I was talking to my wife about it because she came with me that day. Quite difficult to get her to come to cricket, but to see Bradman . . . It was the MCC against the Australians. I remember Laker lured him out of his crease and he should have been stumped and it's best forgotten the name of the one who missed and dropped the ball and I think Bradman went on to get a century. But he obviously wasn't quite the wonderful Bradman he'd been before the war.

In 1985 the Queen was in the *Britannia* in Adelaide and I persuaded her to invite Bradman to lunch. Not that she needed much persuading, he'd have probably come anyway. But I claimed credit for it. And to my enormous delight, the Queen had Bradman on one side and she put me the other side of Bradman. So at last I met him after all these years. I told him the story of how beastly he'd been to the schoolboys in 1930 and he said, 'I do remember it. I was very angry. He totally diddled me, I was sure it was another leg-break and it was a topspinner.' He said, 'Well, I'll make up for it,' and he grabbed the menu of the *Britannia* and signed it. That occupies a very special place in our apartment. So that was 1985.

We talked a lot. He told me one golfing story which I enjoyed. He said, 'Yes I do enjoy the golf and I like to keep it up and I was very excited the other day because I went around Royal Adelaide from the back tees in one less than my age.' I think he was 77 that year, and he holed his putts in 76 and really that was much more important to him than cricket, at least that was the impression I got.

We talked about 1948. 'Yes,' he said, 'we had a good side but as far as I'm concerned, it had gone.' Very interesting. He meant he hadn't got 'the flair' he felt. The unique flair. He was still a wonderful player and the averages will show that he scored a lot of runs.

And he used that expression?
It had gone. 'Yes, Sir Philip, but by then it had gone.' I thought it was fascinating.

The 1948 tour appears to have meant a great deal here.
Oh it did. I think it was marvellous. I think part of the pleasure it gave was that it was such a super side. They really were. I would have said until this present Australian side, that '48 side was the best ever probably. And it was happening that though England was being defeated, cricket seemed to be at its best again.

What was your impression of Sir Donald?
I think rather as I expected. Slightly buttoned up, I would say. Very human in that although he had met the Queen before, he was obviously pleased to be sitting on her right, to be given the place of honour at lunch. It was a big lunch in the *Britannia*. I explained to Her Majesty (who follows cricket a bit) that Don Bradman was by far the most important Australian alive. (laughs) I think fortunately she hadn't the Governor-General to lunch that day.

*David and **Sam Parkinson** have a wholesale sports business in Adelaide, not far from Sir Donald's Kensington Park home. David Parkinson played for the Kensington District Cricket Club and had known Sir Donald since he was a boy. His son Sam played for South Australia. We spoke in Sam's office.*

SAM PARKINSON: I approached him in the early 80s to organise some autographs for a charity, I forget which charity it was. I wrote him a letter and left it in his letterbox and he rang the next day and said, 'Yes, that'll be fine. I'll pop around and see you.' And he was most obliging and very polite. He said any time. Just as if it was no big deal. I gradually got to know him a bit better. Over that period I suppose he called in 20 or 30 times. In early days he'd sign, then leave. But towards the end he'd stay for an hour or so and have a chat, just in his tracksuit, and he was really relaxed and a lot of fun.

I used to look after him with golf balls because he loved his golf. He couldn't get around the course after his stroke so we gave him a golf cart courtesy of our company for a while. From time to time I'd go up there and have a cup of tea and he'd sign things and he was very relaxed and I could not get over his sharpness given his age.

I think he was one of the most intelligent people I've ever met by a long stretch. He was just extremely quick. If I ever asked a question that was futile, he would just ignore it and pretend it didn't happen and talk about something else, which was quite often because as a young man I was very nervous and I'd try and make conversation.

He had a magnificent sense of humour and saw the light side of life enormously. Quite often we had belly laughs with some of the conversations we had, which you didn't see publicly. He was a very private man. I just consider myself fortunate to have known him at all.

You played for South Australia. Was that a bond?

SAM PARKINSON: We didn't really talk a great deal about cricket. But from time to time we'd talk about different personalities. I remember when I was a young lad I played for the South Australian under 16s and I had a great big run-up and the message came from Sir Donald that I should cut my run-up in half. When you're a young lad, you think you're pretty special and I thought, 'He doesn't know anything about bowling, he was only a batsman'. I quickly learned the realities of life as I got older.

He was a wonderful man. I'm sure at times he found it imposing but he was always obliging. I think he understood that we were not selling his bats, we were giving them to charities, all for good causes. All I would ask is that the charities write him a letter of thanks and they nearly always did.

When he was in his mid-70s, he would roll up to the office in a suit with a briefcase and he'd sit down and say, 'Righto, Sam, we've got some business to do,' and open the briefcase and there'd be nothing in it except for three pens: a black texta, a biro and a pencil, depending on what product we had to sign. I thought that was hilarious. That was his business.

DAVID PARKINSON: He used to sign books and bats and photographs and there's one thing he wouldn't sign, and that was a cricket ball. He'd say, 'I'm not a bowler.' We asked him, we had one signed by Lillee. He said, 'No, I don't sign them, Dave.'

I've been involved with his club Kensington for 53 years now. I played my first game for Kensington when I was 12 and as a consequence I knew him when I was a boy. Then I sat on the committee with him at Kensington. He was on the committee for well over 20 years.

He was recruited to Kensington by a fellow called Hodgetts who was the president of the Kensington District Cricket Club. He was a stockbroker and he found out that Don Bradman was a bit disenchanted and was keen on getting into this sort of profession. He came down here in September 1935 and played his first game for Kensington in September/October. And then he played for Kensington on and off when he was able to and captained Kensington.

As a youngster playing in short pants, I used to call him Mr Bradman. He was Mr Bradman when I first knew him and I used to stumble, I couldn't get the Sir Donald out. I used to feel terribly embarrassed but eventually it just rolled off. But we were all a bit stunned to have to call him Sir Donald when he was Mr Bradman to us little kids.

I sat with him on committees at Kensington, only for a year or so, and then I sat on the board with him at the SACA. He was very astute. Whenever he made a statement or a comment, it was always very thoughtful and rarely did anyone debate against it. Because if there was anything contentious, he used to do his homework. I'm not saying he was right all the time and he was beaten in some moves that he had. He wasn't God. But he was a very, very astute man and his brain was very keen right up until the last years. Well, we didn't see him in his last year. In fact we backed off when he became frail. His signature changed from a bold signature to very frail.

He used to just come down here and we'd discuss all sorts of things. Some days he'd talk for half an hour to us, wouldn't he?

SAM PARKINSON: At least. I suppose the best memory is that he was always extremely friendly and polite and obliging. And never ever said no.

DAVID PARKINSON: Except when we asked him to sign the cricket ball.

SAM PARKINSON: He signed a cricket bat that we had already had signed by Harold Larwood, and his comment was I'm not too happy about this or I don't know about signing on the same bat as this bloke, but it was tongue in cheek.

Was he interested in cricket bats?

DAVID PARKINSON: Oh yeah, he was very strong on the fact that the bats young blokes used were too heavy. See, he used to use a 2.2 or a 2.3, and there was a trend (it's reverted back now) to getting into very heavy bats and he used to say they were losing the opportunity to cut and pull. Because the bats are too heavy. All they are doing is front-foot driving, you see, and he had a very strong view on that. He used to say, I used a 2.2 [2 pound 2 ounce] and they're using 2.10 and 2.12. He used to say it's okay for Clive Lloyd, who was a great man. I don't know if you've seen Lloyd's bats. His bats were three pound and the grips – I've got pretty big hands and I could hardly get my hands around them. But he was a great big strong man and Bradman used to say, 'Well, that's fine for big strong blokes but you see little teenagers using them.' He was quite right too. The pendulum has turned now and as bat distributors we are finding that the real heavy bats are lying on the shelves.

SAM PARKINSON: Towards the end he would come in regularly. He said, 'I don't recommend getting old.' He really hated the fact that he couldn't play golf as well as he wanted to, because his mind was so sharp but his body had given up the ghost a bit. One time I took a lot of gear around to his home – in fact, a hundred cricket bats – and I had to go straight from there to Mount Gambier and he was very frail, and he was very disappointed that he couldn't help carry them out to the car.

DAVID PARKINSON: He was a very proud man. He loved his golf. We used to look after him with golf balls. That was the only thing he'd take in recognition. But often he'd say, 'No Dave, I've got plenty, son.' 'What about a glove, Sir Donald?' 'Oh no, I've still got a couple you gave me.' A lot of blokes would have just taken them in any case and given them to blokes they played with, but he wouldn't.

He was very conscious of getting old and losing distance in his drive because he was almost a scratch golfer, you know. I think he might have played scratch – it might have been at Mount Osmond, I don't know whether he got scratch at Kooyie. Anyhow, when he started to lose distance – as you get older you do lose distance in your drive – he was all the time at me to try and get something that would help him. We made up a couple of clubs for him with flex shafts. We made up not lady's shafts but in between, what we call an A shaft which has more flex in it.

Sam Parkinson: It's a senior's shaft now.

David Parkinson: But he was just grasping at straws because he was in his late 70s then or his 80s. But he was such a competitive man. He couldn't abide the fact that he was being out-driven by blokes that were off 20 handicaps. That's the sort of bloke he was.

His capacity to sign autographs seems extraordinary.

Sam Parkinson: The bottom line for my personal view, he didn't need to be going around and signing all these autographs, but he was extremely friendly and polite and I just think that he tolerated my requests. Dad's known him a lot longer than I have, but I suppose the thing he wanted me to remember was his integrity. Well, that was just unbelievable.

David Parkinson: He was a very generous man. You think of the millions of times he signed. He didn't need to do that, he could have pulled the plug 20 years ago, couldn't he? And he really only pulled the plug in the last 18 months of his life, didn't he?

Sam Parkinson: I went around there one day and he said that someone had sent 500 sheets of paper to sign, without even requesting it. Just posted them to him. And he just said, 'It's inhumane how these people can do this to me,' but he signed them and sent them off. I think the tolerance of the man must have been unbelievable, right back from the early days.

DAVID PARKINSON: We never used him up. We were always conscious of that and we used to say him, 'If we're overdoing it Sir Donald . . .' and he'd say no, though not in so many words. And of course it was convenient. That was the other thing. He was only four kilometres from here, from our old office about three.

I've always been of the opinion that once he started to sign, he signed everything. As private as he was in his way, imagine what he'd have signed if he'd been a really private man. Cricket bats with his signature on them would have been worth tens of thousands, whereas now they're only worth thousands because there are so many of them around.

Sir Donald was unimpressed when Bowral solicitor **Garry Barnsley** *first put the idea of the Bradman Museum to him back in the mid-80s. He listened politely then said, 'I'd really prefer to be left alone.' Barnsley and I spoke in his office in the heart of Bowral.*

ONE OF THE APOCRYPHAL stories handed down in the family was about my grandmother and my Uncle Harry who was my father's older brother. He came home from school one day and proudly announced to my grandmother that he'd bowled Don Bradman at school. And of course my grandmother at that stage said, 'That's very nice dear, but who's he?' 'Uh,' he said, 'no one else can get the beggar out.' So we were brought up on those sorts of stories.

When did you first discuss the idea of the Bradman Museum with Sir Donald?
I had progressed quite a bit over more than 12 months, trying to raise awareness of the idea and the word got around that I was pushing this project. Then I had a phone call from Andy George who was the manager of Dormie House over in Moss Vale, which has

now been absorbed within the Moss Vale Golf Club. It's a lovely old building, perched right on the edge of the golf course. Andy said, 'Your hero Sir Donald Bradman will be here in town tomorrow. Not many people know, but I'm letting you know, just in case.'

So screwing up my courage I simply turned up there early one morning and with sweaty hands, I waited in the corridor. It seemed such a sensible thing to do in the beginning but as I waited, I thought this is ridiculous. I'm a person of mature years and a solicitor, why am I breaking out in perspiration? Then I was invited to go into Andy's office and Don was sitting at the desk signing autographs and I introduced myself and said, 'I wonder if you can spare a moment to talk to me about an idea I have?' I said, 'I have this idea to create a museum here in Bowral. It will tell the story of Australian cricket and it will tell your story.' It was very bold of me to ambush him because Lady Jessie was waiting to take him out onto the golf course. But he listened very courteously and then said (I remember his words very clearly), 'I have lived a life where I have been subjected to the most intense publicity imaginable and now that I've retired, I would really prefer to be left alone. Besides which, there is the repository of my material in Adelaide at the Mortlock Library, and there isn't a large quantity of material left that I can offer to you or suggest that will be made available to house in the museum.'

I suggested that museums these days are not necessarily based on collections because the medium of telling the story is mainly film and the objects themselves are merely pegs on which you hang the story. I'd been the secretary of the Berrima Court House Museum since 1973, so I'd been immersed in the museum world. So we had an amiable chat. I can't say that he was at all encouraging, but at the same time he didn't expressly disapprove of the ideas that I was promoting. Then we shook hands and he went off and played golf.

Where did it go from there?

I was at that time an elected member of the Wingecarribee Shire Council, and within the council I continued to push this idea of let's do something with Bradman Park. The focus gradually became on acquiring the house in which he had lived, the one in which Richard Mulvaney lives now, 20 Glebe Street. It was the second of the two Bradman houses, not the one with the tank stand against which he practised as a boy.

There was no hint of outright opposition locally, but the support for it was lukewarm. Then came the bicentennial. I wrote up the idea, put it to the local bicentennial committee, and they ranked it pretty much at the bottom of their list of preferences. Right up the top were things like the new civic centre and the sporting fields, and they got progressively less expensive towards the end. The forecast cost at that stage was $240 000. And that was made up of the purchase price plus the fitting out of the cottage. I remember getting a call one night and it was the chairman of the committee and through gritted teeth he told me that there was wonderful news. 'Your project has received a $110 000 grant.' Of course, I was absolutely ecstatic, I thought it's going to happen after all. So the council then convened a committee of local citizens with me as chairman and that committee was entrusted with the project of overseeing the development of the museum project.

At that stage all hell broke loose because suddenly there was a groundswell of opposition to the project and it took a pretty vitriolic turn from time to time. While it was only a pipedream people dismissed it and thought it would never get off the ground. We didn't know whether it was going to succeed and the grant came within an inch of being withdrawn because we hadn't raised the balance of the funds.

Bruce Collins, a Sydney-based solicitor, persuaded Ron Brierley to come on board through Industrial Equity Limited with more money and finally it was really going ahead. Bruce took over from me as chairman of the committee which then took the form of a trust. The idea had gradually evolved to move from the cottage across the road to the park. The cottage was where the angst was, that we were converting a cottage with neighbours into a museum. So we said we'll move across the road into the park, where it is now, take a lease of the land and we'll build the museum there. The council leased the land to us for $1 a year for 99 years. Bruce then expanded the membership of the committee to bring into focus people such as Bob Radford, representing the NSW Cricket Association, other people representing the ACB, State Bank and so on. So under Bruce's leadership, the project expanded much beyond my original concept. Then when Bruce resigned, Bob Radford took over as chairman with me as the deputy chairman.

When did you next meet Sir Donald?
I made a trip to Adelaide to meet him at his home, which was a very nerve wracking experience. I always found him a person of great courtesy, but at the same time, very intellectually acute. He had an uncanny ability to be able to discern genuineness, and what I might call puffery, which placed me in a slightly difficult position, because I was the person at that stage who was endeavouring to beat up, if you like, the prospects of the success of the museum. I found Don to be slightly on the pessimistic side. He had lots of reasons why things wouldn't work, and a particularly fine mind when it came to analysing the value of a dollar. I'd been to Cooperstown in the United States which was the home of the American Baseball Hall of Fame, and I did quite a bit of research there in order to bolster my own feelings about the prospects of the success of the museum. So I brought these statistics back and I remember sitting in Sir Donald's lounge room, and I actually sat on one of those low poufs, those little cushion things, and sitting

there with Sir Donald and I remember Ron Brierley was also at this meeting and Basil Sellers. As a little boy from Bowral I really felt a little out of my depth among these captains of industry and the great Sir Donald. It was my task to give a report on the prospects of success of the Bradman Museum in Bowral.

Fortunately I was able to say that the American Baseball Hall of Fame had been going since the 1930s, it received hundreds of thousands of visitors a year and it was obviously an enormous financial success, employing umpteen staff and receiving all these visitors, so I think that that provided some reassurance. I remember Don was always a person who, I sensed, very much knew the significance of his accomplishments as a sportsman. He himself would always say that the most important quality of a man is modesty, so he was always very circumspect about what he had accomplished – he was never boastful but at the same time he knew in a very mathematical way what his accomplishments were. I can remember in this particular interview I said, 'There's one other thing, Sir Donald, that I learnt in my visit to the American Baseball Hall of Fame. And that is that probably the best known American baseballer outside America would be Babe Ruth but he's about number five on the all-time batting averages, and the graduations between him and the best are just like every other sports. Sports like swimming, basketball, foot racing, any sport you like to name of human endeavour, the graduations between the best and the next best can often be infinitesimal – a hundredth of a second, a fraction of a millimetre. Except in cricket where the greatest exponent is about twice as good as the next fellow. And you know, I feel sorry for the Americans, that they don't have a Don Bradman.' And there was a definite twinkle in his eye. He actually turned around and glanced at the other two guests with a smile on his face. So that was a very cordial meeting, I remember it very well.

I met him again when he came with Lady Jessie to the opening of stage one. That was in October 1989. So I was standing with him on the balcony and he was able to point out to me where he had played his earliest cricket and it was literally 'down there' on the oval just a little bit away. It was very pleasant standing there as he pointed out the childhood playing grounds and here we were standing on the balcony of this wonderful new museum.

There was a nice touch because the premier had been scheduled to attend and at the last minute was unable to and so he delegated the job of opening the museum to John Fahey who was then a minister in the Greiner cabinet and the local state member. John spoke briefly about Sir Donald's accomplishment and he said, 'The thing to remember is that while Sir Donald was abroad accomplishing these great things he did for Australia and for cricket, Lady Jessie was the one who had to stay behind and I think rather than a politician opening this museum, I think we should ask her to do it.' And that was a lovely gesture by John. So she had the pleasure of pulling the cord and opening the museum. That was a very pleasant occasion. The night before there had been a major banquet in Sydney at the Regent Hotel where Sir Donald had spoken.

Sir Donald took a keen interest in the prospects of the success of the museum and there's no doubt that he was pessimistic about its prospects.

What aspect of the museum interested him most?

I think he took a keen interest in every aspect of it. Some of the things that focused his attention were nuts and bolts and things like: Are you sure you can afford to run the lift? Lifts are very expensive to run, you know. What about the air-conditioning? Air-conditioning is very expensive to run. I think he was a natural born worrier when it came to the prospects of success. By inclination cautious. Very self-contained. These are words and epithets that other people have used about him in his cricket. For example, something that stuck in my mind was that he was never nervous when he went out to play, he was composed. He knew what he had to do. That was one of the first things that I learnt from my first trip to the Mortlock Library, the State Library of South Australia. One of the exhibits I saw was Don Bradman's Royal typewriter, the portable typewriter that he took on the tour with him in 1930. Now think about that – 1930, a 21 year old carrying his portable typewriter in a metal box in order to be able to deal with his correspondence. Discipline, focus.

I keep coming back to his intelligence. The overwhelming thing that I discovered as I met him and got to know him was that he was extremely bright. In the museum, for example, there is a letter he wrote as a 19 year old. The handwriting is immaculate, the composition is superb. There was this combination of factors. Clearly he had physical agility, visual acuity, all of the physical characteristics that would be the things we would first identify with superlative skills as a batsman. But it was his intellect that has perhaps not gained the recognition that it deserves.

It often amuses me that he was criticised because he wasn't the knockabout bloke. Well, Bradman did go rabbiting and he obviously did enjoy country life. But to my mind that makes his accomplishments as a statesmanlike figure in his early 20s even more astonishing. There's film of him making these witty speeches at black tie dinners in England with lords and ladies all round him. I keep thinking to myself, what was I like when I was 25 or 26? Could I have carried that off? Without a sign of nervousness, with poise, timing, humour, absolute sense of the occasion.

We were having a chat and because it's always impressed me, I said, 'You were able to make those speeches at the dinners when you'd been out on the field all day. Whereas if it were me, if I were out on the field batting, I'd be worrying about what I was going to say at the dinner that night.' And he said, 'No, no, I just closed it off. I was able to compartmentalise it' – I don't know if that was quite his word – 'I knew I was going out to bat so I thought of nothing other than batting. When I came off the field, I thought of what I was going to do next.' Discipline. I was just in awe of it.

And he was analytical. I suppose being a lawyer you could see the way his thought pattern worked. Everything was methodical, thought through, and it required a fairly deep intellect to be able to do that. At the same time he was world-wise in his dealings with people. You can sense that I have a most profound admiration for him. But it is less to do with what he accomplished on the field, which is everyone's focus, and more to do with this extraordinary intellectual strength.

And the other factor is his accomplishments as a philanthropist. Can you imagine a major sporting figure today doing what Don did, giving away all the rights associated with his persona freely? Here, take this and do good things with it. I mean, it's almost Biblical, isn't it? If you look at the wealth of some major sporting figures, how have they accumulated it? Out of prize-money? No, it's out of the rights associated with their identity. It's this phenomenon of brand endorsements. The marketeers have worked out that we're very susceptible to the concept of brand association. Don gave it all away. He didn't exploit it. He also gave it away knowing that it might otherwise have been an extraordinary inheritance for his heirs. The revenue stream to the foundation we have turned to valuable account. We have created scholarships. Originally the focus was upon the idea the funding would come from donations from the corporate sector and it was only later that we realised just how valuable this gift was. We started to realise the value of it through endorsements.

We tried to prevail upon Don to recognise that his signature was a valuable commodity and not to give it away quite so freely.

But he was adamant that he would never refuse an autograph. Even in the context where people were coming to the museum, buying 20 postcards, and within a few days we'd get a complaint from Don that, 'You know, that museum of yours over there is generating more work for me. I've just had one fella send me 20 postcards to sign.' And you could see what was happening and when we pointed this out to Don he'd smile wryly, probably in recognition of the shrewdness of the entrepreneur who'd turned it to account and say, 'Well, I just can't refuse.' His self-image was of a person who would never refuse an autograph.

On one of my visits to Adelaide, Don was still driving and he had a very modest little Holden car. We were going to the golf club to have lunch with his son John and he offered to drive me. So he put me in the front and backed out, tootled along, we were going very slowly and came to an intersection and turned around and he said in that slightly croaky voice of his, 'I'm just going to pull over here, I'm just going to post a few letters in the letter box.' Sitting in front of me was this enormous pile of letters all wrapped up neatly with a rubber band, and the letterbox was just there and Don pulled up and I said, 'Don't you worry about getting out, Sir Donald, I'll pop these into the letterbox for you.' No sooner had I said those words than I think, I've just insulted the greatest living Australian by imparting the connotation that he was too old and doddery to post his own bloody letters. I think, ahh. And he said, 'No, no, it's right, I'll do it.' And so he's getting out of the car and he'd swung both legs out and then I realised that the car was starting to go slowly backwards down the hill. I was sitting there thinking, you know how your mind moves at a million miles an hour? Now hang on, do I insult him again by pointing out that he's failed to put the car into park, or do I sit here politely and allow the greatest living Australian to be run over by his own motor car? Of course all this happens in a millisecond and I reached across and discreetly pushed it into park, and he got out and nothing was said. Posted his letters and got back in again and off we went.

Did Sir Donald come to the opening of the second stage of the Museum in 1996?

He's always had an aversion to air travel. Sir Ronald Brierley offered to bring him over in his private jet but he wouldn't accept that. They finally decided that he really wasn't up to the trip. Also, Jessie was unwell at that stage. All of those things conspired to keep him away.

South African batsman **Barry Richards**, *whom Sir Donald compared with Sir Jack Hobbs and Sir Leonard Hutton, played for South Australia in 1970 and returned to coach the state in 1988. We spoke in the ABC Studios at the Melbourne Cricket Ground while he took a break from commentating during the second Test of the 2001–02 South African series.*

I THINK HE WAS A very dominating figure. I don't think he set out to be but just the aura of the man created the domination. You thought, well who am I, a lesser mortal, to argue? I think he exploited that position, and why shouldn't he? There are times when if you sit on the fence for too long no decisions are ever made, so I think he would realise that he could use the aura to get something through or to get a decision made without it dragging on too long. He knew how to use his aura well.

In England and Australia, who were the powerhouse of cricket certainly right up until very recent times, I think what he said counted for an enormous amount. He probably didn't have quite as much influence in places that he hadn't played in, although he still had a tremendous reputation.

He was always very forthright about his views on cricket and he would always articulate his reasons for it. Issues like the eight-ball over, the no-ball issue, the front-foot rule and back-foot rule, were fairly strong in his mind. Not everybody would agree with him but you knew you were in for a good debate and you knew he'd thought it through and he had very valid reasons why he thought a particular rule should be changed.

He was chairman of the Australian Cricket Board when it cancelled the South African cricket tour. Was that something he discussed with you?
No, but I think it would have caused him some angst because he always had a lot of affection for South African players and he had a lot of affection for South African administrators. He got to know quite a few over the years and had a tremendous amount of respect for fellows like Joe Pamensky who had been around the cricketing traps in South Africa for a very long time as an administrator. But in the end I think the political and governmental pressure would have been something that he would have had to take tremendous cognisance of; it had become a wider issue, not just a cricket issue.

What was your initial contact with him?
I struck up quite a warm friendship with him when I went to play for South Australia in 1970, during the games we played at the Adelaide Oval. We used to play a reasonably regular game of golf. He was a very good golfer. In those days he was very sprightly. He used to shoot under his age and go round the course in three and a half hours – he'd be pretty cranky if you took any longer than that and you'd play for a dollar, that's the most you'd play for. He was pretty snappy around the course.

I'd just started in the game essentially, I was very keen to play well and it was something that he had a passion for. I used to love playing. He was not a risk-taker. If you played as his partner, he always assumed the lead role of captain. 'You go there. This is how we are going to play this hole because we want to win it.' Even when he was in his 80s, he wanted to win and you could tell how competitive he must have been. And probably in an era when there was less of that sort of thing going on. He was the ultimate competitor, do you know what I mean?

Sir Donald must have been delighted when you hit 366 in 372 minutes for South Australia against Western Australia in 1970.
People used to say it couldn't be done, and I think that used to irk Sir Donald a little bit. They used to say, 'Oh, they threw the ball up', and all this sort of stuff and I think to him it was a slight slur on his ability of quick scoring. They'd say it's not possible to do again because it hadn't ever been done before. So I think he was quite appreciative when it was actually done again and he could say, 'Well if you're good enough, you can do it'.

I must be honest though, it's hard to imagine that someone could do it now given the number of balls that are bowled. Bradman never did it in Australia, he did it in England. And the time that Ponsford did it, there were 102 eight-ball overs that day, and then when I did it, there were 78. So that's 24 overs less in one day's play, so if you multiply that by four, that's 800 balls per match, so you can understand why the scoring was a lot higher in the 30s because the over rate was just a hell of a lot better. And when I did it in the 70s compared to now, there's even less balls, so as each year goes by, because there's less balls bowled, it's harder for somebody to do it.

How would you describe Sir Donald?
If you were using a word to describe him, I'd say 'meticulous' is the word that comes to mind. Everything is thought out and organised

and that's how it's got to be done and there won't be any argument about it. He was very meticulous on the golf course too.

He was very prolific with protocol and with writing letters – letters of thanks and all that sort of thing. Unfortunately for me, I was more the other way. I'd try and do the right thing but not always do it. You just felt that every time he stepped out of the house, everything was immaculate, polished shoes, the behaviour was immaculate, that there wasn't anything that he didn't do in the correct manner.

My mum and dad wrote to him once when I was very young saying what inspiration that I'd got out of his book *How to Play Cricket* and we've still got the letter at home which Sir Donald wrote to us.

Did you rekindle your relationship with Sir Donald when you went back to Adelaide to coach in 1988?
I got more out of knowing Sir Donald that one season in 1988 when I was in my 40s than when I was in my 20s in 1970. That's when we had reflective conversations of a much more mature nature. He was a very interesting man because he was so well read. It wasn't just a cricket thing. We had conversations about all sorts of issues, it could be art, literature, theatre, his thoughts on cricket, reflecting on what could have been in terms of the South African scenario. How disappointing it was that South Africans were out of the fold for so long. At that stage Nelson Mandela was still in jail so there were some real issues facing South Africa and I think it was an area which really interested Sir Donald from all aspects.

Towards the end he started to mellow a bit. He was out of cricket administration and fully retired when I went back for that season, so he would stay on for a lunch every now and then. You'd have a couple of glasses of wine and he'd loosen up a little bit. But he was never prone to losing any of the aura around him, he was always very conscious of the role modelling he had to do. Even when he'd had a couple of glasses of wine, he would never let the guard down.

The banning of South Africa from test cricket must have contributed to frustration within your own career. Did you receive any support from Sir Donald?

There was obviously an understanding of the frustrations. We discussed that more when I was older. He actually asked my wife at a dinner one night, he said, 'How did Barry ever cope with it? Being potentially one of the true greats of the game and he's only been allowed . . .' He wanted to know what my feeling for that would have been. And in essence I suppose it was something that subconsciously you were very frustrated by and I think he had an understanding of that. He understood ability and he understood where you could be and where you weren't. So I think he had a great deal of sympathy. I think he would have been less critical of things that I did during my career because he would know it's not just pique but there's a bigger picture to it.

*R*etired *sporting commentator* **Norman May,** *a veteran of 10 Olympics and 10 Commonwealth Games for the ABC, rated his radio interview with Sir Donald as one of the most important jobs he did. He was three weeks off 74 when we spoke at his home in Sydney.*

I STARTED BROADCASTING cricket for the ABC in 1958, and we had a broadcast box in the Noble Stand at the Sydney Cricket Ground, which looks straight down the pitch. There was a row of seats in front where the commentators would sit, and the seat in front was for the Australian selectors. That was for Dudley Seddon, Jack Ryder and Don Bradman. And Bradman always sat in the middle.

They would sit there every time a match was played in Sydney. We got quite friendly over a period of years and we used to exchange pleasantries.

When it got to the bicentennial the ABC wrote to Bradman and asked would he do something for us as part of history for the bicentennial. And he wrote back and said yes. This was in September 1987. At the time Alan McGilvray had just retired from the ABC as a broadcaster and I was the only long-term broadcaster left. I'd been around Australia for 17 years with Alan McGilvray before that; he was radio and I was television. So Bradman said he would do it with me, which was quite a thrill. He wouldn't deal with Richie Benaud or Tony Greig or any of the World Series people so it had to be the ABC. I went and saw him at Holden Street, Kensington Park where he lived, and we had a preliminary discussion. He said he would do it but he wanted me to do all the research.

So I went away and I read 24 books about cricket, about all of his life and his career and then sent him 15 pages of typewritten questions as a guide to what we were going to do. Then in January of 1988, we booked the stereo studio in Adelaide for three days to record what we could with him. And we did probably about nine hours of recording over the three days. We used to pick him up by car and drive him back.

If Bradman decided to do something he would give it 100 per cent support and he was very, very good to work with. We had no restrictions on what I asked him at all, except we said, 'It's not going to be about your personal life or your marriage or your children or anything like that. It's going to be about cricket.'

And there was no question he didn't answer. His life story is fascinating. He had a bit of a squeaky voice, Bradman, but he just captivated once you started to listen to him. We took it year by year and his recall was amazing. We started when he first started to play cricket in Bowral. He could recall things that happened to him when he was a kid, how he played and all that sort of thing.

We spent three months beforehand getting maybe 100 little inserts from other people, like Bill O'Reilly; the captain of England, Gubby Allen; and all his co-players such as Keith Miller and Neil Harvey, Bill Johnston, Lindsay Hassett – just little comments. And where the person was dead, we got Paul Jennings to dummy the voices for us, reading extracts from books and things like that. And we progressively played them in, so we were chronologically telling the story of his life from all these books I read and then asking people about it. So we'd play a quote from say Neville Cardus in 1934 and then ask him a question about what was said and he'd come back with the answer. He was amazing when it came to the pure technique of cricket. He just ad-libbed it. Anything to do with scores and facts and figures, he had all the answers there, in accordance with my questions. He was very thorough, he had reams and reams of sheets of answers. It was an amazing experience. It was fantastic.

When we finished the whole thing we both listened to it independently to work out any errors. He was very meticulous about that. He had a great memory and a desire to tell the truth. Any claim about him, it had to be accurate for him to say it was. If it wasn't accurate he wouldn't have any part of it. But on the same token he also wanted credit for what he did. But only what he did, not what people thought he did, you know. I found him very good on that.

So we listened to it independently and we came up with about seven small errors in nine hours. For example, when he made 452 in Sydney, which was the highest-ever score, he thought he was out for a duck in the first innings and I said, 'No, you weren't, you were out for three.' That was a slight correction we had to make.

When we came to edit that nine hours of material, all we did was cut out the small seasons that didn't matter much like 1935–36, which was a Shield season. We virtually ran everything else he said which is an amazing thing because you can't do that with anybody else. Can you imagine making a film and using 80 per cent of the material? We finished up with eight 55-minute programs, about seven and a half hours out of probably just under nine hours.

When we finished the three days with Bradman, the executive producer Alan Marks invited him to come to lunch with us. There's a lot of stories about Bradman being a non-drinker. Now, that's not true. He was an occasional drinker but he always drank good stuff. Max Schubert, who made Grange Hermitage, was a great friend of his. And we took him to a little restaurant and the owner of the restaurant was so delighted to have him there that he produced two bottles of Grange. (laughs) I think The Don drank half a bottle. He would drink the good stuff.

His only concern when it was all finished, he said, 'Well, was I controversial enough?' I said, 'You don't have to worry.' You could just listen to him talk all day long. And we used to play it at 9 o'clock on Saturday mornings and now it's been released again by the ABC on CD, the whole series. And the first release of that has been sold out completely since he's died. So that shows the fascinating interest in him.

He was very suspicious of the media, wasn't he?
He was suspicious of journalists, right, because they write lies about him. You know, Neville Cardus, who was one of the most respected English journalists, wrote a big article saying how he selected some literature for Bradman to read to further his education and Bradman said, 'That's nonsense.' They were doing this sort of thing because if they are instructed to get a story about Bradman and Bradman won't talk to them, what do you do?

Did he reveal a sense of humour?

He had an unusual sense of humour. He seemed to get pleasure
out of other people's discomfort. He would think it funny if you
fell over and sprained your ankle, that type of thing.

*He clearly had an extraordinary sense of concentration. Was that
something he showed when he was being interviewed?*

Yes, he had the ability to sit there and listen to something, and
while other people would start getting impatient and start walking
around, he could listen. He had these extraordinary powers of concentration plus the ability and plus the desire to do well and that's
why he got these huge scores. And he was just efficient in what he
did. He knew he could play well and he was such an entertainer.
When he got his 100th hundred in Sydney, his aim was to entertain the crowd, and he came out with a crook leg and got 75 in
about 40 minutes after that, you know.

He was an amazing character. Can you think of any politician,
or anyone else you can name, who you would put on eight
55-minute programs?

*Lawyer **Jack Clarke** was a South Australian Cricket Association
board member when his friend Michael Brock invited him to play golf
with Sir Donald Bradman. It was the first of a number of encounters.
We spoke in the legal firm's boardroom in Adelaide.*

THE FIRST TIME I played golf with him in 1988, by the second hole
I knew that he just about knew more about me than I knew about
me. He was such a meticulous man. He probably rang up people
and said: 'Who's this bloke I'm playing golf with?'

The first time we played there were three of us: Michael
Brock, he's a local land agent here, and the great cricketer Barry

Richards, and myself. We had three rounds, over a few months, and we had lovely long lunches together which was a fascinating insight to him.

My assessment of Sir Donald's problem was he'd had so many people who had almost betrayed him – betrayed is perhaps too strong a word – but people who had sought to knock him off his perch for whatever reason. And I think he probably got so sick of talking to idiots who wanted to talk cricket to him.

I felt as though you almost had to earn your spurs with him before he would really have a conversation. But once you'd earned your spurs, he was very generous in his thoughts with you. He had just the most erudite memory. He told me that he could remember every innings he'd ever played. Not a problem. Every innings. And a lot of shots he played in every innings. He wasn't saying it in a bragging sense. There were just four of us quietly having lunch and a few wines.

I remember when we first played with him, we tossed the balls and I was his partner in these three golf games. This is a bit intimidating. And it was just marvellous, it really was. I remember thinking, 'don't talk about cricket'. We talked about banking, and we talked about the law and we talked about everything but cricket. It wasn't until the 14th hole I said, 'Oh Sir Donald, you've seen them all but Barry is arguably the best I've seen.' He said, 'Jack, don't let anyone talk you out of that, he's probably the equal of any I've seen.' And then we talked about cricket. Cricket has been a passion of mine and once he'd worked out that I knew what I was talking about, and hopefully I did, we had some great conversations.

That first game, Brocky's got more front than David Jones and what he'd done is he'd written to Sir Donald and said, 'Look would you be interested in playing a game of golf with Barry Richards – he's just come to town – and Jack Clarke, who's a lawyer friend of mine who's on the SACA board?' Brocky gave his number and Sir

Donald rang back and left his silent number with Brocky's wife. And Brocky rang him back. This rather high-pitched voice answered the phone and he said, 'Oh Lady Bradman, is Sir Donald there please?' To which Sir Donald replied, 'It is Sir Donald speaking.' Brocky says he's never felt so embarrassed in his life.

But he said he'd love to have a game of golf and that day's fine. He said a couple of rules: no press, no publicity, otherwise I'm not interested at all. I just want to play with you three guys. Which is what happened.

After the first game we had a drink and he bought a round of drinks and he had to go. We agreed we should have a rematch so a few weeks later Brocky rang Sir Donald and said, 'How about having lunch as well after this?' He said, 'Oh no, Jessie's been pretty crook and I'd better get home.' So Brocky, not to be outdone, then rang Lady Bradman and said, 'Look we'd love to have lunch with Sir Donald,' and she said, 'Michael, what a fantastic idea, I'm sick of him hanging around me, go for it, that would be great.'

So we finished the round of golf and we were playing Kooyonga, and we came into the dressing room and Sir Donald came in, he hadn't said anything at all, then as we were getting out of our golfing togs he said, 'Now Michael, I understand that Jessie's given me a leave-pass to have lunch, is that right?'

So we had this marvellous lunch. He paid for all the drinks, by the way. Stories of him being tight with money were never my experience. And we had a few wines too, I must say.

And we had him for about three and a half hours. At that stage I think because of Barry's presence he'd worked out we weren't going to betray him. We talked about things. He revealed a lot of his inner thoughts. Barry was then coaching South Australia and Sir Donald said, 'Look, every time I come to the ground these days, you've got the players running up and down Montifiore Hill getting fit. Do you reckon that's really necessary?' And Barry said,

'Oh well Sir Donald, my belief is that on the last day of a Shield match or a Test match you've got to be fit enough to make a hundred and bat for a few hours or bowl 20 overs on a hot day or whatever.'

I remember Sir Donald saying to him, 'Barry, look I'm sure you're right.' He said – and he used this word, because I'll never forget it – 'You know, I didn't realise I was a freak until after I retired. You know, I've never run around an oval in my life, but I never once got out batting because I was tired.' He said, 'I always assumed that other people were like that and perhaps I was a bit intolerant of that and it wasn't until after I retired that I realised that I was unique.' And he used the word 'freak'.

Then a few weeks later we had a third game of golf. We were one-all at that stage. I remember distinctly on the 4th at Kooyonga, I had a four-foot downhill putt and I'm an 18 handicapper, I'm no star with the golf club, and he said, 'Jack, we really need this one.' I pulled away and said, 'Listen, I find this game hard enough without you telling me.' (laughs) He turned away and laughed about that. That was the rapport we'd built by that stage. Just four guys playing golf. We won the third game so he and I did get up.

Sir Donald in his speech and mannerism was always very crisp and clean and he always wore a suit. But on the golf course, he didn't have a flash golf bag and he just had an old pair of shoes and an old pair of pants with a torn pocket from memory. And a shirt that was nothing sensational, he was no Beau Brummel. I think because that wasn't important. I think he had a view that what was important was important and what is not is not. He was a most practical man.

After the third game, Brocky had a lunch in his corporate box at the Adelaide Oval, and a few of the people who come to his business lunches, they left, but Sir Don stayed. He stayed for lunch for five or six hours. It was marvellous. I remember he put on a silly hat that someone had left there, and he was sitting back in his chair with his feet on the table late in the day telling stories. But it wasn't just him telling stories, he really wanted to hear what you were doing too, he really wanted to hear what was going on in the modern world.

Subsequently we had a dinner a bit after that. We had an 80th birthday party at the Adelaide Oval, not thinking that he would come. So that would be 1989. Anyway, he said, 'Yeah, I will, thank you.' So we just had the SACA committee and their wives and a few of the key people including Barry, and Les Burdett, the curator. Again he said, 'Look, no speeches, no press,' and that sort of thing.

We came along and I walked into the room and there was this lectern set up for a speech. There were only probably 35 people there, perhaps 40. I said to Barry Gibbs, then the SACA CEO, 'What's the story?' He said, 'Oh,' (he used to call him the Great Man) 'the Great Man rang me this morning and he said I've changed my mind.' Barry thought oh, the dinner's off. And he said, 'No, it's suddenly dawned on me that I'm 80, I may not be around much longer. I've never heard W. G. Grace's thoughts on cricket. I'd like to make a speech and I'd like you to tape it, if you wouldn't mind please.'

He spoke for I've no idea how long, and we were just so transfixed. He spoke about all range of things, about his knighthood, what that meant to him, or what that meant to cricket, more than him, and apologised to Barry Richards for calling off the South African tour in 1971–72 which he knew was going to end his career. He spoke of a lot of letters that had been written. It was the most entertaining speech, just fantastic. Subsequently I understand that at the opening of the Bowral Museum which was the last time he spoke in public, he used a lot of the stuff he'd prepared for that. But it was just incredible. You could have heard a pin drop.

I was sitting alongside Barry at the time and Barry was crying when he said 'I ended your career'. It was really heartfelt stuff.

He had his analytical approach to everything, you know. Where you hit the golf ball, which way you do. Not that he would try and coach you, but if he said, 'Why don't you try this,' his advice to you was always very simple and easy to follow. He didn't talk in riddles. He just talked. He was extraordinary. I've never met anyone in my life, in the law or whatever, who expressed himself so succinctly and with no wastage of words. He could do it. I think he just had a fantastic ability to analyse things and come to a conclusion which was invariably right – well, certainly too difficult to argue against without any apparent effort. That's his great genius to me.

What I also enjoyed about him, he wasn't immodest about his achievements but he wasn't bragging either. He was just a very factual person, he spoke about it as it was. He just didn't mince words. And he was never locked in a time warp. A lot of the old cricketers, they are getting on in years and they want to talk about the good old days when they were playing cricket and they were fit young men. He only did that when you urged him to or perhaps to amplify what he was saying. His comment about being a freak, for instance, was really more aligned to how you train modern players, it wasn't him just talking about himself. That was the analogy. That's why I found him fascinating. Just great company.

Betty Joseph became Sir Donald's housekeeper in 1987. We spoke at her home in Adelaide.

I'D BEEN THERE A good few weeks and I hadn't seen Sir Donald. I'd more or less made up my mind, the poor old thing, he's probably too old to get down the stairs. How wrong I was. My first sight of him, he was in his white painting overalls with a bucket of green paint in one hand and a ladder in the other. A painter came and painted the whole house but Sir Donald still painted the verandah posts out the back. He would have been 78 – older than I am now and I can get up on my kitchen ladder, but that's all. (laughs)

Even then, they could get up and down those stairs better than me, you know. He was a very fit and active man. Right up until about 85, he still did all his own gardening. Lady Bradman used to threaten him. (laughs) She'd say, 'If he doesn't do something in that garden soon, I'll get a gardener,' and he'd get out there.

She was very nice to work for, Lady Bradman. She didn't believe in you working hard. I think I did two days a week at first. I was 63 or 64 when this happened. It gradually got more and more and I just stayed there and enjoyed it and it got to the stage where actually they wanted me to go and live in with them, but I thought no, that's not going to work. So I ended up staying five nights a week.

Lady Bradman had her hip done and it took her a good while to get over that and I think they made her wait 12 or 18 months then she had the other one done. It was about two years after the hip operation that she went to the doctor, and when she came home she said to me, 'Well, do you know what it is?' I said, 'No, what did he tell you?' She said, 'It's cancer.' Just like that. Of course, she just was never well after that. It was an awful time, as you can imagine. She's been gone four years last month.

Then Sir D asked me if I'd stay and look after him. He was a dear man, really. It was the night of Lady Bradman's funeral. We sat in the kitchen and I can see him now. He was sitting on the chair at the end of the kitchen table and I was sitting in the next chair. 'Mrs J,' he said, 'I wonder if you'd stay on and take care of me like you have.' I said yes I would. And he said, 'You won't have to do anything, you won't have to work.' He said, 'All I want you to do is get my meals.'

We respected one another, we got on well. He was a very difficult man to get to know, Sir Donald. I was there for 14 years and I wouldn't say that I was close to him. It was as much my fault as his. I always had in the back of my mind, I'm only a worker here and it might have put a gap. I always felt that Sir Donald was an insecure man, because he wasn't a man to make small talk, and therefore you couldn't get close to him.

Lady Bradman, five minutes and you were close to her. She'd have me rolling . . . in fact Sir Donald came down one day and told us not to make so much noise. We were laughing! I don't know what about now. We had the painter there. He was an Irishman, and she'd invite him in to have a cup of morning tea with us, because he used to tell us jokes. At the time I thought they were marvellous and laughed my head off but it would go in here with me and out there. But she could repeat them (laughs) and the greengrocer would come or the cleaning lady would be there with us for a cup of tea another day, and she'd be telling these jokes. (laughs) We had some lovely times. This time, I think Sir Donald was recording. His den, where he did all his writing and everything, was almost directly above the kitchen and (laughs) we were rolling around the floor just about, you know. Some of these tales Terry used to tell us were a little bit – you know, almost blue, but she would remember them.

And she would also entertain me by telling me about her school days. They lived on a farm just out of Bowral. She was really a lovely person, Lady Bradman.

And Sir Donald had a wonderful sense of humour. He could be very good company at dinner. He used to tell little incidents that happened when he played cricket or golf or whatever.

I didn't do a lot of cooking for others. They did entertain quite a bit in their earlier days. The only thing I remember them doing really was having people in for bridge of a night and they'd have coffee, and I think they'd have sweets or something. And there were a couple of dinner parties. I remember more lunches. You've heard of men that can't boil a kettle? Well, he was one of them. Before Lady Bradman ever got sick, she used to say to me, 'I don't know what's going to happen to him if I go first.' If we went out to lunch or shopping or anything, she'd always leave everything just so. She'd leave him crumpets to cook. He never ate much, he was a very small eater.

Once Lady Bradman died, I only ever remember Alan Jones and Richard Mulvaney coming to lunch and Sir Donald would always tell me to give them a toasted cheese sandwich. I'm sure they thought that was all I could make.

Richard Mulvaney had not much more than a passing interest in cricket when he was appointed curator to the proposed Bradman Museum in 1988. We spoke when he was in Melbourne to address the Melbourne Cricket Club luncheon in celebration of Sir Donald Bradman's birthday.

I WOULD HAVE MET Sir Donald within two weeks of taking on the position in Bowral and it was an unnerving experience. I had just been appointed as the first employee of this organisation, the Bradman Museum Trust, who had a dream to build the museum. I knew Sir Donald had really come on board very reluctantly and even at the time when I saw him, he was very uncertain about the whole thing. My visit was merely a courtesy call on my part. Don really was taking very much a backseat role. He didn't think there was much that he would do or could do for the project.

So I arrived, and I was shaking like a leaf and he answered the door and I said, 'Good morning, Sir Donald,' and so on. He said, 'Look please, don't call me Sir. I'm Don and I'd like to introduce you to Jessie, my wife.' From that moment on I called them Don and Jessie and that's how they liked it.

We sat down and I thought he'd grill me with every cricket question known to man and certainly grill me about his life and he didn't ask a single question, almost to my disappointment because I'd avidly read everything I could and was so armed to answer anything about him. But I spent all day there and unexpectedly, it was an extremely pleasant experience. A far cry from what I expected. He was very affable and sociable as was Jessie and we just seemed to hit off a rapport from that moment on.

How did Sir Donald respond to the early local hostility to the museum in Bowral?

A number of local residents took the committee and the council to the Land and Environment Court, so we had quite a mighty legal battle very early on in the piece. While I wasn't strictly employed then (I couldn't take the position on until March 1989), I was still constantly having meetings and discussions with the committee. At that stage, if they had lost the case, it looked like the museum may be built at the Sydney Cricket Ground or North Sydney Oval or something like that. And had that occurred I think the museum would not have been the success it's become. Bowral and the association with Sir Donald was vital to the whole thing.

I think he was quite hurt by it because there were a number of misinformation stories about it. The idea of having the museum at the oval was because it was the ground that young Donald played all his cricket on as a boy. But some of the residents had powerful connections with the *Sydney Morning Herald* and they ran some pretty persuasive stories, with the assistance of Bill O'Reilly who I think was used.

They tried to run this story that basically it was not the ground that Don had played on so it was silly to build the museum here. I think Don was quite annoyed by all that. Certainly when he opened the pavilion in October of 1989 he went to considerable lengths to describe where he played at all times. When he was a young kid they weren't even allowed on the oval itself, they had to play on a dirt patch where the actual buildings are now sited and it wasn't until later with the men's team that he played on the oval itself.

At the time there was considerable division in Bowral. You have to understand Bowral to appreciate it. Many people feel it's a vital and integral town in Australia and almost the centre of the universe. It's a town people go to, it's not a town people leave and I think there was still an element of people in the town who felt that Don had in some way slighted the community by leaving Bowral. Which is an absurd notion. At that stage he was playing cricket for St George and New South Wales and he was being touted as a potential Australian player. He made the decision very reluctantly to go Sydney in 1928 but I don't think Bowral ever forgave him for that.

And he was always very private. He would come back to Bowral, or Mittagong in particular because Jessie's family had the farm there, and on two occasions after 1934 and in 1941 he spent some months in the district. But he was there to recover, he wasn't there to wave a flag. So I think there was an element in Bowral that felt that Don Bradman had done nothing for the town, so why should we do something for him?

By the time I came on board there was a new chairman, Bruce Collins, and it was Bruce who had the vision to take the project beyond a simple museum and to turn it as much as possible into a complete cricket centre. That was the other thing that interested Don. Don had literally given to cricket all his life, very much in a hands-on way in attending clinics and so on with young kids, even later in life in Adelaide. And I think he really liked the idea of coaching clinics and bursaries and scholarships and kids on Bradman Oval, because he saw that was the future of the game and he liked his name being used to facilitate this whole process.

Was there a time when you noticed he had decided to get behind the museum?

Yeah, there certainly was, within six months of me first meeting him. I would travel to Adelaide very regularly and we started to correspond. I wasn't trying to fill him in too much because I thought that he didn't really want to know. But after each letter I wrote he would write back inquiring about more of this and more of that. And all of a sudden it was becoming clear that he was becoming quite interested in the project – to my astonishment and possibly his own.

I think he was genuinely very buoyed by it. He'd stepped down from cricket, he'd stepped down from the Australian Cricket Board, and I think while he enjoyed the 1980s in relative reclusion, he found he had perhaps dropped out all together. And all of a sudden the museum provided him with a new outlet, a new project. I think he just really started to get involved in it. And as is Sir Donald's character – I don't think he'd ever done anything half-hearted – once he got more involved he did start to give his full support.

Toward the mid-90s, I was getting four or five letters a week from him. In the earlier days, he was writing not so much, but pretty regularly. Sir Donald was a letter writer. It was his principal means of communication. He never seemed to like the phone that much and would use it sparingly. I think he liked to be considered in his thoughts and by the time he would put pen to paper he really had thought through what he was saying.

Was there a point of commitment?

The thing about the Bradman Museum that I find interesting was that they had this idea first to build a museum, but they had nothing to put in it, whereas most museums start because they've built up a collection of something. So when I came to the Bradman Museum, there really wasn't a collection.

We had organised for Sir Donald to come over for our first dinner at the Regent Hotel, which was a magnificent gala night and I think the last time that Sir Donald spoke publicly. There were about 800 guests. The following day we had the opening of the pavilion in the museum.

He came up to Bowral four or five days earlier. They just quietly drove their own car up and did their own thing and stayed with family. We wanted to fly or chauffeur them up and put them up in places, but they really wanted to just mooch about. He said he had a few things to give to the museum. I was, 'Great, fantastic', but I didn't think there'd be anything because he had given most of his possessions to the State Library of South Australia some years earlier.

To my amazement, he just lobbed in with his Australian 1946–47 blazer, a special presentation inkwell trophy that had been given by the Australian players after he first captained the series in 1936–37 and a whole lot of other things that I just did not know he had. And I don't think the State Library knew he had either, he just hadn't given them everything. It was a real seal of approval. I remember being absolutely bowled over. He just quietly decided he wanted to do this. And I know by that stage he was getting firmly committed to the whole idea of the museum and right on board with it. This was October of 1989. Pretty early on in the scheme of things.

And he was a boots and all man, he didn't do things by halves. By that stage he was very much committed to it. And so was Jessie. She had very strong memories of growing up in Bowral and they both enjoyed coming back.

Did you find him a conservative man?
I think he's been labelled as a conservative incorrectly because I never found him so. For a man who did not seem to really receive a high education, he seemed to know and be aware of a lot of things.

He seemed to be very much in tune with current thoughts. There was 50 years age difference between us and I felt there was only five. I didn't feel ever that I was having a conversation with an old man.

He didn't really have many social graces because he was a shy retiring humble sort of person. I have never met a person so unaffected by his place in history. That gap in terms of his social behaviour was really picked up by Jessie. She loved a crowd, she loved people, she loved talking about anything and everything, I think sometimes to Don's annoyance. She would take the conversation to all sorts of places where he didn't really want to go. Things like perhaps what my children were doing and how were they going at school. Probably things that a woman is more interested in than a man, without sounding too funny about it. And I think Don would want to steer it back to more matters of importance. But Jessie was fun and I think she made up for any lacking in the social graces that Don had by just being a wonderful diplomat, almost. She really was a lovely lady.

Perhaps his only conservatism would be in the financial aspect. He was always a man that was very interested in figures. If he'd come back in life, I think he'd want to be a mathematician or something like that. He had a very sound financial mind. In the 1980s there were a lot of gamblers about in big business, Skase and Bond and all those people, and that was never the way Don operated a business or regarded finances. I think he felt in our earlier days that some of our ideas were a bit far-flung and far-fetched.

Was there a point when you became friends?
Yes there was. Certainly in that first year or so, I tried to keep a bit more distance, but gradually I found that we just seemed to be talking more about things and I realised that I was in a very special circumstance that I hadn't expected or chased. Because I think for many people, Don would distance himself. He had a very small

select band of friends that he trusted. But if you violated that trust I think you were 'in trouble'.

And probably because of complete ignorance, I found myself enjoying a friendship with Don because it just evolved. And I treated him like he was just Don, I didn't overtly revere him or tug my forelock or anything, he was just a bloke, and as we became closer I found that he was a man who thought a lot more in life about other things and he enjoyed having the conversations.

He was very careful not to let too many people in but we had a level of trust. And if you had that level of trust with Sir Donald he was a very open and friendly person. We enjoyed a close and personal friendship but also we had a very good working understanding. He seemed certainly to be quite happy with the way the museum was run and how we performed and what we did and I'm glad all that worked out. We differed a lot in many aspects. I was never a Don Bradman.

As his involvement with the museum grew, what was his input?
After a while it became vital. I suppose one of the real turning points was maybe even as early as 1990. Don was always concerned about the financial viability of the museum and I would be constantly grilled on it. Where was the money coming from? I can laugh about it now but it wasn't so easy at the time. On many occasions I found his inquisitiveness into our business hard to handle. Here's this revered world figure and I was happy to provide him with whatever information he wanted but as time got on, it was becoming quite clear that he wanted to know everything.

From the word go I was very conscious of the huge responsibility we had in adopting the name Bradman. He didn't allow that name to be given lightly. It's a very special name and he'd upheld it to such a high level for 80 years and all of a sudden we'd come along. So we always had to be very careful. That was a big burden.

But I found it slightly amusing. (laughs) We'd write regularly and in correspondence it was probably easier to evade things, although Don would certainly ask forthright questions. But I found on my regular visits to Adelaide, I would have to be well versed with everything. In the earlier visits Don would always have a written list of questions to ask. I felt he was going to stick a light in my face, he'd just interrogate me. And I would try and do a Humphrey Appleby on him and evade his questioning, not because I didn't necessarily want to give him the answer, but purely since there were many things that we weren't really too sure about, there was a certain vagueness about the whole operation. And that's not how Don Bradman behaved, you know. Very forthright and knew exactly what was happening. So there was a lot of thinking on my feet, so to speak, but no matter how creative I became in the evasions, eventually he'd get his answer. I had to be careful I didn't play too silly about it, because he'd get a bit grumpy about me trying to evade too much. But there were occasions where I really did try to just not answer him but it just was impossible, he got it out of me.

We would go through his list and we wouldn't finish until he'd put a line through every question he had to ask and any other issues I'd had to present as well. At the end of all that, we were then free to range more widely. But he always in essence quietly in his very Bradman way set the agenda of the day. I have no doubt that that's how he was at committee meetings. He didn't want people wasting time and so if he could cut to the chase, he would.

But the financial thing always concerned him. There is absolutely no doubt that there is not a museum in the country that is a paying concern. You don't set up museums thinking you're going to make money, they are a cost, they are a service to the community. And Don was very aware of this. Here was a man who had never known failure and I do think he was really genuinely concerned that this museum that was setting up in his honour, that by this stage he'd given his boots and all support to, I think his worst nightmare was the fact the thing may just go under.

And Don was to some extent a worrier. He did worry about things, I always thought overly so, and I'd go and calm him down. Jessie was wonderful because he'd grill me and grill me and Jessie would come in and say, 'Don, Don, don't worry about all this. Richard knows what he's doing. Let him run the museum, not you. He's doing a fine job.' And I'd thank my stars that Jessie walked in at the moment and calmed it all down.

And I must say that Don had been very vital in the late-80s and early-90s, particularly in terms of galvanising corporate support. People like Sir Ron Brierley and Basil Sellers (who's an old family friend) and others came on board and were generous with donations because of their awe and respect for Sir Donald Bradman. Many of these people had always wanted to do something for The Don and he always refused. But then all of a sudden he's turned around and said, 'Well, if you want to do something, I'd like you to help my museum.' And it was *my* museum, which was a really nice touch. We were glad he thought that. And so people started to do things, because Don asked them, not Richard Mulvaney or the chairman of the board. So all of a sudden I found Don is my great fundraiser behind the scenes, unasked.

But he always wanted to know about our financial figures. I'd have to go and talk him through and I must say in the early 90s, we were having some real concerns because a number of sponsors that had promised generously had not come through and it was a time of economic recession and not a lot was happening. We'd opened the pavilion with much fanfare in 1989 but found we didn't have anywhere near the monies for the main museum building. We didn't actually open that until 1996, so there was a bit of time between the two.

But the turning point, and I only discovered this recently when I saw the letter, was that he wrote to Ron Brierley who was an old friend and on our board at the time and said, 'I'm thinking of allowing the museum to use my name for commercial purposes so that they can raise moneys to help build the museum. What do you think of the idea?' I didn't ever see Brierley's response. But we had certainly not asked Sir Donald or approached him. Don came forward with the idea of using his name in a commercial sense, which was unheard of. That was in late 1990.

We thought it was a good idea and with pro bono legal support we started to register 'Don Bradman' as a trademark. It was registered in this country and every cricketing country in the world, in a whole range of classes that we thought were probably likely. And the response in some of these countries was amazing. We obviously had to pay various registration fees but in countries like India and Pakistan, they were just in awe to be acting for Sir Donald Bradman and they did donate their legal services to the registrations and so on.

And that had to happen with the full support of Sir Donald.

What was Sir Donald's response to seeing his name used like that?
Don took great pleasure out of all our licensed programs and endorsements and signings. I remember when he was on the Weetbix packets, he thought the whole thing was fun and loved it and Sanitarium sent them whole lots of free samples of their product and he was really grateful for that. A simple gesture, but he was really grateful. I remember when the Australian Mint had the idea for him to be on a coin and he was really chuffed by that. And then later when Australia Post in 1997 wanted him on the stamp, that he was the first living Australian to ever feature on an Australian postage stamp was a huge honour in his eyes. As our licences kicked in and he saw the money that we were making for the project, he'd have this lovely smile on his face, a real sense of contentment.

Do you think Don's success was due to more than his sporting ability?

Don always had a very strong work ethic. He always took whatever task he had in hand very seriously. He didn't ever do anything by half measure, so whatever he did, he thoroughly prepared for it. That was the reason for his success. I don't think to be very honest his time on the field had anything to do with it. I think there was a lot he gained and learnt but he was a man very prepared to take on anything. There's absolutely no doubt that Don would have been a success in anything that he decided to do. He dabbled in all sorts of sports and other pastimes and was very talented.

He seemed to find that he had a particular liking for serving on cricket boards and this sort of thing, which is not everyone's bailiwick. But if you look through the records of the Bowral Cricket Club, he's the team scorer from about eight onwards. When he started to become more involved with the club he became its social secretary at 16, and its treasurer, and said he enjoyed those times, sitting at meetings with the men and going through matters of state.

Was he interested in the minutiae of the museum?

Oh look, (laughs) he would constantly grill me about all aspects of the whole concept. I just couldn't believe he was interested, it was just incredible. I remember vividly having long-ranging discussions about aspects of the building. For example, air-conditioning seemed to worry him considerably. How was the museum going to be heated and cooled, and how were we going to pay for it? He saw this as an extortionate expense and I would have to tell him, 'Look there are two things that we must have in here. One is you must make sure that your patrons are comfortable in your museum and secondly I must insist that the very important and valuable items are adequately cared for, including the optimum environmental conditions for them.' So we'd eventually agree on it.

I enjoyed being involved with the architects from a very early stage in designing the building. And as the building evolved in the planning stages, Don would look at this and look at that and I'd tell him, well, we're not going to have windows here and there because we don't want external light coming in and fading objects, and he got really very interested in these sorts of things. I don't think he'd really had any understanding of what a museum was, which is not necessarily surprising, but he found a lot of it was really to his liking. He enjoyed the challenge of the building and how it was going to work and what was going to be in there. And then when I was able to say things like all this will keep the heating cost down – when he found that we were looking at ways to make the building more affordable in its operation he was absolutely content. And possibly because of his rigorous interest, I found that we ended up with a design of a building which was certainly much more cost effective than it could have been. So yes, he wanted to know where things were and what we were doing. He was extremely interested in the whole thing.

Did aspects of the process make life difficult for him?
There was absolutely no doubt that the whole museum project put Don back into the public gaze. He had been a relative recluse and people were leaving him alone. All of a sudden he came on board with the project and made himself available. To this day I do have a funny feeling about the impact the museum had on Don's final 10 or so years of his life. It was quite considerable.

The mail increased as the museum advanced. As we started to make more noises and people knew more of us, all of a sudden people realised that Don was almost back in circulation and they would write. And because he involved himself so much, there were lots of decisions that had to be made. It got well beyond a mere courtesy. Particularly the use of his name. And any licensed product or any planned promotional thing I would discuss it with him because I didn't want him at any time feeling that the museum had let him down or done the wrong thing by him. I also knew that he was genuinely interested in the whole thing.

The museum was a big burden to him but by the same token I think he was quietly pleased by it all. I could be wrong in that analysis but I think he enjoyed still seeming to matter. Here he is in his 80s and he's still an important person in the community. It wasn't that he felt important but that he was doing something. And while he enjoyed his golf and other leisure pursuits, he was a man that had an incredible work ethic. He was nine to five, right almost up until his death. And the museum provided him with considerable opportunities (laughs) to stay at work.

In some ways we created a harder life for him, but by the same token, he wanted it. He enjoyed that and I think perhaps he had a longer life because of it. He had a reason to get up every day and get on with things and he was really on the ball with most things. I did not really see him much diminished in his ability until close to a year before his death.

He was rocked by the long drawn out final death of Jessie. That obviously affected him. And the sparkle certainly seemed to go out of him once Jessie had died. People were saying he'd die within a few months of Jessie, but he didn't give up. He was never a man to give up. You had to get him out. And that's how he viewed life. Possibly the museum became even more important once Jessie died. I found myself spending much more time with him in that later three years of his life. I think there were others who would do the same, without Jessie there, who would fill a gap.

It was in those years that Don had time to reflect on his early life. We would talk a lot about Bowral and his family life. We hoped to return 20 Glebe Street back to what it was in the 1920s and I would literally ask Don what he remembered. Which was absurd really because here he is, late-80s, early-90s, and I'm asking him to remember a house that he hadn't lived in for 75 years and only lived in relatively briefly.

And could he remember things? He was able to tell me where the piano was, in which room, on which wall. He was able to recount his father getting a bottle of wine, and his father was not a wine drinker. He used to go down to the pub and have a beer with some of his workmates and come back but they didn't drink alcohol at home and that bottle of wine sat on a certain cupboard in a certain room the entire time Don can remember. He just seemed to have incredible recall about his family and the house and I think perhaps it's something a lot of people do at that age. He had a lot of affection for his time in Bowral as a young kid.

And I think that had something to do with the fact that it was of course in Bowral at that time that he was able to live a natural life. He was never able to after leaving Bowral so Bowral was a sort of a sanctuary to him to some extent. And there were just many fond memories he had of mucking about as a young kid.

In January 1995, the British biographer **Charles Williams** *interviewed Sir Donald for his book* Bradman, *which was published the following year. Charles Williams is Lord Williams of Elvel and we spoke at the House of Lords over a cup of coffee.*

THE PREMISE BEHIND the book is that Bradman was not just a great cricketer; that in the 1930s he was a symbol that Australians could turn to as being in some sense the pride of the country at a time when the country was flat on its back. And the fact that he was knocking spots off the Poms in successive Test matches in the 1930s gave Australians encouragement in what was a very, very difficult period.

At what stage in your research did you meet Sir Donald?
Quite early on. I hadn't started drafting. I'd done quite a lot of
work on the background, on sources, and briefed myself in order
to have a starter with Don.

Had you formed an impression at that stage?
No, not really. I always start off books with a clean sheet of paper
in so far as I can. I mean, obviously you come with baggage and by
the time I got to see Don I knew about the controversies and about
some aspects of his personality. But I wouldn't say I had a very
clear impression of him, about what he was like, how he developed, what his childhood was like, what Australia was like in the
1930s. All that came out as I went through.

Did the meeting hold any surprises for you?
I suppose the only surprise was the reverence with which he was
treated by the South Australian Cricket Association. It was as
though I was meeting royalty. I was required to sit down in a certain place at 12 noon and not move until Sir Donald appeared
and then he would do this, I would do that and we'd all do this,
that and the other. And that was the way it happened. I was ushered into a seat and this little man came up, he was bang on time.
But once we got down to business it was all quite different. It
wasn't 'Sir Donald' and all that. He opened up and we got on
famously.

It was quite a long conversation. We had lunch pretty well at
one sharp with members of the committee and then continued the
conversation and at about half past three, he said he ought to be
going off back to Jessie and wandered off.

I think he was vetting me for the first quarter of an hour but
once he realised that (a) I was reasonably intelligent and (b) I knew
something about cricket and (c) that I was actually quite interested

in Australia and what he thought about Australia, rather than just trying to score points or digging out things, I really got down to a serious conversation, not just about cricket but about all sorts of things. And he was prepared to talk about it.

Did your own cricketing background with Oxford University and Essex help?
Oh yes. He had been alerted by SACA that I had actually played some cricket – not to anything like international standard, but I did know something about the game.

And what about the fact that you are a Lord. Was that an influence, do you think?
Yes. You've got to say that Don was a tremendous snob and I think the fact I was a Lord was very important. Lords could get in to see Sir Donald Bradman whereas if I'd been Mr C. C. P. Williams, just a former Essex cricketer, I might have had a problem.

Was Sir Donald forthcoming on every subject?
To be perfectly honest, he didn't much want to talk about his early days in Sydney. I mentioned the Illawarra Regiment, the almost fascistic group in which he enrolled in Sydney in the 1920s, and he brushed that aside. I mentioned Freemasonry and he said, 'Oh well, I only joined that because the captain of St George said you should become a Freemason.' And he gave up 'the craft', as he said, when he went to Adelaide. To use the expression 'the craft' shows that you're a bit more into Freemasonry than having joined it just for the fun of things, so I suspect he was probably a bit more involved.

He didn't want to talk about it at all. Understandably, why should he? He didn't want to talk about Hodgetts [the stockbroker jailed for fraud in 1945 for whom Sir Donald had worked, and whose business he took over] either. You can tell if you're reasonably skilled at this business of writing biographies if your subject is trying to avoid an event. He or she talks glibly about something and you can see in the body language that they'd rather get off the subject.

I faintly suspect, as with Hodgetts, there were things he had buried. I think if you are as single-minded as he was when he was playing cricket, you can bury things. You can simply say, 'That did not happen. Because if it did, that affects what I'm trying to do at the moment, which is hit you through the covers for four'. I suspect he was the sort of person who could be in denial. He was almost like that when we talked about John and his name change. It almost never happened.

Was he pedantic?
No. He was crisp on occasions. The old Bradman came out occasionally, particularly when I mentioned the Ikin incident, for instance. Of course Jack Ikin went to his grave saying he caught the fair catch off Bradman and that he was out. But he was pretty sharp about that. 'If I'd have thought I was out, I'd have walked.' 'Well all right Don. We'll just pass on to other things. No point in pursuing that.'

How would you describe his sense of humour?
It's a waspish, sarcastic put-down type of humour. In most male sporting teams, as a part of the normal masculine bonding, teammates josh each other. 'Ah now, I know you went out with the boys last night and had 10 pints and we saw you come in at 2 o'clock in the morning.' That sort of thing. Don was not like that. He would say, 'I know you went out last night and had three pints. Do you deny it?' (laughs) While he thought it was a joke, the other guy probably didn't. And very quick sarcasm.

You mention in your book that you had your agreements and disagreements and you agreed to disagree.

After the interview we had long correspondence and every point I wanted to check I would write to him and he would write back. We were corresponding the whole time, right up to the final typescript.

And yes, there were certain points. We didn't disagree about the sectarian thing because I'd verified that from other sources, but we somewhat disagreed that Bradman was totally innocent in getting up their nostrils, to put it politely. I kept on saying, 'Well, you did rather provoke them, Don, didn't you?' and he said, 'No I didn't'.

We had a serious dispute, which related to the family. I said I'll tone it down but I'm not going to excise it altogether. And on John changing his name as well. The true story is that they were all sitting around the swimming pool and John came in and announced that he was changing his name. Don told me that verbatim but he didn't want that to be put in such a brutal way because the family were all very shocked. So there were bits and pieces like that.

And there were bits and pieces about his captaincy and what I would call in retrospect the slight brutality of his captaincy. A very hard-balled, tough way of playing cricket which has come down to the present Australian team. (On the other hand, we talked about sledging. He didn't like that and of course the Australian team of today are the greatest sledgers of all time.)

But it is very hard-ball and some of the English gentlemen were repelled. And that's why he . . . I won't say respected Jardine, but he knew what Jardine was about. He understood that absolutely single-minded, 'We're going to bash the bastard and that's what we're here for'. So when I talked about Jardine to him he had that slight Bradman smile on his face, a slightly crooked smile. He'd say, 'It was a difficult period. He's a Scotsman and we sat next to each other 20 years later and didn't talk,' but I could see that he actually quite admired Jardine in that absolute single-mindedness.

He continued to argue in later interviews against the suggestion that he'd been called a coward around the time of the Bodyline series.

That was the whole basis of Bodyline, that they thought he was yellow. That last day of the last Test at the Oval in 1930 when Archie Jackson and Bradman were in and Larwood peppered them around the ribs on a rather wet wicket and Jardine, looking at footage of that, then saying: 'I've got it. He's yellow.' It was absolutely central to the whole thing. And then the Australians thought he was yellow because he developed this technique of stepping outside his leg stump and carving Larwood off outside leg and some of his strokes looked absolutely crazy. And the English thought: 'What's this chap playing at?' But still he averaged over 50 in the series, you see, (laughs) so it was very effective. But they all thought that he just couldn't take Larwood.

I address this slightly obliquely in my book. I think he was scared. Who wouldn't be? I stood facing Peter Loader on a hard Oval wicket, coming in number three for Essex. A hard new ball, no helmet, just a cap on and this chap was bowling bouncers at me at 85 mph and I was scared stupid. If you're not scared there's something wrong with you. (laughs)

You also bring out in your book that he quite probably had at least one mental breakdown during his playing career.

I reckoned that was part of this denial process. You know, the question of being frightened, 'I wasn't frightened, of course I wasn't frightened – I was scared stupid – I wasn't frightened'. And then the fact England got after him and the Australians got after him and Woodfull got after him and wanted to drop him from the team. Yes. A very highly strung gentleman. Very highly strung indeed, but that's what made him a great man.

Did you send Sir Donald the manuscript before the book was published?

I had a big argument with my publisher about whether I should send Don the typescript and the publisher said, 'No, no, no. You can't possibly.' And I said, 'No, really, I've got a relationship with Don. We've exchanged correspondence, he's been very good. He's answered meticulously all my questions. I think I have to do it.' So I did send Don the final typed draft.

I got 15 typed pages in response, almost all of it copy editing. He said (I am quoting from page 10 of his typescript), 'On page 153, you have used the expression "to be sure" three times on this page and I find that inconsistent with your normally good writing style.' (laughs) So most of it was like that. 'There's a comma missing on line 10, page 35.' And he'd gone through it meticulously. There were one or two things he objected to in substance, but on those things we exchanged letters and there's nothing in that final version that offended him. But I told enough of what I wanted to tell without compromising my own honesty.

And did he give an opinion of the book?

It's on the back of the book. He wrote to me and said, 'It would be stupid to say I enjoyed or agreed with every word, every sentence, and every nuance, but I honestly believe it's a splendid production.' And he did let everybody know that he thought it was by far the best book that had been written about him. But also I think what he liked about it was it did actually do what it set out to do, which was to place him, not just as a cricketer but as a great Australian figure on a par with the Flying Pieman and Ned Kelly, to mention just two. The subtitle *An Australian Hero* was meant to portray the whole essence of the book.

*Radio announcer, former Wallabies coach and political adviser **Alan Jones** was befriended by Sir Donald when he spoke at a function at his request more than 20 years ago.*

I spoke at a function in Adelaide, and he was just overwhelming in his endorsement of what I said and his gratitude for what I said and his thanks and he wrote and thanked me and we'd been corresponding ever since. It was when I was working for the prime minister [Malcolm Fraser]. We had met at a function in Adelaide with the prime minister.

After that we regularly had lunch together. That was our occasion. We used to say 'once a month' but it wasn't really once a month, because we missed Christmas and so on. It would be about eight times a year. We had this little arrangement whereby I'd fly down after I came off the air, so we only had about three hours or more and then I'd fly back and that was it. But he knew I'd come and he was very grateful.

John would come with us in the latter years, but earlier on it was just him and me and we'd go to the Kooyonga Golf Club, we wouldn't worry Jessie. I'd meet him at home. Or sometimes we would meet at the golf club and then go home and have a cup of tea with Jessie and we'd just talk. We always had vegetable soup, whiting fillets, apple pie and ice cream, and he ordered a bottle of white wine. And it was the same meal, all the time.

Indeed, one day a very funny thing happened. We always seemed to have the same waiter so of course when he saw us coming, he knew what the order was. We'd arrived at the club and he's come up and he's said, rather sheepishly: 'Oh Sir Donald, I'm sorry but there are no whiting fillets.' This was before we'd ordered because everyone knew, it was routine, we had whiting fillets. And of course normal people would say, 'Oh well, we'll have such-and-such', but not Don. He said, 'Well, where are the whiting fillets?' And he said, oh, they had made a mistake with the order and something else had come . . . 'But the whiting fillets are on their way.' Which is always a fatal thing to say. So, lo and behold, to the great chagrin of this poor chap, Sir Donald said, 'Well then, we'll wait.' So (this is a true story) we sat there! I saw it come 2 o'clock and we still hadn't had an order, and I think these wretched things arrived about ten past two. So we had a very late lunch and we had the same thing: we had vegetable soup, whiting fillets and apple pie. (laughs) I don't know where the whiting fillets had come from. I think we had time to go out and catch them.

He regarded it as a compliment that I'd fly over just for lunch and we'd sometimes have afternoon tea and then latterly, we wouldn't go to the club, we'd have just sandwiches at home, very simple.

Did you consider Sir Donald a friend?
Well I'd like to think that we were friends. Yes, I'm sure we were. But in a sense, what is friendship? I don't know. I think friendship is where you cross certain barriers where the impersonal becomes the personal, so I would often ring and just say, 'I haven't got time to talk, I'm just ringing to see how you are,' and that would cheer him up a bit and he'd say, 'Oh I'm not feeling too well today,' and I'd say, 'Oh come on, come on, come on' because I used to joke with him and say, 'Now remember, Bradman was never dismissed in the 90s. So now you've got to 90 so you've got to get to a 100.' And he'd often say to me, 'Alan, you're too tough on me,' because I'd say, 'Come on.'

He loved Jessie and when Jessie was sick we'd walk to the gate and he'd say, 'Jessie's dying,' and I'd say, 'Well look I know, but I mean so are we. You know we're all dying. We've all got to be strong,' and he'd have a bit of a tear in his eye.

We shared those things and he wrote very personal letters and he was very supportive of me. If I had a bit of success he'd rubbish me, which is always the Australian way, isn't it? You know, 'I saw that you've done such-and-such' (I can't remember what it was) or – this is when I was coaching Australia – 'You might have won but I thought you played badly.' 'I beg your pardon?' He said, 'I thought you played badly.' I said, 'You don't think that at all. You're just saying that to stir me up.' And then he'd change the subject.

So I suppose in that sense, yeah, we were friends, and he in many ways treated me like a son. You know, he was interested in what I did. The interesting point was his overarching political interest, even though obviously he was not in any way either capable of influencing politics or desirous of influencing politics, but he wanted to know, you know. Who's going to win? What do you think of Fraser? What about Hawke? What about this Keating? He was always the local bloke. 'Howard? Howard's no good, how will he win?' And you'd have these very earthy discussions. And it was a very organised and deliberative mind. He was very deliberate about all this. He'd thought about it, you know. 'You can't win an election on the GST,' he said. I said, 'Well I'm not too sure about that.' 'No, you can't win.' We'd have these arguments about the GST.

We had this argument about W. G. Grace. He said W. G. Grace was the greatest cricketer who ever lived. He wrote this long letter about it, explaining to me why, because he'd carry on the discussion after you left. Write a letter. Finish you off over the mail. (laughs) Because he was a wonderful letter writer. I mean, I write hundreds of letters too but I don't write them. Don wrote them. And he would type them on the old rickety typewriter. So a fantastic correspondent.

He was always entertaining, but always challenging, that's the thing. He wasn't argumentative, he would challenge. 'Oh don't tell me you can't . . .' And then they'd be often completely clipped, where he would say, 'I don't think he can play.' 'What did you say?' 'I don't think . . .' That was it. That was the end of the discussion. 'I don't think he can play'. He said, 'You can't win an election on GST. Come on Alan. You can't.' Or then, if I defended, say, a John Howard or a Malcolm Fraser, next time they'd be 'my bloke'. And he'd have a go at you. 'Your bloke's not doing very well'. (laughs) I thought, he's not my bloke.

I've read where you've described him as a man whose accomplishments didn't stop at himself. What quality in him was it that made him reach beyond himself?
I think he shared himself far more than people ever imagined. You know, you can't comprehend what it means to some anonymous person on the other side of the world to have a letter to Sir Donald Bradman answered in his own handwriting. It's totally unnecessary. It's very, very demanding. Sending cricket bats to be signed. But he did this with the firm view that he was in a way obligated. This was his further contribution. And I just thought that was quite noble, because it would drive you nuts, and it was relentless. So in that sense he had this wonderful sense of sharing.

He had a wonderful devotion to Jessie, which was, I think he said, his greatest partnership. But it was active, it wasn't passive. It wasn't rhetoric, it was reality. And that was it, in everything that they did. He really grieved for her before she died, knowing she was going to die, and it was most damaging when she passed on. He had great difficulty accommodating that. So in that sense he gave.

But at times he was a bit of a sook. You know, he'd say, 'I'm not feeling well today' and you'd have to say, 'Oh come on, come on'. Or sometimes he'd drag his feet on the ground so, 'Pick your feet up'. We'd always have a bit of a laugh but he was very loyal to Shirley and to John. Loved the grandchildren. One day he said, 'Alan likes music. Greta will sing for you.' So it was in the dining room, and we were just having a sandwich. Greta loved her grandfather and she stood beside him and sang.

And let's face it, long before I knew him, he ran Australian cricket. He didn't have to be on the Cricket Board (or the Board of Control) and his advice to players was always gentle and constructive so that there was a life beyond Don Bradman.

Did you ever watch cricket with him?
I think we did go to the Adelaide Oval a couple of times. We'd sit and watch on the TV sometimes. Now that is another story, the television. Oh my God! I kept on saying to him to get a new TV. He had a television which was all snow. Couldn't see a thing, and he watched the cricket on TV and expected me to sit there and watch this. I said, 'I can't see a thing!' 'Oh yes,' he said, 'that's Kallicharran (or someone) batting.' Well I couldn't see them. It was one of the most appalling receptions. Tiny little thing. I used to say to him, 'Get Foxtel. Get the pay TV. Because you love your golf and you love your sport and you'll see it all.' But he never did. That was the manifestation of age. You know, you're happy with the circumstances that you enjoy and you don't want to confront something that's new.

It strikes me that for a man of his reputation he lived quite modestly.
Very modestly. Modest car. And never flashy clothes. Neat and plain and tidy and the house bore all the hallmarks of age in the sense that there were lovely old doilies and cushions and it was clear that it was Bradman's house. No ornamentation, no artifice. There was one portrait over the fireplace of him playing or walking out to bat but beyond that, not much.

He was extremely wary of the press. Was that wariness realistic?
Yes. Although he never put it in these terms, I think that he felt that the press had the capacity to invade his life and penetrate areas which he thought were off-limits, Shirley for example, and John and his relationship with John, I'm sure he probably did say they were off-limits. Then, you know, I think there were aspects of the family that he felt should stay as family. I remember once he was very disturbed. When Jessie was very sick at the end, and he was so brave in that he didn't say how sick, there were bouts of her illness which manifested themselves in incidents in the house. It was so very sad for him to see this lovely, lovely human being (she was beautiful, Jessie) whom he loved fading in front of him. He felt that certain sections of the media were hunting his grandchildren to find out, to trap them into getting a story. You know: 'Did your grandmother fall down the steps last night?' that sort of stuff. And it really bothered him and it built up the suspicions that he held.

Yet was that realistic, or was that paranoid?
Well, I suppose it was paranoid. We're all paranoid aren't we? There was a paranoia about it. But at the same time he felt I think a certain paternal responsibility to protect all these people under his wing and I think he often wondered whether they were going to be afforded that protection, and that did bother him. He often audibly worried what would happen to the family after he died. Will they scarify? Will they leave my family alone? Will they let them go on?

It must have been a dreadful burden.
Well, it was a burden. He shouldered it very well. I think for John's children, it's a burden because they've got the name and the outward manifestations of that – but yes.

Were there aspects of his personality that you think were the result of his fame?

Well, not to me. I mean, people said there was an aloofness about him and that that was a manifestation of fame. But it's very difficult when you are famous. If you say a lot to people they think 'Well, who does he think he is? I mean who the hell is interested in his views, for God sake? Why doesn't he shut up?' If he shuts up they say, 'Oh he's just too snobbish to talk to us and of course he's got tickets on himself.' And to straddle the halfway house in all of that is very difficult. And so I think that the sensitivity and almost isolation were manifestations of that. He knew that he would be hounded. Basically he was. I mean he was just mobbed. He was a hero. It was just extraordinary.

I think also that one aspect of 'fame' was his awareness, though he never said it in as many words, that if he said yes today then there would be a veritable tsunami of demands upon his time. So he denied himself things he would like to have done. I'm sure he would have liked to have been present at certain functions but that would have resulted in an inundation of invitations, demands, expectations, so there was almost a blanket thing in the end really.

I remember the 90th birthday party, they wanted to raise money and use his birthday as an occasion and they said that they wanted to have a guest speaker and so on. And he wrote this beautiful letter to say, 'I've told them that I won't have it unless the guest speaker is you. Please notify me if you concur with this.' This beautiful letter which I've framed. He said, 'Oh, they're all saying Sir Colin Cowdrey and the Duke of Edinburgh, but I've told them I only want Alan Jones.' And they yielded to that. So we had the big party. But he said, 'I won't be going, Alan.' And he didn't go. He'd have liked to, but it was invasive.

*Sir Donald maintained his distinctly Australian accent
throughout his career, didn't he?*

Oh yes. At a time when it was not in vogue, when Michael Charlton was reading the news and sounded like an Englishman. He was
proudly and fiercely Australian, and enjoyed Australian success.
I can remember Stephen Waugh played his first Test, against India
in 1985–86, in Melbourne, and he played another one in Sydney.
Anyway, in both of them he'd done poorly, if memory serves me
correctly. I knew Stephen, and I'd gone over for lunch in Adelaide.
Here was this man who was the powerbroker of Australian cricket.
But now he wasn't and when you're out you're out. The curtain
goes down and you get off the stage – and he did that. And he said
to me, which quite amazed me, 'What are they going to do about
Stephen Waugh?' 'I don't know.' He said, 'Do you think they'll
drop him?' And I said, 'Why are you so interested?' He said, 'Oh,
he's the best batsman in the country.' I said, 'What are you telling
me for? Why don't you tell him?' 'No, you tell him.' I said, 'No,
why don't *you* tell him and not me?' So I said, 'Can I use the
phone?' So I got on the phone and I rang Stephen Waugh up and I
said, 'I've got someone here who thinks you can bat.' Of course
Stephen was down, he was about to be dropped, I think. And on
got The Don. It was Don Bradman who told him what he thought.
He loved Stephen Waugh.

*How would you describe the influence Sir Donald has had on
your life?*

Well in a way, you don't know, do you? But it was profound in ways
that perhaps I haven't fully defined and thought of. Our discussion
of the value and meaning of sport and what it means, and of sporting history, was important. We talked a lot about where people
belong in the scheme of things, how you should conduct yourself.
I'd take young people there to see him, to meet him, and he was

very happy about that. And he would make observations which would be telling to them. Nothing to him but telling to them.

And I just felt that I had someone who was interested in me doing well and that was important because in the world in which we all live, normally they're interested in you failing. He was always excited to know that I'd done well or I'd spoken here or my team had won or something had happened or he saw me on television or whatever and he'd have a little critique of it all.

He gave time to interviews. I'm always fascinated to hear that people talk about the only interviews he did were television interviews, because he did an interview with me, at length, which I know the Melbourne *Age* subsequently lifted without any approval from him or from me, and we talked about all of these things, it was a lovely interview. And often he'd come on my program – when Alec Bedser was 80 he came on the program and they talked and then when Alec had another birthday. 'Oh no' he'd say. 'Oh come on,' I'd say. 'It will do you good. Just come on and I'll just talk to you, it won't be a difficulty.' So he'd come on and he'd really love it. He'd never shut up. He and Alec were very close friends. So he and Alec would talk on the program and he knew there was going to be no invasion of his life. So to ask what effect did he have, I think to know that there was someone of that remarkable capacity and who is an indelible part of history who had a little bit of time in his life for you was a bit of a buzz.

Did he keep everything under his control?
Was he a control freak? No, and that's what I liked about him. Often you'd go there and he'd just be in his slippers and dressing gown. It would be winter, he'd be comfortable. He felt comfortable with you, but he wouldn't let other people into the house. I remember a wonderful day, we walked outside and we were talking as I was about to leave. And we were just inside the lawn, where

the brush and the shrubbery was, and this person walked in right next to us. He and I were talking, and this person looked at me and he looked at him and he looked at me again and he said, almost with his head up under Sir Donald's nose, 'Aren't you Don Bradman?' and Don said, 'Yes, that's correct.' (He'd always say it very courteously, but as much as to say, 'Yes, but . . .') 'May I shake your hand?' this fellow said, and Don looked at him and he said, 'Excuse me sir, but this is private property, not the Town Hall.' (laughs) Which I thought was wonderful. I just burst out laughing. Wonderful line. Bloke didn't know what to do. I think he shook his hand though.

Well it's invasive, isn't it? He didn't want that. And I think all of us, the older we get the more we value our own space and he had a lot of telephone and written invasions of his space. But there were certain things he loved. He loved seeing John. Right at the end John would always come over, I don't know when it was, 9 o'clock, but he'd tell me, 'John was here and John was wonderful' and he'd have to tell me what John had done and where he was and how he was and you could see this wonderful pride. They were very simple things but that was what he wanted to do in the end. I mean, I would let him talk about what he wanted to talk about. Before we'd argue, but we didn't in the end, I'd just agree with him, because I could see that he was battling to survive on his own. Once Jessie went, he was ready to go.

Index

A

ABC (Australian Broadcasting
   Corporation) 26, 35, 348,
   349, 429–33
Ackerman, Hylton 346, 369, 389
Adelaide 133, 217, 283
Adelaide Oval 60, 76, 79, 152,
   155, 158, 159, 170, 178, 180,
   185, 234, 239, 244, 257, 268,
   270, 278, 280, 289, 290–2,
   332, 367, 370–1, 426, 436,
   437, 465
   Centenary of Test Cricket at
      the Adelaide Oval 1984
      370–1
Allen, G. O. (Gubby) 5, 6, 20,
   28–9, 33, 38–9, 43, 65, 89,
   102, 132, 148, 209, 220, 221,
   224, 226, 238, 249, 255, 259,
   303, 347, 364, 365, 398, 431
Altham, Harry 149
Anti-Apartheid Movement 337,
   340, *see also* cancellation of
   South African Test series

Argo Investments 196, 216,
   266, 267, 270, 304–5,
   391–7
Arthur Richardson Testimonial
   1949 (Bradman's last first-
   class game) 77–8, 99,
   183–4
Ashes series (1928–29) 115,
   147; (1930) 28, 96, 300,
   459; (1932–33) 262; (1934)
   97; (1936–37) 28, 445;
   (1938) 9,10, 110;
   (1946–47) 56, 61, 106, 445;
   (1948) 87, 96, 107–9, 119,
   120, 123, 140, 242;
   (1950–51) 143, 69, 205;
   (1953) 124, 139, 141, 143;
   (1956) 35, 144, 180;
   (1958–59) 188, 209, 254;
   (1962–63) 64, 249;
   (1970–71) 249, 335; (1972)
   345; (1974–75) 373; (1977)
   361–2; (1978–79) 222, 224,
   366; (1982–83) 230
Ashton, Hubert 220

Australian Cricket Board
(Australian Board of Control
for International Cricket)
16, 66, 77, 80, 85, 89, 101,
103, 113, 161, 164, 179, 182,
186, 203, 204, 207, 222, 223,
234, 237, 241, 245–6, 256,
266, 275–7, 279, 284, 286,
291, 313, 320, 324–5, 338–9,
341, 344, 347, 359–61, 363,
365, 367, 368, 369, 373–6,
387, 388, 419, 444, 465

B

Bacher, Dr Ali 386–7
Bannister, Alex 62, 139–52
Barnes, Alan 182, 331, 332–3
Barnes, Sid 87, 106, 108, 141,
151
Barnett, Ben 11–12, 184, 383
Barnsley, Garry 416–25
Beames, Percy 55–9
Beard, Dr Don 152–60, 177,
386
Bedi, Bishen 157, 344
Bedser, Sir Alec 59–71, 96,
140, 142–3, 151, 184, 232,
250, 260, 263, 469
Bedser, Eric 59–71, 250
Benaud, Richie 36, 85, 87, 145,

161–2, 167, 171, 188, 226,
247, 253, 254, 259, 260, 263,
380, 430
Bodyline series 1932 8, 28, 79,
118, 124, 140, 147–8, 155,
182, 208, 209, 221, 226–7,
397, 398, 459
Bowes, Bill 262
Bowley, Bruce 71–9
Bowral 23–5, 385, 440, 441,
442–3, 445
Bradman, Sir Donald
100th century (Australia v
India 1947) 84, 95, 389,
433
autographs 27, 68, 80–1,
111, 146, 268, 311–12,
317, 318–19, 331, 377,
411–13, 415–16, 417,
423–4, 464
as Board of Control
chairman 62, 113, 166,
171, 182, 207, 225, 320,
323, 325, 332–3, 335,
338, 360, 368, 426
Bowral childhood 24, 117,
327, 431, 451, 453–4
bridge 11, 22, 289, 311,
312, 326, 440
captaincy 14, 15, 55, 86–7,
110–11, 120, 155, 176,
458

correspondence 15, 30, 41,
    68, 86, 102, 103, 111,
    133, 146, 159, 164, 202,
    209–10, 224, 226, 229,
    231, 232, 249, 295, 331,
    337–41, 348, 364, 369,
    371, 378, 386, 396, 404,
    405, 422, 428, 444, 448,
    452, 460, 461, 463, 464
country background 59,
    115, 218
as cricket administrator 44,
    89, 113, 148–9, 166–7,
    174, 182, 237–8, 302–3,
    322, 353
directorships 78, 102, 131,
    152, 196, 215–17, 265,
    267, 272, 274, 282,
    304–6, 319, 393
Don Bradman & Co. 73,
    124–35
fame, effects of 12–13, 49,
    114, 141–2, 208, 216,
    219, 285–6, 293,
    312–13, 326, 347, 467,
    469–70
golf 19–20, 22, 36–7, 43–4,
    50, 89, 100–1, 102,
    120–1, 129, 132, 148,
    156, 157, 167–8, 174,
    201, 204, 206, 207, 211,
    241, 258, 289, 292,

294–300, 316, 317–18,
    319, 331, 390–1, 396,
    410, 414–15, 417, 426–7,
    433–6, 438, 440, 453
health 31–2, 73, 130–1,
    135, 242, 273, 282, 297,
    329, 331, 378, 406, 462,
    464
Holden Street, Adelaide 72,
    129, 134, 155, 159, 171,
    244, 249, 269, 270, 305,
    310, 382, 386, 397, 403,
    419, 430
Ikin incident (1946) 56,
    227, 457
interviews 122, 334–7, 343,
    397, 429–33, 469
and Jessie's illness and death
    135,146, 292, 331, 378,
    435, 439, 441, 453,
    462–3, 466, 470
and John Bradman's change
    of name 216, 315–16,
    346, 457, 458
and John Bradman's illness
    84, 131, 132, 160, 245,
    315, 345
journalism 58, 122, 139,
    142, 144–5, 146–7, 162,
    180, 207, 220
knighthood 21, 77, 162,
    233–4, 437

music 21, 35, 116, 121, 129,
150, 154, 156–7, 179,
189, 193, 244, 288, 315,
326, 396
philanthropy 152, 172, 190,
268, 423
relationship with press 40,
45, 73, 76–7, 121–2, 206,
336–7, 383, 399–400,
432, 466
as selector (national) 56–7,
65, 84, 87, 89–91, 100,
105, 106, 154, 161, 163,
165, 171, 186, 200, 225,
234, 302, 313, 325, 335,
345, 353, 368, 372, 429,
(state) 47, 234, 294
sense of humour 21, 36,
102, 150, 179, 195,
232–3, 235, 249, 261,
263, 274, 275, 289, 310,
411, 433, 440, 457
speeches 21, 32, 86, 111–12,
146, 263, 266, 273, 334,
346, 422–3, 437
wine 45, 103, 113, 157, 178,
197, 235, 273, 287, 313,
326, 331, 394, 403, 432
Bradman, Lady Jessie 17, 27, 33,
35–6, 37, 40, 41, 44, 45, 52,
59–60, 63, 66, 78, 79, 100,
114, 129, 130, 134–5, 143,

145, 146, 148, 150, 156, 167,
172, 177, 178, 179, 180, 189,
190, 191, 192–3, 204, 206,
209, 211, 244, 245, 250,
257–8, 268, 269, 271, 274,
278, 279, 282, 284, 285, 287,
290–4, 305, 308, 309–10, 311,
312–13, 314, 315–16, 317,
318–19, 327, 328, 329, 331,
335, 336, 341, 357–8, 378,
379, 380, 385, 386, 387–8,
397, 399, 400, 404, 417, 420,
421, 435, 439–41, 441–2, 443,
445, 446, 449, 453, 455, 461,
462–3, 464, 466, 470
Bradman, John 17, 29, 36, 37,
42, 60, 63, 72, 77, 83–4, 131,
132, 135, 143, 145, 160, 167,
172, 178, 189–90, 216, 245,
265, 267, 273, 315–16, 318,
328, 424, 457, 458, 461, 465,
466, 470
Bradman, Shirley 65, 131, 132,
145, 149, 150, 172, 268, 269,
270, 273, 315, 328, 388, 465,
466
Bradman Foundation 320, 321,
326, 327, 328, 330, 331, 334,
Bradman Museum 25, 35,
168–9, 175, 320, 328, 398,
405, 406, 416–21, 437,
441–54

Bradman Museum Trust 405,
406, 441

Bradman Oval 25, 443

Brideson, Colin 49–50

Brideson, Hedley 279–83, 306–7

Brierley, Sir Ron 418, 420, 425,
449, 450

Brock, Michael 433, 434–6

Brown, Barbara 3, 17, 21–3

Brown, W. A. (Bill) 3–23, 70,
102, 160

Bullock, Len 125, 126, 128,
131, 133, 264, 265, 267

Burgmann, Dr Meredith
337–41

Burke, Jim 254

Chappell, Ian 91, 356–7, 358,
359, 360, 373, 374, 380

Chappell, Martin 74, 356, 357,
358

Chipp, Don 259–63

Clarke, Jack 433–8

Cole, Brian 304–6

Collins, Bruce 418–19, 443

Compton, Denis 40, 68, 107–8,
109, 143, 151

Coward, Mike 397–400

Cowdrey, Sir Colin 33, 232,
261, 467

Craig, Ian 160–9, 200

Craig, Ros 160, 165

Cutler, Sir Roden 51–2, 329

C

Caldwell, Tim 103, 276, 277,
324, 360, 376

cancellation of South African
1971–72 tour of Australia 39,
65, 166, 323, 325, 338–41,
343, 344, 389, 426, 437

Cardus, Neville 149, 431, 432

Carr, Arthur 148

Centenary Test (Melbourne)
1977 228, 250, 278, 379

Chadwick, Sir Albert 342

Chappell, Greg 353–71, 372, 380

D

Daily Mail 58, 62, 139, 140,
145, 147, 148

Dansie, Neil 81–84

Davidson, Alan 170–5, 256,
262

Dowling, Bill 255, 341

Dwyer, 'Chappie' 57, 106, 116

E

Eccles, Graham 334–7

Egar, Colin 221, 234–48, 249, 250 251, 254

England (MCC) tour of Australia 1946–47 55, 59, 60, 66, 143, *see also* Ashes series

F

Favell, Les 158–9, 177, 353

Fingleton, Jack 4, 6, 7, 8, 9, 58, 59, 63, 140, 181, 208, 231, 242

Fleetwood-Smith, Leslie 16, 23, 58

freemasonry 127

Freer, Fred 93, 102

Frith, David 378–87

G

Gauvin (née Wallis), Jill 281, 306–20

Gauvin, Rob 306, 308–12, 314, 317, 318, 319, 320

Gibbs, Barry 247, 377, 437

Goossens, Eugene 121

Gowrie, Lord 127

Grace, W. G. 144, 149, 437, 463

Grimmett, Clarrie 20, 57, 227, 231, 381

Grout, Wally 173, 253, 260, 263

H

Hamence, Ron 383

Hammond, Walter 37, 55–6, 66–7, 99, 110–11, 143, 382

Harris, Clem 73, 77

Harvey, Neil 84–92, 93, 95, 97, 104, 109, 123, 145, 161–2, 171, 253, 260, 261, 263, 374, 431

Hassett, Lindsay 12, 15, 57, 79, 80, 85, 87, 93, 95, 102, 104, 110, 111, 120, 123, 139, 260, 409, 431

Hobbs, Sir Jack 149, 150, 382, 387, 425

Hodgetts, W. H. 72, 73, 77–8, 124–5, 126, 217, 219, 271, 283, 396, 412, 456–7

Howard, John, 403–7

Hutton, Sir Leonard 11, 38, 40, 108, 140, 148, 151, 163, 346, 387, 425

Hutton, Richard 346

I

Ikin, J. T. 227, 457

Insole, Doug 210, 219–34

International Cricket Council
(Imperial Cricket Council,
ICC) 26, 34, 149, 209, 223,
224, 226, 230

J

Jackson, Archie 383, 398, 459

Jacobs, Bill 341–9

Jardine, Douglas 4, 5, 28, 118,
147–8, 207, 221, 458–9

Jeans, Bill 73, 127

Jenner, Terry 92, 371–8

Johnson, Ian 85, 120

Johnston, Bill 57, 93, 118, 119,
120, 431

Jones, Alan 441, 461–70

Joseph, Betty 438–41

K

Kensington District Cricket
Club 36, 50, 71, 73–8, 81,
83, 153, 175–6, 357, 411,
412–13

Kippax, Alan 4, 5, 6, 99

Kooyonga Golf Club 211, 292,
295, 299, 415, 435, 436, 461

L

Laker, Jim 35, 96, 144

Larwood, Harold 5, 6, 8, 96,
182, 255, 413, 459

Lawry, Bill 91, 165, 302, 372

laws
front-foot rule 37, 226, 238,
249, 278–9, 426
lbw 39, 201, 210, 303
no-ball rule 201, 210, 303,
380, 426

Leveson Gower, Sir H. D. G.
12, 100

Lill, Dr John 176–9, 185

Lill, Rosie 177–9

Lindwall, Ray 57, 103, 109,
119, 120, 150, 199, 252,
330

Lloyd, Clive 345, 414

Lord's 109, 210, 226

Lord's Taverners 40, 158, 159,
378

Loxton, Sam 36, 88, 91,
93–104, 122, 251, 255, 258,
260, 262, 343, 377

M

McCabe, Stan 4, 5, 9, 15, 16,
59, 105, 242, 385

McDonald, Colin 183–8

Mackay, Ken 'Slasher' 172,
253, 260

MacPherson, Mal 294–300

Maddocks, Len 179–83, 255

Mailey, Arthur 20, 382

Mallett, Ashley 154, 371, 373

Martin, Ray 168

Marylebone Cricket Club
(MCC) 4, 26, 34, 65, 89,
187, 208, 209, 210, 220, 238,
329, 409

May, Norman 429–33

Meckiff, Ian 181, 182, 221,
247, 251–9

Melbourne Cricket Club 3,
176, 185, 342

Melbourne Cricket Ground 57,
179, 240, 257, 360, 425

Mellor, Jim 188–90

Menzies, Sir Robert 57, 259,
260, 261, 263, 406

Miller, Keith 57–8, 95, 103,
109, 119, 150, 151, 155, 199,
225, 252, 377, 381, 431

Moore, Lord 408–10

Morris, Arthur 14, 57, 96,
104–14, 199, 200

Mulvaney, Richard 418,
441–54

N

New South Wales Cricket
Association 112, 174, 320,
419

New South Wales cricket team
4, 6, 8, 45,105, 115, 161,
170

Noblet, Geff 'Nobby' 79–81

Norfolk, Duke of 64–5, 263

O

O'Brien, Leo 15, 16, 102

Oldfield, Bert 12, 99

one-day cricket 230, 277, 325,
329, 366, 368, 404

O'Reilly, Bill 4, 15, 16, 25, 46,
58, 59, 63, 105, 107, 110,
140, 172, 181, 208, 230–1,
242–3, 329, 330, 333, 380–1,
385, 431, 442

Oval, The 109, 119, 459

P

Packer, Kerry 39, 65, 66, 168,
169, 203, 204, 207, 223, 224,
276, 286, 324, 362, 363, 365,
388

Pamensky, Joe 364, 426

Parish, Bob 182, 207, 223, 275–9, 324, 325, 360, 362

Parkinson, David 411–16

Parkinson, Sam 411–16

Patterson, Rob 304–5, 391–7

Pentilow, Bob 133, 264, 265, 266, 270

Phelan, Sylv 244, 295, 298, 300

Pollock, Graeme 346, 387, 389–91

Ponsford, W. H. 22, 140, 142, 408, 427

Prime Minister's XI 259–63

Q

Queensland Cricket Association 359, 360

Queensland cricket team 358, 370

R

Radford, Bob 320–34, 419

Rest of the World Xl 1971–72 250, 341, 343, 344–7, 368, 389

Richards, Barry 159, 387, 390, 425–9, 433–8

Richardson, Arthur 77–8, 99, 153, 183, 184

Richardson, Vic 14, 49, 353–4, 356–7

Ridings, Joan 79, 250, 284–94

Ridings, Phil 47, 70, 76, 160, 239, 250, 284–94, 353, 358, 360, 367, 373

Ring, Doug 115–24

Rivett, Nan 190–9, 341, 347

Rivett, Rhyll 190–9

Rivett, Rohan 190–5, 197–9, 341, 347–8

Robins, G. R. V. (Richard) 26–45

Robins, R. W. V. (Walter) 19, 26–35, 37, 38–9, 41, 42–5, 65, 89, 210, 220

Rotary Club 40, 188–90, 202, 250, 279, 280, 307

Rowan, Lou 234, 240, 246, 248–51

Ryder, Jack 56, 57, 90, 91, 100, 106, 116, 160, 255, 257, 302, 337, 429

S

St George Cricket Club 3, 105, 443

Scammell, Bill 215–19

Schubert, Max 235–6, 273, 403, 432

sectarian issue 16, 112, 140, 181, 187, 208, 231, 242–3, 381, 458

Seddon, Dudley 90, 337, 429

selection (national) 62–3, 92,93, 160, 174, 179, 220, 255, 284, 337, 373, 374; (state) 83, 93, 284

Sellars, Basil 420, 449

Sheahan, Paul 301–4

Sheffield Shield competition 7, 46, 47, 56, 57, 93, 99, 106, 124, 163, 179, 180, 183, 184, 252, 257, 270, 385, 427

Shiell, Alan 356

Simpson, Bob 167, 199–205, 325

Sims, Keith 124–35

Sobers, Sir Garfield 298, 344, 345, 387

South African Test series (1949–50) 58, 80, 150; (1963–64) 249, 251, 254, 389, 390; (1966–67) 344, 347; (2001–02) 389, 397, 425

South Australian Cricket Association 45, 47, 73, 78, 79, 80–1,101, 127, 152, 154, 237, 239, 241, 246, 284, 294, 332, 353, 359, 367–8, 369, 370, 377, 381, 413, 433, 434, 437, 455, 456

South Australian cricket team 46, 49, 71, 79, 177, 183, 242, 353, 354, 356, 358, 372, 411, 412, 425, 426, 435

Starr, Cecil 45–9, 73

State Library of South Australia 279, 280–1, 306, 319, 399, 445

Mortlock Collection 279, 282, 308, 309, 417, 422

Statton, John 175–6

Steele, Alison 291, 387–8

Steele, Ray 222, 223, 387–8

Stephens, Alf 23, 24, 25

Sutcliffe, Herbert 221, 226

Swanton, E. W. 107, 206, 209, 210

Sydney Cricket Ground 3, 4, 7, 9–10, 84, 360, 429, 442

Sydney Cricket Ground Trust 112, 166

T

Tendulkar, Sachin 209, 230, 405

Thomson, Jeff 157, 177

throwing 39, 65, 149, 181–2, 187–8, 189, 209, 220–1, 229–30, 245–8, 251, 254–7, 259, 303

dragging controversy 39,
148
Tied Test, Brisbane 1960 161,
170, 173–4, 188, 236, 254,
259, 400
Toshack, Ernie 57, 112
tours of England (1930) 6, 27,
58, 79, 97, 115, 120, 209,
408, 422; (1934) 8, 11, 12,
23, 32, 97, 408–9; (1938) 10,
11, 12, 15, 33, 97; (1948) 11,
18–19, 30–1, 32, 59, 60–1,
68, 84, 85–9, 92, 95–7,
107–12, 115–24, 130, 155,
187, 199, 409, 410
match against Essex 1948
155, 219, 225, 233
see also Ashes series
Trueman, Fred 260, 261
Tummel, Jim 133, 264–74

V

Victorian Cricket Association
57, 341, 347, 387
Victorian cricket team 55, 56,
57, 93, 99, 181
Viljoen, Ken 389
Voce, W. 5, 6, 8

W

Wall, Tim 18, 130, 289
Warne, Shane 230–1, 405
Waugh, Steve 70, 168, 468
West Indies v Australia 1960–61
series 164, 172, 255
Whatman, George 24
Wilkin, John 50–1
Williams, Charles 454–61
Woodcock, John 205–11
Woodfull, Bill 14, 120, 408,
460
World Cup competition 221–2,
373–4, 375, 386
World Series cricket 39, 65,
112, 182, 199, 203–4, 207,
222–4, 240, 276–7, 286,
324–5, 359, 361–6, 388, 430
World War II 17, 30, 32, 33
Wotton, Keith 23–6
Wotton (née Stephens), Peggy
23, 24, 26
Wyatt, R. E. S. 226, 227

Y

Yalumba 101, 103, 114, 329
Yardley, Norman 31